Carl Lumholtz

UNKNOWN MEXICO

Explorations in the Sierra Madre
and Other Regions
1890–1898

CARL LUMHOLTZ

In Two Volumes
VOLUME I

Dover Publications, Inc., New York

Published in Canada by General Publishing Company, Ltd., 20 Lesmill Road, Don Mills, Toronto, Ontario.

Published in the United Kingdom by Constable and Company, Ltd., 10 Orange Street, London WC2H 7EG.

This Dover edition, first published in 1987, is an unabridged republication of *Unknown Mexico: A Record of Five Years' Exploration Among the Tribes of the Western Sierra Madre; in the Tierra Caliente of Tepic and Jalisco; and Among the Tarascos of Michoacan*, originally published by Charles Scribner's Sons, New York, in 1902. The foldouts of the original have been printed over consecutive pages for this Dover edition, except for the color maps, which are now attached to the back cover of the second volume. The color plates of the original have been reprinted in black and white for this edition, and some have been relocated closer to their text references.

Manufactured in the United States of America
Dover Publications, Inc., 31 East 2nd Street, Mineola, N.Y. 11501

Library of Congress Cataloging-in-Publication Data

Lumholtz, Carl, 1851–1922.
  Unknown Mexico.

  Reprint. Originally published: New York : C. Scribner's, 1902.
  Includes index.
  1. Indians of Mexico. 2. Mexico—Description and travel. I. Title.
F1220.L85 1987   972'.00497   86-29335
ISBN 0-486-25364-3 (v. 1)
ISBN 0-486-25413-5 (v. 2)

To

MORRIS K. JESUP, M.A., LL.D.

PRESIDENT OF THE

AMERICAN MUSEUM OF NATURAL HISTORY

OF NEW YORK

THE PATRON AND FRIEND OF SCIENCE

THIS WORK

IS RESPECTFULLY DEDICATED

AS A

TOKEN OF GRATITUDE

AND REGARD

PREFACE

I N the course of my travels in Australia, and especially after my arrival at Upper Herbert River in
Northern Queensland, I soon perceived that it would
be impracticable for me to hunt for zoölogical specimens
without first securing the assistance of the natives of the
country. Thus it came about that for over a year I
spent most of my time in the company of the cannibalistic blacks of that region, camping and hunting with
them ; and during this adventurous period I became so
interested in these primitive people that the study of savage and barbaric races has since become my life's work.

I first conceived the idea of an expedition to Mexico
while on a visit to London in 1887. I had, of course,
as we all have, heard of the wonderful cliff-dwellings in
the Southwest of the United States, of entire villages
built in caverns on steep mountain-sides, accessible in
many cases only with the aid of ladders. Within the
territory of the United States there were, to be sure, no
survivors of the race that had once inhabited those
dwellings. But the Spaniards, when first discovering
and conquering that district, are said to have come upon
dwellings then still occupied. Might there not, possibly, be descendants of the people yet in existence in
the northwestern part of Mexico hitherto so little
explored ?

I made up my mind, then and there, that I would answer this question and that I would undertake an expedition into that part of the American continent. But my ideas were not realised until in 1890 I visited the United States on a lecturing tour. On broaching the subject of such an expedition to some representative men and women, I met with a surprisingly ready response ; and interest in an undertaking of that kind being once aroused, the difficulties and obstacles in its way were soon overcome.

Most of the money required was raised by private subscription. The principal part of the fund was, however, furnished by a now deceased friend of mine, an American gentleman whose name, in deference to his wishes, I am bound to withhold. The American Museum of Natural History of New York and the American Geographical Society of New York contributed, each, $1,000, and it was arranged that I should travel under the auspices of these two learned institutions. Many scientific societies received me most cordially.

The Government in Washington readily furnished me with the official papers I required. The late Mr. James G. Blaine, then Secretary of State, did everything in his power to pave my way in Mexico, even evincing a very strong personal interest in my plans.

In the summer of 1890, preparatory to my work, I visited the Zuñi, Navajo, and Moqui Indians, and then proceeded to the City of Mexico in order to get the necessary credentials from that Government. I was received with the utmost courtesy by the President, General Porfirio Diaz, who gave me an hour's audience at the Palacio Nacional, and also by several members of his cabinet, whose appreciation of the importance and the scientific value of my proposition was truly gratifying. With everything granted that I wanted for the success of my expedition—free passage for my baggage through the Custom House, the privilege of a military escort whenever I deemed one desirable, and numerous letters of introduction to prominent persons in Northern Mexico who were in a position to further my plans —I hurried back to the United States to organise the undertaking. My plan was to enter, at some convenient point in the State of Sonora, Mexico, that great and mysterious mountain range called the Sierra Madre, cross it to the famous ruins of Casas Grandes in the State of Chihuahua, and then to explore the range southward as extensively as my means would permit.

The western Sierra Madre may be considered a continuation of the Rocky Mountains and stretches through the greater part of Mexico into Central and South America as a link of the Cordilleras, which form a practically uninterrupted chain from Bering Strait to Cape Horn. The section occupying Northwestern Mexico is called Sierra Madre del Norte, and offers a wide field for scientific exploration. To this day it has never been surveyed.

The northernmost portion of the Sierra Madre del Norte has from time immemorial been under the dominion of the wild Apache tribes whose hand was against every man, and every man against them. Not until General Crook, in 1883, reduced these dangerous nomads to submission did it become possible to make scientific investigations there; indeed, small bands of the " Men of the Woods " were still left, and my party had to be strong enough to cope with any difficulty from them.

Inasmuch as my expedition was the first to take advantage of the comparative security prevailing in that district, I thought that I could best further the aims of Science by associating with me a staff of scientists and students. Professor W. Libbey, of Princeton, N. J., took part as the physical geographer, bringing with him his laboratory man; Mr. A. M. Stephen was the archæologist, assisted by Mr. R. Abbott; Messrs. C. V. Hartman and C. E. Lloyd were the botanists, Mr. F. Robinette the zoölogical collector, and Mr. H. White the mineralogist of the expedition.

All the scientific men were provided with riding animals, while the Mexican muleteers generally rode their own mounts. Our outfit was as complete as it well could be, comprising all the instruments and tools that might be required, besides tents and an adequate allotment of provisions, etc. All this baggage had to be transported on mule-back. We were, all in all, thirty men, counting the scientific corps, the guides, the cooks, and the muleteers, and we had with us nearly a hundred animals—mules, donkeys, and horses—as we crossed the sierra.

It was a winter campaign, and from Nacori, in Sonora, to Casas Grandes, in Chihuahua, we were to make our own trail, which we did successfully. Ancient remains were almost as rare as in the rest of the Sierra Madre del Norte; yet traces of ancient habitations were found in the shape of stone terraces, which had evidently served agricultural purposes, and at some places rude fortifications were seen. In the eastern part we came upon a considerable number of caves containing house groups, the builders of which, generally, rested in separate burial-caves. In the same local-

ity, as well as in the adjacent plains of San Diego, Chihuahua, we found numerous mounds covering house
groups, similar in construction to those in the caves.
From underneath their floors we unearthed about five
hundred beautifully decorated pieces of pottery.

Among the further results of the expedition may be
mentioned the gathering of large collections of plants,
among them twenty-seven species new to science ; fifty-
five mammals, among which the *siurus Apache* was new
to science, and about a thousand birds. A complete
record was made of meteorological observations.

Thus far, although the question regarding surviving
cliff-dwellers was answered negatively, the field southward in the sierra was so promising that I was eager
to extend my explorations in that direction. The funds
of the expedition, however, began to run low, and in
April, 1891, I had to return to the United States to obtain more money with which to carry on a work that
had opened so auspiciously. I left my camp in San
Diego in charge of one of my assistants, instructing him
to go on with the excavations during my absence. This
work was never interrupted, though the force of men
was now considerably reduced. The law prohibiting excavations without the special permit of the Government
of Mexico had not yet been promulgated.

I was so absolutely confident of the ultimate success
of my efforts, in spite of discouragements, that I twice
crossed the entire continent of North America, went
down to the City of Mexico and came north again—a
journey of over 20,000 miles—seeing prominent people
and lecturing to arouse a public interest. ⸀ Finally, the
American Museum of Natural History of New York
decided to continue the explorations, the funds being

this time supplied mainly through the munificence of
the late Mr. Henry Villard, and toward the end of that
year I was able to return to my camp, and in January,
1892, lead the expedition further south. My scientific
assistants were now: Mr. C. V. Hartman, botanist;
Mr. C. H. Taylor, civil engineer and photographer,
and Mr. A. E. Meade, mineralogist and zoölogical
collector.

This time we came upon Cave-Dwellers. The Tarahumare Indians of the Sierra Madre, one of the least
known among the Mexican tribes, live in caves to such
an extent that they may properly be termed the American Cave-Dwellers of to-day. I determined to study
these interesting people, especially the so-called *gentiles* *
(pagans), and as this was not practical, even with the
present reduced size of the expedition, I gradually dis-
banded the entire company and at last remained alone.

By selling most of my animals, and a large part of
my outfit, and through the untiring efforts of two
American ladies, whose friendship I highly esteem, I was
enabled to continue my researches alone until August,
1893, when I took my Tarahumare and Tepehuane collections to Chicago and exhibited them at the World's
Fair. Extensive vocabularies of the Tarahumare and
Tepehuane languages, as well as a vocabulary of the now
almost extinct Tubares, were among the results of this
expedition, besides anthropological measurements, samples of hair and osseous remains.

The great possibilities Mexico offers to ethnology
proved an irresistible incentive to new researches, and
seeing the results of my previous expeditions, the Amer-

---

* I have used once or twice the expression *gentile* Indians, referring to these
Tarahumares.

ican Museum of Natural History of New York again sent me out on what was to be my third and most extensive Mexican expedition, which lasted from March, 1894, to March, 1897. During these three years I again travelled alone, that is, without any scientific assistants, at first with two or three Mexicans. Soon, however, I found that my best companions were the so-called civilised Indians, or even Indians in their aboriginal state, who not only helped me by their mere presence to win the confidence of their tribesmen but also served me as subjects of observation. As before, I stopped for months with a tribe, discharging all alien attendants, and roughing it with the Indians. In this way I spent in all a year and a half among the Tarahumares, and ten months among the Coras and Huichols. At first the natives persistently opposed me ; they are very distrustful of the white man, and no wonder, since he has left them little yet to lose. But I managed to make my entry and gradually to gain their confidence and friendship, mainly through my ability to sing their native songs, and by always treating them justly.

Thus I gained a knowledge of these peoples which could have been procured in no other way. When after five or six months of such sojourns and travel my stock of "civilised" provisions would give out, I subsisted on what I could procure from the Indians. Game is hard to get in Mexico, and one's larder cannot depend on one's gun. As in Australia, my favourite drink was hot water with honey, which, besides being refreshing, gave a relish to a monotonous diet.

All along my route I gathered highly valuable material from the Tarahumares, the Northern and the Southern Tepehuanes, the Coras, the Huichols, and the

Tepecanos, all of which tribes except the last named dwell within the Sierra Madre del Norte; also from the Nahuas on the western slopes of the sierra, as well as from those in the States of Jalisco and Mexico; and, finally, from the Tarascos in the State of Michoacan. Of most of these tribes little more than their names were known, and I brought back large collections illustrating their ethnical and anthropological status, besides extensive information in regard to their customs, religion, traditions, and myths. I also completed my collection of vocabularies and aboriginal melodies. On my journey through the Tierra Caliente of the Territory of Tepic, and the States of Jalisco and Michoacan, I also obtained a number of archæological objects of great historical value and importance.

In 1898 I made my last expedition to Mexico under the same auspices, staying there for four months. On this trip I was accompanied by Dr. Ales Hrdlicka. I revisited the Tarahumares and Huichols in order to supplement the material in hand and to settle doubtful points that had come up in working out my notes. Sixty melodies from these tribes were recorded on the graphophone.

Thus from 1890 to 1898 I spent fully five years in field researches among the natives of northwestern Mexico. The material was collected with a view to shedding light upon the relations between the ancient culture of the valley of Mexico and the Pueblo Indians in the southwest of the United States; to give an insight into the ethnical status of the Mexican Indians now and at the time of the conquest, and to illuminate certain phases in the development of the human race.

So far the results of my expeditions to Mexico have been made public in the following literature :

CARL LUMHOLTZ : "Explorations in Mexico," Bulletin of the American Geographical Society, 1891.

CARL LUMHOLTZ : Letters to the American Geographical Society of New York, "Mr. Carl Lumholtz in Mexico," Bulletin of the American Geographical Society, Vol. III., 1893.

J. A. ALLEN : "List of Mammals and Birds Collected in Northeastern Sonora and Northwestern Chihuahua, Mexico, on the Lumholtz Archæological Expedition, 1890–1892," Bulletin of the American Museum of Natural History, Vol. V., Art. III., 1893.

B. L. ROBINSON and M. L. FERNALD : "New Plants Collected by Mr. C. V. Hartman and Mr. C. E. Lloyd upon the Archæological Expedition to Northwestern Mexico under the Direction of Dr. Carl Lumholtz," Proceedings of the American Academy of Arts and Sciences, Vol. XXX., 1894.

CARL LUMHOLTZ : "American Cave-Dwellers ; the Tarahumares of the Sierra Madre," Bulletin of the American Geographical Society, Vol. III., 1894.

CARL LUMHOLTZ : "The Cave-Dwellers of the Sierra Madre," Proceedings of the International Congress of Anthropology, Chicago, 1894.

CARL LUMHOLTZ : Four articles in SCRIBNER'S MAGAZINE : "Explorations in the Sierra Madre," November, 1891 ; "Among the Tarahumares, the American Cave-Dwellers," July, 1894 ; "Tarahumare Life and Customs," September, 1894 ; "Tarahumare Dances and Plant Worship," October, 1894.

C. V. HARTMAN : "The Indians of Northwestern Mexico," Congrès International des Americanistes, Dixième Session, Stockholm, 1894.

CARL LUMHOLTZ : "Blandt Sierra Madres huleboere," Norge, Norsk Kalender, Kristiania, 1895.

CARL LUMHOLTZ and ALEŠ HRDLIČKA : "Trephining in Mexico," American Anthropologist, December, 1897.

CARL LUMHOLTZ : "The Huichol Indians in Mexico," Bulletin of the American Museum of Natural History, Vol. X., 1898.

TARLETON H. BEAN : "Notes on Mexican Fishes Obtained by Carl Lumholtz," Bulletin of the American Museum of Natural History, Vol. X., 1898.

CARL LUMHOLTZ and ALES HRDLICKA : "Marked Human Bones from a Prehistoric Tarasco Indian Burial-place in the State of Michoacan, Mexico," Bulletin of the American Museum of Natural History, Vol. X., 1898.

ALEŠ HRDLIČKA : "Description of an Ancient Anomalous Skeleton from the Valley of Mexico, with Special Reference to Super-numerary Bicipital Ribs in Man," Bulletin of the American Museum of Natural History, Vol. XII., 1899.

CARL LUMHOLTZ : "Symbolism of the Huichol Indians," Memoir of the American Museum of Natural History, Vol. III., May, 1900 ; 228 royal quarto pages and 3 coloured plates.

IN PREPARATION :

CARL LUMHOLTZ : "Conventionalism in Designs of the Huichol Indians," Memoir of the American Museum of Natural History.

The present volumes give a succinct account of my travels and work among the remote peoples of the Sierra Madre del Norte and the countries adjacent to the south and east as far as the City of Mexico. Most of what I tell here refers to a part of the Republic that is never visited by tourists and is foreign even to most Mexicans. Primitive people are becoming scarce on the globe. On the American continents there are still some left in their original state. If they are studied before they, too, have lost their individuality or been crushed under the heels of civilisation, much light may be thrown not only upon the early people of this country but upon the first chapters of the history of mankind.

In the present rapid development of Mexico it can-not be prevented that these primitive people will soon disappear by fusion with the great nation to whom they belong. The vast and magnificent virgin forests and the mineral wealth of the mountains will not much longer remain the exclusive property of my dusky friends; but I hope that I shall have rendered them a service by setting them this modest monument, and that civilised man will be the better for knowing of them.

That I have been able to accomplish what I did I owe, in the first place, to the generosity of the people of the United States, to their impartiality and freedom from prejudice, which enables foreigners to work shoulder to shoulder with their own advance guard. I wish to extend my thanks in particular to the American Geographical Society of New York, and still more especially to the American Museum of Natural History of New York, with whom I have had the honour of being connected more or less closely for ten years. To its public-spirited and whole-souled President, Mr. Morris K. Jesup, I am under profound obligations. I also take pleasure in acknowledging my indebtedness to Mr. Andrew Carnegie, who initiated my Mexican ventures with a subscription of $1,000; furthermore to the Hon. Cecil Baring, Mr. Frederick A. Constable, Mr. William E. Dodge, Mr. James Douglass, Mrs. Joseph W. Drexel, Mr. George J. Gould, Miss Helen Miller Gould, Mr. Archer M. Huntington, Mr. Frederick E. Hyde, Mr. D. Willis James, Col. James K. Jones, the Duke of Loubat, Mr. Peter Marié, Mr. Henry G. Marquand, Mr. F. O. Matthiessen, Mr. Victor Morawetz, Mr. J. Pierpont Morgan, Mrs. Edwin Parsons, Mr. Archibald Rogers, Mr. F. Augustus Schermerhorn, Mr. William C. Schermerhorn, Mr. Charles Stewart Smith, Mr. James Speyer, Mr. George W. Vanderbilt, Mr. William C. Whitney, of New York; to Mr. Frederick L. Ames, Mrs. John L. Gardner, Mrs. E. Mason, Mr. Nathaniel Thayer, Mr. Samuel

D. Warren, Dr. Charles G. Weld, of Boston; to Mr. Allison D. Armour and Mr. Franklin MacVeagh, of Chicago; to Mrs. Phœbe Hearst, Mr. Frank G. New-lands, Mrs. Abby M. Parrot, Mr. F. W. Sharon, of San Francisco; to Mr. Adolphus Busch, of St. Louis; to Mr. Theo. W. Davis, of Newport; and to the late Mr. E. L. Godkin.

Much valuable support or assistance I have also received from Mrs. Morris K. Jesup; Mrs. Elizabeth Hobson, of Washington, D. C.; Miss Joanna Rotch, of Milton, Mass.; Mrs. Henry Draper, of New York; Mrs. Robert W. Chapin, of Lenox; the late Mr. E. L. Godkin; Professor Alexander Agassiz; Professor F. W. Putnam, Curator of the American Museum of Natural History in New York; Dr. S. Weir Mitchell, of Phila-delphia; Professor Franz Boas, Curator of the American Museum of Natural History in New York; Dr. B. L. Robinson and Dr. M. L. Fernald, of Harvard Univer-sity; Professor J. A. Allen and Mr. L. P. Gratacap, Curators of the American Museum of Natural History.

I am under obligation to Mr. Marshall H. Saville, Curator of the American Museum of Natural History, especially for the placing of the names of the ruins of Southern Mexico on one of the maps; to Miss Alice Fletcher, of Washington, D. C., and Mr. Edwin S. Tracy for transcribing from the graphophone three of the songs rendered in this book, and to Mrs. George S. Bixby for aid in transcribing the native music. Finally I desire to express my appreciation of the untiring ser-vices of my private secretary, Mrs. H. E. Hepner.

The upper illustration on page 65 is a reproduction of a photograph kindly furnished me by Mr. Frank H. Chapman, and the illustration in Vol. I., pages 145–146, is made from a photograph acquired through the late Dr. P. Lamborn. The illustration in Vol. II., pages 464–465, I owe to the courtesy of Mr. D. Gabriel Castaños, of Guadalajara.

The coloured illustrations are represented as the objects appear when the colours have been brought out by the application of water.[*]

The maps do not lay claim to an accuracy which, under the circumstances, it was impossible to obtain, but they will, I hope, be found to be an improvement on the existing ones.[†]

Dr. Aleš Hrdlička, who has just returned from the Hyde expedition, informs me that in visiting the western part of Sonora he found pure Opata spoken west of Rio de Sonora and north of Ures, *e.g.*, in Tuape.

Wherever dollars and cents are given Mexican currency is meant.

In the Indian Songs II., 10 and 18, I have made an attempt at rendering the native words in English in such a form that the translations could be sung, without, however, deviating from the original.

In the native words " x " should be given the sound of the Greek χ.

---

[*]All the illustrations are in black and white in this Dover edition.
  [†]In this Dover edition, the maps are attached to the inside back cover of the second volume.

CONTENTS

CHAPTER I

Preparations for the Start—Our Dry Goods Relished by the Cattle—I Become a " Compadre"—Beautiful Northern Sonora—Mexican Muleteers Preferable in Their Own Country—Apache Stories—Signs of Ancient Inhabitants—Arrival at Upper Yaqui River—Opata Indians now Mexicanised—A Flourishing Medical Practice—Mexican Manners—Rock-carvings —How Certain Cacti Propagate, ... Pages 1–16

CHAPTER II

A Remarkable Antique Piece—A New Species of Century Plant—Arrival at Nacori, at the Foot of the Sierra Madre—Trincheras—A Mommoth Tusk Secured—Climbing the Sierra Madre—A New Squirrel Discovered—Solitude—Apache Monuments—Arrival at Upper Bavispe River, ... Pages 17–40

CHAPTER III

Camping at Upper Bavispe River—Low Stone Cabins, Fortresses, and Other Remains Indicating Former Habitation—The Animals Starve on the Winter Grass of the Sierra and Begin to Give Out—A Deserted Apache Camp—Comfort at Last—The Giant Woodpecker—We Arrive at the Mormon Settlements of Pacheco and Cave Valley, . . Pages 41–59

CHAPTER IV

A Splendid Field Prepared for Us by the Ancient Agriculturists of Cave Valley—House Groups in Caves Along a Pretty Stream—Well-preserved Mummies Found in Caves—More Trincheras—Our Excavations in Caves and Mounds Confirm to the Mormons their Sacred Stories—We Move to the Plains of San Diego—Visit to Casas Grandes and the Watch-tower— Successful Excavations of the Mounds near San Diego, . Pages 60–98

CHAPTER V

Second Expedition—Return to the Sierra—Parrots in the Snow—Cave-dwellings at Garabato, the most Beautiful in Northern Mexico—A Superb View of the Sierra Madre—The Devil's Spine Ridge—Guaynopa, the Famous Old Silver Mine—Aros River—On Old Trails—Adventures of " El Chino"—Cure for Poison Ivy, ... Pages 99–117

CONTENTS

CHAPTER VI

Fossils, and One Way of Utilising Them—Temosachic—The First Tarahu-mares—Ploughs with Wooden Shares—Visit to the Southern Pimas—Aboriginal Hat Factories—Pinos Altos—The Waterfall near Jesus Maria—An Adventure with Ladrones, ... Pages 118–135

CHAPTER VII

The Uncontaminated Tarahumares—A Tarahumare Court in Session—The Power of the Staff—Justice has its Course—Barrancas—Excursion to the Gentiles—Tarahumare Costumes Simple and Inexpensive—Trincheras in Use Among the Tarahumares, ... Pages 136–155

CHAPTER VIII

The Houses of the Tarahumares—American Cave-dwellings of To-day—Frequent Changes of Abode by the Tarahumare—The Patio or Dancing Place—The Original Cross of America—Tarahumare Storehouses, ... Pages 156–178

CHAPTER IX

Arrival at Batopilas—Ascent from Batopilas to the Highlands of the Sierra—A Tarahumare who had been in Chicago—An Old-timer—Flight of Our Native Guide and its Disastrous Consequences—Indians Burn the Grass All Over the Country—Travelling Becomes too Difficult for the Animals—Mr. Taylor and I Go to Zapuri—Its Surroundings—The Pithaya in Season, ... Pages 179–189

CHAPTER X

Nice-looking Natives—Albinos—Ancient Remains in Ohuivo—Local Traditions, the Cocoyomes, etc.—Guachochic—Don Miguel and " The Postmaster "—A Variety of Curious Cures—Gauchochic Becomes My Headquarters—The Difficulty of Getting an Honest Interpreter—False Truffles—The Country Suffering from a Prolonged Drought—A Start in a Northwesterly Direction—Arrival at the Pueblo of Norogachic, Pages 190–202

CHAPTER XI

A Priest and His Family Make the Wilderness Comfortable for Us—Ancient Remains Similar to those Seen in Sonora—The Climate of the Sierra—Flora and Fauna—Tarahumare Agriculture—Ceremonies Connected with the Planting of Corn—Deterioration of Domestic Animals—Native Dogs of Mexico, ... Pages 203–217

CHAPTER XII

The Tarahumares Still Afraid of Me—Don Andres Madrid to the Rescue—Mexican Robbers Among the Tarahumares—Mode of Burial in Ancient Caves—Visit to Nonoava—The Indians Change their Minds about Me, and Regard Me as a Rain-god—What the Tarahumares Eat—A Pretty Church in the Wilderness—I Find at Last a Reliable Interpreter and Proceed to Live à l'Indienne, ... Pages 218–234

CHAPTER XIII

The Tarahumare Physique—Bodily Movements—Not as Sensitive to Pain as White Men—Their Phenomenal Endurance—Health—Honesty—Dexterity and Ingenuity—Good Observers of the Celestial Bodies and Weather-forecasters—Hunting and Shooting—Home Industries—Tesvino, the Great National Drink of the Tribe—Other Alcoholic Drinks, ... Pages 235-257

CHAPTER XIV

Politeness, and the Demands of Etiquette—The Daily Life of the Tarahumare—The Woman's Position is High—Standard of Beauty—Women Do the Courting—Love's Young Dream—Marriage Ceremonies, Primitive and Civilised—Childbirth—Childhood, . . , Pages 258-275

CHAPTER XV

Many Kinds of Games Among the Tarahumares—Betting and Gambling—Foot-races the National Sport—The Tarahumares are the Greatest Runners in the World—Divinations for the Race—Mountains of Betting Stakes—Women's Races, ... Pages 276-294

CHAPTER XVI

Religion—Mother Moon Becomes the Virgin Mary—Myths—The Creation—The Deluge—Folk-lore—The Crow's Story to the Parrot—Brother Coyote—Beliefs about Animals, ... Pages 295-310

CHAPTER XVII

The Shamans or Wise Men of the Tribe—Healers and Priests in One—Disease Caused by Looks and Thoughts—Everybody and Everything has to be Cured—Nobody Feels Well without His " Doctor"—Sorcery—The Powers of Evil are as Great as those of Good—Remarkable Cure for Snake-bite—Trepanning Among the Ancient Tarahumares, Pages 311-329

CHAPTER XVIII,

Relation of Man to Nature—Dancing as a Form of Worship Learned from the Animals—Tarahumare Sacrifices—The Rutuburi Dance Taught by the Turkey—The Yumari Learned from the Deer—Tarahumare Rain Songs—Greeting the Sun—Tarahumare Oratory—The Flowing Bowl—The National Importance of Tesvino—Homeward Bound, Pages 330-355

CHAPTER XIX

Plant-worship—Hikuli—Internal and External Effects—Hikuli both Man and God—How the Tarahumares Obtain the Plant, and where They Keep It—The Tarahumare Hikuli Feast—Musical Instruments—Hikuli Likes Noise—The Dance—Hikuli's Departure in the Morning—Other Kinds of Cacti Worshipped—" Doctor" Rubio, the Great Hikuli Expert—The Age of Hikuli Worship, ... Pages 356-379

CHAPTER XX

The Tarahumare's Firm Belief in a Future Life—Causes of Death—The Dead are Mischievous and Want Their Families to Join Them—Therefore the Dead Have to be Kept Away by Fair Means or Foul—Three Feasts and a Chase—Burial Customs—A Funeral Sermon, ... Pages 380–390

CHAPTER XXI

Three Weeks on Foot Through the Barranca—Rio Fuerte—I Get My Camera Wet—Ancient Cave-dwellings Ascribed to the Tubar Indians—The Effect of a Compliment—Various Devices for Catching Fish—Poisoning the Water—A Blanket Seine, ... Pages 391–407

CHAPTER XXII

Resumption of the Journey Southward—*Pinus Lumholtzii*—Cooking with Snow—Terror-stricken Indians—A Gentlemanly Highwayman and His " Shooting-box "—The Pernicious Effect of Civilisation Upon the Tarahumares—A Fine Specimen of the Tribe—The Last of the Tarahumares, ... Pages 408–421

CHAPTER XXIII

Cerro de Muinora, the Highest Mountain in Chihuahua—The Northern Tepehuanes—Troubles Cropping Out of the Camera—Sinister Designs on Mexico Attributed to the Author—Maizillo—Foot-races Among the Tepehuanes, and *Vice Versa*—Profitable Liquor Traffic—Medicine Lodges—Cucuduri, the Master of the Woods—Myth of the Pleiades, ... Pages 422–436

CHAPTER XXIV

On to Morelos—Wild and Broken Country—The Enormous Flower-spike of the Amole—Subtropical Vegetation of Northwestern Mexico—Destructive Ants—The Last of the Tubars—A Spectral Ride—Back to the United States—An Awful Thunder-storm—Close Quarters—Zape—Antiquities—When an " Angel " Dies—Mementos of a Reign of Terror—The Great Tepehuane Revolution of 1616—The Fertile Plains of Durango, ... Pages 437–450

CHAPTER XXV

Winter in the High Sierra—Mines—Pueblo Nuevo and Its Amiable Padre—A Ball in My Honour—*Sancta Simplicitas*—A Fatiguing Journey to the Pueblo of Lajas and the Southern Tepehuanes—Don't Travel After Nightfall!—Five Days Spent in Persuading People to Pose Before the Camera—The Regime of Old Missionary Times—Strangers Carefully Excluded—Everybody Contemplating Marriage is Arrested—Shocking Punishments for Making Love—Bad Effects of the Severity of the Laws, ... Pages 451–470

CONTENTS

CHAPTER XXVI

Pueblo Viejo—Three Languages Spoken Here—The Aztecs—The Musical Bow—Theories of Its Origin—Dancing Mitote—Fasting and Abstinence—Helping President Diaz—The Importance of Tribal Restrictions—Principles of Monogamy—Disposition of the Dead, . Pages 471–483

CHAPTER XXVII

Inexperienced Help—How to Acquire Riches from the Mountains—Sierra del Nayarit—The Coras—Their Aversion to " Papers "—Their Part in Mexican Politics — A Dejeuner à la Fourchette — La Danza, ... Pages 484–495

CHAPTER XXVIII

A Glimpse of the Pacific from the High Sierra—A Visionary Idyl—The Coras Do Not Know Fear—An Un-Indian Indian—Pueblo of Jesus Maria—A Nice Old Cora Shaman—A Padre Denounces Me as a Protestant Missionary—Trouble Ensuing from His Mistake—Scorpions, ... Pages 496–507

CHAPTER XXIX

A Cordial Reception at San Francisco—Mexicans in the Employ of Indians—The Morning Star, the Great God of the Coras—The Beginning of the World—How the Rain-clouds were First Secured—The Rabbit and the Deer—Aphorisms of a Cora Shaman—An Eventful Night—Hunting for Skulls—My Progress Impeded by Padre's Ban—Final Start for the Huichol Country—A Threatened Desertion, . . . Pages 508–530

LIST OF ILLUSTRATIONS

Portrait of the Author . . . . *Frontispiece*

PAGE

A Dasylirion, ... I
Cottonwood, ... : - . . . 4
Cereus Greggii, a small cactus with enormous root, ... 5
Fronteras, ... 7
Remarkable Ant-hill, ... 8
Church Bells at Opoto, ... 10
Also a Visitor, ... 11
A Mexican from Opoto, ... 12
Rock-carvings near Granados, ... 15
The Church in Bacadehuachi, ... 17
Aztec Vase, Found in the Church of Bacadehuachi, ... 18
Agave Hartmani, a new species of century plant, ... 19
Ancient Pecking on a Trachyte Boulder one foot square, . . . 20
In the Hills of Northeastern Sonora, ... 24
Adios, Señor! 27
View toward the Northwest from Sierra de Huehuerachi, . . . 29
Our Principal Guide Leaving Us, ... 32
A Mule with its Pack of Crates, ... 33
The Photographic Mule, ... 34
On the Crest of the Sierra, ... 37
Apache Monument, ... 39
Camp in the High Sierra, ... 47
Bringing in Deer, ... 51
The Largest Woodpecker in the World, ... 54
Distant View of Cupola-shaped Granary in Cave, ... 58
Single Wall in Cliff, ... 61
Ground Plan of House Groups in Granary Cave, ... 62
Cupola-shaped Granary in Cave, ... 64
Granary in Tlaxcala, ... 65
Bases of Granaries in Cave, ... 65
Ground Plan of House Groups in Cave on East Side of the River, . 66

PAGE

Sandal Plaited from Yucca Leaves, ... 67

Heel of a Sandal, Showing Plaiting, ... 68

Piece of Wood Showing Drill Mark, ... 68

Pendant of Wood, ... 69

Implement for Throwing, ... 69

Burial Caves in Cave Valley, ... 70

A Mummified Body, ... 71

Rock Paintings in White on the Inside of a Burial Cave in Cave Valley, 72

A Trinchera in Cave Valley, ... 73

Ancient Cave-dwellings in Strawberry Valley, ... 75

Interior View of Cave-dwellings Shown on Page 75, ... 76

Exterior View of Cave-dwellings in Strawberry Valley, . . . 77

Objects Found in Mounds at Upper Piedras Verdes River, . . . 81

Painting on Rock on Piedras Verdes River, ... 82

Figures on Walls of a Cave-house on Piedras Verdes River, . . 83

Figure on Rock on Piedras Verdes River, ... 83

Hunting Antelope in Disguise, ... 84

Casas Grandes, ... 85

Ceremonial Hatchet with Mountain Sheep's Head. From Casas Grandes.
 Broken, ... 88

Earthenware Vessel in Shape of a Woman. From Casas Grandes, . 89

Cerro de Montezuma and the Watch Tower Seen from the South, . 91

Double Earthenware Vessel, from San Diego, with Hollow Connection
 at Base, ... 92

Extension of Designs on Plate I., *a*, ... 95

The Horned Toad Jar, Seen from Above and Below. Plate I., *c*, . 95

Extension of Designs on Plate I., *d*, ... 95

Extension of Designs on Plate III., *e*, ... 95

Extension of Designs on Plate V., *e*, ... 97

Black Ware, Highly Polished, ... 97

Extension of Design on Plate IV., *a*, ... 98

Extension of Design on Plate IV., *b*, ... 98

Extension of Designs on Plate IV., *c*, ... 98

Extension of Designs on Plate IV., *f*, ... 98

Extension of Designs on Plate V., *c*, ... 98

Ancient Cave-dwelling at Garabato, ... 101

Part of Cave-dwellings at Garabato, ... 103

Design in Red on Second-story Wall, ... 105

PAGE

Piece of Matting from Garabato Cave, ... 107
Ancient Cave-houses and Granaries near Aros River, ... 111
Tarahumare, ... 119
Tarahumare Plough with Wooden Share, ... 121
Tarahumare Ploughshare Made of Oak, ... 122
Tarahumare Ploughshare of Stone, ... 122
Young Southern Pima, ... 123
Middle-aged Southern Pima, ... 124
Southern Pimas Living in a Brushwood Inclosure, ... 125
Pine Cone Serving as a Comb, ... 127
Southern Pima Arrow Release, ... 128
Small Crosses Placed in a Log in Front of Southern Pima House, . 128
The Waterfall of Basasiachic, ... 129
Tarahumare Ploughman. 133
Ancient Stone Hammer Seen in the Presidente's Yard, . . . 134
Tarahumare Indians from Pino Gordo, ... 137
Tarahumare Court in Session at Cusarare, ... 140
Barranca de Urique, ... 145
Our Tarahumare Carriers and the Gobernador, ... 148
Tarahumare Men, ... 149
Tarahumare Woman, ... 150
Necklace of Seeds of *Coix Lachryma-Jobi*, ... 151
Tarahumare Ear-ornament; one seed *Coix Lachryma-Jobi* at top.
    Natural size, ... 151
Tarahumare Ranch near Barranca de Cobre, showing ploughed fields
    supported by stone walls, ... 152
Tarahumare House near Barranca de Cobre, ... 157
Tarahumare House in the Hot Country, ... 158
Cappe of Sandstone Pillar, showing effect of erosion, ... 159
Tarahumare Family Camping under a Tree, ... 161
Inhabited Cave, the Home of a Tarahumare Belle, . . . 162
The Belle of the Cave, ... 163
Side View of Cave on Page 165, Showing Store-houses and Inclosure, . 164
Inhabited Cave, Showing Store-houses, Inclosure, and Extended Floor, 165
Cave with Wooden Ladder Leading to a Store-room, . . . 169
Crosses Made from the Natural Growth of Pine-trees in Front of Tara-
    humare House, ... 172
Crosses in Front of Tarahumare House, ... 173

PAGE

Cross, ... 174

Tarahumare Store-house of Stones and Mud, ... 175

Caves Used as Store-houses, ... 176

Tarahumare Store-houses Made of Logs, ... 178

Cactus Flowers, ... 179

Making Larvæ Ready for the Pot, ... 182

Gathering Pithaya, ... 188

In the Highlands of the Sierra, ... 194

Tarahumare Interpreters, ... 201

Indian Trail Cut in a Ridge of Tuff, ... 202

Pecking on Rock in the Neighbourhood of Norogachic, . . 203

Tarahumare Girl from the Neighbourhood of Norogachic, . . 205

Pecking on Rock in the Neighbourhood of Norogachic, . . 207

Winter Morning in the Sierra, ... 209

Dogs of Chihuahua, ... 216

Tarahumare Girdles, ... 219

Aspect of the Tarahumare Country in Humarisa, ... 227

Taking My Baggage Down an Indian Trail in the Barranca de San
    Carlos, ... 231

Tarahumare Woman, ... 236

Tarahumare Man, ... 237

Usual Crouching Position of the Tarahumare, ... 238

Tarahumare Man, ... 239

Tarahumares Sunning Themselves, ... 240

Tarahumare Girl. The Hair Worn in Mexican Fashion, . . 242

Weaving a Girdle, ... 249

Patterns of Tarahumare Belts, ... 249

Woman Pottery Maker and Some Results of Her Labour, . . 250

Tarahumare Pottery from Panalachic, ... 252

Basket for Straining Tesvino, ... 254

Tarahumare Blanket, ... 259

A Tarahumare Call, ... 260

Tarahumare Arrow Release, ... 262

Tarahumare Baskets, ... 263

Tarahumare Girl Carrying Water, ... 265

Tarahumare, Showing Mode of Wearing Blanket, . . . 268

Tarahumare Blankets, ... 274

Stone Disk for Playing, ... 277

PAGE

Sticks Used by Tepehuanes for Playing, ... 278
Value of the Different Sides of a Knuckle-bone, ... 278
Tarahumares Playing Quinze, ... 279
Cross Marking the Track of the Foot-runners, ... 283
Tarahumares Racing by Torch-light, ... 285
Making Wagers at a Foot-race, ... 288
Part of Tarahumare Rattling Belt, ... 290
Tarahumare Foot-runners, Photographed after the Race, . . . 291
Tarahumare Women Crossing a Stream in Their Race, . . . 293
Fork and Wooden Ball Used in Women's Game, ... 294
Stick and Ring Used in Women's Game, ... 294
The Coyote, *Canis Latrans*, ... 303
Tarahumare Shaman's Rattles, ... 313
Rubio, the Shaman, ... 316
Rubio, the Shaman, and His Wife at Home in Their Cave, . . 319
Shaman Rubio's Cave, Seen from the Outside, ... 320
Rubio, the Shaman, Examining a Man Accused of Sorcery, . . 324
Trepanned Tarahumare Skull, Female, ... 328
The Beginning of the Rutuburi and the Yumari Dance, . . . 335
Dancing Yumari, ... 341
Sacrificing Tesvino after a Yumari Dance, ... 345
Ready to Begin Eating and Drinking after a Night's Dancing of
    Rutuburi, ... 349
Echinocactus, ... 357
Hikuli or Peyote, the principal sacred cacti, ... 358
Dry Hikuli, ... 359
Shaman's Notched Stick, ... 366
Ancient Notched Sticks, ... 366
Tarahumare Women Dancing Hikuli at Guajochic Station, . . 369
Mammilaria fissurata, ... 373
Shaman Rubio and His Company at a Hikuli Feast. Photographed
    after a Night's Singing and Dancing, ... 376
Tarahumare Medicine Figure, Mexico, ... 378
Ancient Ritualistic Petrograph, Arizona, ... 378
Mourning, ... 380
View from the North across Barranca de San Carlos, near Guachochic, . 392
Barranca de San Carlos, in its Upper Part, ... 395
One of My Companions in Barranca de San Carlos, . . . 397

PAGE

The Widow Grinding Corn in Her Camp, ... 399
Bow and Throwing-stick for the Fish-spear, ... 401
The Amole, a Species of Agave, ... 402
Tarahumares on the Rio Fuerte Fishing with Their Blankets, . . 405
Pinus Lumholtzii, ... 409
Civilised Tarahumare Boy, ... 417
Juan Ignacio and His Son, Pagan Tarahumares, ... 419
A Tepehuane Family, ... 423
Old Log-houses near Nabogame, ... 424
Tepehuanes from Nabogame, ... 427
Tepehuane Medicine Lodge near Mesa de Milpillas, ... 432
A Well-known Tepehuane Shaman, ... 434
Salvia elegans, var. *sonorensis*, ... 438
The Flower-spike of the Amole, ... 439
Cereus cæspitosus, ... 440
Tubar Man, ... 442
Tubar Women, ... 443
Beads of Burnt Clay, from Tubar Tombs, ... 444
Tepehuane Sling made from Maguey Fibre, ... 458
Tepehuane Pouch made from Maguey Fibre, ... 459
Tepehuane Store-house, near Lajas, ... 461
The Musical Bow of the Tepehuanes of the South, and of the Aztecs, 475
Rattle for Ankle, made from Empty Pods of a Palm, ... 477
Cora Men and Women from Santa Teresa, ... 489
Cora Pouch, of Unusual Shape, made of Wool. Patterns represent
    Flying Birds and a row of Deer, ... 492
Cora Indians from Mesa del Nayarit, ... 501
The Sacred Dancing-place of the Coras, called Towta, the supposed
    residence of the great Taquat of the East of the same name. Pho-
    tographed after the Dancing was over, ... 517
God's Eye, made by the Cora Tribe as a Prayer for My Health and Life, 521

PLATES

PLATES I., II., III., IV. Pottery from San Diego . . *facing page* 94
PLATE V. Pottery from San Diego and Casas Grandes . *facing page* 94
PLATE VI. A Tarahumare Beauty . . . . . *facing page* 266

Two maps are attached to the inside back cover of the second volume.

UNKNOWN
MEXICO

UNKNOWN MEXICO

CHAPTER I

PREPARATIONS FOR THE START—OUR DRY GOODS RELISHED BY THE
CATTLE—I BECOME A "COMPADRE"—BEAUTIFUL NORTHERN
SONORA—MEXICAN MULETEERS PREFERABLE IN THEIR OWN
COUNTRY—APACHE STORIES—SIGNS OF ANCIENT INHABITANTS
—ARRIVAL AT UPPER YAQUI RIVER—OPATA INDIANS NOW
MEXICANISED—A FLOURISHING MEDICAL PRACTICE—MEXICAN
MANNERS—ROCK-CARVINGS—HOW CERTAIN CACTI PROPAGATE.

HEAVY floods in the southern part of Arizona and
New Mexico, with consequent wash-outs along
the railroads, interfered with my plans and somewhat

A Dasylirion.

delayed my arrival at Bisbee, Arizona, a small but
important mining place
from which I had decided
to start my expedition. It
is only some twenty odd
miles from the Mexican
border, and the Copper
Queen Company main-
tains there well-supplied
stores, where the neces-
sary outfit, provisions, etc.,
could be procured. The
preparations for the start consumed more than two
weeks. Animals had to be bought, men selected and
hired, provisions purchased and packed. In the mean-

time I was joined by the various scientific assistants appointed to take part in the expedition.

The horses and mules were bought in the neighbourhood. In purchasing animals much caution is required in that part of the country, as even men who pose as gentlemen will try to take advantage of the situation. One such individual not only raised his prices, but delivered unbroken animals. Much loss of time and endless annoyance were caused, first in the camp and later on the road, by unruly mules, that persistently threw off their packs and had to be subdued and reloaded.

Gradually, I had succeeded in finding the necessary men. This was another hard task to accomplish. There are always plenty of fellows, ready for adventures, greedy to earn money, and eager to join such an expedition. But to select the right ones among the cow-boys and miners of the border lands is most difficult.

By what appears, furthermore, to be the compensating justice of Nature, the treasures of the earth are always hidden in the most unattractive, dismal, and dreary spots. At least all the mining places I ever visited are so located, and Bisbee is no exception. To get away from the cramped little village and its unsavoury restaurant, I established my first camp four miles south of it on a commodious and pleasant opening, where we could do our own cooking. But here a new annoyance, and rather a curious one, was met with. The cattle of the region evinced a peculiar predilection for our wearing apparel. Especially at night, the cows would come wandering in among our tents, like the party who goes about seeking what he may devour, and on getting hold of some such choice morsel as a sock, shirt, or blanket, Mrs. Bossie would chew and chew, "gradually," to quote Mark Twain, "taking it in, all the while opening and closing her eyes in a kind of religious ecstasy, as if she had never tasted anything quite as good as an overcoat before in her life." It is no use arguing about tastes, not even with a cow. In spite of this drawback, it was pleasant to be out in the country, which was growing delightfully green after the rains, and gave us a foretaste of what we might expect.

The last thing to do, after all other preparations had been completed, was to get into the camp three small bags containing seven hundred and fifty Mexican dollars, since among the Mexican country population paper money is hardly of any use. There was some talk about a raid on the camp by some toughs in the neighbourhood, but we made our start unmolested, on September 9, 1890.

Thanks to my letters from the Mexican Government, I had no trouble at the custom-house in San Pedro. I stopped a few days there, nevertheless, to buy some Mexican pack-saddles, called aparejos, which, roughly speaking, are leather bags stuffed with straw, to be fastened over the mules' backs. Through the courtesy of the Mexican custom officials I also secured two excellent and reliable Mexican packers, to take the place of some Americans who had been fighting in the camp and proved themselves unfit for my purpose.

As a mark of regard, one of the custom officers invited me to act as godfather to his child. I had to support the baby's head during the ceremony, while an elderly woman held the little body. According to custom, I gave twenty-five cents to every member of the party, and to the child a more adequate present. From now on I was called compadre by most of the people in the village, and that sacred relationship was established between myself and the baby's family, which is deemed of so much importance in the life of the Mexi-

cans.   During ten years of travel and ethnological activity I have never met the child again, but I hope that he
is getting on well.

How beautifully fresh the country looked as we travelled southward in Northern Sonora ! The dreary plains
of Arizona gave way to a more varied landscape, with
picturesque hills studded with oaks and mountain cedars.
Along the rivers cottonwood
was especially noticeable.
There was also an abundance
of wild-grape vines.   Everywhere near the shady creeks
I saw the evening primrose,
brilliantly yellow, while the
intense, carmine-red flowers
of the lobelia peeped out
from under the shrubs.   But
of all the flowers on the
banks of the streams, the
most remarkable was the
exquisitely beautiful *Datura
meteloides*, with its gorgeous white crown, six inches
long and four inches wide.   We saw one cluster of this
creeper fully fifty feet in circumference.   It is well
known among the Navajo Indians that the root of this
plant, when eaten, acts as a powerful stimulant ; but the
better class among the tribe look upon it with disfavour,
as its use often leads to madness and death.   The effect
of the poison is cumulative, and the Indians under its
influence, like the Malays, run amuck and try to kill
everybody they meet.

Cottonwood.

There is also found a species of cactus, with a
root which looks like an enormous carrot.   One small
plant had a root four feet long.   It is used as soap.

Among the birds, doves and flycatchers were most

commonly seen, one species of the latter frequently dazzling our eyes with its brilliant vermilion plumage.

The men I had hired before crossing the border did not work at all well with the Mexicans. They generally considered themselves vastly superior to the latter, whom they did not recognise as "white men." Personally, I preferred the Mexicans, who were obedient, obliging, and less lawless than the rough, mixed-white citizens of the American Southwest. As an illustration of the moral status of the frontier population, I may relate that when about sixty miles south of the border, a custom-house official stationed in the neighbourhood insisted upon examining all my baggage, which, of course, would have involved a lot of trouble. He was neither worse nor better than other custom officers, who seem to exist only to annoy people, and by the exertion of a little patience I

Cereus Greggii. A small cactus with enormous root.

succeeded in settling the matter satisfactorily. But one of my foremen, who had noticed my annoyance, came up to me and asked if I desired "to get rid" of him; if I did, said he, he knew how he could serve me so that nothing more would be heard from the Mexican !

I gradually weeded out this unscrupulous element among the men, and replaced most of the American with Mexican muleteers, who are far superior in that particular line of business. In hiring them, only one precaution had always to be observed : never to accept one unless he had a good recommendation from his

village authorities or some prominent man in the neighbourhood.

The first village of any importance we passed was
Fronteras. It is built on the summit and slopes of an
elevated plateau and looks extremely picturesque at a
distance. Seen close, however, it turns out to be a
wretched little cluster of adobe, or sun-dried brick,
houses. Not only the town itself, but also all the
ranches in the neighbourhood are erected on elevations,
a precaution from former days against the bloodthirsty
Apaches.

Not so very long ago Fronteras was quite an important place, numbering, it is said, some 2,000 inhabitants. But the Apaches, by their incessant attacks,
made the life of the villagers so miserable that the place
became depopulated. Once it was even entirely abandoned. Many stories of the constant fights with these
savages are related by the survivors of those struggles.
Never was it safe in those days to venture outside of the
town limits. Yet the conflicts did not always end in
one way, and the Mexicans sometimes got the better of
the raiders, although it may be doubted whether the
methods by which these results were brought about
would come under the rules of modern warfare.

One bright moonlight night an old man, who had
himself taken part in many an Apache fight, led me to
a deep gorge where seven Apaches once met their
doom. The story he told was as follows :

A large band of warriors came threateningly into the
town. They had killed two hawks and, decorated with
their feathers, were on the warpath. As they were in
such numbers the Mexicans realised that it would be
useless to attempt resistance, and therefore sued for
peace, which was granted. A peace-banquet followed,
during which mescal, the Mexican brandy, flowed freely,

distributed without stint to the warriors by their wily hosts, who were abiding their time. When the Apaches were intoxicated the villagers fell upon them and captured seven men ; most of the band, however, managed to escape. Next day the prisoners were taken to the

Fronteras.

ravine and speared, charges of powder being deemed too good for them. Only el capitan, pointing to his head, requested, as a special favour, to be shot, which was done. Their bodies were buried in the ravine where they fell, but too long a time had already elapsed since the event to enable me to secure for my collections the specimens for which I had been on the lookout. Yet I was told by the inhabitants that the ground about the town was so full of Apache remains that I should have no difficulty in gaining my object in places close by. A number of Apaches, men and women, I was informed, had once been dumped into a well. I set to work at the place indicated, and our efforts were rewarded by the exhumation of eight skulls in perfect condition, besides many typical bones. The last raid of the Apaches on Fronteras was in 1875.

Passing Cochuta about a hundred miles south of Bisbee, we came upon a deposit of fossils. It was

Remarkable Ant-hill.

scarcely more than a mile in extent, but many bones were said to have been taken away from it as curiosities. I had already observed isolated fossil bones along the creeks on several occasions during our travels, but we could find nothing here of value.

Signs that the country was in former times occupied by another race than its present inhabitants are seen everywhere throughout the region we traversed following the road to the south. Here they appear frequently as remarkable groupings of stones firmly embedded in the ground. Only the tops of the stones (the total length of which is about one foot) are seen above the surface, much as stones are used in parks and gardens for ornamental purposes. They are arranged in circles or in rectangles. I saw two circles close to each other, each six feet in diameter. One rectangle measured fifty feet in length by half that in width. Low walls divided it into three indistinct partitions. There was never any wall built underneath these surface stones, nor were there any traces of charring. Among the ruins found on top of the hills we collected a lot of broken pottery and some flint arrowheads. In several places in this district we found gold and coal, but not in paying quantities.

Some forty miles south of Cochuta we turned in a southerly direction, ascending a hilly plateau 3,200 feet above sea-level. Here we observed the first orchids, yellow in colour and deliciously fragrant, and in the cañon below we met the first palms. The rocks continued to show volcanic and metamorphic formation.

About 130 miles south of Bisbee we caught the first glimpse of the Sierra Madre rising above the foot-hills some forty miles off to the east. Its lofty mountain peaks basking in the clear blue ether, beckoned to us inspiringly and raised our expectations of success. This, then, was the region we were to explore! Little did I think then that it would shelter me for several years. It looked so near and was yet so far, and as we travelled on southward the sight of it was soon lost again.

We gradually descended to the Bavispe River, a name here given to the Yaqui River, in accordance with the custom which the Mexicans have in common with people in other parts of the world of giving different names to one river in its course through different districts. It was a treat to catch the first sight of the magnificent sheet of water the river forms near the town of Opoto, as it slowly wends its way through green shrubs. It is the largest river of the west coast of Mexico and is here about 1,400 feet above the level of the sea.

Following the river to the south, we soon passed the towns of Guasavas and Granados. The vegetation

along the river banks is in strong contrast to the land
in general.   Here are fields of sugar-cane, and in the
orchards, orange, fig, and lime trees grow in abundance.
The country, though fertile, is dry, and the heat is great.
Even at the end of October the thermometer sometimes
registered 100° F. in the shade.   The grass had become

Church Bells at Opoto.

dry and scarce, and it was difficult to keep the animals
in satisfactory condition.

This territory was once in the possession of the
large tribe of Opata Indians, who are now civilised.
They have lost their language, religion, and traditions,
dress like the Mexicans, and in appearance are in no
way distinguishable from the labouring class of Mexico
with which they are thoroughly merged through frequent intermarriages.

As we passed the hamlets, our large party and outfit created quite a sensation and aroused the people from the uneventful routine of their daily existence. They used to surround my tent, especially mornings and evenings, as if an auction had been going on inside. Some of them wanted to sell things that would come in handy, such as fowls or panoche (brown sugar). One woman offered me three chickens for one dollar. I told her she charged too high a price, as chickens were not

Also a Visitor.

worth more than twenty-five cents apiece; but she insisted that she wanted a dollar, because she had promised that amount to the padre for reading a mass for a man who had died in the time of Hidalgo at the beginning of the century.

But most of the crowd flocked to my tent to consult me about their ailments. It was useless to tell them that I was not a medical man, or that I had not much medicine to spare, carrying only what I expected to use for my own party. If I had given them all they wanted, our little stock would have been exhausted on the first day ; but in order to soften my heart they would send me molasses, sugar-cane, and similar delicacies. One poor old woman who was suffering from cancer even offered me her donkey if I would cure her—an offer in a way equivalent to a Wall Street magnate's millions, for the donkey was her sole possession on earth.

They all were anxious to have me feel their pulse, whether there was anything the matter with them or not. They firmly believed that this mysterious touch enabled me to tell whether they were afflicted with any kind of disease and how long they were going to live. A woman in delicate condition wanted me to feel her pulse and to tell her from that when

A Mexican from Opoto.

her child was going to be born. I only hope that my practical advice and the little medicine I could give them relieved some of their backaches and sideaches, their felons, croups, and fevers and agues, and above all, their indigestion, which is the prevailing trouble in that section of the country. But I confess that I was nearly tired out with these consultations. In consequence of frequent intermarriages there are many deaf and dumb persons among them, and epilepsy and insanity are by no means rare.

On the other hand, I was assured that such a character as a thief was here unknown. However this might be, it was certain that the Mexicans of Eastern Sonora were a nice class of people. They were pleasant to deal with, very active and obedient, and I never wish for better men than those I then had in my camp, nearly all of whom were from these parts. The people were poor, but genuinely hospitable. Of course they were ignorant, and might not, for instance, recognise a check unless it was green. In each town, however, I found one or two men comparatively rich, who knew more of the world than the others, and who helped me out in my difficulties by going from house to house, collecting all the available cash in town, or what coffee and sugar could be spared to make up the deficiency. One thing is certain, I should never have gotten on so well had it not been for the friendly and obliging attitude of the Mexicans everywhere. As an instance, when the great scarcity of grass began to tell seriously on the animals, I was efficiently helped out by the courtesy of some influential men. Without any personal letters of introduction I received many services whenever I showed my letters of recommendation from the Governor of the State, and had a hearty welcome.

I was so much impressed with the readiness of the people to accommodate and serve me that my notebook contains the remark : " I find the Mexicans more obliging than any nation I have ever come in contact with." It has been my lot to travel for years in Mexico, and my experience with her people only tended to deepen the pleasant impression I received at the outset. Anyone who travels through Mexico well recommended

and conducts himself in accordance with the standard
of a gentleman is sure to be agreeably surprised by the
hospitality and helpfulness of the people, high and low,
and it is not a meaningless phrase of politeness only by
which a Mexican " places his house at your disposal."

It is of the utmost importance to have as your chief
packer a man who thoroughly understands how to take
care of the animals. It is not the custom in Mexico,
as it is everywhere in Australia, to wash the backs
of the animals as soon as the packs or saddles are
taken off—a precaution which is very beneficial, as it
strengthens the skin and prevents inflammation and
sores. In the Southwest they do not wash their
beasts of burden until the mischief is done and they
have to allay the swelling and heal up the cuts. If not
properly cared for from the beginning, the animals
will soon be ailing ; some grow unfit for service, and
much time is lost mornings and evenings curing their
sores. Through the carelessness of some packers I lost
several valuable mules from such wounds. In summer
the blue-bottle fly aggravates the annoyance, as it lays
its eggs in the open spaces of the skin, and maggots
develop in a very short time. Of course there are many
ways of ridding an animal of this pest, but here, as
everywhere, the proverbial ounce of prevention is
better than the pound of cure.

A curious case of a man whose life was threatened
by a blue-bottle fly and its maggots came to my notice.
He was a soldier, and once in a fight he had his nose
cut off so that the nostrils became entirely exposed.
One night when he was asleep, drunk, a fly laid its eggs
in his nose, and when these were hatched it seemed
as if the man was to be eaten up alive. I gave him
some relief by syringing the parts with a solution of
corrosive sublimate. Then an intelligent Mexican, who

had an extensive knowledge of the numberless native medicinal plants (many of which, no doubt, are very valuable), treated the patient, and in two days the poor wretch seemed to be in a fair way to be saved.

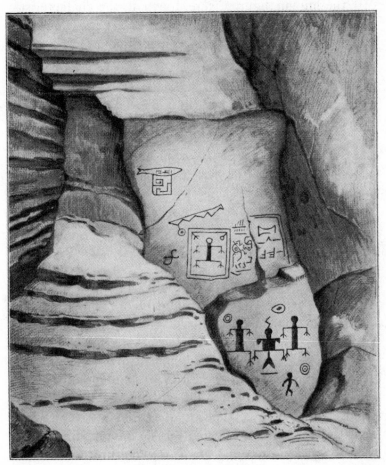

Rock-carvings near Granados.

Near Granados I heard of some petroglyphs, or rock-carvings, and sent Mr. Stephen to examine them. The Mexicans called them "Painted Face." They were to be found only two miles and a half to the northwest of the town, and were interesting. The designs were rudely pecked on the moderately smooth felsite cliffs on a nearly perpendicular wall in the foot-hills, about forty feet above the bed of the arroyo, or gulch. All the human figures were drawn in the characteristic style that we find farther north, the hands and feet being defined with three radiating lines, like a bird's track. The size of the figure, carved in something like a frame, is about twenty by twenty-four inches, and each of the three figures in the group close below is about eighteen inches high. Some of the drawings evidently represent the deified dragon-fly found almost everywhere among the ruins of Arizona and Northern Mexico. There are also the concentric circles, the conventionalised spiral, and the meander design, so common among the North American Indians, and still in use among the Moquis.

Our botanist, Mr. Hartman, drew my attention to an interesting cactus, which is beautifully shaped like a candelabra, and attains a height of three to five feet. As it grows old, the top joints of the branches become thick and heavy and are easily broken off by the wind. The joints, like all other parts of the plant, are beset with numerous inch-long spines, and many of them fasten in the loose, moist soil and strike root. In this way many new plants are formed, standing in a circle around the mother plant. On sloping ground the young plants form rows, some forty feet long. There was a fruit to be observed, but very scarce in comparison with that of other species of *Cereus* growing in the vicinity.

CHAPTER II

A REMARKABLE ANTIQUE PIECE—A NEW SPECIES OF CENTURY
PLANT—ARRIVAL AT NACORI, AT THE FOOT OF THE SIERRA
MADRE—TRINCHERAS—A MAMMOTH TUSK SECURED—CLIMBING
THE SIERRA MADRE—A NEW SQUIRREL DISCOVERED—SOLITUDE
—APACHE MONUMENTS—ARRIVAL AT UPPER BAVISPE RIVER.

FROM Granados we took an easterly course, being
at last able to cross the Bavispe River, which,
owing to heavy rains in the sierra, had for some time
been overflowing. Starting from this point, the ground

The Church in Bacadehuachi.

gradually rising, we arrived at Bacadehuachi, a small
village remarkable for its church, a massive adobe structure, the grand style of which looked somewhat out of
proportion in these mountains. It had been built by

the Franciscans more than 100 years ago, on the site of an older Jesuit church, remains of which are still in existence, and which in turn had been erected on the ruins of an ancient temple.

While inspecting the church Professor Libbey discovered that one of the holy water fonts or stoups was a

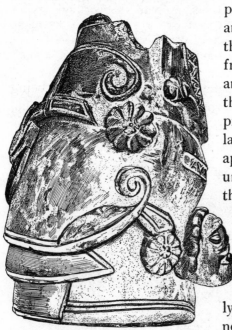

piece of great antiquity, and we were informed that it had been dug up from the débris of the ancient temple when the foundations for the present building were laid. Its æsthetic value appealed even to the unscientific builders of the church, who deemed the vessel worthy of a place in the new cathedral, where it served as a bénitier. Unfortunately, it had been found necessary to engrave on the ancient carving some Roman letters

Aztec Vase, found in the Church of Bacadehuachi.   Height, 37 ctm.

dedicating the vessel to its new purpose. Though this somewhat mars its general character, the vase is a most valuable relic of prehistoric Mexico, not only as a masterpiece of ancient art, but still more as a way-mark or sign-post showing the trend of Aztec migrations.

It was not possible to obtain it right away, but a few days later I sent a messenger to a gentleman in Granados, whose wife had been relieved from illness by some remedy of mine, requesting him to use his influence with the priest, and in due course I had the satisfaction of possessing this valuable relic of history. The vase is made of a soft, unctuous stone resembling steatite (soapstone); it is true agalmatolite, a mineral popularly called pagoda stone. Through the mouth of the human head carved out in front passes a copper tube, which once no doubt pierced the thick wall of the vessel and penetrated into its interior. This tube had been stopped up to make the piece available for its new purpose.

Marching for several days through oaks and mesquites, over hills and rising country, we reached Nacori, a poor village in the foot-hills of the Sierra Madre. It is scarcely forty miles from Granados, and lies at an ele-

Agave Hartmani, a new species of century plant.

vation of 3,700 feet. Our camp, about two miles outside of the village, was permeated with a delicious odour of acacia blossoms, and water in the neighbouring mountains, though strongly impregnated with iron, was quite palatable.

In this region Mr. Hartman found a new form of

agave with delicate stripes of white on the lanceolate
leaves that constitute the basal rosette of the plant.
The flower stalk is only twelve or thirteen inches high,
and I should not wonder if this diminutive and beautiful
century plant some day became fashionable in green-
houses.   It grows in large numbers in the crevices of
the rocks, the perpendicular walls of cañons often being
studded with the bright little rosettes when the drought
has withered all herbaceous vegetation.

From here I made an excursion to an ancient pueblo
site.   As usual, there were traces of small dwellings,
huts of undressed stone, and fragments of pottery.   We
found three mortars and one pestle, a remarkable number of metates (the stone on which corn is ground), and
the corresponding grinding stones, showing that a large
population must have once lived here, huddled together
in a small space.

But the most striking feature of antiquity met thus
far on our journey were curious stone terraces built
across the small gullies.   They are called trincheras
(trenches).   Some of them do not appear to be very old,
and many present the ap-
pearance of tumble-down
walls, but the stones of
which they are construct-
ed were plainly used in
their natural state.   Although many of the
boulders are huge and
irregular in shape, they

Ancient pecking on a trachyte boulder
one foot square.

were used just as they were found.   The building material
always conformed to the surroundings : in places where
conglomerate containing water-worn boulders abounded,
this was used ; where porphyry was prevalent, blocks
of that material were employed.   There is no trace of

dressing or cutting, but in the mason work considerable skill is evident. The walls are not vertical, but incline somewhat toward the slope on which they are erected. The terrace thus formed is often filled with soil to the height of the wall-top for a space of from fifteen to twenty feet. Earth taken from them does not show any colours. Some of these trincheras measure thirty feet in length by four feet in height, while the smallest ones I saw were only five feet long and three feet high. Naturally enough, the largest ones are in the lower part of the gullies; then, some twenty-five feet back and above, others almost as large may be found. As the arroyo rises and narrows, the walls, each placed a little higher up the slope than the preceding one, are necessarily smaller.

In the mountains near Nacori, especially on their eastern and southeastern sides, trincheras were encountered in every gulch as high up as six thousand feet, though steep crests and the mountain tops bear no traces of them. In one arroyo, which was about a thousand feet in length and of comparatively gentle slope, twenty-nine trincheras were counted from the bed of the main drainage to the summit of the mountain. Some of them were quite close together, three being within eighteen feet of one another.

These trincheras somewhat resemble the small terrace gardens of the Moqui Indians, and have undoubtedly been used for agricultural purposes, just as they are used by the Tarahumares to this day (page 152). It is true that they are built in great numbers, sometimes in localities that would appear unsuitable for farming; but, on the other hand, they are seldom, if ever, found far from the remains of habitations, a fact from which it may also reasonably be inferred that the ruined houses, as well as the trincheras, were originally built by

the same race. Some of the terraces were, no doubt,
erected as a protection of the crop against enemies and
wild animals ; but it is impossible to think that they
were intended for irrigation dams, though we did see
water running through some, coming out of a marsh.
Still less likely is it that they had been used as mining
dams.

As soon as the plains of Northern Sonora were left
behind, and the country became hilly and broken, these
peculiar structures were conspicuous. At first they appeared more like walls built simply along the slopes
of the hills, and not crossing gulches. They seem to be
more numerous in the western and central part of the
sierra, its spurs and foot-hills, than in the eastern part
of the great range. As regards their southern extent,
they are not found further south than the middle part
of the state of Chihuahua. Captain Bourke, in his
book, "An Apache Campaign," mentions that "in
every sheltered spot could be discerned ruins, buildings,
walls, and dams, erected by an extinct race once possessing these regions." Mr. A. F. Bandelier, on his journey to the Upper Yaqui River, in 1885, which took
him as far as Nacori, also refers to them, and Professor
W. J. McGee, on his expedition in 1895, found in Northeastern Sonora ruins locally known as *Las Trincheras*,
which he considered the most elaborate prehistoric work
known to exist in Northwestern Mexico. They com-
prise, he says, terraces, stone-walls, and inclosed fortifications, built of loose stones and nearly surrounding
two buttes.

I must not omit to mention that in a week's exploration in the mountains near Nacori, Mr. Stephen and
his party did not find any pottery fragments, nor flint
flakes, nor grinding stones. They reported that there
was in that region no other trace of an early people

than the hundreds of trincheras in the lower portions of the arroyos.

Noteworthy, however, was the frequent occurrence of old trails across the hills, some quite plainly traceable for three and four hundred yards. Old oaks stretched their limbs across many of them quite close to the ground.

While at Nacori I learned from the inhabitants that at no great distance from their town there were several deposits containing *huesos giganteos* (giants' bones), a name given to fossils in this part of the world, where the people imagine that the large bones were originally those of giants. I had then neither time nor men to make excavations of any importance; but Mr. White, the mineralogist of the expedition, whom I sent to look into the matter, and who devoted a week to the examination of the deposits, reported that one of them, in a valley sixteen miles south of Nacori, was a bed of clay thirty feet thick and about a mile and a half long. On the edge of this field he discovered a tusk six feet eight inches long and twenty-six inches at its widest circumference, and having almost the curve of a circle. It was not petrified and had no bone core, but the hole filled in with clay, and its colour was a rich mahogany. It was undoubtedly the tusk of a mammoth.

From the beginning it had surprised me how very ignorant the people of Sonora were regarding the Sierra Madre. The most prominent man in Opoto, a town hardly forty miles from the sierra, told me that he did not know how far it was to the sierra, nor was he able to say exactly where it was. Not even at Nacori, so close to this tremendous mountain range, was there much information to be gotten about it. What the Mexicans know about that region may be briefly summed up thus: That it is a vast wilderness of mountains most difficult of approach; that it would take eight days to climb some of the high ridges; that it contains immense pine forests alive with deer, bear, and wonderfully large wood-peckers, able to cut down whole trees; and that in its midst there are still existing numerous remains of a people who vanished long ago, but who once tilled the

In the Hills of Northeastern Sonora.

soil, lived in towns and built monuments, and even bridges over some of its cañons.

This general ignorance is mainly due to the fact that until very recently this entire part of the sierra, from the border of the United States south about 250 miles, was under the undisputed control of the

wild Apache Indians. From their mountain strong-
holds these marauders made raiding expeditions into the
adjacent states, west and east, sweeping down upon the
farms, plundering the villages, driving off horses and
herds of cattle, killing men and carrying off women and
children into slavery. Mines became unworkable; farms
had to be deserted ; the churches, built by the Spaniards,
mouldered into decay. The raiders had made themselves absolute masters, and so bold were they that at
one time a certain month in the year was set apart for
their plundering excursions and called "the moon of the
Mexicans," a fact which did not prevent them from rob-
bing at other seasons. Often troops would follow them
far into the mountains, but the " braves " fought so skil-
fully, and hid so well in the natural fortresses of their
native domain, that the pursuit never came to anything,
and the Mexicans were completely paralysed with fear.
The dread of the terrible pillagers was so great that even
at the time when I first went into the district, the Mexicans did not consider it a crime to shoot an Apache at
sight.

Such a scourge did this tribe become that the
Governor of Chihuahua had a law passed through the
Legislature, which put a certain price upon the head
of every Apache. But this law had soon to be re-
pealed, as the Mexicans, eager to get the reward, took
to killing the peaceful Tarahumares, whose scalps, of
course, could not be distinguished from those of the
Apaches.

It was not even now safe for a small party to cross
the Sierra Madre, as dissatisfied Apaches were constantly breaking away from the San Carlos Reservation
in Arizona, and no Mexican could have been induced to
venture singly into that vast unknown domain of rock
and forest, about which lingered such painful memories

of bloodshed and terror.*　　In the early part of our journey a Mexican officer had called on me to offer, in the
name of the Governor of the State of Sonora, his services
as escort and protection against the Apaches; but I declined the courtesy, preferring to depend rather upon my
own men.　I am happy to say that I had no personal en-
counter with the dreaded "Shis Inday," or Men of the
Woods, as they call themselves, though on one occasion
we came upon fresh tracks near one of our camps, and
also upon small bunches of yucca leaves tied together in
a peculiar way known to the Mexicans as signs intelligi-
ble only to the Apaches.

The only precaution I had taken against possible attacks was to augment my force of trustworthy Mexican
muleteers.　Among the new recruits was an honest-
looking Opata Indian, who joined the camp one evening,
clad in the national costume of white cotton cloth, and
carrying in his hand a small bundle containing his wife's
petticoat (probably intended to do duty as a blanket)
and a pair of scissors.　This was his whole outfit for a
winter campaign in the Sierra Madre.　They are hardy
people, these Indians!　This man told me that he was
thirty years old; his "señora," he said, was twenty-five;
when he married her she was fifteen, and now they had
eleven children.

Finally I succeeded in securing two guides.　One of
them was a very intelligent man, who had been several
times in the sierra; the other one had been only as far
as Chuhuichupa, and, although he did not remember the
way very well, still he thought that with the help of the
other man he would be able to make out the route.　As
we could do no better, we had to take him as the best
guide available.

* Several years after my expedition passed through those regions the Apaches on
more than one occasion attacked outlying Mormon ranches and killed several persons.

After having received some supplementary provisions from Granados, I at last, on December 2, 1890, began the ascent. It was a beautiful day; the air was clear and warm and the sun shone bright, as it always does at this time of the year in this favoured region. The genius of spring seemed to hover about, and snow, frost and scarcity of grass seemed far removed contingencies. Everything looked promising.

As I left the town, following the pack-train after having made the last settlements with the natives, I

Adios, Señor!

passed a little hut, the last homestead on this side of the sierra. In front of it stood a young girl, her hand raised to shade her eyes against the rays of the sinking sun. She had watched the expedition go by, and was much excited by the strange sight of so many men, the wonderful array of animals and great quantity of baggage never before seen in those parts of the world. With her fine dark eyes, her loose wavy hair and graceful figure, she made a strikingly beautiful picture, and as she called out in a sweet, melodious voice, "*Adios, Señor!*" I took this kindly greeting from a pretty girl

as a good omen for my journey. On the spur of the
moment I dismounted and perpetuated the auspicious
scene by means of a kodak which I carried fastened to
the pommel of my saddle.   I wish it had been possible
for me to send her that picture as a token of my gratitude for her cheery greeting.   She surely would have
appreciated it, as all Mexicans delight in seeing their
photographs.   Then I turned my face to the east and
soon overtook my men.

To reach the Sierra Madre from the Bavispe River
by way of Nacori, two—or, as the Mexicans consider it,
three—sierras have to be crossed, all running, generally
speaking, in a northwesterly to southeasterly direction.
The first two ranges are quite easy to climb.   The third
is the Sierra Madre proper, which the Mexicans here
call Sierra de Nacori, as the upper Bavispe River from
its source makes a great detour toward the north around
it, thereby partly separating it from the main chain.
Even this range does not really present any unsur-
mountable difficulties if the weather is fine ; in bad
weather, I admit, some parts of the trail we made would
be all but impracticable.

Having reached the second range called the Sierra
de Huehuerachi, near its northern terminus, and looking backward, we see the Sierra de Bacadehuachi lying
farthest to the west.   On its eastern flank tower steep-
tilted broken masses of conglomerate, and the frowning
row of hog-backs just north and east of Nacori are
only a continuation of that range.   But looking east
from where we were we obtained the first close view
of the main range of the Sierra Madre (Sierra de Nacori).   It rises bold and majestic on the opposite side
of the valley, at the bottom of which runs the little river
of Huehuerachi.

In this valley we camped for two days, being de-

View toward the Northwest from Sierra de Huehuerachi.

layed by rains. It was early in December, but we found *Helianthus* ten to twelve feet high in bloom everywhere in the cañons. A *Salvia* with a blue corolla, dotted with red glands, was very striking, a new variety, as it proved. We also observed elders with flowers and leaves at the same time, and the *Bambusa* formed a thick light-green undergrowth in beautiful contrast to the darker shades of the oaks, elders, and fan palms. The latter were the last of their kind we saw on this side of the sierra.

We then went six miles further to the northeast. At first the trail followed the little river, whose clear and rapid water is about a foot deep and on an average six feet wide. Frequently its bed had to be cleared of palm trees to make it passable for the pack train, and big boulders and heavy undergrowth made travel rough. Then, ascending a cordon which led directly up to the main range, we followed for a while a dim trail on which the Apaches used to drive the herds of cattle they had stolen, and which is said to lead to a place so inaccessible that two Indians could keep a whole company at bay. The surface soil we had lately been travelling over was covered with boulders and fragments of conglomerate.

The Sierra Madre was now so close that the tilted masses of its rocks seemed to overhang our tents threateningly where we had pitched them at its foot. From this camp we had about the same splendid view as from the ridge of Huehuerachi we had just left behind ; and between us and the foot-hills of the Sierra de Bacadehuachi stretched out a vast mass of barren-looking rocks and hills. The Mexicans call them *agua blanca*, a designation also applied to the small water course that runs through them in a northerly and southerly direction, but which from our point of view could not be

made out in the chaotic confusion. Away off toward
the north, at a distance of from fifteen to twenty miles,
could be seen a high chain of sharp peaks.

I may mention here that I found the water of many
streamlets and brooks throughout the western mountains of Mexico to have a slightly whitish colour and a
dull, opalescent look, like a strong solution of quinine.
The Mexicans call it *agua blanca*, or *agua zarca*, and
consider it the best water they have. Many places, especially ranches, are named after it. In the locality
where we now found ourselves the water had a slightly bitter taste, owing to a strong admixture of iron and
other minerals, but generally it was very palatable.

Here, only twenty-three miles from Nacori, and at
an elevation of 4,000 feet, we were obliged to make
camp for three days. Dense fogs and occasional hard
showers made travel impossible. Besides, our principal
guide, Agustin Rios, became dangerously ill. He was
sixty-five years old, and I decided to send him back.

Our Principal Guide Leaving Us.

When I hired him I
had not been aware
that he was afflicted
with an incurable dis-
ease, and that on this
account his wife had
tried to keep him at
home. Now he had
to be carried on a sort
of palanquin construct-
ed for the occasion,
and I regret to state
that he died before he reached his home in Nacori. He
had been a reliable man, and his loss was very deplorable.

Before he left he gave me directions for finding a
rather large ancient pueblo, which he had come across

once in the sierra, and of which he frequently spoke to us. However, our search for it proved fruitless, and I am inclined to think that it would probably not have differed much from those we found later on Bavispe River.

From now on I made it a rule to send three or four men about two days ahead of the main body of the ex-

A Mule with its Pack of Crates.

pedition, to make a path. Occasionally they were guided by Apache tracks, but for the most part we cut our own way through the wilderness. Instead of adopting the Mexican method of going uphill as straight as practicable, I had the trail cut zigzag, and to this I attribute the fact that I was able to pull through at all, as it saved the animals an immense amount of strain. The steepest inclination we ascended was 40°, while for the most part we climbed at an angle of about 30°. On some of the ridges, in order to help an animal up, one man had to drag it by a line, while two others pushed it from behind. In many places the mules had to be led one by one along the narrow edge of chasms.

To look at these mountains is a soul-inspiring sensation; but to travel over them is exhaustive to muscle and patience. And the possibility of losing at any moment perhaps the most valuable part of your outfit is a constant and severe strain on your mind. Nobody except those who have travelled in the Mexican mountains can understand and appreciate the difficulties and anxieties attending such a journey. Not only the animals themselves, but everything they carry is vital to the success of the expedition, and there is always a danger that, for instance, your camera and photographic outfit, and the priceless collection of negatives already taken, may roll down a precipice.

A mule with its bulky pack is, to a certain extent, helpless on these narrow mountain trails. Old and experienced animals often manœuvre their packs with a cleverness that is almost human : yet, whenever a mule runs accidentally against some projection, or its foot slips, the poor beast invariably loses its balance, and over it goes, down the hill with ever-increasing velocity.

The Photographic Mule.

On one occasion I heard a noise coming from above without being at first able to discern what caused it. A few stones came tumbling down, and were presently followed by a donkey, pack and all, turning over and over with astounding speed. It cleared a perpendicular rock some twenty feet high and landed at its base, rolling over twice. Then, to my amazement, it rose to its feet in the midst of its scattered cargo. And do you know what that cargo consisted of ?—a case of dynamite and our tool chest ! As fast as their legs could carry them, two Mexicans were by its side, promptly reloading the donkey and leading it up to the trail as coolly as if nothing had happened. A very fine mule, raised on the plains of Arizona, was naturally giddy, and met with such a mishap three times in one day, tumbling down 150 to 200 feet without, however, being seriously hurt. At first I was greatly shocked to see the animals thus rolling over and over with their packs, down the mountain sides, never stopping until checked by some large tree or rock, sometimes 200 feet below. But the Mexicans were evidently quite accustomed to such happenings, which seemed to be in the regular line of their travel.

I could not help admiring the agility as well as the valour of my Mexican packers and muleteers on such occasions. They moved about as sure-footed and quick as sailors on their ship, and always on the alert. Whenever one of the poor beasts lost its foothold, the men would instantly run after it, and as soon as some obstacle stopped its downward career they would be by its side and relieve it of its burden. Of course, sometimes the animal was badly bruised about the head, and unable to carry a pack for a few days; but, *mirabile dictu!* in the majority of cases it rose to its feet. Then, after giving it a few moments' respite, the packers would strap the cargo again on its back, unless they deemed it proper to take a part of it upon themselves, so that the beast might more safely climb the declivity. The men really seemed indefatigable. One of them once took upon his head a large case of honey and carried it up the ridge on a run. Strange as it may sound, on my first journey across the Sierra Madre I did not lose one animal by such accidents.

Climbing, climbing, climbing, one massive cordon after another, at the start through dense oak thickets, and over hills flattened and eroded with countless deep, precipitous gashes seaming the rock in every direction.

Numerous springs oozed and trickled from the stratified conglomerate along the edges, sides, and bottoms of the ravines. The tops of some of these truncated knolls were quite swampy in the depressions, and covered with a thin-stemmed feathery grass. Here and there was a clump of scrub oaks ; sparsely scattered about were small pines. We found great numbers of *Opuntia Missouriensis*, called by the Mexicans nopal ; small mesquite shrubs, too, are seen everywhere, while the resurrection plant covers great areas, like the heather on the Scotch hills. Here are also found century plants, or agaves, and many species of small ferns, such as the graceful maidenhair. In the larger watercourses are poplars and maples, now presenting their most brilliant hues, and carrying the thoughts of the Americans back to their Northern homes.

Thus we advanced for about six miles and made camp, at an elevation of 6,300 feet, on some old trincheras, with a fine view over the vast country we had left below. Large flocks of gray pigeons of remarkable size squatted on the pine trees near-by, and two specimens of the gigantic woodpecker we here observed for the first time. Here, too, Mr. Robinette shot a new species of squirrel, *Sciurus Apache*. It was large, of a pale grayish-yellow color varied with black, and having a long, full and bushy tail.

We had now arrived in the pine region of the sierra. The Mexican scouts reported that the country ahead of us was still more difficult of access ; but the track having been laid out well by Professor Libbey along the pine-covered slopes, we safely arrived at the crest of the sierra, which here has an elevation of 8,200 feet. The steep slopes of the valleys and crevices were covered with slippery pine needles eight to twelve inches long, while the pines rose up to a

height of a hun-
dred feet or more.
The forest, never
touched by a wood-
man's axe, had a
remarkably young
and fresh look
about it. Now and
then, however, at
exposed places we
came upon trees
broken off like
matches, telling of
what terrific storms
may rage over
these solitary re-
gions that received
us calmly enough.
Not until we had
reached the top did
we feel the wind
blowing pretty hard
from the east and
encouraging us in

On the Crest of the Sierra.

our hopes that the fine weather would continue, although
the moon appeared hazy.

Having ascended the sierra, we made a picturesque
camp on the top of the cordon, in the midst of forests
so dense that we did not get any view of the landscape.
While here, Mr. Stephen discovered, on the summit of
a peak, about four hundred and twenty feet above the
brow of the ridge, a small circular structure about four
feet in diameter. Four or five large fragments of
scoria, each about fifteen inches high, were set around
in a circle, and the space between them was filled in

with small fragments.   No nicety was shown in the work, but the arrangement of the stones was not accidental.   It was, however, quite old, for in several places the fragments were cemented together with a thick coat of lichen.   The purpose of the circle is a matter of conjecture.

We were now obliged, as the guide did not seem to know any more of the country, to explore ahead of us before the main body of the expedition could proceed further.   Several of us went out in different directions, and I happened to strike the right course, which here unexpectedly goes first northward.   Accompanied by my dog " Apache," I walked in the fresh morning air through the sombre pine woods, the tops of which basked in glorious sunshine, and along the high cordon, which ran up to a height of 8,900 feet (the highest point reached on my first expedition over the Sierra Madre), until I came to a point where it suddenly terminated.   But I soon ascertained that a spur branching off to the east would lead us in the right direction.

I sat down to gaze upon the magnificent panorama of the central part of the Sierra Madre spread out before me.   To the north and northeast were pine-covered plateaus and hills in seemingly infinite successions ; on the eastern horizon my eyes met the dark, massive heights of Chuhuichupa, followed towards the south by ridge upon ridge of true sierras with sharp, serrated crests, running mainly from northwest to southeast. And between them and me was an expanse of gloomy, pine-hidden cordons, one succeeding close upon another, and running generally in the same direction as the sierras.   Primeval stillness and solitude reigned all over the woodland landscape.   I like the society of man, but how welcome and refreshing are occasional moments of undisturbed communion with Nature !

On the following day the pack train moved along the path I had walked over. We were pleasantly surprised to find at this season, the middle of December, and at this elevation, a species of violet in bloom, while *Lupinus* and *Vicia* were already in seed. We made our camp at a place 7,400 feet above sea level, and here we noticed trincheras close by, with water running through them from a marsh.

We also happened to come upon some stone piles made of rough stones laid on top of each other to a height of about three feet. The Mexicans called them

Apache Monument.

"Apache Monuments," and I saw here eight or ten, three at a distance of only twenty yards from each other and lying in a line from east to west. On the next day we found an Apache track with similar monuments. Some of these piles did not seem to be in places difficult to travel, and therefore could hardly have been intended for guide-posts, though others might have served that purpose ; nor is it easy to see how they could have been meant for boundary marks, unless they were erected by some half-castes who kept company with the Apaches, to divide off the hunting grounds of various families. It seems to me more likely that they are connected with some religious rite.

We had some little difficulty in making our descent to the Bavispe River, but at last we discovered, and travelled down, an old but still practicable trail, dropping nearly 1,000 feet. A little further northward we came down another 1,000 feet, and thus we gradually reached Bavispe, which is here a rapid, roaring stream, girth-deep, and in many places deeper. It here flows northward, describing the easterly portion of the curve it forms around the Sierra de Nacori.

I selected as a camping ground a small mesa on the left bank of the river, among pines and oaks and high grass, about forty feet above the water edge. A meadow set park-like with pines extended from here nearly three-quarters of a mile along the river, and was almost half a mile wide. Near our camp we found several old and rusty empty tin cans, such as are used for putting up preserved food. One of them was marked " Fort Bowie." Doubtless this spot had been used before as a camping ground, probably by some of General Crook's scouts.

CHAPTER III

CAMPING AT UPPER BAVISPE RIVER—LOW STONE CABINS, FORTRESSES
AND OTHER REMAINS INDICATING FORMER HABITATION—THE
ANIMALS STARVE ON THE WINTER GRASS OF THE SIERRA AND
BEGIN TO GIVE OUT—A DESERTED APACHE CAMP—COMFORT
AT LAST—THE GIANT WOODPECKER—WE ARRIVE AT THE MOR-
MON SETTLEMENTS OF PACHECO AND CAVE VALLEY.

A T Bavispe River we had to remain for some little
time to allow the animals to recuperate, and to
get them, as far as possible, in condition for the hard
work still ahead. I also had to send back to Nacori
for fresh provisions. Of course, not much was to be
gotten there, but we got what there was in the line of
food stuffs, panoche (brown sugar) and corn. My messengers had orders to bring the latter in the form of
pinole, that is, toasted corn ground by hand into a fine
meal. This is the most common, as well as the most
handy, ration throughout Mexico. A little bag of it is
all the provisions a Mexican or Indian takes with him
on a journey of days or weeks. It is simply mixed
with water and forms a tasty gruel, rather indigestible
for persons not accustomed to it. When boiled into a
porridge, however, pinole is very nourishing, and forms
a convenient diet for persons camping out. Aside from
this we still had a supply of wheat flour sufficient to
allow the party fifteen pounds a day, and our stock of
canned peas and preserved fruit, though reduced, was
not yet exhausted. The jerked beef had given out even
before we reached the main sierra, and we had to de-

pend on our guns for meat.   Luckily, the forest was
alive with deer, and there were also wild turkeys.
Thus there was no difficulty about provisions, although
the Americans sighed for their beloved bacon and hot
biscuits.

Fish seemed scarce in this part of the Bavispe
River ; at least we did not succeed in bringing out any
by the use of dynamite.   We got only five little fish—
one catfish, and four suckers, the largest six inches
long.

On Christmas Day the black bulb thermometer rose
in the sun to 150° F., although that very night the
temperature fell to 22.9° F., a difference of nearly 130°.
The warmth was such that even a rattlesnake was deceived and coaxed out by it.

We made every effort to celebrate Christmas in a
manner worthy of our surroundings.   We could not
procure fish for our banquet, but one of the Mexicans
had the good luck to shoot four turkeys ; and Kee,
our Chinese cook, surprised us with a plum pudding the
merits of which baffle description.   It consisted mainly
of deer fat and the remnants of dried peaches, raisins,
and orange peel, and it was served with a sauce of
white sugar and mescal.   The appreciation of this delicacy by the Mexicans knew no bounds, and from now
on they wanted plum pudding every day.

On the upper Bavispe we again found numerous
traces of a by-gone race who had occupied these regions
long before the Apaches had made their unwelcome appearance.   In fact, all along on our journey across the
sierra we were struck by the constant occurrence of
rude monuments of people now long vanished.   They
became less numerous in the eastern part, where at last
they were replaced by cave dwellings, of which I will
speak later.

More than ever since we entered the Sierra de Nacori, we noticed everywhere low stone walls, similar to
those we had seen in the foot-hills, and evidently the
remains of small cabins. The deeper we penetrated
into the mountains, the more common became these
hut-walls, which stood about three feet high, and were
possibly once surmounted by woodwork, or, perhaps,
thatched roofs. All the houses were small, generally
only ten or twelve feet square, and they were found in
clusters scattered over the summit or down the slopes
of a hill. On one summit we found only two ground
plans in close proximity to each other.

The stones composing the walls were laid with some
dexterity. They were angular, but never showed any
trace of dressing, except, perhaps, by fracture. The
interstices between the main stones were filled in with
fragments to make the walls solid. Neither here nor
in any other stone walls that we saw were there any indications of any mud or other plaster coating on the
stones.

On top of a knoll in the mountains south of Nacori,
at an elevation of 4,800 feet, well preserved remains of
this kind of dwelling were seen. The house, consisting of but one room about ten feet square, was built
of large blocks of lava. The largest of these were eighteen inches long, and about half as thick, and as wide.
The walls measured about three feet in height and
one foot and a half in thickness, and there was a sufficient amount of fallen stone debris near-by to admit of
the walls having been once four or five feet high.
There were the traces of a doorway in the northwest
corner of the building. Numerous fragments of coarse
pottery were scattered around, some gray and some red,
but without any decoration, except a fine slip coating
on the red fragments.

In the Sierra de Nacori, on the summit of a steep
knoll, and at an elevation of about 6,500 feet, we found
two huts of such laid-up walls. The rough felsite
blocks of which they were composed were surprisingly
large, considering the diminutive size of the cabins.
We measured the largest block and found it to be two
feet long, ten inches wide, and eight inches thick.
There were many others almost as large as this one.
But there was only one tier of stones left complete
in place. Although there were well-built trincheras in
all the surrounding arroyos, there were no traces of either
tools or pottery on that hill.

On the western slope of the Sierra de Nacori, on
top of another knoll, and at an elevation of 6,400 feet,
we found numerous rude ground plans, some of which
showed rubble walls fifteen inches thick. They formed
groups of four or five apartments, each ten by twelve
feet. But on the north side of that summit there was a
larger plan, nearly eighteen feet square; however, the
outlines of the entire settlement were not distinct enough
to enable us to trace its correct outlines.

Many fragments of pottery lay about, but neither in
number nor in interest could they be compared with
those found near the ruins in the southwest of the United
States, for instance, near the Gila River. Some of the
potsherds were one-third of an inch thick, and large
enough to show that they had been parts of a large jar.
They were made of coarse paste, either gray or brown
in colour. Some had a kind of rude finish, the marks of
a coarse fibre cloth being clearly discernible on the outside. Others were primitively decorated with incisions.
One sherd of really fine thin red ware was picked up,
but there was no trace of ornamentation on it. We
found, besides, a few cores of felsite and some shapeless
flakes and several fragments of large metates.

In the valley formed between the mountains on the upper Bavispe River we met with very many such houses. The clusters which we came across seemed to have been composed of a larger number of houses. Parapets, also built of undressed stones and surrounding these villages, now became a constant feature. Even within sight of our camp was such a parapet, six feet high, and house ruins were near by. We also discovered an ancient pueblo consisting of thirty houses, all of the usual small dimensions, but not all alike in shape. Some were round, others triangular, but most of them were rectangular, measuring eight by ten feet. Along two sides of this village ran a double wall, while the other two sides were bound by a single wall constructed on the same principle. Evidently these walls were built for the protection of the people in time of war.

About five miles south of our camping place the river turns eastward, and again two miles below this point it receives a tributary from the west. One day I followed the broken cordon on its eastern bank, then turned north and ascended an isolated mountain, which rises about fifteen hundred feet high above the river. There is a small level space on top, and on this there has been built, at some time, a fortress with walls of undressed stones from two to six feet high and three feet thick. It was about fifty paces long in one direction, and about half that length in the other. Remains of houses could be traced, and inside of the walls themselves the ground plan of three little chambers could be made out.

On the Bavispe River we photographed a trinchera which was about eight feet high and thirty feet long; and one of the foremen observed one which was at least fifteen feet high.

I decided to move the camp one and a half miles

down the river, and to its right bank, on a cordon, where Mason, one of my Mexican foremen, had discovered some ruins. It was very pleasant here after the rather cool bottom of the valley, which in the morning was generally covered with a heavy fog. On this ridge were many traces of former occupancy, parapet walls and rude houses divided into small compartments. The parapets were lying along the north and south faces of the houses, and just on the brink of the narrow ridge. On the south side the ridge was precipitous, but toward the north it ran out in a gentle shallow slope toward the next higher hill. The building material here is a close-grained felsite, and huge fragments of it have been used in the construction of the parapets. These boulders were, on an average, thirty-five inches long, twenty-five inches thick and fifteen inches wide; while the stones used in the house walls measured, on the average, fourteen by nine by seven inches.

On the western end of the ridge is a small house group, which, for convenience sake, I will designate as "Mason's Ruins." They showed a decidedly higher method of construction, and the walls were better preserved, than in any we had seen so far. The ground plans could be readily made out, except in a small part of the southwest corner. These walls stood three to five feet high, and the stones here too were dressed only by fracture. They were laid in gypsiferous clay, a mass of which lay close to the southwest corner. This clay is very similar to the material used by the Moquis in whitening their houses. The stones themselves were felsite, which abounds in the locality. The blocks have an average size of twelve inches square by six inches thick. It should be noted that no regard was paid to the tying of the corners and the partition walls; but considerable care had been taken in making the walls vertical, and

Camp in the High Sierra.

the angles were fairly true. The walls were almost twelve inches thick, and on the inner side they had evidently never been plastered.

Being coated with some white plaster, these ruins look white at a distance, and the Mexicans therefore called them *casas blancas.* I heard of an extensive group of such buildings near Sahuaripa, and there are also some ruins of this category near Granados, and in the hills east of Opoto. Undoubtedly they belong to a more recent period than the rude stone structures described before. Most of the ancient remains of the Sierra are remnants of tribes that expanded here from the lowlands, and only in comparatively recent times have disappeared. I also perceived that they were built by a tribe of Indians different from those which erected the houses in the caves of the eastern and northern Sierra Madre, and in the country east of it, and may safely be ascribed to Opatas.

In spite of the rest here, the animals did not seem to improve on the grama and buffalo grass. It was rather perplexing to note that they grew weaker and weaker. The grass of the sierra, which was now gray, did not seem to contain much nourishment, and it became evident that the sooner we proceeded on our journey, the better. To save them as much as possible, we loaded only half the regular weight on the mules and donkeys, and sent them back the next day to fetch the balance of the baggage. In this way, and by strengthening the poor beasts with a judicious use of corn, I managed to pull through and overcome this most serious of all difficulties, which, at one time, threatened to paralyse the entire expedition.

On December 31st we moved up a steep zigzag trail cut out by us, and then went north and east through broken foot-hills. We got into a series of cordon mesas, but the breaks between them were not at all difficult to pass. On the mountain sides grew oaks and, higher up, pines.

The country was wild and rugged. Everywhere we encountered fallen rocks, and there was a scarcity of water. It was a kind of comfort to see now and then some trincheras in these desolate regions. At four o'clock we camped on a steep place amidst poor grass, and only a trickling of water in the bed of a little rill.

Here, at last, the men whom I had sent to Nacori for provisions overtook us, bringing eighteen dollars' worth of panoche, and two and a quarter fanegas of pinole. Measuring by fanegas was then still in vogue in Mexico ; a fanega equals about sixty-four kilograms.

This, the messengers stated, was all that the women would grind for us. Twenty of them had been set to work to fill our order, and when they had laboured until their hands were tired, they declared they would grind no more ; and if the *caballeros* in the mountains wanted further quantities, they should come and make mills of themselves. From this we judged that their tempers had risen in proportion to the heaps of pinole they were producing, and that they did not bless the day when we had come into their peaceful valley, since it meant so much hard work for them.

Though we were now provisioned for some time to come, I was anxiously looking forward to the day when we should reach the eastern side of the sierra. The animals were rapidly giving out, and it was the opinion of the packers that they could not last longer than a week ; but what little corn we could spare for them each day worked wonders, and in this way we enabled them to carry us through.

The most noticeable among the plants in the valleys was the madroña or strawberry tree (*Arbutus Texana*)

growing singly here and there. Its beautiful stem and
branches, ash-grey and blood-red, are oddly twisted
from the root to the top. Now and then, in this world
of pine trees, we came upon patches of grama grass.
We also observed piñon trees, a variety of pine with
edible seeds.

Apache monuments were plentiful in this part of the
sierra, and after four days of travel, on January 5, 1891,

Bringing in Deer.

we arrived at an old Apache camping place, called by the
Mexicans "Rancheria de los Apaches." It was a sheltered place, and we decided to stop again and rest, as
now we could not be very far from the Mormon colonies
in the eastern part of the sierra. We had, on the day
before, heard a shot, which had not been fired by anyone of our party, and we had met some short-horn cattle that must have belonged to some settlers.

We halted on a bare conglomerate scalp near a little

creek, which we called " Bonito," and which shortly
below our camp joins the Gabilan, an affluent of the
Bavispe River which probably has its origin near Chuhuichupa.   The elevation of our camp was 6,620 feet.
The summit of the sierra toward the east appeared to
be 2,000 feet high, and the first ridge, at the foot of
which we camped, rises here almost perpendicularly
about a thousand feet.   The little stream already mentioned originates in a deep cañon and adjoining it are
four large cordons descending from the ridge east of us
and spreading themselves out like a gigantic fan, which
we had noticed from some distance on the previous day.
From our camp led a track eastward, up along one of
these cordons, and a reconnoitring party found a Mormon settlement ten or twelve miles off.

The day after our arrival I went out to take a look
at the country.   South of us, at no great distance from
the camp, I found patches of fertile black soil partly
cultivated with corn and turnips that did not appear to
be flourishing, and with potatoes which were doing well.
An old horse stood there, and I also noticed a small tent.
Going up closer I found a plough standing outside.
This made quite a queer impression in these solitary
mountains, but the implement was apparently not out of
place, judging from the beautiful black soil near-by.   In
the tent I saw a heap of bed-clothes piled up on some
tin pails, and there were also some pots with potatoes
and corn.   The owner of all this was not at home ; but
the atmosphere was American, not Mexican.   I had evidently come upon an outpost of one of the Mormon
colonies.

Throughout January the days continued to be fine,
though at times a southerly cold wind was blowing ; but
at night it was cold and the water in our buckets was
often frozen.   Then we felt what a real comfort a large

camp-fire is. Before sundown we would gather the fallen trees and such sorts of wood, and roaring fires were built in front of each tent. The smoke, to be sure, blackened our faces, but the fire made the tents wonderfully comfortable, filling them with light and warmth. For beds we used fragrant pine boughs.

We also had several falls of snow, the heaviest two and a half inches, and on the coldest night, on January 10th, the thermometer went down to 6° F. As the rays of the sun partly melted the snow in the course of the day, the animals could at least get a meagre meal. On January 15th a cup of water froze inside of my tent, but during the day we had 57° F.

We soon found out that in the river Gabilan, some four miles south of our camp, there were immense quantities of fish, which had come up to spawn. No one ever interfered with them, and their number was simply overwhelming. As the task of feeding thirty men in these wild regions was by no means a trifling one, I resolved to procure as many fish as possible, and to this end resorted to the cruel but effective device of killing them by dynamite. I trust that the scarcity of provisions in the camp will serve as my excuse to sportsmen for the method I employed. We used a stick of dynamite six inches long, and it raised a column of water twenty feet in the air, while the detonation sounded like a salute, rolling from peak to peak for miles around. In two hours three of us gathered 195 fish from a single pool. Most of them were big suckers; but we had also thirty-five large Gila trout. All were fat and of delicate flavour, and lasted us quite a long time.

Never have I been at any place where deer were so plentiful. Almost at every turn one of them might be seen, sometimes standing as if studying your method of approach. I sent out five men to go shooting in the northwesterly direction from the camp, and after a day and a half they returned with ten deer. At one time we had fifteen hanging in the kitchen.

One morning our best marksman, a Mexican named Figueroa, brought in three specimens of that superb bird, *campephilus imperialis*, the largest woodpecker in

the world. This splendid member of the feathered tribe is two feet long ; its plumage is white and black, and the male is ornamented with a gorgeous scarlet crest, which seemed especially brilliant against the winter snow. The birds go in pairs and are not very shy, but are difficult to kill and have to be shot with rifle. One of their peculiarities is that they feed on one tree for as long

The Largest Woodpecker in the World.

as a fortnight at a time, at last causing the decayed tree to fall. The birds are exceedingly rare in the museums. They are only found in the Sierra Madre. On my journeys I saw them as far south as the southernmost point which the Sierra Madre del Norte reaches in the State of Jalisco, above the Rio de Santiago. I frequently observed them also in the eastern part of the range.

Here, too, a great many specimens of the rare Mexican titmouse and some beautiful varieties of the duck tribe were procured.

A few days after our arrival at the Rancheria de los Apaches, Professor Libbey left our camp, returning to the United States by way of Casas Grandes. After bidding him good-bye, I made an excursion of a week's duration to the north of our camp, to look for possible antiquities, especially a *casa blanca*, of which I had heard considerable from the people in Nacori.

The woods, considering that it was midwinter, were quite lively with birds. Everywhere I saw bluejays; crested titmice, too, were plentiful, as well as cross-beaks. A large yellowish squirrel also attracted my attention. It was of the same kind as that recently found by our expedition. The country was hilly and full of small cañons, and well watered by springs. Outcroppings of solidified volcanic ash looked in the distance like white patches in the landscape. We searched diligently for some twenty-five miles to the north of the main camp, and also toward the east and west, but no trace of former habitation was found except trincheras and house ruins such as we had seen before. Near one of the group of houses I saw three metates in an excellent state of preservation.

While out on this trip I was one day surprised by the appearance of a Mormon in my camp. It was really a pleasure to see someone from the outside world again ; and this was a frank and intelligent man, very pleasant to talk to. He told me that he had never been farther north than where he was now ; nor had he ever been farther west than the little creek about two miles west of the place where he met me, which he called the "Golden Gulch." This creek probably originates in the mountains near by; there was still another creek west of us which joined the Golden Gulch near the Mormon's tent, and this he called "North Creek." The ranch near our main camp he had taken up only about three years ago, and he considered agriculture in this region successful, especially with potatoes. Maize, too, may also ripen. Furthermore, he told me of some interesting cave dwellings near the Mormon settlement on the eastern edge of the sierra, which I decided to investigate.

When the Mormons had come to colonise parts of northern Mexico, an American called "Apache Bill," who had lived for a number of years with the Apaches, told them of a large, fertile valley showing many evidences of former cultivation. Probably he referred to a locality that had once been inhabited by a remnant of the Opata Indians, who had become christianised and had received fruit trees from the missionaries. The trees, when found, were said to be still bearing fruit, while the people had vanished—having probably been killed off by the Apaches.

I returned to the main camp, leaving, however, two men behind to search still further for the *casa blanca*. When they returned after a few days, they reported that nothing could be found, and that the country was difficult of access. On my return I found the men who had gone to Casas Grandes back already, bringing with them some provisions and the first mail for three months.

Two miles east of our camp obsidian was found *in situ*. It was not in the natural flow, but in round, water-worn pebbles deposited in the conglomerate. Many of these had been washed out and had rolled down the hill, where a bushel of them might be collected in a few hours. The outcrop does not extend over a large area, only about two hundred yards on one side of the bank.

On January 22d I started eastward toward the Mormon settlement, passing the watershed at a height of 8,025 feet. After fifteen miles of travel we arrived at the Mormon colony called Pacheco, and situated on the Piedras Verdes River. It consists of small wooden houses lying peacefully on the slope, surrounded by pine forests, at an elevation of seven thousand feet. A saw-mill bore evidence of industry. There were sixteen families living here, and as we arrived some eighty children were just streaming out of school. Near by stood a kindly looking old man, possibly their teacher. The children, who ranged in age from seven to eighteen years, were all studying in one class. They showed remarkably varied physiognomies, yet all looked healthy and sturdy, and were demure and well-behaved.

We made camp one and a half miles from the village, and in the evening we were visited by my friend from the sierra and another Mormon. Both expressed their readiness to serve us in every way they could ; we bought some potatoes and half a hog.

As is the custom with the Mormons, they have several colonies outlying from a central one. Among these is Cave Valley, about five miles east to north from Pacheco, immediately upon the river already mentioned. On the following day I went there with the scientific corps to examine the cave dwellings of which the Mormons had been speaking. The settlement (having an elevation 6,850 feet) consisted of eight houses. Knocking on the door of one of these I walked in, introduced myself, and stated the purpose of my visit. " How do you do ? " said my host ; " my name is Nelson"—as if he had been accustomed to receive strangers every day.

Mr. Nelson was quite a charming old man, more than seventy years old, but hardy. In spite of the cold, he walked out in his shirt sleeves in the full moonlight to select a camping place for me. The animals, he suggested, might be left in the field for the night; he would see about them in the morning, and he did not think there would be any difficulty about keeping them there. We got a fine camp on top of a hill with a view of the valley in which the caves are.

Distant View of Cupola-shaped Granary in Cave.

Mr. Nelson told us of two interesting caves on this side of the river; also, that there were numerous "inscriptions" (petroglyphs), that the country was full of mounds, and that skeletons and mummies had been found but had been buried again. From his statement it was evident that we had a rich field before us, and the results of the following day more than came up to our expectations.

The old man, acting as our guide, showed us on the way to the valley a primitive kind of corn-mill driven by water power, and with some pride he pointed out to us an "infant industry," the product of which so far was a dozen wooden chairs with seats of interwoven strips of green hide, instead of cane.

A number of caves were found to contain houses. One of them especially made a great impression on us on account of an extraordinary cupola-shaped structure, which from a considerable distance sprang into view from the mouth of the cave. Most of the caves were found on the western side of the river; but there were also some on the eastern bank, among them a number of burial caves. In one of the latter a well-preserved mummy was shown to us. It had already been taken up two or three times to be looked at; but our guide intimated that the influential Mormons in Utah did not want to have the skeletons and caves disturbed. I therefore left it for the present, but thought that in time we might get this, with whatever others might be found there.

I was introduced to a Mormon in the neighbourhood, who invited me to excavate a large mound close to his house. He would even help to dig, he said, and I was free to take whatever I might find inside of it. He was sure that there would be no difficulty about the mummies I might want to remove from the burial caves.

CHAPTER IV

A SPLENDID FIELD PREPARED FOR US BY THE ANCIENT AGRICUL-
TURISTS OF CAVE VALLEY—HOUSE GROUPS IN CAVES ALONG
A PRETTY STREAM — WELL-PRESERVED MUMMIES FOUND IN
CAVES—MORE TRINCHERAS—OUR EXCAVATIONS IN CAVES AND
MOUNDS CONFIRM TO THE MORMONS THEIR SACRED STORIES—
WE MOVE TO THE PLAINS OF SAN DIEGO—VISIT TO CASAS
GRANDES AND THE WATCH-TOWER—SUCCESSFUL EXCAVATIONS
OF THE MOUNDS NEAR SAN DIEGO.

FINDING the locality so inviting for research, I de-cided to remain here, returning to Pacheco only to despatch the rest of my party to make excavations at the ranch of San Diego, thirty miles to the east, down on the plains of Chihuahua. The ranch was temporarily leased by an American, Mr. Galvin, who received my expedition hospitably, and invited the members to remain as long as they pleased and to make excavations wherever they wanted.

Cave Valley is the widening of a long, low-walled cañon through which the Piedras Verdes River flows. As its name implies, it contains many caves in the felsitic conglomerate overlying the region. It is from one-quarter to half a mile wide, and has a fine, rich, loamy soil. The stream is ten to twenty feet wide and from one to three feet deep. Fine forests of pine, oak, cedar, and maple surround it, and make it an ideal dwelling-place for a peaceful, primitive people.

The little knoll on which we were encamped rises on the north side of a brook which empties itself in the river. It was in equally close proximity to the dwellings of the living and the dwellings of the dead.

Up the main stream, on the western wall of the cañon, and about a mile from our camp, is a large cave containing the curious cupola-shaped structure already mentioned. The cave is easy of approach up a sloping

Single Wall in Cliff.

bank from its south side, and arriving at it we found it quite commodious and snug. It is about eighty feet wide at its mouth, and about a hundred feet deep. In the central part it is almost eighteen feet high, but the roof gradually slopes down in the rear to half that height.

A little village, or cluster of houses, lies at its back and sides. The interior of most of the rooms must have been quite dark, though the light reaches the outside of all the houses. The walls are still standing about six feet high. The compartments, though small, are seldom kennel-like. Some of the houses have shallow cellars.

The roof of the cave was thickly smoked over its entire surface. From traces of walls still remaining on it, we may infer that a second story had been built toward the centre of the cave, though this could only have been five feet high. These traces of walls on the roof further prove the important fact that this second story had been

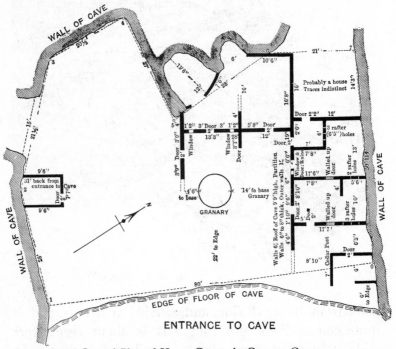

Ground Plan of House Groups in Granary Cave.

built in terrace-fashion, receding about four feet back from the front of the ground story.

The cave had evidently been occupied for a very long time, the houses showing many alterations and additions, and on the walls I counted as many as twelve coatings of plaster and whitewash. The conventional design of the ear of corn is well preserved in every doorway. Rude scrawlings of soot and water cover nearly all the front walls, mixed here and there with a few traces of red ochre. There are meander designs, lightning, and drawings of cows and horses ; but the latter were doubtless put on after the walls were demolished, and their general appearance denotes recentness.

Several of the cyclopean riffles lead from the cave cliff to the stream.

The houses here, as well as in all other caves we examined, were built entirely of a powdery substance, the decomposed material of the cave itself. Great quantities of it were found on the floors of caves which had not been occupied by man. It is not of a sandy nature, and its colour is light brown, sometimes almost grey, or even white. The ancient builders simply had to mix it with water and mould it into bricks, which, though fairly uniform in thickness, were very irregular in size. There were no marks of implements on the walls ; all the work seems to have been done by hand and smoothed over with some wetted fabric. In one cave of this valley the walls show finger-marks on the plaster. Occasionally we found a small boulder of hard stone embedded in the wall.

The most unique feature of this cave, however, is the cupola-shaped structure which stands in an open space in front of the house group, near the mouth of the cave, but still under its roof. Its height, measured inside, is twelve feet, and its widest inside diameter is eleven feet. Its walls average eight inches in thickness. It has one aperture three feet wide at the top, another one of the same dimension near the base, and there are several others nearly opposite each other. In the two upper ones are seen distinct impressions of timber in the plaster.

The building was made by twisting long grass into a compact cable and laying it up, one round upon another. As the coil proceeded, thick coats of plaster were laid on inside and outside. This plaster, which is the same material as that of which the houses are con-structed, got thoroughly mixed with the straw during the process of building, and the entire structure was finished without any opening except the one at the top. The other apertures were undoubtedly cut out after-

Cupola-shaped Granary in Cave.

ward. There is no trace of withes or other binding material to hold the straw cables in place. They are kept in position only by the plaster, which here, as in the houses, is almost as hard as the conglomerate of the surrounding rocks.

My Mexicans from Sonora called it *olla*, a jar, and insisted that it was a vessel used for keeping water; but this is entirely improbable, for several reasons, mainly because the river is in close proximity and easy of access. It was without the slightest doubt a granary. Similar structures, used for that purpose to the present day, may be seen in the States of Vera Cruz and Tlax-

Granary in Tlaxcala.

cala. In a cave only a short distance away, the rear portion of which also contained a group of houses, we found between the mouth of the cave and the house

Bases of Granaries in Cave.

walls the remains of five of these peculiar buildings which I call granaries. They, too, were made of straw and plaster, similar to the one described, but the walls

here were only two inches thick.   The remains showed
that they had not been set up in any special arrangement, nor were all five alike.   Two of them were deeply
sunken into the floor of the cave, and inside of them we

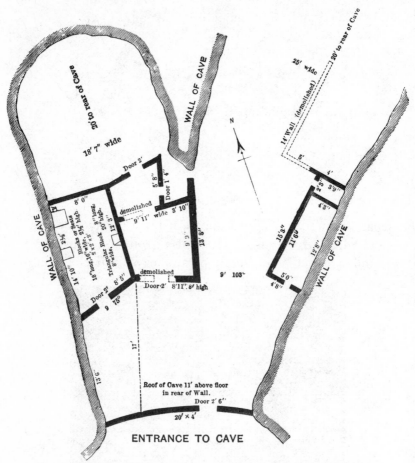

Ground Plan of House Groups in Cave on East Side of the River.

found, between the rubbish and debris that filled them,
several grains of corn and some beans.

The other caves which we examined in this valley
were of the same general character as these two, although we found no granaries in them.   On this page

is shown the ground plan of a cave on the east side of the river, and attention is drawn to the singular concrete seats or blocks against the wall in the house on the west side of the cave. A floor of concrete had been made in this cave extending inward and fairly level.

Evidence of two-storeyed groups of houses was clearly noticeable in many caves; but our investigations were somewhat impeded by the destruction wrought by some Mormon relic-hunter, who had carried off almost everything removable. He had even taken away many of

Sandal Plaited from Yucca Leaves. Heel is Shown on Left. Length, 21 ctm.

the door lintels and hand-grips, in fact, most of the woodwork, from the houses.

In the rear of some of the caves it was so dark that we had to light a candle to find our way, crawling from house to house. In one instance we found a stone stairway of three steps.

In spite of the tremendous dust which is raised by digging into the ground, and which makes the work very arduous, we searched diligently and succeeded in bringing to light a number of objects which fairly well illustrate the culture of the ancient people. Among them were needles and awls of bone; a complete fire drill with a stick showing drilling, basketry work covered

with piñon pith, mats and girdles, threads of fibre or hair, and sandals plaited of yucca leaves. Wads of cotton and pieces of pottery were found in many places; and an interesting find was a "boomerang" similar to that used to this day by the Moqui Indians for killing rabbits.

Heel of a Sandal, Showing Plaiting.

The handle is plainly seen, but the top is broken. The implement, which is made of very hard, reddish wood, has but a slight curve. We discovered many smooth pieces of iron ore that had probably been used for ceremonial purposes, and a bow that had been hidden away on a ledge.

That the ancient cave-dwellers were agriculturists is evident from the numerous corn-cobs, as well as grains of corn and beans, that we came upon. Datems, a green, sweet fruit still eaten by the Mexicans, were identified everywhere in the cave-dwellings.

Having effectually started the work of investigation here, I went to look after the second section of my expedition, which had been sent to San Diego. I covered the thirty-five miles with four pack mules in one day. There is a charming view from the brow of the sierra over the plains of San Diego, which are fully ten miles wide; but after descending to them I found a hard, cold wind blowing. The weather here is not at all as pleasant as in the sheltered Cave Valley up in the mountains.

Piece of Wood Showing Drill Mark. Length, 22.5 ctm.

I went to Casas Grandes, a village of 1,200 souls, six miles north of San Diego, and succeeded in getting a draft cashed. On learning that Mr. Moses Thatcher, a prominent Mormon apostle from Utah, was on a tour of inspection of the colonies, I proceeded to Colonia Juarez, a prosperous Mormon settlement on the Piedras Verdes River, ten miles from Casas Grandes and six miles from San Diego. It was only four years old, but had already a number of well laid-out broad streets, set on both sides with cottonwood trees, and all the houses were surrounded by gardens. I explained to Mr. Thatcher that I desired to make excavations in Cave Valley, and he courteously acceded to my wishes, adding that I might take away anything of interest to science.

Pendant of Wood.
Length, 14 ctm.

To reduce expenses, I paid off many of my Mexican men, who then returned to their homes in Sonora, going over the sierra by the trail we had made in coming east. A few months later several of them returned, bringing others with them, and asked to work again in the camp, which remained in San Diego for about nine months longer—long enough for us to see quite a little trade in oranges, sugar, tobacco, etc., developing between Sonora and Chihuahua by way of the road cut out by us, and called, after me, *el camino del doctor.*

Implement for Throwing. Length, 67 ctm.

Excavations in Cave Valley were continued, and the burial caves gave even better results than the cave-dwellings. They were located in the eastern side of the cañon, which is rarely touched by the sun's rays. With

Burial Caves in Cave Valley.

one exception the ceilings and sides of these caves were much blackened by smoke. There was not the slightest trace of house walls, and no other sign that the place had ever been inhabited; therefore, a fire here could have had no other purpose than a religious one, just as the Tarahumares to this day make a fire in the cave in which they bury their dead. Indeed, at first sight there was nothing in the cave to indicate that they had ever been utilised by man; but below the dust we came upon a hard, concrete floor, and after digging through this to a depth of three feet, we fortunately struck a skull, and then came upon the body of a man. After this we disinterred that of a mother holding a child in her arms, and two other bodies, all lying on their left sides, their knees half drawn up, and their faces turned toward the setting sun. All were in a marvellous state of preservation, owing to the presence of saltpetre in the dust. This imparted to the dead a mummy-like appearance, but there was nothing to suggest that embalming or other artificial means of preservation of the bodies had been used. The entire system was simply desiccated intact,

A Mummified Body.

merely shrunken, with the skin on most of the bodies almost unbroken. The features, and even the expression of the countenance, were in many cases quite distinct. Some had retained their eyebrows and part of their hair, and even their intestines had not all disappeared.

The hair of these people was very slightly wavy, and softer than that of the modern Indian; in fact, almost silky. The statures were quite low, and in general appearance these ancients bear a curious resemblance to the Moqui Indians, who have a tradition that their ancestors came from the south, and who, to this day, speak of their "southern brethren"; but it would be

very rash to conclude from this that the cave-dwellers of
northwestern Chihuahua are identical with the Moqui
ancestors.   I afterwards brought to light several other
bodies which had been interred under similar conditions.

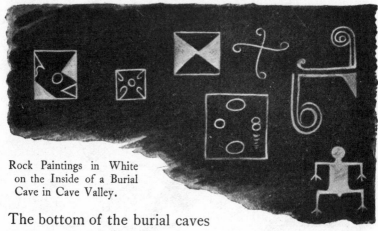

Rock Paintings in White
on the Inside of a Burial
Cave in Cave Valley.

The bottom of the burial caves
seems to have always been overlaid
with a roughly level, concrete floor.   There was no
trace here of cysts, or other formal sepulture.

None of the remains wore ornaments of metal, but
various shell ornaments, anklets and bracelets of beautifully plaited straw, which, however, crumbled into dust
when touched.   Their clothing consisted of three layers
of wrappings around the loins.   Next to the body was
placed a coarse cotton cloth; then a piece of matting,
and over that another cotton cloth.   Between the legs
was a large wad of cotton mixed with the feathers of the
turkey, the large woodpecker, and the bluejay.   In a
few instances, the cotton cloth was dyed red or indigo.
Near the head of each body stood a small earthenware
jar of simple design ; in some cases we also found drinking gourds placed at the head, though in one instance
the latter had been put on the breast of the dead.
Buried with the person we found a bundle of " devil's

claws" (*Martynia*). These are used by the Mexicans of
to-day for mending pottery. They drill holes through
the fragments to be joined and pass into them one of
these claws, just as we would a rivet. The claw is

A Trinchera in Cave Valley.

elastic and strong, and answers the purpose very well.
My Mexicans understood at once to what use they had
been put.

As already alluded to, trincheras were also found in
Cave Valley, where they were quite numerous. There
was one or more in every ravine and gully, and what
was a new feature, some were built across shallow
drainages on the very summit of a hill. This summit
was a bald conglomerate, about 150 feet above the valley. In one place we observed eight trincheras within
150 feet of each other, all built of large stones in the

cyclopean style of masonry. The blocks were lava and hard felsite, measuring one and a half to three feet. As a rule, these trincheras had a lateral extent of thirty feet, and in the central part they were fifteen feet high. After all the great labour expended in their construction, the builders of these terraces had secured in each only a space thirty feet long and fifteen feet wide; in other words, these eight terraces yielded together barely 3,000 square feet, which means space enough for planting five or six hundred hills of corn. People who do not know the Indians would consider this too small a result to favour the theory that these terraces were erected for agricultural purposes. But the Indian's farming is, in proportion to his wants, conducted on a small scale, and he never thinks of raising more corn than he actually needs ; in fact, many tribes, as for instance the Tarahumares, seldom raise enough to last the family all the year through.

Further groups of cave-dwellings were found some ten miles higher up the river, in what is called the "Strawberry Valley," probably through the prevalence of the strawberry tree, of which several beautiful specimens were seen. The largest cave there contained fourteen houses. Unlike the dwellings in the Cave Valley, here a gallery ran in front of the houses. The woodwork here was fresher than that of the Cave Valley houses, and as the walls had only three coats of plaster and whitewash, and the corners did not show much wear, these dwellings were undoubtedly of more recent origin. But the general character of the structures was similar to those we first investigated. No implements were found in these caves. In the same locality were quite a number of smaller caves containing houses in demolition. In one of them the walls were composed of stones and mud, and here we also saw the first circular-shaped house in a cave.

By digging below the concrete floor of one of the rooms, we came upon the skeletons of five adults. This was a singular fact, showing that these ancient cave-dwellers observed the custom of burying their dead under the floors of their houses when conditions permitted it. Cave-dwellings comprising twenty rooms were also seen by the Mormons at the head of Bavispe River.

My relations with

Ancient Cave-Dwellings in Strawberry Valley.

the Mormons continued to be friendly, and in my dealings with them I found them honest and business-like. While thriftily providing for the material requirements of this life, they leave all their enjoyment of existence for the future state. Their life is hard, but they live up

Interior View of Cave-Dwellings Shown on Page 75.

to their convictions, though these, in some points, date from a by-gone stage in the development of the human race.

They were much interested in our work, never doubting but that it could only be to their advantage to have light thrown upon the mysteries buried in their caves, as, in their opinion, our researches would only confirm the statements made in the "Book of Mormon," which mentions the prehistoric races of America. They

Exterior View of Cave-Dwellings in Strawberry Valley.

told me that the book speaks of the arrival of three races in America. The first landing was made at Guaymas in Sonora, the people being fugitives from the divine wrath that destroyed the Tower of Babel. They were killed. The second race landed in New England, coming from Jerusalem ; and the third, also coming from Jerusalem, landed in Chile.

We spent altogether about six weeks in Cave Valley, and the weather, as far as our experience went, was pleasant enough, although in February, for several days, a strong, cold wind was blowing, so as to interfere with our work in the mounds at daytime and with our sleep at night. In addition to the discomforting feeling that at any moment my tent might be blown down, I was worried by the possibility of its falling on the results of our excavations, the pottery and skeletons, which, for safety's sake, I kept in my tent. The situation was not improved by some indiscreet burro (donkey), who would stray into the camp and get himself entangled in the tent ropes.

On January 30th nearly seven inches of snow fell. One day a flock of twenty-five turkeys was observed near our camp; but our efforts to get within shooting distance proved futile, as these cunning birds, who apparently move about so unconcernedly, always disappeared as if they had vanished into the ground, whenever one of us, no matter how cautiously, tried to approach them.

News of Apaches was again afloat, and one day a Mexican officer called at the camp obviously in pursuit of Apaches from whom he had recently taken twelve horses; but unfortunately the men had escaped. The presidente of Casas Grandes had been advised of the killing of two Americans near San Bernardino by some Apaches, and had also ordered some men to look for the miscreants in the sierra.

Having thoroughly investigated the caves, we turned our attention to the mounds, which are very numerous in this part of the country. They are always covered with grass, and sometimes even trees grow on them. When excavated they disclosed the remains of houses of a type similar to that of the cave-dwellings. Some of the mounds were high enough to justify the supposition that the houses had two stories, each six or seven feet high, and containing a number of rooms. From the locality in which the mounds were found it becomes at once evident that the houses which once stood there were not destroyed by inundations and covered by diluvial deposits. The mounds are composed of gravelly cement and fine debris of house walls, and the rooms left are completely filled with this material. It is easy to imagine how the mounds were formed by the gradual demolition of the ceilings, plastering, and roofs, forming a heap which to-day appears as shapely as if it had been made by man for some definite purpose.

The houses were communal dwellings, each consisting of one room, which generally was not quite ten feet square. The walls, eight to nine inches thick, built of a mixture of clay and earth, were fairly well preserved in places. In one house, which had unusually solid compartments, the walls were twenty, and in some places even thirty-three, inches thick. Here nothing could be found, either in the rooms or by excavating below the floor. The same conventional doorways were met with in all the mound houses, but there was hardly any trace of woodwork.

Excavations in one of the mounds near our camp disclosed very interesting composite structures. One part of the walls consisted of large posts set in the ground and plastered over, forming a stuccoed palisade. At right angles with this was a wall of cobblestones, and among the buried debris were fragments of adobe bricks.   In one room of this group, at a depth of less than five feet, we struck a floor of trodden concrete.   Breaking through we found a huddle of six or seven skeletons, which, however, were not entire.

Objects Found in Mounds at Upper Piedras Verdes River.   An Earthenware Vessel in Shape of a Gourd is Seen in the Middle.   Length of the Double Grooved Axe, 16 ctm.

Rarely if ever was any object found in these rooms, except, perhaps, some stray axe, or some metates and grinding stones, and in one case a square stone paint pot.   But by digging below the concrete floors we came upon skeletons which seemed to have been laid down without regard to any rule, and with them were invariably buried some household utensils, such as earthenware jars and bowls, beautifully decorated ; axes and mauls, fairly carved and polished.   One very rare object was secured : a doubled-grooved axe.   The skeletons were badly preserved, but we were able to gather several skulls and some of the larger bones.

The floor material was so hard that only by means of heavy iron bars could we break through it.   As it was

impracticable for us to make complete excavations, the
number of rooms each mound contained cannot be
stated.   There were in the immediate neighbourhood of
Cave Valley at least ten or twelve separate groups, each
of which had from four to eight rooms on the ground
floor.   The entire district is richly studded with mounds.
On an excursion three or four miles down Piedras
Verdes River I saw several groups of mounds, some of
which, no doubt, contained many objects of antiquity.
On top of one low hill was a large group, and half a

Painting on Rock on Piedras Verdes River.   The Colour is White Except
One Line in Red.   Height of Lowest Figure, about 60 ctm.

mile north of this another, 160 paces long and containing two oblong mounds.   Some of the mounds were ten
or twelve feet high.

A very trustworthy Mormon informed me that there
were no ruins, in caves or otherwise, along the river between this settlement and Colonia Juarez ; nor were
there any, he said, for a hundred miles south of Pacheco,
though mounds could be seen in several places.   Therefore when I at last departed from Cave Valley, I took
his advice and did not follow the course of the Piedras
Verdes River down to San Diego, but led the pack
train the safer, though longer, way over the regular

road. The country along the river was afterward explored by members of my expedition. They came upon
several small caves high up on the side of the cañon,

Figures on Walls of a Cave House, on Piedras Verdes River. They are
painted red except those indicated by white lines, that signify pecking.
Figure to right is about 60 ctm. high.

some of which had once been inhabited, to judge from
the many potsherds and the smoky roofs; but no cave-
houses were found until higher up the river, where some
were seen in the sandstone cliffs.

I broke camp in Cave Valley on March 11th, and
arrived on the same day at Old Juarez, a few miles
from my camp at San Diego. Now
the weather was warm; the grass
was sprouting, and I noticed a flock
of wild geese going northward.

The plains of San Diego used
to swarm with antelopes, and even
at the time of my visit herds of
them could be seen now and then.
One old hunter near Casas Grandes
resorted to an ingenious device for
decoying them.

Figure on Rock on Piedras
Verdes River. White
lines indicate peck-
ing, the rest is coloured
red.

He disguised himself as an antelope,
by means of a cloak of cotton cloth (manta) painted to

resemble the colouring of the animal.   This covered his
body, arms, and legs.   On his head he placed the antlers
of a stag, and by creeping on all fours he could approach
the antelopes quite closely and thus successfully shoot
them.   The Apaches, according to the Mexicans, were
experts at hunting antelopes in this manner.

We excavated a mound near Old Juarez and found

Hunting Antelope in Disguise.

in it a small basin of black ware.   There were twelve or
fifteen other mounds, all containing house groups.   The
largest among them was 100 feet long, fifty feet wide,
and ten feet high ; others, while covering about the
same space, were only three or four to six feet high.
They were surrounded, in an irregular way, by numerous stone heaps, some quite small, others large and
rectangular, inclosing a space thirty by ten feet.

Casas Grandes.

From an archæological point of view, the district we now found ourselves in is exceedingly rich, and I determined to explore it as thoroughly as circumstances permitted. One can easily count, in the vicinity of San Diego, over fifty mounds, and there are also rock carvings and paintings in various places. Some twenty miles further south there are communal cave-dwellings, resembling those in Cave Valley, which were examined by members of the expedition at the San Miguel River, about eight miles above the point at which the river enters the plains. Inside of one large cave numerous houses were found. They had all been destroyed, yet it was plainly evident that some of them had originally been three stories high.

But the centre of interest is Casas Grandes, the famous ruin situated about a mile south of the town which took its name, and we soon went over to investigate it.

The venerable pile of fairly well preserved ruins has already been described by John Russell Bartlett, in 1854, and more recently by A. F. Bandelier ; a detailed description is therefore here superfluous. Suffice it to say that the Casas Grandes, or Great Houses, are a mass of ruined houses, huddled together on the western bank of the river. Most of the buildings have fallen in and form six or eight large mounds, the highest of which is about twenty feet above the ground. Low mesquite bushes have taken root along the mounds and between the ruins. The remaining walls are sufficiently well preserved to give us an idea of the mode of building employed by the ancients. At the outskirts of the ruined village the houses are lower and have only one story, while in its central part they must have been at one time at least four stories high. They were not palaces, but simply dwellings, and the whole village, which probably once housed 3,000 or 4,000 people, resembles, in its general characteristics, the pueblos in the Southwest, and, for that matter, the houses we excavated from the mounds.   The only features that distinguish these from

either of the other structures are the immense thickness of the walls, which reaches as much as five feet, and the great height of the buildings.   The material, too, is different, consisting of enormous bricks made of mud mixed with coarse gravel, and formed in baskets or boxes.

A striking fact is that the houses apparently are not arranged in accordance with any laid-out plan or regularity.   Nevertheless they looked extremely picturesque, viewed from the east as the sun was setting.   I camped for a few days on top of the highest mound, between the ruined walls.

Ceremonial Hatchet with Mountain Sheep's Head. From Casas Grandes. Broken.   Length, 12.16 ctm.

No circular building, nor any trace of a place of worship, could be found.   The Mexicans, some of whom have nestled on the eastern part of the ruins, have from time to time come upon beautiful jars and bowls, which they sold to relic hunters or used themselves. Such pottery is far superior in quality and decoration to anything now made in Mexico.   The ancient metates of Casas Grandes, which are much appreciated by the present inhabitants of the valley, are decidedly the finest I have ever seen.   They are square in shape, resting on four legs, and well finished.   There have also been taken out some stone axes and arrowheads, which are much like those found in the Southwest of the United States.

Some years ago a large meteorite was unearthed in a small room on the first floor of one of the highest of the buildings. When discovered it was found carefully put away and covered with cotton wrappings. No doubt it once had served some religious purpose. On account of its glittering appearance, the Mexicans thought it was silver, and everybody wanted to get a piece of it. But it was taken to Chihuahua, and the

Earthenware Vessel in Shape of a Woman. From Casas Grandes.
Height, 15.8 ctm.

gentleman who sent it to Germany told me that it weighed 2,000 pounds.

There are still traces of well-constructed irrigation ditches to be seen approaching the ruins from the northwest. There are also several artificial accumulations of stones three to fifteen feet high and of various shapes. One of them has the form of a Latin cross measuring nineteen feet along its greatest extent. Others are rectangular, and still others circular. About three miles off, toward the west, are found pictures pecked on large stones, one representing a bird, another one the sun.

An interesting relic of the population that once prospered in Casas Grandes Valley is a watch tower, plainly visible on a mountain to the southwest, and about five miles, in a straight line, from the ruins. Well-defined tracks lead up to it from all directions, especially from the east and west. On the western side three such trails were noticed, and several join at the lower part of the ridge, which runs southward and culminates in the promontory on which the watch tower stands 1,500 feet above the plains.

The western side of the ridge is in some places quite precipitous, but there is a fairly good track running along its entire extent to the top. Sometimes the road is protected with stones, and in other places even with walls, on the outer side. Although the ascent is, at times, steep, the top can be reached on horseback.

The path strikes a natural terrace, and on this is seen a ruined house group built of undressed stones on the bare rock. Some of the walls are twenty-four inches thick. And a little to the south of it is a large mound, from which a Mormon has excavated two rooms. A very well-built stone wall runs for more than 100 paces from north to south on the western, or most easily accessible, side of the pueblo.

After leaving this ancient little village, we made a pleasant ascent to the top, where a strikingly beautiful panorama opened up before us on all sides. The summit commands a view of the fertile valleys for miles around in every direction. To the west is the valley of the Piedras Verdes River, and to the east the valley of Casas Grandes; and in the plains to the south the snakelike windings of the San Miguel River glitter in the sun. Toward the north the view is immense, and fine mountains form a fitting frame for the landscape all around the horizon.

What a pre-eminently fine position for a look-out! As I contemplated the vast stretches of land commanded from this point, I pondered for how many centuries sentinels from this spot may have scanned the ho-

Cerro de Montezuma and the Watch Tower Seen from the South.

rizon with their eagle eyes to warn their people of any enemy approaching to disturb their peaceful occupations.

The fort is circular and about forty feet in diameter. The surrounding wall is on one side about eleven feet high and very broad, while in other places it is much lower and narrower. There are four clearly outlined chambers in the centre; but by excavations nothing could be found in them, except that the flooring was one inch thick.

It was quite warm here. Some birds were about, and there were a few flowers out. Wild white currant bushes were growing inside of the fortress, breathing delicious fragrance. But aside from the top, the mountain was all but barren of vegetation.

A few days afterward I went on an excursion up the Casas Grandes Valley, as far as the Mormon colony Dublan. This valley, which is about fifteen miles long and equally as broad, is very fertile where properly irrigated, and maize and wheat fields delight the eye. Naturally, the country is well populated, and the mounds which are met with everywhere prove that this was already the case in ancient times. In fact, mounds, in groups or isolated, are numerous as far north as Ascension.

How richly the apparently poor soil repays the labour which man expends on it may be seen in the flourishing colony the Mormons have here. Wherever they go,

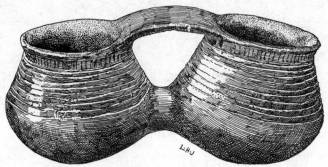

Double Earthenware Vessel, from San Diego, with Hollow Connection at Base. Length, 24.8 ctm.

the Mormons transform waste land into scenes of prosperity, so much so that the Mexicans attribute the success of these indefatigable developers to a gold mine, which they are supposed to work secretly at night.

As I found it imperative to return to the United States in the interest of the expedition, I considered it expedient to reduce my scientific corps to three. My camp at San Diego I left in charge of Mr. H. White, who later on was relieved by Mr. C. V. Hartman. During my absence they conducted excavations of the mounds along the southern bank of the Piedras Verdes River, near its junction with San Miguel River, and in convenient neighbourhood to the camp. Neither the mounds themselves nor the houses inside of them differ much from those already described on the upper part of the river, except that some of the mounds here were somewhat larger. Judging from the beams left, they probably contained a few three-story houses. However, in either locality most of the mound houses were only one story high, and where second or third stories were indicated, they were never found intact. In neither place were circular houses observed. The mounds here were located on a rich, alluvial clay soil.

Here, as on the upper part of the river, the treasures we secured were taken from underneath the floors of the houses, where they had been buried with the dead. Here, as there, they consisted of beautifully decorated earthenware jars and bowls, some of them in bizarre representations of animal and human forms, besides stone implements, shell beads, pieces of pyrites and turquoise, all being generally unearthed intact.

The things were found alongside of skeletons, which were huddled together in groups of from two to five in one of the corners. The jars, bowls, etc., had generally been deposited close to the body, as a rule near the head. The skulls of the skeletons were mostly crushed, and crumbled to dust when exposed to the air. There was no trace of charring on the bones, although in some cases charcoal was found close to the skeletons.

To excavate such mounds is slow and tedious work, requiring much patience. Sometimes nothing was

found for weeks.   Small mounds gave results as good
as, if not better than, some large ones.   In shape they
are more or less conical, flattened at the top; some are
oblong, a few even rectangular.   The highest among
them rose to twenty or twenty-five feet, but the majority
varied from five to twelve feet.   The house walls inside
of them were from eight to sixteen inches thick.

The pottery which was excavated here may be
judged by the accompanying plates.   It is superior in
quality, as well as in decoration, to that produced by the
Pueblos of the Southwest of the United States.   The
clay is fine in texture and has often a slight surface
gloss, the result of mechanical polishing.   Though the
designs in general remind one of those of the Southwestern Pueblos, as, for instance, the cloud terraces, scrolls,
etc., still most of the decorations in question show
more delicacy, taste, and feeling, and are richer in colouring.

This kind of pottery is known only from excavations in the valleys of San Diego and of Piedras Verdes
River, as well as from Casas Grandes Valley.   It forms
a transition from the culture of the Pueblos of Arizona
and New Mexico to that of the Valley of Mexico, a
thousand miles farther south.   In a general way the
several hundred specimens of the collection can be
divided into four groups :

(1) The clay is quite fine, of white colour, with a
slightly grayish-yellow tinge.   The decorations are black
and red, or black only.   This is the predominant type,
and may be seen in Plates I. and II. ; also Plate III., *a.*

(2) Of a very similar character, but somewhat
coarser in texture, and heavier.   See Plate III., *b* to *g*,
and Plate IV., *f.*   Both these groups include variations
in the decorative designs, as may be seen in the rest of
Plate IV.

PLATE I.

a

d

b

e

c

f

PLATE II.

b

a

c

PLATE III.

PLATE IV.

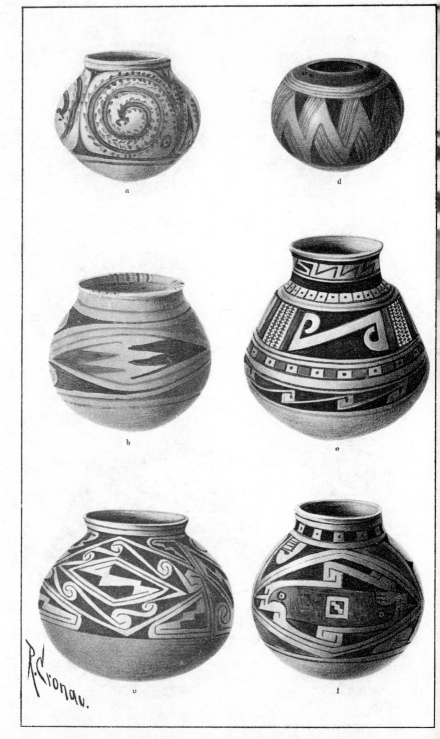

PLATE V.

a

b

e

c

f

d

g

R. Cronau.

Extension of Designs on Plate I., *a*.

The Horned Toad Jar, Seen from Above and Below.   Plate I., *c*.

Extension of Designs on Plate I., *d*.

Extension of Designs on Plate III., *e*.

(3) Brown pottery with black decorations. See Plate V., *a*, *b*, *c*, and *e*.

(4) Black ware.

Here follows a condensed description of the more important specimens shown in the plates:

PLATE I

Heights: *a*, 18.5 ctm.; *b*, 15.2 ctm.; *c*, 16.2 ctm.; *d*, 18.8 ctm.; *e*, 11.3 ctm. ; *f*, 8.5 ctm.

a, particularly graceful in outline and decoration, is a representative type that is often found.

c, from Colonia Dublan, is made in the shape of a horned toad, the lizard so familiar to anyone who has visited the Southwest of the United States. The head with its spikes, and the tail as well, are well rendered; the thorny prominences of the body are represented by the indentations around the edge.

d, the principal decoration here is the plumed serpent with a bird's head.

e, a vase in the shape of a duck.

f, a bowl decorated only around the edge and in the interior.

PLATE II

Height, 16.5 ctm.

Here is shown what, in regard both to manufacture and to decoration, is the best specimen in the collection. Its principal ornaments are the plumed serpent and two birds, all clearly seen in the extension of the design above and below the vase. The lower section is a continuation of the upper one.

The birds are represented as in flight. Mr. M. H. Saville is probably right in considering them as quetzals, though the habitat of this famous trogon is Central America and the southernmost part of Mexico. The bird and the serpent form the decoration of other jars of this collection and would indicate that the makers of this pottery were affiliated with the Aztecs in their adoration of the great deity Quetzalcoatl.

Plate III

Heights : *a*, 18.5 ctm.; *b*, 18 ctm.; *c*, 17 ctm.; *d*, 11 ctm.; *e*, 14.5 ctm.; *f*, 15.3 ctm.; *g*, 24.2 ctm.

c, a jar in the shape of a conventionalised owl.

d, a jar in the shape of a fish.

f is a much conventionalised representation of four horned toads.   Around its upper part it has two serpents, apparently coral snakes, attached in high relief.

Plate IV

Heights : *a*, 14 ctm.; *b*, 16.8 ctm.; *c*, 18.6 ctm.; *d*, 12.2 ctm.; *e*, 22 ctm.; *f*, 18.5 ctm.

a, a very realistic representation of the rain-grub.

c has a black slip.

d is very strong and highly polished, and differs also in colouring from the rest.

Plate V

Heights : *a*, 3.7 ctm.; *b*, 9.8 ctm.; *c*, 25.6 ctm.; *d*, 17 ctm.; *e*, 20.7 ctm.; *f*, 19.3 ctm.; *g*, 19.3 ctm.

Extension of Designs on Plate V., *e*.

This brown ware is very handsome, and its ornamentation is strikingly artistic in its simplicity.   See, for instance, Plate V., *e*.   *D*, *f*, and *g* represent pottery from Casas Grandes, distinguished by a certain solidity and a higher polish.

Black Ware, Highly Polished.   Heights, 12.5 ctm.; 14 ctm.; 7.8 ctm.

Extension of Design on Plate IV., *a*.

Extension of Design on Plate IV., *b*.

Extension of Designs on Plate IV., *c*.

Extension of Designs on Plate IV., *f*.

Extension of Designs on Plate V., *c*.

CHAPTER V

SECOND EXPEDITION—RETURN TO THE SIERRA—PARROTS IN THE SNOW—CAVE-DWELLINGS AT GARABATO, THE MOST BEAUTIFUL IN NORTHERN MEXICO—A SUPERB VIEW OF THE SIERRA MADRE — THE DEVIL'S SPINE RIDGE — GUAYNOPA, THE FAMOUS OLD SILVER MINE—ARROS RIVER—ON OLD TRAILS—ADVENTURES OF "EL CHINO"—CURE FOR POISON IVY.

WHEN in the middle of January, 1892, I resumed my explorations, my party was only about one-third as large as it had been the year before. In pursuance of my plan, I again entered the Sierra Madre, returning to it, as far as Pacheco, by the road on which we had come down to San Diego. We travelled over freshly-fallen snow a few inches deep, and encountered a party of eight revolutionists from Ascension, among whom I perceived the hardest looking faces I had ever laid eyes on. All questions regarding their affairs they answered evasively, and I could not help feeling some anxiety for three of the men, who with a Mexican guide, had for some weeks been exploring the country around Chuhuichupa, a discarded cattle range some forty miles south of Pacheco. Next day I sent a man ahead to warn them against the political fugitives. The Mormons told me that for more than a fortnight they had been keeping track of these suspicious-looking characters who had been camping in the neighbourhood.

There were repeated falls of snow, and the sierra assumed a thoroughly northern aspect. Only the multitude of green parrots with pretty red and yellow heads, chattering in the tree-tops and feasting on pine cones, reminded us that we were in southern latitudes. As all tracks had been obliterated by the snow, I secured a Mormon to guide us southward.

About ten miles south of Pacheco we passed Mound Valley, or "Los Montezumas," so named after the ex-traordinary number of montezumas, or mounds, found in the locality, probably not far from a thousand. Looking at them from a distance, there seemed to be some plan in their arrangement, inasmuch as they formed rows running from north to south. They are small, and nearly all of them are on the south side of a sloping plain which spread itself over about 500 acres in the midst of densely pine-covered highlands.

On making camp a few miles south of this plateau we found that one of the mules had strayed off. My dismay over the loss of the animal was not alleviated by the news that the mule was the one that carried my blankets and tent, and that I had a good prospect of passing at least one uncomfortable night on the snow. The American who had been intrusted with keeping count of the animals on the road immediately went back to look for the lost one; but not until next day did a Mexican, who had been sent along with him, bring back the pack, which the mule had managed to get rid of. The animal itself and its aparejo were never re-covered by us.

On my arrival at Chuhuichupa I found everything satisfactory. There are extensive grass-lands here, and a few years after our visit the Mormons established a colony. The name Chuhuichupa is interesting, as it is the first one we came upon that was of undoubted Tarahumare origin, "chuhui" being the Spanish cor-ruption of "Chu-i," which means "dead." The name signifies "the place of the dead," possibly alluding to burial caves.

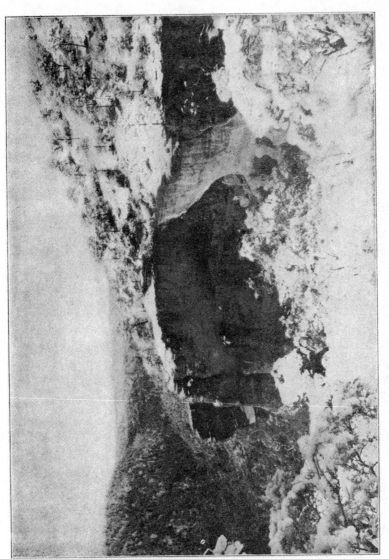

Ancient Cave-Dwelling at Garabato.

Here Mr. Taylor had discovered very interesting cave-dwellings, fifteen miles southeast to east in a straight line from the camp, but fully twenty-five miles by the track he had followed. The Mexicans called the cave Garabato, a Spanish word, which in Mexico is used in the sense of " decorative designs," and refers here to ancient paintings or scrawlings on the house walls. The cave is situated in a gorge on the north-

Part of Cave-Dwellings at Garabato.

ern slope of the Arroyo Garabato, which drains into the Rio Chico. It is in conglomerate formation, faces east, and lies about 215 feet above the bottom of the gorge. The ascent is steep and somewhat difficult. At a little distance the high, regular walls of the houses, with their many door and window openings, presented a most striking contrast to their surroundings of snow-covered jagged cliffs, in the lonely wilderness of pine woods. Some of the walls had succumbed to the

weight of ages, but, on the whole, the ruins are in a
good state of preservation, and although I found cave-
dwellings as far south as Zapuri, Chihuahua, none
of them were nearly as well preserved nor on such
an extensive scale.   Time would not allow me to
visit the cave myself, and the following description
is based on notes taken by Mr. Taylor on the spot,
as well as on his photographs and his verbal explana-
tions.

The space covered by the houses and fallen walls
was 125 feet from side to side, and at the central part
the dwellings were thirty-five feet deep.   The roof of the
cave, or rather, the overhanging cliff, was at the highest
point eighty feet above the floor.   The houses were
arranged in an arc of a circle so large as hardly to deviate
from a straight line.   The front row seems to have been
of but one story, while the adjoining row back of it had
two stories.   The roof of the houses at no place reached
the roof of the cave.   Each room was about twelve feet
square, and the walls, which showed no evidence of
blocks or bricks, varied in thickness from fifteen inches
at the base to seven inches at the top of the highest.
At some places large stones were built into the walls;
in another wall wooden posts and horizontal sticks or
laths were found.   The surface of the walls, which
were protected against the weather, was smooth and
even, and the interior walls showed seven or eight coatings of plaster.   The floors, where they could be examined, were smoothly cemented and so hard as to ef-
fectively resist the spade.   The pine poles which formed
the roof were smooth, but not squared ; they were three
to four inches in diameter, and some of them were
twenty-four feet long.   According to all appearances,
they had been hewn with a blunt instrument, as they
were more hacked than cut.   Many of them were

nicely rounded off at the ends, and several inches from the ends a groove was cut all around the pole.

In the centre of the back rooms of the ground floor there was usually a pine pole, about ten inches in diameter, set up like a rude pillar. Resting on this and the side walls of the rooms in a slight curve was a similar pole, also rounded, and running parallel to the front

Design in Red on Second Story Wall.

of the houses ; and crossing it from the front to the rear walls were laid similar poles or rafters about four inches in diameter. The ends of these were set directly into the walls, and covering them was a roofing of mud, some three inches thick, hard, and on the upper surface smooth. The second story, where it had not caved in, was covered in the same manner. None of the lower story rooms had an outlet to the apartments above, and the evidence tended to prove that

the second story houses were reached from the bottom
of the cave over the roofs of the front row of houses
by means of ladders.

Most of the rooms were well supplied with apertures
of the usual conventional form ; sometimes there were
as many as three in one room, each one large enough
to serve as a door. But there were also several small
circular openings, which to civilised man might appear
to have served as exits for the smoke ; but to the Indian the house, as everything else, is alive, and must have
openings through which it can draw breath, as otherwise it would be choked. These holes were three or
four inches in diameter, and many of them were blocked
up and plastered over. A large number of what
seemed to have been doorways were also found to
be blocked up, no doubt from some ulterior religious
reason.

A peculiar feature of the architecture was a hall not
less than forty feet long, and from floor to rafters seven
feet high. Six beams were used in the roof, laid between the north and south walls. There were rafters of
two different lengths, being set in an angle of about ten
degrees to each other. The west wall contained twelve
pockets, doubtless the cavities in which the rafters had
rested. They were, on an average, three inches in diameter, and ran in some six inches, slanting downward in
the interior. The east wall was found to contain upright poles and horizontal slats, forming a framework for
the building material. The interior was bare, with the
exception of a ledge running along the southern side
and made from the same material as the house walls.
It was squared up in front and formed a convenient
settee.

At the end of this hall, but in the upper story, was
found a house that was distinguished from the others by

a peculiar decoration in red, while the space around the door was painted in a delicate shade of lavender.

There seems to have been still another hall of nearly the same length as the one described, but which must have been at least one foot and a half higher. It is now almost entirely caved in.

No objects of interest were found that could throw

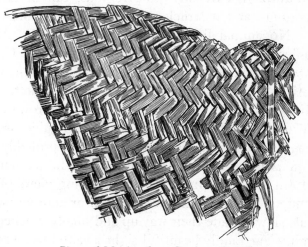

Piece of Matting from Garabato Cave.

any light on the culture of the builders of these dwellings, except the fragment of a stone axe and a piece of matting.

The day after my arrival at Chuhuichupa I continued my journey, now accompanied by Mr. Taylor and Mr. Meeds. We had as a guide an old Mexican soldier, who had been recommended to us as a man who knew the Sierra Madre better than anyone else. He had, no doubt, lived a wild life; had taken part in many a "scrap" with the Apaches, as his body showed marks of bullets in several places, and he had prospected for gold and silver, traversing a good deal of ground in the mountains at one time or another. But topographical knowledge *per se* does not necessarily make a good guide.   Although " Don Teodoro," by something like instinct, always knew where he was, it did not take us long to discover that he had not judgment enough to guide a pack-train, and his fatuous recklessness caused us a good deal of annoyance, and even loss.

After leaving the grass-lands of Chuhuichupa, we passed through extensive pine regions, full of arroyos and cordons, and it struck me how silent the forest was here.   No animal life could be seen or heard.   About ten miles south we caught sight of the Sierra de Cande-laria, which suddenly loomed up in the southeast, while the Arroyo de Guaynopa yawned on our left.   We slowly ascended a beautiful cordon running toward the southwest.   The track we followed, our guide assured us, was *el camino de los antiguos*, but it probably was only an Apache trail.   The cordon was rather narrow, and from time to time gave us sweeping views of the stupendous landscape in one direction or another, as the animals slowly made their way up and finally reached the summit.   A grandly beautiful sight awaited us ; we went a little out of our way to gain a promontory, which, our guide said, was designated " Punto Magnifico."   It was at an elevation of 8,200 feet, and gave us certainly the most strikingly magnificent view of the Sierra Madre we yet had enjoyed.

An ocean of mountains spread out before and be-low us.   In the midst of it, right in front of us, were imposing pine-clad mesas and two weathered pinnacles of reddish conglomerate, while further on there followed range after range, peak after peak ; the most distant ones, toward the south, seeming at least as far as eighty miles away.   The course of the rivers, as they flow deep down between the mountains, was pointed out to us. The principal one is the Arros River, which from the west embraces most of the mesas, and then, turning south, receives its tributaries, the Tutuhuaca and the Mulatos, the latter just behind a pinnacle. West of the Arros River stretches out the immense Mesa de los Apaches, once a stronghold of these marauders, reaching as far as the Rio Bonito. The plateau is also called "The Devil's Spine Mesa," after a high and very narrow ridge, which rises conspicuously from the mesa's western edge and runs in a northerly and southerly direction, like the edge of a gigantic saw. To our amazement, the guide here indicated to us where the camino real from Nacori passes east over a gap in the "Devil's Spine" ridge, and then over several sharp buttes that descend toward the mesa. An odd-looking mesa lay between Rio Bonito and Rio Satachi. Farthest to the west were the big hogbacks near Nacori, standing out ominously, like a perpetuated flash of lightning. The sun was nearing the horizon ; the air was translucent, and the entire panorama steeped in a dusky blue.

Immediately below us, to our left, lay Guaynopa. The mountainside looked so steep that it seemed impossible for us to descend from where we were. But we already heard the voices of our muleteers singing out to the animals 1,000 feet below, and that reminded us that we also had better reach camp before darkness should overtake us. We descended 2,500 feet, and, leaving the pines behind, found ourselves in a warmer climate. It never snows here, according to our guide. That the precipitation took the shape of rain we learned when we were impeded by it for two days.

There were yet eighteen miles between us and the deserted mines of Guaynopa. It was a laborious journey over the hills, mostly ascent. Finally we came to a steep slope covered with oaks, along which there was a continuous descent toward Guaynopa. While zigzagging our

way down, we caught sight of a large cave with houses
and some white cone-shaped structures staring at us
across an arroyo midway up the opposite side, which
was at least two thousand feet deep.   Through my field
glasses I could make out very distinctly a group of
houses of the usual pattern ; and the large, white structures could without difficulty be recognised as granaries,
similar to those observed in Cave Valley.   It was my
intention to go back and examine this cave more closely,
as soon as I had found a camping place; but circumstances interfered.   Several years later the cave was
visited by Mr. G. P. Ramsey, to whom I owe the following brief description.

The cave is situated about twenty-five miles in a
straight line south of the Mormon colony of Chuhuichupa.   There are indications of a spring in the cave,
and there is another one in the arroyo itself.   The
buildings are in a very bad condition, owing to the
action of the elements and animals ; but fifty-three
rooms could be counted.   They were located on a rocky
terrace extending from the extreme right to the rear
centre of the cave.   This extreme right extended slightly
beyond the overhanging cliff, and contained groups of
two-storied houses.   In the central part of the cave were
a number of small structures, built of the same material
and in a similar manner as those I described as granaries in Cave Valley.   They were still in excellent condition, and, as will be seen at a glance, they are almost
identical with the granaries used to the present day in
some southern States of Mexico.

We continued our descent, and, having dropped altogether some 2,000 feet, at last found ourselves alongside some lonely and unattractive old adobe houses.
They were built by the Spaniards and are reputed to
have once been the smelter of the now abandoned silver

Ancient Cave Houses and Granaries near Aros River.

mine of Guaynopa. Only the naked walls remain
standing on a decline, which was too steep to give us
sufficient camping ground. So we went still a little
further, to the top of a hill near by, where we made a
tolerably good camp.

This then was the famous locality of Guaynopa,
credited with hiding such fabulous wealth. There was
still another mine here of the same repute, called
Tayopa, and both of them are said to have been worked
once by the Jesuits, who before their expulsion from
Mexico were in possession of nearly all the mines in the
country. According to tradition, the Apaches killed
everybody here, and the mines were forgotten until recent times, when ancient church records and other
Spanish documents revealed their existence. Several
expeditions have been sent out, one, I believe, by the
Government for the purpose of locating them ; but being situated in the roughest and most inaccessible part
of the Sierra Madre, they are still awaiting their redis-
covery, unless, contrary to my knowledge, they have been
found in recent years. There is no doubt that the
country carries very rich silver ore, and we ourselves
found specimens of that kind ; but the region is so difficult of access that it probably would require too great a
capital to work the mines.

There was now a plain track leading along the hillside down toward the Rio Aros, which is scarcely two
miles off; but the country was so wild and rugged that
the greatest care had to be exercised with the animals
to prevent them from coming to grief. The path runs
along the upper part of a steep slope, which from a perpendicular weathered cliff drops some 400 feet down
into a gorge. As the declivity of the slope is about
forty-five degrees, and the track in some places only
about a foot wide, there is no saving it if an animal loses

its foothold, or if its pack slips. All went well, however, until we reached a point where the track commenced to descend, when our villain of a guide tried to
drive some burros back on the track, instead of leading
each one carefully. The result was that one of the poor
beasts tumbled down, making immense bounds, a hundred feet at a time, and, of course, was killed.

We had no difficulty in fording the Guaynopa
Creek near its junction with the Aros River, and selected a camping place on a terrace 200 feet above it.
The stream, which is the one that passes the cave-dwellings, carries a good deal of limpid water, and there are
abundant signs that at times it runs very high. The
elevation of the ford, which is here about the same as
that of Aros River, 3,400 feet, was the lowest point we
reached in our crossing of the Sierra Madre between
Chuhuichupa and Temosachic. It took us almost the
entire day to move the animals the one mile and a half
to this camp. On the way we had found some good
quartz crystals in the baryte, about four inches high and
one inch in width.

The country before us looked more forbidding than
ever, as if it did not want us to penetrate any further
into its mysteries, but our guide seemed to be quite at
home here.

Our march toward Rio Chico was about thirty miles
of ups and downs, ascending to a height of 7,600 feet
and descending again some 3,000 feet. In the beginning it was almost impossible to make out the track;
where it did not lead over bare rocks, it was nearly obliterated by overgrown grass. The first ascent was over
a mile long in a straight line; then, after a little while,
came the most arduous climbing I had until then ever
attempted. Following the slope of the mountain, the
track rose higher and higher in long zigzags, without any

chance for the animals to rest, for at least three-quarters of a mile. It was necessary to push them on, as otherwise the train would unavoidably have upset, and one or the other have rolled down the declivity. One large white mule, El Chino, after it had almost climbed to the top, turned giddy at the "glory-crowned height" it had reached, and, sinking on its hind legs, fell backward and rolled heels over head down, with its two large canvas-covered boxes, like a big wheel. As luck would have it, it bumped against a low-stemmed old oak that cropped out of the hillside in an obtuse angle to it, some ninety feet below. Making one more turn up the stem, the mule was nicely caught between the forked branches, which broke the momentum, loosened the cargo, and caused the animal to fall back into the high grass. One box landed close by, the other, containing our library, pursued its course downward 200 feet further, bursting open on the way and scattering the wisdom of the ages to the winds, while the mule escaped without a scratch.

The burros came into camp three hours after us, and the drivers explained how they had succeeded in bringing them up the long slope only by constantly punching them to prevent them from "falling asleep."

As we continued our journey toward Rio Chico the panorama of the sierra changed continuously. We got a side view of the big Mesa de los Apaches, and many weathered pinnacles of eroded conglomerate were seen standing out like church spires in this desert of rock, varying in colour from red to lead gray. Once we caught sight of a stretch of the Rio Aros deep down in a narrow, desolate valley, some 3,000 feet below us. The geological formation of the region is mostly volcanic; then follows conglomerate, and on the high points porphyry appears.

We camped on the crest of the eastern side of the

Rio Chico Cañon, in an ideal place with bracing air. A fine, sloping meadow afforded quite an arcadian view with the animals peacefully grazing and resting ; but looking westward, the eye revelled in the grand panorama of the sierra. The two sides of the Rio Chico Valley rise here evenly from the bottom of the gorge so as to suggest the letter V. In many places its brow is overhung by precipitous cliffs, and further down still more steeply walled chasms yawn up from the river bed.

My chief packer now became ill from the effects of poison ivy. He was one of those unfortunate individuals who are specially susceptible to it. According to his own statement it sufficed for him to pass anywhere near the plant, even without touching it, to become afflicted with the disease. In this case he did not even know where he had contracted it, until the cook showed him some specimens of the plant near an oak tree close by the kitchen tent. The poor fellow's lips were badly swollen ; he had acute pains in his eyes, and felt unable to move. Sometimes, he said, the disease would last ten days, and his skin become so tender that he could not endure the weight or contact of his clothes. But by applying to the afflicted parts of his body a solution of baking soda in water, I was able not only to relieve his suffering, but to enable him, after two days, to continue with us on our journey.

In the meantime we had investigated some caves in the conglomerate of the steep cañon side, about 250 feet above the bottom of the gorge, and rather difficult of access. The house group occupied the entire width of a cave, which was eighty feet across, and there was a foundation wall made of stone and timber underneath the front part. The walls were made of stone, with mortar of disintegrated rock that lined parts of the cave and were plastered inside and out with the same material. Lintels of wood were seen in the windows, and rows of sticks standing in a perpendicular position were found in two of the walls inside of the plastering. On one side of the cave, some two feet off, was a small tower, also in ruins, measuring inside four feet in diameter, while the walls were about six inches thick.

Pinnacles of eroded conglomerate are a prominent characteristic of the landscape west of the Rio Chico; further on, the usual volcanic formation appears again. After fully twenty miles of travel we found ourselves again in pine forests and at an altitude of 7,400 feet. Here we were overtaken, in the middle of February, by a rain and sleet storm, which was quite severe, although we were sheltered by tall pine trees in a little valley. It turned to snow and grew very cold, and then the storm was over. Here a titmouse and a woodpecker were shot, and the bluebirds were singing in the snow.

Travelling again eleven miles further brought us to the plains of Naverachic, where we camped. It was quite a treat to travel again on comparatively level land, but, strange to say, I felt the cold so much that I had to walk on foot a good deal in order to keep warm. The word Naverachic is of Tarahumare origin; nāvé means "move," and ráchi refers to the disintegrated trachyte formation in the caves.

We had just emerged from a district which at that time was traversed by few people; perhaps only by some illiterate Mexican adventurers, though it had once been settled by a thrifty people whose stage of culture was that of the Pueblo Indians of to-day, and who had vanished, nobody knows how many centuries ago. Over it all hovered a distinct atmosphere of antiquity and the solemnity of a graveyard.

CHAPTER VI

FOSSILS, AND ONE WAY OF UTILISING THEM—TEMOSACHIC—THE
FIRST TARAHUMARES—PLOUGHS WITH WOODEN SHARES—VISIT
TO THE SOUTHERN PIMAS—ABORIGINAL HAT FACTORIES—PINOS
ALTOS—THE WATERFALL NEAR JESUS MARIA—AN ADVENTURE
WITH LADRONES.

ABOUT thirty miles from the village of Temosachic (in the Tarahumare tongue Remosachic
means Stone Heap) we entered the plain of Yepomera, and came upon an entirely different formation,
limestone appearing in an almost horizontal layer some
thirty feet deep. In this bed the Mexicans frequently
find fossils, and at one place four large fossil bones have
been utilised as the corner posts of a corral or inclosure. We were told that teeth and bones were accidentally found at a depth of from twenty to thirty feet and
some bones were crystallised inside. This formation,
which stretches itself out toward the east of Temosachic, but lies mainly to the north of this place, has an
extent of about fifteen miles from north to south, and
from three to four miles from east to west.

Fossils picked up by Mr. Meeds in the cutting of a
creek near Yepomera consisted of some fragmentary
teeth and pieces of bones from some small animal.
They were found in the hard clay that underlies the
lime-stone. Large fossil bones also are said to have
been gathered near the town of Guerrero, Chihuahua,
quite recently. It seems to be a custom with the common people to make a concoction of these "giants'
bones" as a strengthening medicine; we heard of a

woman who, being weak after childbirth, used it as an invigorating tonic.

Here in Temosachic we were joined by Mr. Hartman, who had brought part of our baggage from San Diego by wagon in order to enable us to travel as unencumbered as possible.

From now on, until as far as the southern border of the State of Chihuahua, the country is occupied by the large Indian tribe of the Tarahumares. They are now confined to the Sierra Madre, but in former times they also occupied the entire plain of Chihuahua, as far west as the present capital of that State, and in a narrow strip they may have reached as far as 100 miles north of Temosachic. They were the main tribe found in possession of the vast country which is now the State of Chihuahua, and although there are still some 25,000 left, the greater

Tarahumare.

part of them have become Mexicanised, adopting the language and the customs of the whites, together with their dress and religion. Father Ribas, in the seventeenth century, speaks of them as very docile and easily converted to Christianity.

The high plateau of the Sierra Madre for a couple of hundred miles southward is not difficult to follow. Most of it is hilly and clad in oaks and pines; but there are also extensive tracts of fine arable land, partly under cultivation, and fairly good tracks connect the solitary villages and ranches scattered over the district. The country of the aborigines has been invaded and most of the descendants of the former sovereigns of the realm have been reduced to earning a precarious living by working for the white and mixed-breed usurpers on their ranches or in their mines. The native language, religious customs, and dress are being modified gradually in accordance with the new régime. Only in the less desirable localities have the Tarahumares been able to hold their own against the conquerors.

There is not much interest attached to the study of half-civilised natives, but the first pure-blooded Tarahumares I met on their little ranch about ten miles south of Temosachic were distinctly Indian and very different from the ordinary Mexican family. There was a kind of noble bearing and reserve about them which even the long contact with condescending whites and half-breeds had not been able to destroy. The father of the family, who, by the way, was very deaf, was a man of some importance among the native ranchers here. When I approached the house, mother and daughter were combing each other's hair, and did not allow themselves to be disturbed by my arrival. The younger woman wore her long glossy tresses plaited in Mexican fashion. She evidently was in robust health and had well-moulded, shapely arms and an attractive face, with an eagle nose. She was beautiful, but I could not help thinking how much better she would have looked in her native costume.

On the road we had several times overtaken donkey trains carrying corn to the mines of Pinos Altos. In the small Rio Verde we caught three kinds of fish : suckers, catfish, and Gila trout, which grow from one to three feet long, and, according to Tarahumare belief, change into otters when they are old.

The name of the village of Tosanachic is a Spanish corruption of the Tarahumare Rosanachic, which means

"Where there is White," and alludes to a number of white rocks or cliffs of solidified volcanic ash, which rise to a height of some fifty feet and give to the little valley quite a striking appearance. There are caves in these rocks, and three poor families of Pima Indians lived in some of them.

In the village we noticed the first Tarahumare plough, the share of which was made of a section of oak. In its general appearance it is an imitation of the ordinary Mexican plough, in other words, is simply a tree stem

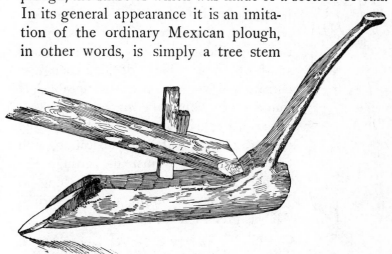

Tarahumare Plough with Wooden Share.   Length, 1 Metre.

with a branch as a handle.   But, however primitive in design and construction, the civilised man's implement always has an iron share.   Of course, such among the Tarahumares as can afford iron shares, never fail to get them ; but in several parts of their country ploughs made entirely of wood, that is to say, ploughs with wooden shares, are seen.   The foremost part of such a plough is cut to a point, and into a groove made for the purpose a section of tough oak is inserted, to serve as a share.   It is held in place by the tapering of the groove, and some wedges or plugs.   The share has

Tarahumare
Ploughshare
Made of Oak.
Length, 20.5 ctm.

naturally to be renewed quite frequently, but it serves its purpose where the ground is not stony. Later on, in Cusarare, Nararachic and other places, I found ploughshares of stone applied in the same manner as were the wooden ones.

Here at an elevation of 7,600 feet, and at the end of February, I saw the first flowers of the year, some very fresh-looking yellow *Ranunculus*. On crossing the ridge to Piedras Azules, sixty-odd miles south of Temosachic, a decided change of climate and vegetation was noticeable. I found another kind of *Ranunculus*, as well as various other flowers, and as we passed through a small but gorgeous cañon, with the sun shining against us through the fresh leaves of the trees, everything in Nature made the impression of spring. All was green except the ground, which was gray. The road was stony, and bad for the feet of the animals ; altogether the country presented a new aspect with its small volcanic hills, many of them forming cones.

A few Indian hamlets surrounded by peach trees in full bloom were found here. The Indians here are

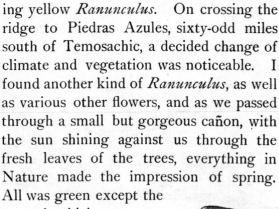

Tarahumare Ploughshares of Stone.
Length, 9 and 10.5 ctm.

Pimas, who, in their general characteristics, resemble the Tarahumare, although they impress you as being less timid and suspicious, and more energetic, perhaps also more intelligent, than the latter.   We had no diffi-

Young Southern Pima.

culty in taking some photographs.   Among those who agreed to have their pictures taken was a dignified, courteous old man, who thought he was a hundred years old, but was probably only eighty.   He showed me some scars on his body, which were a souvenir from a fight he once had with a bear.

In order to see more of the Southern Pimas I went

to the near-by village of Yepachic, which I think
is also a Tarahumare name, yēpá meaning snow.
There are, however, more Mexicans than Pimas in the
village, and the presidente was a half-caste Tarahumare;

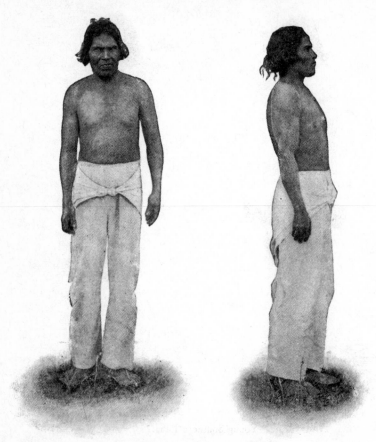

Middle-aged Southern Pima.

he was once a shepherd, but had made money by trading mescal to the natives—six bottles for a cow.

Although the Pimas whom I visited in the neighbourhood, were very reserved, and even more Indian-like
than the Tarahumares I had seen so far, still in their
dress they showed more traces of advancing civilisation

Southern Pimas Living in a Brushwood Inclosure.

than the latter tribe. Everything here betrays the
nearness of the mines, with the characteristic accompaniment of cheap clothes, cheap, tawdry jewelry, and
a slight influx of iron cooking utensils. The Pimas,
like the Tarahumares, use pine
cones for combs; and we
picked up several discarded
ones near their houses.

I went still fifteen miles
further northward, but found
that most of the Indians there

Pine Cone Serving as a Comb.

had gone to the Pinos Altos mines to look for work.
That "March comes in like a lion" I realised even here
in the sierra, when, on this excursion, on which I had not
taken my tent along, I was overtaken by a snow-storm.
We had gone to bed with the stars for a canopy, clear
and beautiful; we woke up under blankets of snow,
which turned to rain, drenching us to the skin and
making us shiver with cold.

I saw several small, shallow caves, and learned that
many of them were utilised by the Pimas during the
wet season. I also passed a rock-shelter, which served
as a permanent home. The housewife was busy making straw hats. She was very shy, as her husband was
away ; but I elicited the information that she gets two
reales (25 cents) for each hat. The making of straw
hats and mats is quite an industry among the Pimas.
In the houses they have a cellar-like dug-out outside
of the dwelling and covered with a conical roof of dry
grass. These cellars, in many cases, serve not only as
the work-rooms, but also as store-rooms for their stock
in trade.

In one or two instances I found Pima families
living in open inclosures, a kind of corral, made from
cut-down brushwood. I noticed two small caves that

had been transformed into storehouses, by planting poles along the edge and plastering these over with mud,

Southern Pima Arrow Release.

to make a solid wall, behind which corn was stored.

In Yepachic I estimated there were about twenty Pima families. I had some difficulty in inducing them to pose before the camera; the presidente himself was afraid of the instrument, thinking it was a diabolo (devil).

There are probably not more than sixty Pima families within the State of Chihuahua, unless there are more than I think near Dolores. Some twenty-odd families of these live in caves during the wet season, and a few of them are permanent cave-dwellers. I understand that the Pimas in Sonora utilise caves in the same way.

I made an excursion from the mine of Pinos Altos (elevation 7,100 feet) to Rio Moris, about ten miles west, where there are some burial caves; but they had already been much disturbed by treasure seekers, and I

Small Crosses Placed in a Log in Front of Southern Pima House.

could secure only a couple of skulls. An interesting feature of the landscape near Rio Moris is a row of large reddish pinnacles, which rise perpendicularly from the river-bed up along the hillside, and form a truly imposing spectacle. An excited imagination may see in them so many giants suddenly petrified while walking up the mountain. Around Pinos Altos and Jesus Maria the rock is of blue porphyry, quite hard in places, and speckled with little white patches. It is in this rock that the gold- and silver-bearing quartz occurs.

Through the courtesy of the bullion-convoy I was enabled to dispatch some of my collections via Chihuahua to the museum at New York, among other things eight fine specimens of the giant woodpecker.

Then, sending my train ahead, I made with a guide a little detour to visit the

The Waterfall of Basasiachic.

beautiful waterfall near Jesus Maria. It is formed by
the River Basasiachic, which, except during the wet
season, is small and insignificant. Before the fall the
stream for more than a hundred yards runs in a narrow
but deep channel, which in the course of ages it has worn
into the hard conglomerate rock. The channel itself is
full of erosions and hollowed-out places formed by the
constant grinding and milling action of the rapidly rushing water, and the many large pebbles it carries. Just
at the very brink of the rock, a low natural arch has been
eroded, and over this the stream leaps almost perpendicularly into the deep straight-walled cañon below. The
height of the cascade has been measured by a mining
expert at Pinos Altos, and found to be 980 feet. Set in
the most picturesque, noble environments, the fall is
certainly worth a visit.

I arrived at its head just as the last rays of the setting
sun were gilding the tops of the mountains all around.
The scenery was beautiful beyond description. Above
and around towered silent, solemn old pine-trees, while
the chasm deep down was suffused with a purple glow.
About midway down the water turns into spray and
reaches the bottom as silently as an evening shower, but
as it recovers itself forms numerous whirlpools and
rapids, rushing through the narrow gorge with an incessant roar. When the river is full, during the wet season,
the cascade must present a splendid sight.

I wanted to see the fall from below. The guide, an
elderly man, reminded me that the sun was setting, and
warned me that the distance was greater than it seemed.
We should stumble and fall, he said, in the dark. But
as I insisted on going, he put me on the track, and I
started on a rapid run, jumping from stone to stone,
zigzagging my way down the mountainside. The entire
scenery, the wild, precipitous rocks, the stony, crooked

path, the roaring stream below—everything reminded me of mountains in Norway, where I had run along many a *säter* path through the twilight, alone, just as I was running now.

As luck would have it, I met an Indian boy coming up from the river, where he had been trout fishing, and I asked him to accompany me, which he did. About half-way down we arrived at a little promontory from which the fall could be seen very well. The rock seemed to be here the same as on top, showing no sign of stratification. A few yards from the point we had reached was a spring, and here we made a fire and waited for the moon to rise. To make him more talkative, I gave the boy a cigarette. He spoke only Spanish, and he told me that he had neither father nor mother, and when his uncle died he was quite alone in the world; but a Mexican family brought him up, and he seemed to have been treated well. At present he was paying two dollars a month for his board, earning the money by selling grass in Pinos Altos.

At nine o'clock we began to ascend through the moonlit landscape. I had left my mule some hundred yards from the fall, and here I also found the guide. At two o'clock in the morning I arrived at my camp.

The road continued through rather monotonous country, the altitude varying from 6,300 to 7,700 feet. Grass began to be scarce, and the animals suffered accordingly. It is the custom with Mexican muleteers to select from among themselves a few, whose business throughout the journey it is to guard the animals at night. These men, immediately after having had their supper, drive the animals to a place where suitable pasture is found, never very far from the camp, and bring them back in the morning. They constitute what is called la sabana. Comparatively few men suffice for this duty,

even with a large herd, as long as they have with them
a leader of the mules, a mare, preferably a white one.
She may be taken along solely for this purpose, as she
is often too old for any other work.   The mules not infrequently show something like a fanatic attachment for
their yegua, and follow blindly where they hear the tink-
ling of the bell, which is invariably attached to her neck.
She leads the pack-train, and where she stops the mules
gather around her while waiting for the men to come
and relieve them of their burdens.   Sometimes a horse
may serve as a leader, but a mare is surer of gaining the
affection of all the mules in the train.   This is an important fact for travellers to bear in mind if they use
mules at all.   In daytime the train will move smoothly,
all the mules, of their own accord, following their
leader, and at night keeping close to her.   In this way
she prevents them from scattering and becomes indispensable to the train.

But in spite of the vigilance of the sabana and the
advantage of a good yegua, it may happen, under favourable topographical and weather conditions, that robbers
succeed in driving animals away.   While giving the
pack-train a much-needed rest of a day in a grassy spot,
we woke next morning to find five of our animals missing.   As three of the lot were the property of my men,
they were most eagerly looked for.   The track led up a
steep ridge, over very rough country, which the Mexicans followed, however, until it suddenly ran up against
a mountain wall ; and there the mules were found in
something like a natural corral.

Not until then did our guide inform me that there
lived at Calaveras (skulls), only three miles from where
we were stopping, a band of seven robbers and their
chief, Pedro Chaparro, who was at that time well-known
throughout this part of the Tarahumare country.   I had

no further experience with him, but later heard much of this man, who was one of a type now rapidly disappearing in Mexico. He did not confine his exploits to the Mexicans, but victimised also the Indians whenever he got an opportunity, and there are many stories in circulation about him.

On one occasion he masqueraded as a padre, a black mackintosh serving as his priestly garb. Thus attired he went to the unsophisticated Tarahumares in the more remote valleys and made them send out messengers to advise the people that he had come to baptise them, and that they were all to gather at a certain place to receive his blessings. For each baptism he charged one goat, and by the time he thought it wise to retire he had quite a respectable herd to drive home. When the Indians found out that they had been swindled, they caught him and put him into jail, intending to kill him; but unfortunately some of his Mexican confrères heard of his plight and came to his rescue. However, a few years later, this notorious highwayman, who had several murders to answer for, was caught by the government authorities and shot.

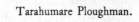

Tarahumare Ploughman.

On the road, as we travelled on, we met many Tarahumares carrying on their backs trays (*huacales*) with apples, which they were taking to market. The price per tray was $2, and the apples were delicious.

At night it was very cold, the thermometer falling to

13° below the freezing point. I was sorry to learn from my men that the prospects of grass further south were small.

At the village of Bocoyna (elevation 7,100 feet) we were 400 miles from San Diego by the track we had made. Bocoyna is a corruption of the Tarahumare Ocoina (ŏcó=pine ; ína=drips ; meaning Dripping Pine, or Turpentine).   Here I had to stop for two days, be-

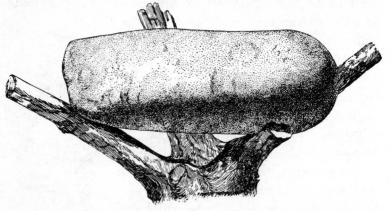

Ancient Stone Hammer Seen in the Presidente's Yard.   Length, 44.5 ctm.

cause no less than six of us, including myself, were suffering from the grippe, which a piercing, dry, cold wind did not tend to alleviate.   However, as the worst cases did not last more than five days, we soon were all well again, though the Mexicans were almost overcome by the effects of the disease.

The presidente here was a powerful-looking half-caste and very original.   After I had read to him twice my letter from the governor of the state, in which the people were told, among other things, to promote the success of the expedition in every way, especially by selling us what provisions we needed and not to overcharge us, he, by way of obeying the orders of his superior, immediately ordered that not more than $6 should be charged for a fanega of corn.   He also had at once four nice, fat hens killed and sold them to us at the market price.

After we passed Bocoyna, the country for ten miles was flat, but fertile. It was gratifying to observe that here the Indians had some ranches with considerable land still left to them. We passed several such home-steads lying close together, and as many as four yokes of oxen were ploughing, each attended by a Tarahu-mare, whose entire clothing consisted of a breech-cloth. The Indians here are very numerous and they are still struggling to resist the encroachments of the whites upon their land, though the ultimate result is in all cases the same.

CHAPTER VII

THE UNCONTAMINATED TARAHUMARES—A TARAHUMARE COURT
IN SESSION—THE POWER OF THE STAFF—JUSTICE HAS ITS
COURSE—BARRANCAS—EXCURSION TO THE GENTILES—TARA-
HUMARE COSTUMES SIMPLE AND INEXPENSIVE—TRINCHERAS IN
USE AMONG THE TARAHUMARES

WE were lucky enough to secure a guide who
spoke the Tarahumare language very well, and
our next stop was at the pueblo of Cusarare (a Spanish
corruption of Usarare, usáka = eagle), an Indian village
situated in a rather rough country full of weathered porphyry rocks. We made camp a few miles outside of
the village and sent the guide to prepare the people for
our coming. There had recently been considerable talk
among the Mexicans of the wild people in the deep
gorges, called barrancas, and it was with no little antici-
pation that I approached the country now immediately
before us. There were no Mexicans living in Cusarare,
nor in the country ahead of us ; in fact, with the exception of the small mining camp in Barranca de Cobre,
there were none within fifty miles to the south, and
almost an equal distance from east to west.

Indian pueblos throughout Mexico are almost abandoned for the greater part of the year. I refer, of
course, only to those which have not yet become Mexican settlements. The first thing the missionaries in the
early times had to do was to force the Indians to leave
their scattered ranches and form a pueblo. To make a
place a pueblo they had to build a church. The Indians

were pressed into service to erect the building, and kept
at work, if necessary, by a troop of soldiers who often

Tarahumare Indians from Pino Gordo.

accompanied the missionaries and in this way assisted
them in spreading the gospel.

From the missionaries' point of view this was a very
practical arrangement; but the purpose of having the
Indians remain in the villages has not been accomplished

to this day. Only the native-chosen authorities, who are obliged to reside there during their term of office, form something like a permanent population in the pueblos. The natives come together only on the occasion of feasts, and on Sundays, to worship in the way they understand it. Someone who knows the short prayer, generally the gobernador, mumbles it, while the congregation cross themselves from time to time. If no one present knows the prayer, the Indians stand for a while silently, then cross themselves, and the service is over.

After church they meet outside for the second purpose that brings them to the village, namely, the transaction of whatever judicial business may be on hand, generally the adjustment of a theft, a marriage, etc.

I arrived in the pueblo on a Sunday, and a great many Indians had come in. Easter was approaching, and every Sunday during Lent, according to early missionaries' custom, the so-called "Pharisees" make their appearance. These are men who play an important part in the Easter festival, which always lasts several days. They paint their faces hideously, tog themselves up with feathers on their sombreros, and carry wooden swords painted with red figures. Such ceremonies were a clever device of the Jesuits and Franciscan missionaries to wean the Indians from their native feasts by offering them something equally attractive in the new religion they were teaching. The feasts are still observed, while the teachings are forgotten.

I found the people assembled before the old adobe church, where they had just finished their service. The gobernador at once attracted my attention as he stood with his large white blanket wrapped around him, Indian fashion, up to his chin—a fine, almost noble personality, with a benign expression on his eagle face.

The Indian never allows anything to interfere with

whatever business he may have on hand, be it public or private. Presently all rose, and eight men, the authorities of the pueblo, marched in two rows to the court house, followed by the rest of the people. There is always found near the church a commodious building, called La Comunidad, originally intended as city hall, court house, and hotel. In this case it was so dilapidated that the judges and officers of the court about to be held took seats outside on the lawn in front of one of the walls. They were preparing to administer justice to a couple of offenders, and as this is the only occasion on which I have seen the details of Indian judicial procedure carried out so minutely as to suggest early missionary times, I am happy to record the affair here in full.

The gobernador and four of the judges seated themselves, white man's fashion, on a bench erected for the purpose, where they looked more grand than comfortable. Two of them held in their right hands canes of red Brazil wood, the symbol of their dignity. The idea of the staff of command, sceptre, or wand, is wide spread among the Indians of Mexico; therefore, when the Spaniards conquered the various tribes, they had little difficulty in introducing their batons (*la vara*), as emblems of authority, which to this day are used by the gobernadors and other officials. They are made much in the same way as the ancient staffs, and of the same material, the heavy, red Brazil wood. Below the head of these canes there is always a hole bored, and through this a leather thong is passed, by which the staff is hung up on the wall when not in use. Those of the highest authorities are ornamented with silver caps; the lesser officers have smaller canes, in proportion to the degrees of their dignity, while the lowest officials have only a thin stick, about a foot and a half long, through the hole of which a red ribbon is passed. The small canes are not carried in the hand, but stuck in the girdle on the left side. Nobody summoned before the judges by a messenger carrying a staff of red Brazil wood dares to disobey the command. The most desperate criminal meekly goes to his doom, following often a mere boy, if the latter has only a toy vara stuck in his belt with the red ribbons hanging down. It is the vara the Indians respect, not the man who carries it.

No supreme court in any civilised community is so

Tarahumare Court in Session at Cusarare.

highly respected and so implicitly obeyed as were the simple, grave men sitting in front of the crumbling adobe wall and holding on to their canes with a solemnity that would have been ridiculous, if it had not been sublime.

Four "soldiers" formed a line on each side. There was nothing to distinguish them from ordinary civilians, except their "lances," or bamboo sticks to which bayonet points had been fastened. These lances they planted in the ground and seated themselves. Presently the two culprits, a man and a woman, came forward, with never a suggestion in their placid faces that they were the chief actors in the drama about to be enacted. They seated themselves in front of the judges, while the witnesses took their places behind them. The mother of the woman sat close by her guilty daughter, but there was no other exhibition of sentiment. The judges did most of the talking, addressing questions to the defendants, who made a few short answers ; the rest of the assemblage observed a decorous silence. There were neither clerks nor lawyers.

I was, of course, not able to follow the testimony, but it was very short, and it was explained to me that the woman had run away with a married man. They had provided themselves with plenty of corn from the man's former home, and furthermore had stolen some beans, and lived very happy in a cave for a year. The man could not be captured, even though on several occasions he visited his family. But they frequently made native beer, and got drunk, and while in this condition they were caught and brought before this tribunal.

While the trial was going on, one of the "soldiers" got up and went some twenty yards off, dug a hole in the ground and planted a thick pole or post in it. No sooner had he completed his task, when the accused man rose with a queer smile on his face, half chagrined, half sarcastic. Dropping his blanket, he walked deliberately up to the pole, flanked by two soldiers, each of whom took hold of his hands, and by putting them crosswise on the further side of the pole, made the culprit hug the pole very tightly. Now another man, wrapped closely in his blanket, stepped briskly up, drew as quick as a flash a leather whip from under his garment, and dealt four lashes over the shoulders of the prisoner, who was then released, and stolidly walked back to his seat, as if nothing had happened.

Now came the woman's turn to be punished for her part in the thefts. They took off her blanket, but left on a little white undergarment. She was marched to the pole and held in the same manner as the man ; but another man acted as executioner. She, too, received four lashes, and wept a little when they struck her ; but neither she nor her fellow-sufferer made any attempt at, or sign of, revolt against the sentence of the court. While the chastising went on, the audience rose and stood reverently. After returning to her seat, the woman knelt down, and both delinquents shook hands with the chief judge.

There still remained the second part of the accusation to be dealt with, the one relating to the marital complications. The man asked permission to leave his first wife, as he wanted to marry the woman with whom he ran away. But no divorce was granted to him. He was ordered to return to his legitimate spouse, who was present at the proceedings with her child in her arms. Evidently disappointed, he slowly stepped over to where she was standing and greeting him with a happy smile.

But the woman with whom he had been living had now to be provided with another husband. Who would take her ? The judge addressed the question to a young man, a mere boy, standing near by, and he replied that he would marry her, if she were willing. She said yes, so he sat down beside her. Their hands were placed together, the gobernador said a few admonishing words to them, and they rose, man and wife, duly married. How was this for rapid transit to matrimonial bliss ?

The next day the guide took us up along some higher ridges, and after ten or twelve miles of slow ascent, we arrived at the summit of Barranca de Cobre, where we made a comfortable camp about half a mile back of the point at which the track descends into the cañon. Here we had an inspiring view; deep gorges and ravines, the result of prolonged weathering and erosion, gashing the country and forming high ridges, especially toward the south and west. In other words, here we observed for the first time barrancas, which from now on form an exceedingly characteristic feature of the topography of the Sierra Madre. These precipitous abysses, which traverse the mighty mass of the sierra like huge cracks, run, as far as Sierra Madre del Norte is concerned, mainly from east to west. In the country of the Tarahumare, that is to say, the State of Chihuahua, there are three very large barrancas. They are designated as Barranca de Cobre, Barranca de Batopilas, and Barranca de San Carlos. The Sierra Madre del Norte runs at an altitude of from 7,000 to 8,000 feet, at some points reaching even as high as 9,000 feet. It rises so gradually in the east, for instance, when entered from the direction of the city of Chihuahua, that one is surprised to be suddenly almost on top of it. The western side, however, falls off more or less abruptly, and presents the appearance of a towering, ragged wall. In accordance with this general trait of the mountain system, the beginnings of the barrancas in the east are generally slight, but they quickly grow deeper, and before they disappear in the lowlands of Sinaloa they sometimes reach a depth of from 4,000 to 5,000 feet. Of course, they do not continue equally narrow throughout their entire length, but open up gradually and become wider and less steep.

Besides these large barrancas, which impede the

traveller in the highlands and necessitate a course toward the east, there are innumerable smaller ones, especially in the western part of the range, where large portions of the country are broken up into a mass of stupendous, rock-walled ridges and all but bottomless chasms. A river generally flows in the barrancas between narrow banks, which occasionally disappear alaltogether, leaving the water to rush between abruptly ascending mountain sides.

As far as the first of the large barrancas was concerned, near the top of which we were standing, we could for some little distance follow its windings toward the west, and its several tributaries could be made out in the landscape by the contours of the ridges. Barranca de Cobre is known in its course by different names. Near the mine of Urique (the Tarahumare word for barranca), it is called Barranca de Urique, and here its yawning chasm is over 4,000 feet deep. Even the intrepid Jesuit missionaries at first gave up the idea of descending into it, and the Indians told them that only the birds knew how deep it was. The traveller as he stands at the edge of such gaps wonders whether it is possible to get across them. They can in a few places be crossed, even with animals if these are lightly loaded, but it is a task hard upon flesh and blood.

It was in these barrancas, that I was to find the gentile (pagan) Indians I was so anxious to meet. From where I stood looking at it the country seemed forgotten, lonely, untouched by human hand. Shrubs and trees were clinging to the rocky brows of the barrancas, and vegetation could be seen wherever there was sufficient earth on the mountain and the sides of the ravines ; but, on the whole, the country looked rather barren and lifeless.

Still, it did not take us long to find traces of human

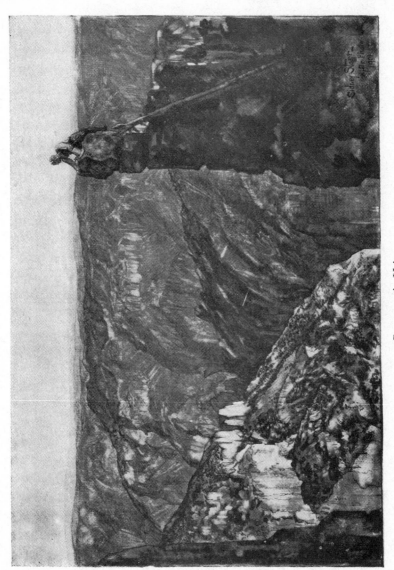

Barranca de Urique.

beings. Our tents were pitched on an old trinchera. Cut deep into a rough ledge not far off was the rough carving of a serpent, sixty feet long, that must have been left here by a race antecedent to the Tarahumares. And a little further off we came upon the ruins of a modern Tarahumare house. It seems as if the Indians must extract a living out of the rocks and stones; though when we got down into the barranca and into the ravines we came upon patches of land that could be cultivated; and there were some small areas of pasture, although extremely precipitous.

The first thing to do was to despatch the guide into the valleys and gorges below, which from our camping place could not be seen, only surmised, that he might persuade some Tarahumares to act as carriers on an excursion I contemplated making through the region. In a couple of days a party was made up, consisting, besides myself, of Mr. Taylor, the guide, two Mexicans, and five Tarahumares with their gobernador. Bundles weighing from forty to seventy-five pounds were placed on the backs of the Indians and the Mexicans; even the guide took a small pack, though it would have been beneath the dignity of the gobernador to take a load upon himself. But his company was valuable on account of his great influence with his people.

It was an exceedingly interesting excursion of several days' duration. Owing to the presence of the gobernador the Indians received us well. Nobody ran away, though all were extremely shy and bashful, and the women turned their backs towards us. But after a while they would offer us beans from a pot cooking over the fire. They served them in earthenware bowls with a couple of tortillas (corn cakes). In another vessel, which they passed around among us, they offered the flavouring, coarse salt and some small chile (Spanish peppers), which vegetable is cultivated and much relished by the Tarahumares.

But the most interesting dish was iskiate, which I now tasted for the first time. It is made from toasted

Our Tarahumare Carriers and the Gobernador.

corn, which is mixed with water while being ground on the metate until it assumes the consistency of a thick soup. Owing to certain fresh herbs that are often added to the corn, it may be of a greenish color, but it is always cool and tempting. After having tramped for several days over many miles of exceedingly rough country, I arrived late one afternoon at a cave where a woman was just making this drink. I was very tired and at a loss how to climb the mountain-side to my camp, some 2,000 feet above; but after having satisfied my hunger and thirst with some iskiate, offered by the hospitable Indians, I at once felt new strength, and, to my own astonishment, climbed the great height without much

effort. After this I always found iskiate a friend in
need, so strengthening and refreshing that I may almost claim it as a discovery, interesting to mountain
climbers and others exposed to great physical exertions.
The preparation does not, however, agree with a seden-
tary life, as it is rather indigestible.

The dress of the Tarahumare is always very scanty,
even where he comes in contact with the whites. One

Tarahumare Men.

may see the Indians in the mining camps, and even in
the streets of the city of Chihuahua, walking about
naked, except for a breech-cloth of coarse, home-spun
woollen material, held up around the waist with a girdle

woven in characteristic designs.   Some may supplement
this national costume with a tunic, or short poncho ;
and it is only right to add that most of the men are provided with well-made blankets, which their women
weave for them, and in which they wrap themselves
when they go to feasts and dances.   The hair, when not
worn loose, is held together
with a home-woven ribbon, or
a piece of cotton cloth rolled
into a band ; or with a strip of
palm leaf.   Often men and
women gather the hair in the
back of the head, and men may
also make a braid of it.

The women's toilet is just
as simple.   A scrimpy woollen
skirt is tied around the waist
with a girdle, and over the
shoulders is worn a short
tunic, with which, however,
many dispense when at home
in the barranca. The women,
too, have blankets, though
with them they are not so
much the rule as with the
men.   Still, mothers with
babies always wear blankets,
to support the little ones in an
upright position on their backs,

Tarahumare Woman.

the blanket being tightly wrapped around mother and
child.   The women nowadays generally wear sandals
of the usual Mexican cowhide pattern, like the men ;
but there is ample evidence to prove that such was not
the case in former times.

The people are, for Indians, not especially fond of

ornaments, and it is a peculiar fact that mirrors have no special attraction for them. They do not like to look at themselves. The women often wear ear-ornaments made of triangular pieces of shell attached to bead strings, or deck themselves with strings of glass beads, of which the large red and blue ones are favourites; and necklaces made from the seed of the *Coix Lachryma-Jobi* are used by both sexes,

Tarahumare Ear-Ornament: one seed *Coix Lachryma-Jobi* at top. Natural size.

chiefly for medicinal purposes. The men wear only single strings of these seeds, while the necklaces of the women are wound several times around the neck. The shaman, or medicine-man — a priest and doctor combined — is never without such a necklace when officiating at a feast. The seed is believed to possess many medicinal qualities, and for this reason children, too, often wear it.

Necklace of Seeds of *Coix Lachryma-Jobi.*

Peasant women in Italy and Spain use the same seed as a protection against evil, and even American women have been known to put strings of them on teething children as a soothing remedy.

An important fact I established is that the Indians

in the barrancas, in this part of the country, use something like trincheras for the cultivation of their little crops. To obtain arable land on the mountain slopes the stones are cleared from a convenient spot and utilised in the construction of a wall below the field thus made. The soil is apt to be washed away by heavy rains, and the wall not only prevents what little earth there is on the place from being carried off, but also

Tarahumare Ranch near Barranca de Cobre, showing ploughed fields supported by stone walls.

catches what may come from above, and in this way secures sufficient ground to yield a small crop. Fields thus made can even be ploughed. On the slopes of one arroyo I counted six such terraces, and in the mountainous country on the Rio Fuerte, toward the State of Sinaloa, chile, beans, squashes, *Coix Lachryma-Jobi*, and bananas are raised on trincheras placed across the arroyos that run down the hills. There they have the form of small terraces, and remind one of similar ones found

Tarahumare Ranch near Barranca de Cobre, showing agriculture on terraces.

farther north as ancient ruins, to such an extent that one might suppose that the Tarahumares have made use of the relics of antiquity. Mr. Hartman in one long arroyo thereabouts observed four at some distance from one another. They were from four to ten feet high, and as broad as the little arroyo itself, some eight to sixteen feet.

CHAPTER VIII

THE HOUSES OF THE TARAHUMARES—AMERICAN CAVE-DWELLINGS OF TO-DAY—FREQUENT CHANGES OF ABODE BY THE TARAHUMARE—THE PATIO OR DANCING PLACE—THE ORIGINAL CROSS OF AMERICA—TARAHUMARE STORE-HOUSES.

THE houses we saw on this excursion were of remarkable uniformity, and as the people have had very little, if any, contact with the whites, it is reasonable to infer that these structures are original with them. On a sloping mesa six families were living in such buildings not far from one another.

These houses have a frame of four forked poles, planted firmly into the ground, to form a square or rectangle. Two joists are laid over them parallel to each other. Under one of them, in the front of the house, is the doorway. The joists support the flat roof of loose pine boards, laid sometimes in a double layer. The rear joist is often a foot or so lower than the front one, which causes the roof to slant towards the back. The boards may simply be logs split in two and with the bark taken off. The walls are made by leaning boards, ends up, against the roof, while the door consists of a number of boards, which are removed or replaced according to convenience. In most instances the doorway is protected from the outside against wind and weather by a lean-to. Access to the house is gained sideways, even where a small vestibule is built, extra poles being driven in the ground to support the porch-roof boards.

While this style of architecture may be said to be typical throughout the Tarahumare country, there are

156

many variations. Generally attempts are made to con-
struct a more solid wall, boards or poles being laid
lengthwise, one on top of the other, and kept in place
by sliding the ends between double uprights at the
corners. Or they may be placed ends up along the
side of the house; or regular stone walls may be built,
with or without mud for mortar. Even in one and the
same house all these kinds of walls may be observed.
A type of house seen throughout the Tarahumare coun-

Tarahumare House near Barranca de Cobre.

try, as well as among the pagan Tarahumares in the
Barranca de Cobre, is shown in the illustration.

It is also quite common to see a frame work of only
two upright poles connected with a horizontal beam,
against which boards are leaning from both sides, making the house look like a gable roof set on the ground.
There are, however, always one or more logs laid horizontally and overhung by the low eaves of the roof,

while the front and rear are carelessly filled in with boards or logs, either horizontally or standing on ends. In the hot country this style of house may be seen thatched with palm-leaves, or with grass.

The dwelling may also consist only of a roof resting on four uprights (*jacal*); or it may be a mere shed.

Tarahumare House in the Hot Country.

There are also regular log-cabins encountered with locked corners, especially among the southern Tarahumares. Finally, when a Tarahumare becomes civilised, he builds himself a house of stone and mud, with a roof of boards, or thatch, or earth.

It is hardly possible to find within the Tarahumare country two houses exactly alike, although the main idea is always easily recognised. The dwellings, though very airy, afford sufficient protection to people who are

by no means sensitive
to drafts and climatic
changes. The Tarahu-
mares do not expect
their houses to be dry
during the wet season,
but are content when
there is some dry spot
inside. If the cold
troubles them too
much, they move into
a cave. Many of the
people do not build
houses at all, but are
permanent or transient
cave - dwellers. This
fact I thoroughly in-
vestigated in subse-
quent researches, ex-
tending over a year
and a half, and cover-
ing the entire width
and breadth of the
Tarahumare country.

In this land of
weather-worn porphy-
ry and inter-stratified
sandstone, natural
caves are met with
everywhere, in which
the people find a con-
venient and safe shel-
ter. Although it may
be said that houses are
their main habitations,

Cappe of Sandstone Pillar, showing effect
of erosion.

still the Tarahumares live in caves to such an extent that they may be fitly called the American cave-dwellers of the present age.

Caves were man's first abode, and they are found in certain geological formations in all parts of the globe. Human imagination always peopled the deep, dark caverns with terrible monsters guarding treasures, and legends and fairy tales still cling about many of them. Shallow caves, however, have from the earliest time attracted man to seek shelter in them, just as the animals took refuge in them against the inclemency of the weather. Prehistoric man in Europe was a cave-dweller, and modern investigations have given us a clear and vivid picture of the life of the ancient race, who existed in France while the mammoth and the reindeer were roaming over the plains of western Europe.

As civilisation advanced, under changing climatic conditions, and as man began to improve his tools and implements, he deserted the caves and preferred to live in houses of his own building. But a long time after the caves had been abandoned as abodes of the living, they were still used for interring the dead. Do we not remember the story told in Genesis, how Abraham bought for 400 shekels a cave from Ephron that he might bury Sarah there and have a family tomb?

The cave-dwellers of France vanished many thousand years ago; but there are yet in several parts of the globe, for instance, in Tunis and in Central Africa, races who still adhere to the custom of living in caves, although their condition of life is different from that of the antediluvian cave-dwellers.

In Mexico the cave-dwellers are in a transitory state, most of them having adopted houses and sheds; but many of them are still unable to perceive why they should give up their safe and comfortable natural shel-

ters for rickety abodes of their own making.   Padre
Juan Fonte, the pioneer missionary to the Tarahumares,
who penetrated into their country eighteen leagues from
San Pablo, toward Guachochic, speaks of the numerous
caves in that country and relates that many of them
were divided into small houses.   Other records, too,

Tarahumare Family Camping under a Tree.

allude to the existence of cave-dwellers in that part of
the Sierra Madre.   Still, the fact of there being cave-
dwellers to-day in Mexico was until recently known
only to the Mexicans living in their neighbourhood,
who regard this condition of things as a matter of
course.

While most of the Tarahumares live permanently on
the highlands, a great many of them move for the winter down into the barranca, on account of its warmer
temperature, and, if they have no house, they live
wherever they find a convenient shelter, preferably a
cave; but for want of better accommodations they content themselves with a rock shelter, or even a spreading
tree.   This would suit them well enough were it not

Inhabited Cave, the Home of a Tarahumare Belle.

that, at least in recent years, there has not been rain
enough in the barrancas to enable the people to raise
there the corn they need.   They therefore go back to
the highlands in March, because in the higher altitudes
rainfall can be depended upon with more certainty.
The general custom among the Indians living near to a
barranca is to plant two crops of corn; one in early
March on the crest, and the other one in June, at the
beginning of the rainy season, down in the barranca,

and after having harvested at both places they retire to their winter quarters to enjoy themselves. Sometimes the cave of a family is not more than half a mile from their house, and they live alternately in one or the other abode, because the Tarahumares still retain their nomadic instincts, and even those living permanently on the highlands change their domicile very frequently. One reason is that they follow their cattle; another that they improve the land by living on it for a while; but there are still other reasons for moving so much about, which are known only to themselves. In summer many people leave their caves on account of the scorpions, tarantulas, and other pests that infest them.

The Belle of the Cave.

In front of the entrance to the cave there is generally a wall of stone, or of stone and mud, raised to the height of a man's chest, as a protection against wind and weather, wild beasts, etc. The cave is fitted up just like the houses, with grinding stone, earthen jars and bowls, baskets, gourds, etc. The fire is always in the middle, without hearth or chimney, and the jars in which the food is cooked rest on three stones. A portion of the ground is levelled and made smooth for the family

Side View of Cave on Page 165, Showing Store-Houses and Inclosure.

to sleep on. As often as not there are skins spread out on the floor. Sometimes the floor space is extended by an artificial terrace in front of the cave. In a few cases the floor is plastered with adobe, and I have seen one cave in which the sides, too, were dressed in the same way.

Inhabited Cave, Showing Store-Houses, Inclosure, and Extended Floor.

Generally there are one or two store-houses in the caves, and these constitute the chief improvement. Of course, there are a good many caves where there are no store-houses; still they are the striking feature of the cave. A few times I found walls of stone and mud erected inside of the cave, breast high, to partition off one or two rooms for the use of the family, as well as for the goats and sheep. Often, inclosures are built of wooden fences for the domesticated animals and occupy the greater part of the cave.

The largest inhabited cave I have seen was nearly a hundred feet in width and from twenty to forty feet in depth. If caves are at all deep, the Indians live near the mouth. They never excavate caves, nor do they live in dug-outs. I heard of one arroyo, where six inhabited caves, only thirty or fifty yards apart, can be seen at one time; but this is a rare case. Generally they are farther apart, maybe a hundred yards to a mile, or more; and that suits the Tarahumares very well, each family preferring to live by itself.

In one place I saw a cave, or rather a shelter under a big boulder, utilised as a dwelling; and here a kind of parapet had been built of stone gravel, terrace fashion, to enlarge the area of the cave floor.

Inhabited caves are never found in inaccessible places, as is the case with cliff-dwellings in the southwestern part of the United States. Where caves are difficult of access, the Indians may place a wooden ladder, or rather, a notched tree trunk, which is the national style of staircase. Once I saw steps cut into the soft "rock" (solidified volcanic ash), leading up to a dwelling. There was also a kind of settee cut out of the cave-wall.

Many of the caves are remarkably symmetrical in shape, and naturally quite comfortable. Caves may be found in the arroyos in the highlands, as well as in the barrancas. If I were to designate a region where they are more plentiful than elsewhere, I should mention the country from Carichic towards Urique, and also to the north and west of Norogachic. Many caves have within the memory of man been permanently abandoned, owing to the occupancy of the land by the Mexicans, as the Indians dislike to be near the whites.

The Tarahumares are not the only tribe still clinging to caves. As we have seen, the Pimas, too, are, to a limited extent, cave-dwellers, and the same is the case with the northern Tepehuanes, as well as with the allied Huarogios in their small area.

Are these cave-dwellers related to the ancient cliff-dwellers in the southwestern part of the United States and northern Mexico? Decidedly not. Their very aversion to living more than one family in a cave and their lack of sociability mark a strong contrast with the ancient cliff-dwellers, who were by nature gregarious. The fact that the people live in caves is in itself extremely interesting, but this alone does not prove any connection between them and the ancient cliff-dwellers. Although the Tarahumare is very intelligent, he is backward in the arts and industries. It is true that the women weave admirable designs in girdles and blankets, but this seems to be the utmost limit of their capabilities. In the caves they sometimes draw with ochre clumsy figures of animals and women, and on some rocks may be seen outlines of feet scratched with stone "in order to leave their imprint in this world when they die." Tarahumare pottery is exceedingly crude as compared with the work found in the old cliff-dwellings, and its decoration is infantile as contrasted with the cliff-dwellers' work. The cliff-dwellers brought the art of decoration to a comparatively high state, as shown in

Cave with Wooden Ladder Leading to a Store-Room.

the relics found in their dwellings. But the cave-dweller of to-day shows no suggestion of such skill. Moreover, he is utterly devoid of the architectural gift which resulted in the remarkable rock structures of the early cliff-dwellers. These people as far as concerns their cave-dwelling habits cannot be ranked above troglodytes.

The Tarahumare never lives all his life in one house or cave ; nor will he, on the other hand, leave it forever. He rarely stays away from it for more than two or three years. A family, after inhabiting a house for a time may suddenly decide to move it, even if it is built of stone. The reason is not always easy to tell. One man moved his house because he found that the sun did not strike it enough. After a death has occurred in a dwelling, even though it was that of a distant relative incidentally staying with the family, the house is destroyed, or the cave permanently abandoned ; and many other superstitious apprehensions of one kind or another may thus influence the people. Very often a man moves for the sake of benefiting the land, and after tearing down his house he immediately plants corn on the spot on which the house stood. A family may thus change its abode several times a year, or once a year, or every other year. The richest man in the Tarahumare country, now dead, had five caves, and moved as often as ten times in one year.

A never absent feature of the Tarahumare habitation, be it house or cave, is a level, smooth place in front of it. This is the dancing place, or patio, on which he performs his religious exercises, and he may have more than one. The formation of the land may even oblige him to build terraces to obtain space enough for his religious dances.

On this patio, which measures generally about ten

yards in every direction, one, two, or three crosses are
planted, as the central object of all ceremonies (except
those in the cult of the sacred cactus híkuli*). The
cross is generally about a foot high ; sometimes it stands
two feet above ground. It is made of two sticks of
unequal length, preferably sticks of pine wood, tied
together in the form of the Latin cross. I saw two
crosses raised outside of a
man's house, which were
formed by the natural
growth of small pine trees,
and these were four feet
high. The shamans, for
their curing, use small
crosses — three or four
inches long.

Crosses Made from the Natural
Growth of Pine-trees in Front of
Tarahumare House.

It is a well-known fact
that on their arrival in
America the Spaniards to
their amazement found
Indians in possession of
the cross. Omitting here
the cross of Palenque, the
symbol of a tree, the tree
of life, it is safe to say that the original cross of most
Mexican tribes is the Greek cross, though the Latin was
also used. To them the former is of fundamental religious moment, as indicating the four corners of the
world ; but a word for cross, or anything corresponding
to it, does not occur in the language of any of the tribes
known to me. Nevertheless the cross (the Greek),
to the Indian the symbol of a cosmic idea, is pecked
on the rocks, or drawn on the sand, or made in corresponding strokes with medicine over the patient's body.

* See page 356.

With the Tarahumare the cross is the pivot around which all his ceremonies and festivals move. He always dances to the cross, and on certain occasions he attaches strings of beads, ears of corn, and other offerings to it. It is used by the heathen as well as by the Christian Tarahumares. The question is whether this tribe has changed its form since its contact with the whites or whether the cross was originally like the one in use to-day. From many of the Tarahumares' utterances I incline to think that their cross represents a human figure with arms outstretched, and is an embodiment of Father Sun, the Perfect Man. When two crosses are placed on the patio, the smaller stands for the moon. This conception also explains the custom of setting up three crosses at the principal dance, the rutuburi,

Crosses in Front of Tarahumare House.

the third cross representing probably the Morning Star. Among Christianised natives the three crosses may come gradually to mean the Trinity.

On one occasion I saw a cross at least ten feet high with a cross beam only one foot long, raised next to two crosses of ordinary size, all standing on the patio of a well-to-do Indian, and the inference was easily drawn that the high cross was meant for Father Sun. The Northern Tepehuanes say that the cross *is* Tata Dios, the Christianised Indian's usual designation of God.

The impression that the cross represents a human figure gains further probability by the fact that a cross is erected on the special patio of the dead, and I have noticed that this cross is moved in the course of the ceremonies to the principal dancing place "to see the

Front View.　　　　　　　　　Rear View.

Cross.　Height, 65 ctm.; width, 27.5 ctm.

dancing and drink tesvino," as the Indians explained it. Surely, this cross represented the dead.

On this page are seen the front and rear view of a cross which is of great interest, although its shape is evidently an exaggerated imitation of a Catholic cross or crucifix. I came upon it in the mountainous country east of Morelos, and the Tarahumares near the Ranch of Colorados present-ed it to me. It had apparently not been made long ago, and was paint-ed with red ochre. The arms have been tied on in the usual fashion with a twine of fibre, the mode of fastening it appearing most distinctly on the back of the cross.

Seen from the front the designs on the head, or the uppermost part, represent the Morn-ing Star, the dots being his compan-ions, the other stars. But it is significant that this constella-tion is also called the " eyes " of the cross. The dots on the other side of the cross are also meant for stars, in order that, as the

Tarahumare Store-house of Stones and Mud.

Indian explained to me, Tata Dios may see the stars where they are dancing; he lives in the stars—a belief evidently arising from Catholic influence. The human figures painted on the cross are intended to emphasise

Caves Used as Store-houses.

its meaning. The most important of these human-like contours are those directly below the junction of the arms with the vertical stem. They are evidently repetitions of the main cross, the arms being expressed in the crude carvings. What the various' pairs of curved side lines mean, I am unable to say.

What is of more importance to the Tarahumare than his dwelling is his store-house, which he always builds before his domicile. In fact, his personal comfort is made secondary even to that of his domestic animals. As a survival of the time when he had no house at all may be noted the fact that husband and wife, after having been away on a journey for several days or longer, do not on the first night after their return sleep in the house or cave, but at some convenient place near the store-house.

These store-houses are always well put together, though many of them are not large enough to accommodate a medium-sized dog, the Tarahumares preferring number to size. In them he stores what little property he has beyond that in actual use, chiefly corn and beans, some spare clothing and cotton cloth, hikuli, herbs, etc. The door of the house is made from one or more short boards of pine wood, and is either provided with an ingeniously constructed wooden lock, or the boards are simply plastered up with mud along the four edges. The Tarahumare rarely locks his house on leaving it, but he is ever careful to fasten the door of his store-house securely, and to break open a store-house sealed up in the manner described is considered the most heinous crime known to the tribe. Mexicans have committed it and have had to pay for it with their lives.

The most common kind of store-house is from four to six feet high, round, and built of stones and mud, with a roof of pine boards, weighed down with earth and stones. Other store-houses of similar size are square and built of boards with corners interlocked. They, too, are covered with boards. These diminutive buildings are often seen inside of caves; or else they are erected in places difficult of access, on tops of boulders, for instance. Sometimes they are seen in lonely places, more often, however, near the dwellings; and the little round structures make a curious effect when erected on boulders in the vicinity of some hut, looking, as they do, like so many diminutive factory chimneys. They proclaim more clearly than anything else the fact that when the people reach that stage in their development in which they begin to till the soil, they soon become careful of the little property they have, in marked distinction to the savage and no-madic tribes, who are always lavish and improvident. I have seen as many as ten store-houses of the kind de-

Tarahumare Store-houses Made of Logs.

scribed, and once even fourteen near one dwelling, but generally one or two only are found near by.

Small caves, especially when difficult to reach and hidden from view, may be utilised as store-houses, and are then sealed up in the same way as the other varieties are. Sometimes regular log-houses are used.

CHAPTER IX

ARRIVAL AT BATOPILAS—ASCENT FROM BATOPILAS TO THE HIGH-
LANDS OF THE SIERRA—A TARAHUMARE WHO HAD BEEN IN
CHICAGO—AN OLD-TIMER—FLIGHT OF OUR NATIVE GUIDE AND
ITS DISASTROUS CONSEQUENCES — INDIANS BURN THE GRASS
ALL OVER THE COUNTRY—TRAVELLING BECOMES TOO DIFFI-
CULT FOR THE ANIMALS—MR. TAYLOR AND I GO TO ZAPURI—
ITS SURROUNDINGS—THE PITHAYA IN SEASON.

WE continued our way toward the south, crossing
Barranca de Cobre where it is 3,300 feet deep.
The track we followed was fairly good, but led along
several dangerous precipices, over which two burros
rolled and were killed. The
highest point we reached on
the track over the highlands
south of the barranca was
8,300 feet. There seemed to
be a divide here, the climate
being cool and moist, and the
farthest ranges toward the
south and west enveloped in
mist and fog. Although Barranca de Batopilas is not as
narrow and impressive as the
barranca we had just left, still
the mighty gap, as we looked
into its hazy bottom from the

Cactus Flowers.

highlands, presented an imposing, awe-inspiring sight.
Following the windings of the well-laid-out road we
descended into the cañon and made camp a few miles

this side of the town of Batopilas. The silver mines here, which are old and famous, were discovered in the seventeenth century. I was cordially received by Mr. A. R. Shepherd, the well-known mining expert, whose courtesy and kindness were much appreciated by the members of the expedition.

My recent experience had convinced me that the only way to study the natives properly was to live among them for a length of time, and as such a thing was out of the question with so large a party as I still had with me, I made up my mind to discharge as soon as possible everybody and to remain alone.

The country was now suffering from a relentlessly scorching sun. The heat increased as the wet season approached, and, as the animals were getting weaker and weaker, I disposed here of about half of them, and the number of attendants and the amount of baggage were correspondingly reduced. On continuing the journey with the weak and hungry mules, we found the ascent of the southern side of Barranca de Batopilas quite laborious; but on the crest we enjoyed the fresh breeze, the more gratefully after the enervating heat in the bottom of the cañon.

Thus we arrived at the village of Yoquibo (yōkí= bluebird; ívo=mesa : bluebird on the mesa). Here I had to stop for a few days to reconnoitre the road. I was told that the grass had been burned by the Indians almost as far as the ranches of Guachochic, our main objective point. The Indians at that time (May) always burn the grass, and the entire country is wrapped in smoke. This, they think, is necessary to produce rain; smoke-clouds and rain-clouds, in their opinion, bringing about the same ultimate result. But it is exceedingly trying for travellers, man and beast. Only by accident is some little spot of grass spared here and there, and progress becomes almost an impossibility.

Immediately upon our arrival I went to see the gobernador, and, strange to say, I found him engaged in teaching his young wife how to weave. Three months ago his first wife had died of smallpox. Old bachelors and widowers have a hard time in getting wives, because the Tarahumare belles have a decided preference for young men. But the wifeless Indian feels very unhappy, as it means that he has to do all the woman's housework, which is very laborious, and therefore thoroughly distasteful to him. By way of fascinating this young girl, the gobernador had to exert himself to the extent of teaching her how to make girdles and wearing apparel.

The next day this gentleman returned my call, carrying his bow and arrows. I had already learned in Batopilas that the party of Indians who, about two years ago, had been exhibited by a now deceased traveller as representative cave-dwellers, had been gathered mainly in the neighbourhood of Yoquibo. My visitor had been one of the troupe, and I was eager to find out what impression the civilised world had made on this child of nature, who had never known anything but his woods and his mountains. Therefore, almost my first question was, "How did you like Chicago?" "It looks very much like here," was the unexpected reply. What most impressed him, it seemed, was neither the size of the city nor its sky-scrapers, though he remembered these, but the big water near which those people dwelt. He had liked riding in the railroad cars, but complained that he had not had enough to eat on the journey.

His experience on the trip had familiarised him with the white man and his queer, incomprehensible ways, and

made him something of a philosopher. I wanted him
to accompany me on my visits to the few houses here,
as the people were very shy and timid.   Although he
was very much engaged, as I could see, having to look
after his animals as well as his wife, he obligingly went
with me to two houses.   We saw a woman with twins;

Making Larvæ Ready for the Pot.

one of them a miserable-looking specimen, suffering
from lack of food.

There were also some cave-dwellings near Yoquibo,
one or two of which were occupied.   In the afternoon,
when I went out alone, the people all disappeared the
moment they saw me approaching, except one group of
strangers who had come to beg and did not pay any

attention to me.   They were too busily engaged in
making ready for the pot a certain kind of larvæ, by
extracting them from the cocoon, a small white sac of
silky texture found on the strawberry tree.

The guide told me that Indians like these, who beg
for food, always return, to those who give them alms,
the amount of the gift, as soon as their circumstances
allow.

Here in Yoquibo I met one of those Mexican adventurers who under one pretext or another manage to
get into the Indian villages and cannot be routed out
again.   Certain of them ply some little trade, generally
that of a blacksmith, others act as " secretaries," writing
what few communications the Indians may have to send
to the government authorities ; some conduct a little
barter trade, exchanging cheap cotton cloth, beads, etc.,
for sheep and cattle ; but most of them supply the Indians with Mexican brandy, mescal.   The one in Yoquibo
had established himself in the only room left intact in
the old dilapidated vicarage, and eked out a living by
selling mescal to the Indians.

This fellow's appearance, especially his unsteady,
lurking eyes, suggested the bandit.   No doubt, like
most of his class, he was in hiding from the government authorities.   He was something of a hypochon-
driac, and among other ailments he thought he had an
animal in his stomach, which he got in there by way of a
knife-stab he had received some time ago.   When he
came to me to get some remedy, he carried a rather
fine rifle, and in spite of all his suffering, real or imaginary, the bandit nature asserted itself, when I made some
complimentary remark regarding his weapon.   His half-
closed eyes slurred in a crafty, guileful manner from side
to side as he drawled :   " *Despues de Dios, mi rifle !* "
(" Next to God, my rifle ! ")

After considerable looking about, I at last found an Indian willing to act as guide for the next stage of our journey. He was an elderly man, and at dusk he was quietly sitting near the camp fire, eating his supper, when the tall figure of Mr. Hartman appeared on the scene, wrapped in a military overcoat. He probably looked to the Indian very martial and threatening as he approached through the twilight. At any rate, his appearance had a most unexpected effect on our guide. I suddenly heard a noise behind me, and on looking around, I saw him running as fast as his legs would carry him, leaving his supper, dropping his blanket, splashing through the creek and disappearing in the night, never to be seen again by us. He imagined that a soldier was coming to seize and kill him ; that the meat-pot in which he was to be cooked was already on the fire, while the skulls of other unfortunates that had been eaten were lying in a heap near one of the tents. He alluded apparently to four skulls which I had taken out of an ancient burial cave. In explanation I will say that some time ago he had been arrested for some crime and had broken away from jail; soldiers, or rather, the police, were after him, and he mistook Mr. Hartman for one of his pursuers and ran for safety.

The incident proved somewhat unfortunate for us. In consequence of the wild stories he told about us, the Indians, of a suspicious nature anyway, sent messengers all over the sierra, warning the people against the man-eaters that were coming. Our strange proceedings in Cusarare, namely, the photographing, had already been reported and made the Indians uneasy. The terrible experience of our runaway guide seemed to confirm their wildest apprehensions, and the alarm spread like wildfire, growing in terror, like an avalanche, the farther

it went. We found the ranches deserted on every hand,
women and children hiding and screaming whenever
they caught a glimpse of us. At every turn our progress
was impeded. Wherever I came I was abhorred as the
man who subsisted on babies and green corn, and the
prospect of my ever gaining the confidence of the Indians was exceedingly discouraging for the next four or
five months.

Though it was impossible to secure a new guide, I
still made a start next day, following a fairly good track
which leads south toward Guachochic. Yet further
obstacles presented themselves. The animals began to
give out. It was the season of the year when they
change their coats, and are in poor condition even under
the best circumstances, and mine were exhausted from
lack of food. They would not eat the dry grass, and
the green pasture was still too scanty to suffice for their
maintenance. The information that the natives had
burned all the grass proved correct to its fullest extent,
so there was nothing for me to do but to establish a
camp, scarcely a day's journey off, at Tasajisa, where
there was some pasture along the ridges that had as yet
escaped the fire of the Indians. Leaving the larger part
of my outfit and about half of my mules in charge of
my chief packer, Mr. Taylor and I continued the journey with the best and strongest of the animals, making
a circuitous tour to the little mining town of Zapuri, in
the neighbourhood of which were some caves I wanted
to investigate.

After a day's journey we turned westward and got
beyond the range of the fires. Turkeys were seen close
to our camp and appeared plentiful ; I also saw a giant
woodpecker, but just as I got ready to shoot, it flew
away with a great whirr of its wings. We soon began
to descend, and after a long and fatiguing day's travel

over cordons and sierras, and through a wide barranca surrounded by magnificent towering mountains, we arrived, late in the afternoon, at Zapuri. The superintendent of the mine, to whom I brought a letter of introduction from the owner of the property, received us with cordial hospitality. Here the climate was splendid; the nights were just pleasantly cool, the mornings deliciously calm; they were all the more enjoyed after the windy weather of the sierra.

Immediately upon my arrival here I had a chance, through the courtesy of the superintendent, to secure a Mexican and some strong mules, which took Mr. Taylor over to Parral on his way back to the United States. Mr. Hartman remained with the expedition two months longer, to join me again the following year for a few months. I also got a guide for myself and made an excursion to the caves in the neighbouring barrancas. After we had gone some ten miles over very bad roads, we came to the home of an old Tarahumare woman, who was reputed to be very rich. Knowing Mexican exaggeration in this regard, I computed that the twelve bushels of pesos she was supposed to have hidden might amount, perhaps, to $50 or $100 Mexican money. Whatever her wealth was, she showed it only in a lavish display of glass beads around her scrawny neck; they must have weighed at least six or eight pounds. But then, her homestead was composed mainly of four or five substantial circular store-houses.

The wealth of the Tarahumare consists in his cattle. He is well off when he has three or four head of cattle and a dozen sheep and goats. There is one instance where a man had as many as forty head of cattle, but this was a rare exception. They rarely keep horses, and never pigs, which destroy their cornfields; and are believed, besides, to be Spaniards (*Gachupines*). Pork, though sometimes eaten, is never sacrificed. No tame turkeys are kept, but occasionally the people have some hens, and in rare cases a family may keep a turtle dove or a tame quail. When a man has oxen, he is able to plough a large piece of land and raise enough corn to sell some. But corn is seldom converted into money.

Here we packed the most necessary things on our best mule, and with the guide and two Indians, who carried bundles, we descended to the river. The road was fairly good, but as we approached the river we came to several bad places. In one of these the mule's aparejo struck a rock, which caused the animal to lose its foothold. Unresistingly it slid down the steep slope for about seven yards and came against a tree, forefeet on one side, hindfeet on the other. The boy who led it, eager to do something, managed to get the halter off, so that there was nothing by which to hold the animal except its ears. I held fast to one of these, steadying myself on the loose soil by grabbing a root sticking out of the ground. The intelligent animal lay perfectly still over the trunk. Finally I managed to get out my bowie-knife and cut the ropes off the pack, which rolled down the hill, while the mule, relieved of its bulky burden, scrambled to its feet and climbed up. It was born and bred in the barranca, otherwise it would never have been able to accomplish this feat.

Toward evening we arrived at the section of a barranca called Ohuivo (Ōví = return, or "the place to-which they returned") on the Rio Fuerte. The Indians here, although many of them have been affected by the nearness of the mines, are reticent and distrustful, and our guide evidently had not much influence with them. They refused to be photographed, and even the gobernador ran away from the terrible ordeal.

During the several days I remained in this valley the

heat never varied from 100°, day and night, which was rather trying and made doing anything an exertion. The country looked scorched, except for the evergreen cacti, the most prominent of which was the towering pithaya. Its dark-green branches stand immovable to

Gathering Pithaya.

wind and storm. It has the best wild fruit growing in the north-western part of Mexico, and as this was just the season when it ripens, the Indians from all around had come to gather it. It is as large as an egg and its flesh soft, sweet, and nourishing. As the plant grows to a height of twenty to thirty-five feet, the Indians get the fruit down with a long reed, one end of which has four prongs, and gather it in little crates of split bamboo, which they carry by straps on their backs. It is a sight to see men, women, and children start out gaily at daybreak, armed with slender sticks, climbing rugged heights with grace and agility, to get the pithaya, which tastes better when plucked at dawn, fresh and cool, than when gathered during the heat of the day. The fruit, which lasts about a month, comes when it is most needed, at the height of the dry season (June), when the people have a regular feasting-time of it. Mexicans also appreciate the pithaya, and servants frequently abscond at that time, in order to get the fruit. The beautiful white flowers of the plant are never found growing on the north side of the stem.

With the Indians, the pithaya enters, of course, into religion, and the beautiful macaw (guacamaya), which revels in the fruit, is associated with it in their beliefs. The bird arrives from its migration to southern latitudes when the pithaya is in bloom, and the Indians think that it comes to see whether there will be much fruit; then it flies off again to the coast, to return in June, when the fruit is ripe. The following gives the trend of one of the guacamaya songs: "The pithaya is ripe, let us go and get it. Cut off the reeds!* The guacamaya comes from the Tierra Caliente to eat the first fruits. From far away, from the hot country, I come when the men are cutting the reeds, and I eat the first fruits. Why do you wish to take the first fruits from me? They are my fruits. I eat the fruit, and I throw away the skin. I get filled with the fruit, and I go home singing. Remain behind, little tree, waving as I alight from you! I am going to fly in the wind, and some day I will return and eat your pithayas, little tree!"

* With which the fruit is brought down.

CHAPTER X

NICE-LOOKING NATIVES—ALBINOS—ANCIENT REMAINS IN OHUIVO
—LOCAL TRADITIONS, THE COCOYOMES, ETC.—GUACHOCHIC—
DON MIGUEL AND "THE POSTMASTER"—A VARIETY OF
CURIOUS CURES—GAUCHOCHIC BECOMES MY HEAD-QUARTERS—
THE DIFFICULTY OF GETTING AN HONEST INTERPRETER—
FALSE TRUFFLES—THE COUNTRY SUFFERING FROM A PRO-
LONGED DROUGHT—A START IN A NORTH-WESTERLY DIREC-
TION—ARRIVAL AT THE PUEBLO OF NOROGACHIC.

I FOLLOWED the river a day's journey up and noticed some small tobacco plantations on the banks. I met some good-looking people, who had come from Tierras Verdes, the locality adjoining on the south. Their movements were full of action and energy. Their skins showed a tinge of delicate yellow, and as the men wore their hair in a braid, they had a curious, oriental appearance. The women looked well in black woollen skirts and white tunics. The people from that part of the country are known for their pretty, white, home-made blankets, and it was evident that in those inaccessible parts the Indians had still something for the white man to take away.

The natives of this valley had a curious habit, when they were made to dive for fish, of afterward throwing themselves in a row on the sun-heated sand to warm their stomachs for a minute or two.

Near Ohuivo, in the mountains toward Morelos, there used to live a family of ten albinos. When I was there only two survived, smallpox having made havoc among them. Their skin was so delicate that

even the contact with their clothing irritated it. Mr.
Hartman visited one of them, an old woman who lived
in a cave with her husband, a small, dark-skinned fellow, and the two certainly were "mated, but not
matched." Her features were entirely Indian, but her
complexion was unique in Mexico, even among the
white population. She reminded one of a very blond
type of Scandinavian or Irish peasantry. Her hair was
yellowish-white, but her eye-brows and -lashes were
snow-white. The face and body were white, but dis-
figured with large red spots and small freckles. She
kept her eyes more than half shut, and as she was very
shy it was not possible to ascertain the color of the iris;
but Mr. Hartman was assured by the husband that it
was bluish.

Most of the Indians in Ohuivo live in houses. The
few caves that are occupied are not improved in any
way. One cave contained ancient habitations, and tradition says that there the Tubares had once established
themselves. The cave is nothing but a nearly horizontal
crack in the rock, situated on the southern side of the
river, some 300 feet above the bottom of the valley. It
runs from south-east to north-west to a length of about
200 feet, interrupted perpendicularly by a crevice. Entering the cave at the southernmost end I found twelve
low-walled rooms, standing singly, but closely side by
side. They were square with rounded corners. The
walls were built of stone and mud and one foot thick,
and the floors were hard and smooth. A store-room, in
a good state of preservation, resembled in every detail
the store-houses used by the Tarahumares of the present
day, being square and built of stone and mud. In
none of these rooms was it possible for me to stand
upright. Apart from this group, a few yards higher up
in the cave, were two small houses. The floor of the

cave was getting higher and higher.   I had to crawl on
my stomach for about ten yards and came suddenly to
the edge of a precipice ; but a track led around it to
the other side, where I found the main portion of the
houses, eighteen in all, the largest having a side thirteen
feet long, though the others were considerably smaller.
They were arranged just like those of the first section,
in one row, and were made of the same material, except
a few, which were built of adobe.   In these the walls
were only eight inches thick.   One of the rooms was
still complete, had square openings, and may have been
a store-room.   The others seem to have had the conventional Indian apertures.   In two chambers I noticed
circular spaces sunk into the floor six inches deep and
about fourteen inches in diameter.   What I took to be
an estufa, nineteen feet in diameter, was found in the
lowest section.   Behind it was only a small cluster of
five houses higher up in the cave.

Though this is the only ancient cave-dwelling I visited in Ohuivo, I was assured that there were several
others in the neighbourhood.   The broken country
around Zapuri is interesting on account of the various
traditions which, still living on the lips of the natives,
refer to a mysterious people called the Cocoyomes,
regarded by some Tarahumares as their ancient enemies, by others as their ancestors.   They were the first
people in the world, were short of stature and did
not eat corn.   They subsisted mainly on herbs, especially a small agave called tshāwí.   They were also can-
nibals, devouring each other as well as the Tarahumares.
The Cocoyomes lived in caves on the high cliffs of the
sierra, and in the afternoon came down, like deer, to
drink in the rivers.   As they had no axes of iron they
could not cut any large trees, and were unable to clear
much land for the planting of corn.   They could only

burn the grass in the arroyos in order to get the fields ready. Long ago, when the Cocoyomes were very bad, the sun came down to the earth and burned nearly all of them ; only a few escaped into the big caves.

Here in Zapuri the Cocoyomes had four large caves inside of which they had built square houses of very hard adobe ; in one of the caves they had a spring. The Tarahumares often fought with them, and once, when the Cocoyomes were together in the largest cave, which had no spring, the Tarahumares besieged them for eight days, until all of the Cocoyomes had perished from hunger. From such an event the name of Zapuri may have been derived. Intelligent Mexicans, whom I consulted, agree that it means " fight " or " contest " (Spanish, *desafío*).

From a place called Tuaripa, some thirty miles farther south, near the border of the Tepehuane country, and in the same mountainous region, I have the following legend, about the Cocoyomes and the serpents :

Two large serpents used to ascend from the river and go up on the highlands to a little plain between Huera-chic and Tuaripa, and they killed and ate the Cocoyomes, returning each time to the river. Whenever they were hungry they used to come up again. At last an old man brought together all the people at the place where the serpents used to ascend. Here they dug a big hole and filled it with wood and with large stones, and made a fire and heated the stones until they became red hot. When the serpents were seen to make their ascent on the mountain-side, the men took hold of the stones with sticks, and threw them into the big, wide-open mouths of the serpents, until the monsters were so full with stones that they burst and fell dead into the river. Even to this day may be seen the marks on the rocks where the serpents used to ascend the mountain-side.

Once having again ascended to the highlands, I found rather level country as far as Guachochic, some forty-five miles off by the track I followed. The name of the place signifies "blue herons," and the fine water-

In the Highlands of the Sierra.

course, which originates in the many springs here, was formerly the abode of many water-birds. The locality thus designated is to-day a cluster of Mexican ranches, most of them belonging to one family. There is an old church, but at present no independent Indians live in Guachochic; the aborigines found about the place are servants of the Mexicans.

Guachochic lies at an elevation of 7,775 feet and at the southern end of a mesa, the largest one in the

Sierra Madre del Norte, being twelve miles long and
three miles wide.   Except on the southern end this
plateau is bordered with stately pine forests.   Many Indians live on the mesa and in the numerous valleys adjoining it, but they are all "civilised"; that is, contam-
inated with many Mexico-Christian notions, and have
lost their pristine simplicity.

I had a letter of introduction to the principal personage in Guachochic, Don Miguel, who enjoys the rare
reputation of being just and helpful toward the Indians ;
and, being a large land-owner, he is a man of considerable influence also with his fellow-countrymen.   To those
in need he lends money on liberal terms out of the pile of
silver dollars buried under the floor of his house.   Robbers know from sad experience that he is not to be
trifled with.   Once, when a band of marauders had taken
possession of the old adobe church and were helping
themselves to the buried cash of the inhabitants of the
ranches, he rallied the terrorised people, gave the robbers
battle and routed them effectually.   He upholds authority against lawlessness, and wants justice to have its
course, except when one of his own relatives has done
the shooting—I was sorry to learn that in this regard he
was probably not beyond rebuke ; but his many good
deeds to the needy and oppressed, whether Mexican or
Indian, should make us lenient toward this failing.
The Indians appeal to him of their own accord.   Three
ruffians once went to the house of a well-to-do Indian,
recently deceased, and told his mourning relatives that
they had come to see to the division of the property
among the heirs, and that they must have good things
to eat and plenty to drink while thus occupied ; calling
upon the relatives to brew plenty of beer and kill an ox.
Their orders were promptly obeyed ; but in addition
they charged the heirs a fee of three oxen, one fanega

of corn, and some silver money. This struck the simple and patient Indians as rather excessive, for what would then be left to divide between themselves? So they took their grievance to Don Miguel to be settled. I do not know of any white man in those parts who would have taken the trouble, as he did, to protect the poor Indians' rights against the wily schemers.

The old gentleman was not at home when I arrived at his ranch, but I met one of his sons, who lives at Guachochic.

"I am the postmaster," he said proudly, stepping forward and showing me, at the same time, his credentials, which he evidently always carried in his pocket. The mail from the lowlands to the mining towns passes over this place, and the mail-carrier sleeps in this house. In the course of the year he may also bring a few letters to the inhabitants of this part of the country. We soon entered into a conversation about postal matters, which naturally interested me greatly, as I was anxious to communicate as often as possible with the outside world. In spite of the great pride this man took in his office, his notions regarding his duties were rather vague. Being desirous of knowing what was going on among his neighbours, he had no compunction about opening the few letters they got; not that he destroyed them after reading them—he very coolly handed them over opened. The people did not like this, and considered it rather high-handed on his part; but then, what was there for them to do about it?

He said he had heard that I could cure people. When a man is called Doctor, the Mexican peasantry expect him to possess comprehensively all useful knowledge in the world. Looking at me for a moment, this healthy, ruddy-cheeked man suddenly, without saying a word, took hold of my hand and pressed it against his forehead for a little while ; then, all the time in silence, he carried it backward until my fingers touched a small excrescence on his back.   Now was the chance to find out whatever was the matter with him !

On my next visit to his office he received me with a queer, hesitating expression on his face, and suddenly blurted out, " Can you cut out trousers? "   For some time he had had a piece of cloth in his house, and he said he would pay me well if I could help him to have it made into trousers.   To cure people, mend watches, repair sewing-machines, make applejack, do tailoring, prognosticate the weather—everything is expected from a man who comes from far away.   And the good people here are astonished at a confession of ignorance of such matters, and take it rather personally as a lack of good-will toward them.   It is the old belief in the medicine man that still survives in the minds of the people, and they therefore look upon doctors with much greater respect than on other persons.

People who live outside of civilisation are thrown upon their own resources in cases of sickness.   The daughter of my Mexican guide was confined and the coming of the afterbirth was delayed.   I give here, for curiosity's sake, a list of the various remedies applied in the case :

1. The carapace of the armadillo, ground and taken in a little water.   This is a Tarahumare remedy, said to be very effective for the trouble mentioned.

2. The skunkwort (the herb of the skunk).

3. The patient to hold her own hair in her mouth for half an hour.

4. The wood of *Palo hediondo*, boiled.

5. *Urina viri*, half a cup.   This remedy is also externally used for cuts and bruises.

6. Fresh excrement from a black horse.   A small

quantity of water is mixed with it, then pressed out through a piece of cloth and taken internally.

7. Perspiration from a black horse. A saddlecloth, after having been used on the horse, is put over the abdomen of the woman.

8. A decoction of the bark of the elm.

9. Pork fat.

After a number of days the patient recovered. Whether it was *propter hoc* or merely *post hoc* is a matter of conjecture.

Guachochic served admirably as a central point from which excursions in various directions could be made, as it lies in the very midst of the Tarahumare country. It is true that the Mexicans have appropriated all the best land round about, and their extensive and fertile ranches lie all around Guachochic. Toward the east, in the direction of the pueblos of Tonachic and Lagunitas, the broad strip of good arable and pasture land as far as Parral is owned exclusively by Mexicans.

But in the immediate neighbourhood of Guachochic toward the west and south lie the ridges and barrancas that run toward Sinaloa, and these are inhabited by pagan Tarahumares. Toward the north the Indians hold undisputed sway over that extensive region of mountains, pine-covered plateaus and well-watered arroyos around the pueblos of Norogachic, Pamachic and Nararachic, and here are found the most independent Tarahumares that are left, who still defy the whites to take their land away from them. They are more valiant than the rest and not easily intimidated.

The first thing for me to do, after establishing camp near Guachochic, was to secure strong mules and the necessary men to bring up the outfit that had been left behind in Tasajisa, and after a week's absence they returned with all the animals and goods intact.

Guachochic is an uninteresting place at its best, and at this season it seemed especially dreary, on account of the crop failure from which the sierra had been suffering for the last two years. There is never much to get here, but now even corn and beans could hardly be bought. It was therefore quite a treat to have a square meal with Don Miguel, whose wife was a clever cook, and who, considering all circumstances, kept a fair Mexican table. He could also give me some general information about the Indians ; but not only here, but in many other parts of Mexico, I was often astonished at the ignorance of the Mexican settlers concerning the Indians living at their very doors. Aside from certain conspicuous practices, even intelligent Mexicans know little of the customs, much less of the beliefs, of the aborigines. Regarding the pagans in the barrancas, I could get absolutely no information beyond a general depreciation of them as savages, *bravos* (fierce men) and *broncos* (wild ones). One Mexican whom I interviewed about certain caves thought that the only thing I could be looking for was the silver possibly hidden in them, and therefore told me that there were 12,000,000 pesos buried in a cave near the mining town Guadalupe y Calvo, waiting to be recovered. Thus it was exceedingly difficult in the beginning to determine just which would be the best way to start my investigations, and all that was left for me to do was to find out for myself where my best field was by making extensive excursions into the domains of the Tarahumare in company with an intelligent interpreter. And there was the rub! There are in this part of the sierra a certain number of men who make a living by dealing with the Indians, and who, having been born and bred in the country, speak the difficult language of the Tarahumares as well as the Indians themselves. But as each man operates in a certain district and has a monopoly of the trade with the Indians within its confines, the temptation to cheat the unsophisticated natives out of their little property is naturally very great, and by far the greater number of the dealers succumb to it. As soon, however, as one of them is found out, he loses his influence with the Indians, and to go with a man of that stamp would have been disastrous to my purpose. The duty of the *lenguaraz*, as the interpreter is called, is to smooth the traveller's way among the distrustful Indians with skilful words, to get provisions, make bargains, and explain to the Indians the purpose of his visit. Last but not least, he must obtain all possible information from them. This may mean one day's hard work, and the trying of his patience with many apparently futile questions which are made to get at the Indian's real meaning. Thus it may be understood how one is completely at the mercy of one's lenguaraz, and how important it is for the success of an expedition to find the right man. There is nothing else to do but to try and try again, one after another.

The Indians near Guachochic seemed all to be depressed, poor, and hungry. Most of their animals had died from lack of food, and the few that had not succumbed to starvation had to be sold in exchange for corn. A couple of Indians who were on their way to Parral to buy wheat died of starvation before they reached their destination. The Indians ascribed the hard times to the presence of the whites, who had deprived them of their lands as well as of their liberty. The gods, as they put it, were angry with the whites and refused to send rain.

In the summer, especially in July, a false truffle is found on the highlands of Guachochic, which serves as a food to the Indians. It grows abundantly a couple

of inches below the ground, raising the earth a little;
and is found also under the limb of a fallen tree.   The
dogs help in finding this fungus, and they are so fond of
it that they go of their own accord to look for it.
Pigs grow fat on this food, and coyotes, bears, and grey
foxes also eat it.   It is considered by Professor W. G.
Farlow as a variety of *Melanogaster variegatus*, which he
calls *Mexicanus*.   It tastes
like an over-ripe pear, with a
flavour of onion when one
first bites into it.   The ordinary *Melanogaster variegatus* is eaten in Europe, and
esteemed for its pleasant
taste.

It was disagreeable to
travel during the dry season,
on account of the difficulty
in getting provisions and
finding pastures for the animals.   But I made up my
mind to start under any circumstances on an excursion
toward the north-east, knowing that the fresh grass would

Tarahumare Interpreters.

come up quickly after a few of the thunder-storms
not infrequent at that season.   Toward the end of June
I selected a few of my strongest animals, and, leaving
one of my Mexicans to take care of the remainder,
started out with two.   As luck would have it, a heavy
storm drenched our first camp, and afterward the rain
seemed almost to pursue me, much to the delight of the
Indians I visited, who had been praying and dancing
for rain for a long time.   One day I had the imposing
spectacle of three thunder-storms coming up from dif-

ferent directions. The one in the south sent flashes of lightning out of its mass of dark clouds over the clear sky ; but after all, not much rain resulted.

There was no difficulty in finding one's way from Guachochic to Norogachic. At one place I noticed an Indian trail leading up a ridge apparently consisting of volcanic tuff. To facilitate the ascent, steps, now worn and old, had been cut for a distance of a couple of hundred feet. I made my way among the Indian ranches to Norogachic, the residence of the only priest living at present in the Tarahumare country. The name of the place contains an allusion to a certain rock in the vicinity. There is another priest who pays some attention to the Tarahumares, but he lives in Nonoava, and makes only annual visits to baptise infants or marry their elders who wish for the blessings of the Church.

Indian Trail Cut in a Ridge of Tuff.

CHAPTER XI

A PRIEST AND HIS FAMILY MAKE THE WILDERNESS COMFORTABLE
FOR US—ANCIENT REMAINS SIMILAR TO THOSE SEEN IN SO-
NORA—THE CLIMATE OF THE SIERRA—FLORA AND FAUNA—
TARAHUMARE AGRICULTURE—CEREMONIES CONNECTED WITH
THE PLANTING OF CORN—DETERIORATION OF DOMESTIC ANI-
MALS—NATIVE DOGS OF MEXICO.

I CALLED on the padre and found him to be a very
social, nice, energetic-looking person with a tinge
of the " red man " in his veins.

He complained to me that the Indians were lazy
about coming to mass. None of them paid taxes, and
there was no way
of forcing them.
Nearly all of them
he considered hea-
thens, and only
about a thousand
came to the feasts.
They arrive in the
village on the even-
ing before, and hear
vespers. Then they
give themselves up
to drinking, and on
the feast day prop-
er are not in a con-
dition to go to
church.

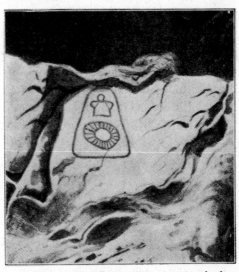

Pecking on Rock in the Neighbourhood of
Norogachic.

He thinks there are some great men among the
Tarahumares, but that, their mental faculties being en-

tirely uncultivated, they are, as it were, rough diamonds. In the padre's opinion not only all the Indians, but also the Mexicans living among them, will soon relapse into paganism altogether.

Living under rough conditions as he does, it is a lucky thing for the padre that his physique is equal to emergencies. Once at the neighbouring village of Tonachic (= where there are pillars) he admonished the people, in a powerful sermon, to mend their ways. As they were coming out of the church, a scoundrel who resented the charges attacked him with a stick, but the padre managed to disarm him and gave him such a sound thrashing with his assailant's own weapon that the latter had to keep his bed for a fortnight.

He showed me his stately old adobe church, built in missionary times. The ceiling, however, was infested with myriads of bats, the smell of which was quite sickening, and I was glad to get out again. With him in this uttermost outpost of Christendom lived his aged mother and six sisters, and they treated us with all the hospitality their very limited means permitted. We especially enjoyed their home-made macaroni.

In the family of the good priest lived a little Indian orphan girl, about five years old, as nice and sweet a child as one might wish to see. He was teaching her how to read and write, and she had learned her letters in two months.

The padre, good-natured to officiousness, helped me to get Indians to be photographed. He also would insist upon arranging them before the camera. His efforts, however, were directed more toward achieving artistic triumph than scientific truth, and he wanted, for instance, to decorate the Indians with peacock feathers. He yielded, however, to my suggestion that turkey feathers would be more appropriate, and straightway ordered one of his turkeys to be caught and deprived of some of its tail feathers. The only way in which I could show my appreciation of the disinterested kindness of the family was by photographing them, too. It was a new sensation to them, and the ladies asked to have it done next day, as they wanted to arrange their hair and prepare themselves properly.

After them it was the turn of the presidente of the village "to look pleasant," but at this juncture the camera met with an accident. The ring holding the lens broke and fell out. This happening miles away from civilisation was decidedly annoying. But the sisters proved themselves equal to the occasion. Their father having been a tinsmith, they had picked up the trade and had tools; and the ring was

Tarahumare Girl from the Neighbourhood of Norogachic.

soldered on so well that it lasted until I returned to the United States the following year.

Norogachic is situated in the most populous part of the Tarahumare country, and its presidente exercises authority over the large surrounding district. He told me that his municipality counted 4,168 souls, among them about 300 Mexicans. With the help of a very intelligent Mexican I made a rough calculation of the number of Indians belonging to Tonachic and Guachochic, next neighbours of Norogachic, and estimated in the former 350, and in the latter 250 families. Counting

each family as consisting of eight members, this would
give us a population of 4,800.   Thus the most populous
part of the Tarahumare country, including the three
municipalities of Norogachic, Tonachic, and Guachochic,
would contain a population of about 8,500 Indians.

As the presidente of Norogachic is an honourable
man and speaks the native language, he exercised great
influence over them, and on one occasion, when they
had gathered in large numbers and threatened to avenge
some abuse, he was able to avert disaster.   Nature had
endowed him with the doubtful blessing of bloodshot
eyes, a feature generally attributed to powerful sorcerers,
and this was perhaps more a point in his favour than
otherwise with the Indians.

One day he took us to the top of a hill where there
were some stones set in circles, about one foot above
and half a foot under the ground.   They reminded us of
similar stone arrangements we had come upon in Sonora, but these were larger and more primitive.   Altogether there were nine circles, varying in size from nine
to thirteen feet in diameter.   One, however, measured
only five feet across, and the stones forming it were fully
two feet above the ground.   Close by was another similar small circle, and some little distance off still another.
On a small mesa I found a flint arrow-point.   There
were also some potsherds there, but of the same kind as
those used by the people of to-day.

The natives rightly count only three seasons—the
dry, the rainy, and the winter.   The first lasts from
March till June, and is very warm and windy.   Throughout July and August one can generally count on thunder-storms and heavy rains, while the mornings are bright.
The rains then rarely extend over a large territory, but
are confined to local showers, a circumstance very annoying to the agricultural inhabitants, who often see

dark clouds rolling up, apparently full of moisture, yet resulting in nothing but gusts of wind. A ridge may change the course of the clouds. Sometimes one valley may be flooded with rain, while not far away the heat is drying up everything. During September and October more constant rains occur, and may last more or less for a week at a time.

In the beginning of the wet season (July and August) the rains come from the south-west, but later

Pecking on Rock in the Neighbourhood of Norogachic.

on north-eastern winds bring rain. In winter there are constant winds from the south-east to the north, somewhat trying until one gets used to them. Snow is by no means unknown, and Indians have been known to freeze to death when caught out intoxicated.

The climate in the sierra, although not so pleasant on account of the constant winds, is extremely salubrious, the heat never exceeding 97° F., while the nights are deliciously cool. Lung diseases are here unknown. When I asked an old American doctor in Guadalupe y Calvo about his experience in regard to the health of the people, he said, " Well, here in the mountains

they are distressingly healthy.   Despite a complete de-
fiance of every sanitary arrangement, with the grave-
yards, the sewers, and a tannery at the river's edge, no
diseases originate here.   When cholera reached the
mountains some years ago, nobody died from it.   The
people simply took a bath in Mexican fashion, and recovered."   Down in the barrancas, however, where the
heat often becomes excessive, the climate is far from
healthy, and I have seen even Indians ill with fever and
ague, contracted generally during the rainy season.

Between these two extremes, on the slopes of the
sierra, toward the warm country, at an elevation of 5,000
feet, I found the most delightful climate I ever knew.   It
was like eternal spring, the air pure and the temperature
remarkably even.   There is a story of a Mexican woman, who, settling in this part of the country, broke her
thermometer because the mercury never moved and she
therefore concluded that it was out of order.   The
pleasantness of the climate struck me particularly on
one occasion, after a prolonged stay in the invigorating
though windy climate of the sierra.   I had caught a
cold the night before, and was not feeling very well as I
dozed on the back of my mule while it worked its way
down the mountain-side, but the sleep and the delightful balmy air made me soon feel well again.   At times
a mild zephyr played around us, but invariably died out
about sunset.   The night was delightfully calm, toward
morning turning slightly cooler, and there was nothing
to disturb my sleep under a big fig-tree but the bits of
figs that were thrown down by the multitudes of bats in
its branches.   They were gorging themselves on the
fruit, just as we had done the afternoon before.

Journeying on the pine-clad highlands, the traveller
finds nothing to remind him that he is in the southern
latitudes, except an occasional glimpse of an agave

Winter Morning in the Sierra.

between rocks and the fantastic cacti, which, although so characteristic of Mexican vegetation, are comparatively scarce in the high sierra. The nopal cactus, whose juicy fruit, called tuna, and flat leaf-like joints are an important article of food among the Indians, is found here and there, and is often planted near the dwellings of the natives. There are also a few species of *Echinocactus* and *Mammilaria*, but on the whole the cacti form no conspicuous feature in the higher altitudes of the sierra.

Along the streamlets which may be found in the numerous small valleys we met with the slender ash trees, beside alders, shrubs, *Euonymus* with brilliant red capsules, willows, etc. Conspicuous in the landscape was still the madroña, with its pretty, strawberry-like, edible berries.

Flowers on the whole are not abundant in the sierra. The modest yellow *Mimulus* along the water-courses is the first to come and the last to go. Various forms of columbine (*Aquilegia*) and meadow rue (*Thalictrum*) should also be remembered. In August and September I have seen the sloping hills of the sierra north-west of the pueblo of Panalachic (Banalachic; banalá = face, *i. e.*, the outline of a prominent rock near by), covered with large crimson flowers, and also certain yellow ones, called *baguis*, making the country appear like a garden. I noticed in the same locality two kinds of lovely lilies, one yellow and one containing a single large red flower. The Tarahumare have names for all these plants.

Before all, however, should be mentioned the carmine-red *Amaryllis*. Like the crocus and the snowdrops of northern climates it appears before the grass is green. It is a perfect treat to the eye to meet now and then in this dry and sandy country, and at such a chilly elevation, this exquisitely beautiful flower, which is here appreciated only by the humming-birds.   Edible plants, species of *Mentha, Chenopodium, Cirsium*, for instance, and the common water-cress, are, at a certain time of the year, numerous; but fruits and berries are rare, blackberries being the most common ones.

Animal life is not particularly plentiful in the sierra. Still, deer, bears, and mountain lions are fairly common, and there are many kinds of squirrels and rats.   The jaguar (*felis onza*) is found now and then on the summits of the barrancas.   Eagles, hawks, turkeys, blackbirds, and crows are the most noticeable birds.   The turkey is called by the Tarahumares, tshīví; by the Mexicans of the sierra of Chihuahua, *guajolote;* while farther south he is designated *cocono*.   Now and then the brilliant green trogon is met with.

There are many species of woodpeckers, all familiar to and named by the Tarahumares.   The giant woodpecker is seen in the more remote parts, but it is on the point of being exterminated, because the Tarahumares consider his one or two young such a delicacy that they do not hesitate to cut down even large trees to get at the nests.   The Mexicans shoot them because their plumage is thought to be beneficial to health.   It is held close to the ears and the head in order to impart its supposed magnetism and keep out the maleficent effects of the wind.   In the pairing season these birds keep up a chattering noise, which to my ears was far from disagreeable, but very irritating to a Mexican whom I employed.   He used to shoot the birds because they annoyed him.

Corn is the most important agricultural product of the Tarahumares.   The average crop of a family may be estimated at six or twelve fanegas.   One exceptionally rich Tarahumare, now dead, is said to have raised as much as four hundred fanegas a year, but this was a fact unique in the history of the tribe. The people also raise beans, squashes, chile, and tobacco, all on an exceedingly small scale. On the highlands, the primitive plough already described (page 121) is still used sometimes, though it is rapidly being superseded by ploughs of Mexican pattern. In the arroyos and barrancas, where the condition of the land makes ploughing impossible, the Indians use the ancient mode of agriculture, still in vogue among remote natives of Mexico and called *coamillar*. They cut down the trees, clear a piece of land from brushwood, and leave it in this condition until just before the wet season sets in. Then they burn the wood, which by that time is well dried up, and plant the corn in the ashes. They simply make a hole in the earth with a stick, drop a few grains of corn into it, and close it up with the foot. Of the usual number of grains I am not aware. The Tepehuanes use four. Their hoes are generally bought from the Mexicans or else home-made, the natural knotted growths of tree limbs being utilised. Women never assist in ploughing, though they may be seen helping in the fields with the weeding and hoeing, and even with the harvesting.

In the sierra a piece of land may yield good crops for three years in succession without manure, but in the broad mountain valleys and on the mesas a family can use the same field year after year for twenty or thirty seasons. On the other hand, down in the barrancas, a field cannot be used more than two years in succession, because the corn-plants in that time are already suffocated with weeds. The planting is done from the middle of April to the first week in July, and the harvest begins about the first week in October and lasts until the beginning of December.

Communal principles prevail in clearing the fields, in ploughing—each furrow in a field is ploughed by a dif-

ferent man—in corn planting, in hoeing, weeding, harvesting, gathering wood for feasts, in fishing and in hunting.

If a man wants to have his field attended to, the first
thing he has to do is to prepare a good quantity of the
national stimulant, a kind of beer called tesvino. The
more of this he has, the larger the piece of land he can
cultivate, for the only payment his helpers expect and
receive is tesvino.

The master of the house and his sons always do first
one day's work alone, before their friends and neighbours
come to help them. Then they begin in earnest to clear
the field of stones, carrying them in their arms or blankets, and cut down the brushwood. Tesvino is brought
out into the field, and iskiate, and the men, all very
much under the influence of the liquor, work with the
animation of a heap of disturbed ants.

When the work of hoeing and weeding is finished,
the workers seize the master of the field, and, tying his
arms crosswise behind him, load all the implements, that
is to say, the hoes, upon his back, fastening them with
ropes. Then they form two single columns, the land-
lord in the middle between them, and all facing the
house. Thus they start homeward. Simultaneously the
two men at the heads of the columns begin to run rapidly
forward some thirty yards, cross each other, then turn
back, run along the two columns, cross each other again
at the rear and take their places each at the end of
his row. As they pass each other ahead and in the rear
of the columns they beat their mouths with the hollow
of their hands and yell. As soon as they reach their
places at the foot, the next pair in front of the columns
starts off, running in the same way, and thus pair after
pair performs the tour, the procession all the time advancing toward the house.

A short distance in front of it they come to a halt,

and are met by two young men who carry red handkerchiefs tied to sticks like flags. The father of the family, still tied up and loaded with the hoes, steps forward alone and kneels down in front of his house-door. The flag-bearers wave their banners over him, and the women of the household come out and kneel on their left knees, first toward the east, and after a little while toward each of the other cardinal points, west, south, and north.

In conclusion the flags are waved in front of the house. The father then rises and the people untie him, whereupon he first salutes the women with the usual greeting, " Kwīra! " or " Kwirevá! " Now they all go into the house, and the man makes a short speech thanking them all for the assistance they have given him, for how could he have gotten through his work without them? They have provided him with a year's life (that is, with the wherewithal to sustain it), and now he is going to give them tesvino. He gives a drinking-gourd full to each one in the assembly, and appoints one man among them to distribute more to all.

The same ceremony is performed after the ploughing and after the harvesting. On the first occasion the tied man may be made to carry the yoke of the oxen, on the second he does not carry anything.

The southern Tarahumares, as well as the northern Tepehuanes, at harvest time, tie together some ears of corn by the husks, two and two. The ears are selected from plants which have at least three or four ears, and after a while tesvino is made from them. At the harvesting feast, the stalks of these plants are strewn on the ground, as well as stalks of squash plants, and over them the people dance kuvála.

The Tarahumare takes good care of his domestic animals and never kills one of them, unless it be for a sacrifice. Sheep and goats are kept at night in enclosures or caves. The shepherd follows his flock wherever the animals choose to find their food, and there are no better herdsmen than the Tarahumares, who wisely trust to the natural instinct of the beasts. They do not pride themselves on breeds. It is astonishing to notice the number of rams with two pairs of horns among the tribe. In every flock two or three specimens may be observed, one pair bending forward the other to the side. I have seen some with three pairs of horns. Near Nonoava, where the Indians are much Mexicanised, they make butter and cheese, using the rennets from the cow, sheep, and deer, but they do not drink the milk, saying that it makes them stupid, and they are watchful to prevent their children from drinking it. Dogs are not much liked except for hunting. A great number of them hang around the houses, but they have to make their own living as best they can. They are of the same mongrel class found everywhere among the Indians of to-day. They are generally of a brownish color and not large, but some of them are yellow and with ears erect.

Dogs of Chihuahua.

The so-called dogs of Chihuahua, which command quite a price among dog-fanciers, are found only in the capital of the state. They are small pet dogs and very timid, with large ears and prominent eyes. I understand that the yellowish-brown are considered the purest breed, but they are found in many different colors, from snow-white and black-and-white to dark-brown. They are said to have a small cavity on the top of the head, though according to some authorities this is not an unfailing mark of the breed, which seems to be indigenous. The illiterate Mexican, in his tendency to connect everything good with Montezuma, thinks that the pure dogs of Chihuahua are descendants of those which were left behind by that regent near Casas Grandes at the time when he started south, which afterward became wild and degenerated into the prairie-dogs of to-day.

Another dog indigenous to Mexico is the hairless dog, also a pet, found throughout the republic among the Mexicans. It is credited with possessing curative properties, for which reason people keep them in their beds with them at night.

CHAPTER XII

THE TARAHUMARES STILL AFRAID OF ME—DON ANDRES MADRID
TO THE RESCUE—MEXICAN ROBBERS AMONG THE TARAHU-
MARES—MODE OF BURIAL IN ANCIENT CAVES—VISIT TO NO-
NOAVA—THE INDIANS CHANGE THEIR MINDS ABOUT ME, AND
REGARD ME AS A RAIN-GOD—WHAT THE TARAHUMARES EAT
—A PRETTY CHURCH IN THE WILDERNESS—I FIND AT LAST
A RELIABLE INTERPRETER AND PROCEED TO LIVE À L'IN-
DIENNE.

AS I travelled along I found the natives unobliging
and afraid of me. One man who had hid himself, but was after a while forced to reappear, bluntly
asked, "Are you not the man who kills the fat girls
and the children?" At another time I was taken for
Pedro Chaparro, the famous robber, who had notori-
ously deceived the Indians. The guide took only a
half-hearted interest in me, as he feared that by being
seen with me he was ruining his trade with the natives, who were especially suspicious about my writing in
my note-book, taking it as a proof of my design to take
their land away from them. Still, I accomplished a
good deal and made interesting observations, though
the difficulties under which I had to labour were quite
exasperating.

It was a positive relief, when in the beginning of
August, six weeks after my start from Guachochic, I
arrived at Guajochic (guajo = *sancudo*, a small mos-
quito), one of the stations where the bullion trains stop
on their travels between Batopilas and Carichic. The
man then in charge of this rather lonely looking place,

Andres Madrid, turned out to be very interesting. Born of Tarahumare parents, in the town of Carichic, he had received quite a liberal Mexican education and was virtually a Mexican, though in hearty sympathy with his native tribe. His grandfather had been a noted shaman, or medicine man, whom Don Andres, as a boy, had accompanied on his travels. He was intelligent, lively and imaginative, of a strong humourous vein, and very entertaining. Generous in giving information about the Indians, and speaking the native language, he would have made an ideal interpreter, except for the fact that he grew tired too easily. Only by piecemeal and when having an abundance of time could an ethnologist expect to take advantage of his accomplishments. As he was honest, and helpful to the Indians, and besides was a representative of the Mexican authorities, the Indians had unlimited respect, nay, adoration, for him.

Tarahumare Girdles.

Knowing all that happens in the sierra, he had already heard of me some time ago, and laughed at the cannibalistic propensities attributed to me. He immediately sent a messenger to el capitan at Nararachic, to advise him of my arrival, and to request him to tell the Indians to present themselves to be photographed by a man who came from Porfirio Diaz, a name to conjure with in Mexico, who wanted to know all about the Tarahumares. Nararachic is an insignificant pueblo, to which the Indians of this locality belong. The name means "where one was weeping."

Being taken under the wing of Don Andres benefitted me in many ways. When the Indians from the hills all around could see my white tent close by his little home, they understood that I could not be so bad, or else the good Don Andres would not have anything to do with me.

The Indians in the vicinity had recently gone through the sensation of fighting with four real robbers, who had several times succeeded in plundering store-houses while the owners were off at some feast. At last the Indians had caught them. The thieves travelled on foot, but had a pack-horse which carried all the blankets and handkerchiefs stolen, the total value of which ran up to $112. Sixty-five Tarahumares had banded together in the course of four or five hours, and obliged the robbers to take refuge in a cave, from which they defended themselves with rifles for several hours. The Tarahumares first threw stones at them, as they did not want to waste their arrows. Finally Don Andres, who had been sent for, arrived at the place, and induced the robbers to surrender; but only with difficulty could he prevent the Tarahumares from attacking them. "What does it matter," they said, "if one or two of us are killed?" Cowards as the Tarahumares are when few in number, they do not know fear when many of them are together. They are harmless when not interfered with, but neither forget nor forgive an injury. On several occasions they have killed white men who abused their hospitality, and they even threatened once, when exasperated by abuses, to exterminate all the whites in some sections of their domain.

The robbers were taken by an escort of Indians to the little town of Carichic, and from there sent to Cusihuiriachic ("where upright pole is") to be tried. This place is about a hundred miles from Nararachic, and as the Indians during the next weeks were called to be present at the trial as witnesses, it annoyed them not a little. They were sorry they had not killed the evil-doers; and it would even have been better, they said, to have let them go on stealing.

In the fight the gobernador had got a bullet through his lung. I saw him a fortnight afterward, smoking a cigarette and on the way to recovery, and after some days he, too, walked to Cusihuiriachic. A few months later the robbers managed to dig themselves out of the prison.

On an excursion of about ten miles through the picturesque Arroyo de las Iglesias, I passed seventeen caves, of which only one was at present inhabited. All of them, however, had been utilised as dwellings before the construction of the road to Batopilas had driven the Indians off.

I saw also a few ancient cave-dwellings. Of considerable interest were some burial-caves near Nararachic, especially one called Narajerachic (= where the dead are dancing). A Mexican had been for six years engaged there in digging out saltpetre, with which he made powder, and the cave was much spoiled for research when I visited it. But I was able to take away some thirty well-preserved skulls and a few complete skeletons, the bodies having dried up in the saltpetre. Some clothing with feathers woven in, and some bits of obsidian and of blue thread were found, but no weapons or utensils. According to the miner, who appeared to be trust-worthy, he had excavated more than a hundred corpses. They were generally found two and a half feet below the surface, and sometimes there were others under-neath these. With many of them he found ear orna-ments made of shells, such as the Tarahumares of to-day use, besides some textile made of plant fibre, and a jar with beans.

A few months later at Aboreachic (Tarahumare : Aoreachic = where there is mountain cedar) I exam-ined a burial-cave in which the dead were interred in a different manner from that described before. The cave is somewhat difficult of access. The ascent of 300 feet has to be made over a track at some places so steep that holes have been cut for the feet, to enable a person to climb up. On reaching the top I found a spacious cave, which had been used as a kind of cemetery, but unfortunately the peculiarity of the cave had attracted treasure-seekers, whose destructive work was every-where to be seen. Still I could see that the corpses had been placed each by itself in a grave in the floor of the cave. The graves were oblong or circular basins lined with a coating of grass and mud and about three feet deep. Apparently no earth had been placed im-mediately over the body, only boards all around it laid lengthwise in a kind of box. The bodies were bent up and laid on their sides. Over the top boards was spread a layer of pine bark about an inch thick, which in turn was covered with earth and rubbish three inches deep, and this was overlaid with the coating of grass and mud so as to form a solid disk four or five inches thick. The edge of the basin was slightly raised, thus making the disk a little higher than the level of the floor. I secured four skulls from here, besides a piece of excellently woven cloth of plant fibre, another piece interwoven with turkey feathers, and a fragment of a wooden needle.

Don Andres told me that he had observed similar modes of burial in the neighbourhood of Nararachic. It may be worth mentioning that the miner who excavated in the burial-cave near Nararachic mentioned above, told me of having met with somewhat similar structures in his cave ; the material was the same, but they were of different sizes, not larger than two feet, and he found them empty.

The ancient modes of burial that I have come upon in the Tarahumare country are either like those in Nararachic or in Aboreachic. There scarcely seems any doubt that the bodies buried here were Tarahumares. The Indians of to-day consider the dead in the ancient burial-caves their brethren, and call them Anayáuli, the ancients.

From Guajochic I went to Nonoava (in Tarahumare : Nonoa, nōnó = father), although this town is outside of the Tarahumare country proper. The natives here, as may be expected, are pretty well Mexicanised, and losing their customs, religion, and language. The Apache raids were well remembered here, as they were in Carichic, Cusarare, and Bocoyna.

I came upon a Mexican here who had married a Tarahumare woman. His predilection for her tribe was also attested by his dress, which was exactly like that worn by the natives. He had a dark, almost swarthy complexion, but otherwise he did not resemble an Indian. His big stomach and short arms and legs betrayed his real race, and contrasted strangely with the

slender limbs and graceful movements of the Tarahumares.

Near Nonoava I photographed a magnificent fig-tree
of the kind called *beyota*, the fruit of which is appreciated
even by the Mexicans. It was 116 feet across, and the
leaves, as in other trees of the species, were very small.
There are larger trees of this kind to be found, but they
are rare. In the wet season, when the figs are ripe, the
Tarahumares have a habit of singing under the trees while
gathering the fruit.

I noticed some beautiful mezquites in the bed of
a creek, the bottom of which was clayish. Although
the season for it was late, Indians were gathering the
fruit. The proper season is before the rain sets in.
The Indians throw the seeds away, but boil the fruit,
grinding it between stones and mixing it with water.
This drink is also used through Sonora and Chihuahua
by the Mexicans.

On my return I again spent some time in Guajochic.
The Indians came to visit me every day, and following
my rule of giving to every visitor something to eat,
I was making satisfactory progress in cultivating their
friendship. Some of them after eating from my plates
and cups, went to the river to rinse their mouths and
wash their hands carefully, to get rid of any evil that
might lurk in the white man's implements. To be generous is the first step toward gaining the confidence of
both the Indians and the Mexicans, and a gift of food
is more eloquent than a long speech. The Indian, however, before he knows you, always wants to see you eat
first.

I interviewed many of the shamans, and began to
gain some little knowledge of their songs, which helped
to bring me nearer to them. Shortly after my first arrival here it happened that rain fell, and precipitations

continued quite frequently during my stay. The Indians, who are intensely interested in rain, to obtain which they make so many exertions and sacrifices, evidently began to connect my presence with it. Before my departure they confided to Don Andres that " It was no good that that man went away ; it might happen that he carried the rain with him." They even seemed to delight now in posing before my mysterious camera, which they imagined to be a powerful rain-maker. I heard no more excuses for not wanting to be photographed. They no longer told me that it would cause their death, and that their god would be angry with them ; nor was there any more of that unwillingness expressed by one Indian who told me that, inasmuch as he did not owe me anything, he did not want to be photographed. Thus, almost without knowing it, I established friendly relations with the people.

However, it must not be thought that all my troubles were ended yet. The Indians are very clannish, and, although my damaged prestige was now almost restored, and, no doubt, favourable rumours heralded me wherever I went, still the good-will of each district had in a way to be won. Many months later, when I found myself among the pagans farther south, I was interpellated quite persistently on the subject of the skulls in Yoquibo. They wanted to know why I had dug them up. My Mexican interpreter, whom they took to task on the subject, advanced an explanation, which was no doubt strictly in accordance with his best knowledge and belief. He declared that my object had been to find out whether those people had been properly baptised—a reason which apparently perfectly satisfied the Indians.

I travelled in a southeasterly direction, making my way back to Guachochic, over the highlands of Humarisa (húmashi = to run). This locality is of considerable elevation, with the Indian ranches lying about here and there on strips of level land, which run in among the rocky hills like *fjords.*   Bears are quite common here, and the Indians have difficulty in guarding their fields against them.   They are not even to be frightened by stones, and at night they will eat corn until they have enough, and then walk away.

The time of the year in which it is most difficult for the Indians to subsist had passed, and the copious rains of the past months had developed ears of corn.   Rarely or never do the Indians plant corn enough to last them all the year round, and they have, therefore, during the summer to depend for support mainly on herbs, roots, fruits, etc.   The leaves and flowers of the ash-tree are cooked and eaten, and the flowers of the pine-tree.   They never suffer from hunger when living near a river, where they can fish, but in the highlands they have been known to die of starvation.

These natives are fonder of corn than of any other food, and when working for the whites would leave without a word if no more corn or flour were forthcoming. They like, too, to have meat every day, though they cannot always get it.   They rarely, if ever, kill any of their domestic animals for food, as, according to their views, man is only the manager for the gods to whom these creatures really belong, and cows, sheep, and the like can be killed only as sacrifices and eaten at the feasts. But any kind of animal in the forest and field, in the air and the water, is acceptable.   I once asked a strong and healthy-looking Indian how he managed to keep in such good condition, when food was so scarce, and he said that he ate meat.   "What kind of meat?" I asked, and he replied, "Mice, gophers, and small birds."   Their favourite meat, however, is deer, mice, and skunks.

Chunks of meat are simply laid upon the coals to

Aspect of the Tarahumare Country in Humarisa.

roast, or turned before the fire on a wooden spit, the ends of which rest on stones. This, by the way, is the universal method of cooking meat in Mexico. These Indians often eat their meat almost raw, nor have they any repugnance to blood, but boil and eat it. Fish and frogs are broiled by being placed between two thin sticks tied together at the ends to do duty as a gridiron.

The flowers of the maize are dried in the sun, ground and mixed with water; if not required for immediate consumption they are put in jars and kept for the winter. Many herbs are very palatable, as, for instance, the makvásari (of the *Cruciferæ*), which is also kept for winter use after having been properly dried. In the autumn the Indians sometimes eat potatoes, which, when cultivated at all, are planted between the corn, but grow no larger than pigeon eggs. The people eat three kinds of fungi, and they have an extensive knowledge of the poisonous ones. Salt and chile are used as relishes.

A peculiar delicacy is ārí, the secretion of a scale insect, *carteria mexicana*. In the months of July and August it is gathered from the branches of certain trees in the barrancas, rolled by hand into thick brown sticks, and thus preserved for the winter. A small portion is boiled in water and eaten as a sauce with the corn porridge. Its taste is sweetish acid, not particularly pleasant to the palate, but very refreshing in effect, and it is said to be efficacious in allaying fever. The Indians prize it highly, and the Mexicans also buy it.

Just a few miles before reaching Guachochic, one passes the pueblo of Tonachic, from whence the Indians have been more or less driven off by the whites. In missionary times the village appears to have been of some importance, to judge from the church, which is quite pretty, considering its location in the middle of the sierra.

In the sacristy I saw lying about three empty cases, but the silver crucifixes and chalices they once contained had been carried off by Mexican thieves. The man in charge of the building showed me three immense drawers full of gold- and silver-embroidered silken robes of exquisite fineness and great variety. There were at least several dozens of them.

The altar-piece was arranged and painted very tastefully in red and gold. Several oil paintings were hanging in the church, but so darkened by the hand of time that it was impossible to make out whether they were of any artistic merit. Wonderful men those early missionaries, who brought such valuables into this wilderness, over hundreds and thousands of miles, on the backs of mules or Indians. It was rather anomalous to see the poor, naked Indians outside the door, for whose benefit all this had been done. A woman was sweeping away the dirt from the swarms of bats that nested in the ceiling.

The richest and most prominent man in the village enjoyed the reputation of being a great ladron. When I called on him I found him in bed suffering from a tooth-ache. He had his head wrapped up and was completely unnerved, and many people came to sympathise with him in his affliction. When I told him that I liked the Tarahumares, he answered, "Well, take them with you, every one of them." All he cared for was their land, and he had already acquired a considerable portion of it. His wife was the only person in the village who knew how to recite the prayers in the church. This made the husband feel proud of her, and he evidently considered her piety great enough to suffice for the family.

On my return to Guachochic I discharged the Mexicans who had been with me since my travels through

Taking my baggage down an Indian Trail in the Barranca de San Carlos.

Sonora ; they were here of little use to me, as they did not know the country.   I also disposed of the greater number of my mules, keeping only about half a dozen.

With the kind permission of Don Miguel I installed most of my baggage in one of his houses, and considered his ranch a kind of headquarters from which I made several long excursions in various directions. Thanks to my pack and riding mules I could take along, as barter, corn, glass beads, tobacco, and cotton cloth, and bring back collections made on the road.   I was accompanied by a couple of Mexicans from this part of the country and some Indians who acted as carriers.   Of course, whenever I went down into the barrancas, I had to leave my mules and cargo in some safe place on the highlands and take along only the most necessary stores as we proceeded on foot.   On such trips I had to depend entirely on the natives ; they secured the food, and selected the cave or rock shelter, or the tree under which we slept.

Our bill of fare was made up mainly of corn and beans, with an occasional sheep or goat, and some herbs and roots as relishes.   Corn was prepared in the styles known to the Indians, either as corn-cakes (tortillas) or, more often, by simply toasting the grains on a piece of crockery over the fire.   The dish is easy enough to prepare and does not taste at all bad, but it is hard work for one's teeth to make a meal of it, as the kernels assume the consistency of little pebbles, and many months of such a diet lengthens your dentist's bill at about the same ratio as that in which it shortens your molars.   You will ask why I did not carry provisions along with me.   Simply because preserved food is, as a rule, heavy to carry, to say nothing of its being next to impossible to secure more when the supply is exhausted. Some chocolate and condensed milk which I ordered from Chihuahua did not reach me until seven months after the date of the order. Besides, the Indians are not complaisant carriers, least of all in this exceedingly rough country.

For over a year I thus continued to travel around among the Tarahumares, visiting them on their ranches and in their caves, on the highlands and in the barrancas. There are few valleys into which I did not go in this central part of the Tarahumare country, that is, from the Barranca de Batopilas and Carichic in the north toward the regions of the mining place Guadalupe y Calvo in the south. By and by I also found a suitable lenguaraz, Don Nabor, who lived a day's journey from Guachochic. He was a tall, lank, healthy-looking fellow, some fifty years old, very poor and blessed with a large family of sons and daughters, some of them full grown. All his life he had been intimate with the Indians; he spoke their language as well as he did Spanish, and really liked the Tarahumares better than his fellow Mexicans. Being a great hunter but a poor shot he brought home but little game, and made his living chiefly by trading with the Indians. He was the picture of good-nature, laughing with the Indians at their jokes, and weeping with them at their sorrows. Among them he passed as a wit, and being very honest was a general favourite. He never took anything without asking, but was not backward about that. Of his teeth he had hardly any but two of his upper incisors left, which was rather hard for a man of his ravenous appetite; but he utilised them with such squirrel-like dexterity as almost to keep pace with others.

CHAPTER XIII

THE TARAHUMARE PHYSIQUE—BODILY MOVEMENTS—NOT AS SENSI-
TIVE TO PAIN AS WHITE MEN—THEIR PHENOMENAL ENDUR-
ANCE — HEALTH — HONESTY — DEXTERITY AND INGENUITY —
GOOD OBSERVERS OF THE CELESTIAL BODIES AND WEATHER-
FORECASTERS—HUNTING AND SHOOTING—HOME INDUSTRIES—
TESVINO, THE GREAT NATIONAL DRINK OF THE TRIBE—OTHER
ALCOHOLIC DRINKS.

THE Tarahumare of to-day is of medium size and more muscular than his North American cousin, but his cheek-bones are equally prominent. His colour is light chocolate-brown. I was rather surprised often to find the faces of the people living in the warm barrancas of a lighter colour than the rest of their bodies. The darkest complexions, strange to say, I encountered on the highlands near Guachochic. In the higher altitudes the people also develop higher statures and are more muscular than in the lower portions of the country.

Both men and women wear long, flowing, straight black hair, which in rare cases is a little wavy. When a woman marries, I am told, she cuts her hair once. When the hair is cut because it has grown too long and troublesome, they place it under a stone or hang it in a tree. A shaman once cut his hair short to get new thoughts with the new hair, and while it was growing he kept his head tied up in a piece of cotton cloth to keep his thoughts from escaping. When the people are very old, the hair turns gray ; but they never grow bald. Beards are rare, and if they appear the Indians pull them

235

out. Their devil is always represented with a beard, and they call the Mexicans derisively shabótshi, "the bearded ones." Much as they enjoy tobacco, an Indian would not accept some from me, because he feared that coming from a white man it would cause a beard to grow on his face.

Tarahumare Woman.

There are more women in the tribe than men. They are smaller, but generally just as strong as the other sex, and when angered, for instance by jealousy, the wife may be able to beat her husband. Hands and feet are small. Many of the women have surprisingly small and well-shaped bones, while the men are more powerfully built. The corner teeth differ from the front teeth in that they are thicker, and, in spite of exceptionally fine teeth, tooth-ache is not unknown in the tribe. Men, even those who are well nourished, are never stout. The women are more inclined to corpulency.

Eight people with hair-lip, seven hunchbacks, six men and four women with six toes to their feet, and one or two cases of squint-eyes came under my notice. One boy had a club-foot with toes turned inside, and I saw one man who had only stumps of arms with two or three finger-marks on each. I have observed one case of insanity among these Indians.

Pediculi (lice) from the heads and clothing of the

Front View.   Side View.

Tarahumare Man.

Tarahumare are blackish in colour, but the claw is not different from that of the white men's parasites.

When at ease, the Tarahumare stands on both legs, without stiffness. In micturition he stands, while the Tepehuane sits down. The body is well balanced. The gait is energetic. He swings his arm and plants his foot firmly, with the toes generally in, gliding along smoothly with quick steps and without swaying to and fro, the body bent slightly forward. The palm of the hand is turned to the rear. Tarahumares climb trees by

embracing the tree as we do ; but the ascent is made in jumps, the legs accordingly not embracing the tree as much as is the case with us. In swimming they throw their arms ahead from one side to another. They point with the open

Usual Crouching Position of the Tarahumare.

hand or by protruding the lips and raising the head at the same time in the desired direction. Like the Mexicans they beckon with their hands by making downward movements with their fingers.

To the casual observer the native appears dull and heavy, so much so that at first it would seem hopeless to get any intelligent information out of him ; but on better acquaintance it will be found that their faces, like those of Mexican Indians in general, have more variety of feature and expression than those of the whites. At the same time it is true that the individual does not show his emotion very perceptibly in his face. One has to look into his eyes for an expression of what passes in his mind, as his face is not mobile ; nor does he betray his feelings by involuntary actions. If he blushes, as he sometimes does, the colour extends down the neck and is visible in spite of his dusky skin. Laughter is never immoderate enough to bring tears to the eyes. The head is nodded vertically in affirmation and shaken laterally in negation only by the civilised Tarahumares.

There is a slight though undefinable odour about the Tarahumare. He is not aware of it; yet he will tell

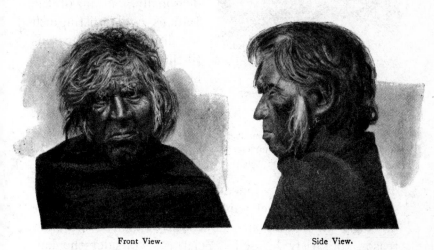

Front View.   Side View.
Tarahumare Man.

you that the Mexican smells like a pig, and the American like coffee, both offensive odours to Tarahumares. They all love to feel warm, and may often be seen lying in the sun on their backs or stomachs. Heat never seems to trouble them. Young babies sleep on their mothers' backs without any covering on their heads to protect them from the fierce rays of the summer sun. On the other hand, the Tarahumare endures cold unflinchingly. On an icy winter morning, when there are six inches of snow on the ground, many a man may be seen with nothing on but his blanket fastened around his waist, pursuing rabbits.

While their senses are keen, I do not consider them superior to those of any well-endowed white man. To test eyesight, Sir Francis Galton directs us to cut out a square piece of white paper one and a half inches a side, paste it on a large piece of black paper, and mark

Tarahumares Sunning Themselves. In the foreground is seen an implement for carrying burdens on the back.

how far a person can distinguish whether the square is held straight or diagonally. None of the Indians could distinguish the different positions until they were within seven hundred and ten feet. On another occasion, however, when I tested six individuals, four men could tell the position of the square at a distance of nine hundred and five feet. One of these had syphilis. They certainly do not feel pain in the same degree as we do. On this point any collector of hair could have reason to satisfy himself. Scientists consider the hair a particularly distinguishing feature among the races of men, not only in regard to its colour, but also as to its texture. In fact, the human race is by some classified according to the character of the hair of the head. Compared under the microscope a section of the hair of a Chinaman or an American Indian is found to be circular, that of a European oval in shape. As a rule, the flatter the hair the more readily it curls, the perfectly cylindrical hair hanging down stiff and straight. A section of the straight hair of a Japanese, for instance, forms a perfect circle. So much importance being attached to the structure of the hair, I made a collection from different individuals. They were willing enough to let me have all the samples I wanted for a material consideration, of course, but the indifferent manner in which they pulled the hair from their heads, just as we should tear out hairs from the tail of a horse, convinced me that inferior races feel pain to a less extent than civilised man. I once pulled six hairs at a time from the head of a sleeping child without disturbing it at all; I asked for more, and when twenty-three hairs were pulled out in one stroke, the child only scratched its head a little and slept on.

They are not so powerful at lifting as they are in carrying burdens. Out of twelve natives, ten of whom were eighteen and twenty years old, while two owned to fifty years, five lifted a burden weighing $226\frac{2}{5}$ pounds (102 kilograms). I was able to lift this myself. The same five lifted $288\frac{3}{5}$ pounds (130 kilograms), as also did two strong Mexicans present, aged respectively eighteen and thirty years. In order to test their carrying capacity, I had them walk for a distance of 500 feet on a pretty even track. One very poor and starved-looking Tarahumare carried $226\frac{2}{5}$ pounds (102 kilograms) on his back, though tottering along with some difficulty; two others carried it with ease, and might have taken it farther. All three were young men.

Their endurance is truly phenomenal. A strong young man carried a burden of over 100 pounds from Carichic to Batopilas, a distance of about 110 miles, in seventy hours. While travelling with such burdens they eat nothing but pinole, a little at frequent intervals.

The wonderful health these people enjoy is really their most attractive trait. They are healthy and look it. It could hardly be otherwise in this delightful mountain air, laden with the invigorating odour of the pines combined with the electrifying effect of being close to nature's heart. In the highlands, where the people live longer than in the barrancas, it is not infrequent to meet persons who are at least a hundred years old. Long life is what they all pray for.

They suffer sometimes from rheumatism, but the most common disease is pleurisy (*dolor de costado*), which generally proves fatal. Syphilis rages in some parts of the country. There was at the time of my visit to Pino Gordo hardly a native there who had not, at one time or another, been afflicted with it; but the victims get quickly over it without special treatment, sometimes within a year. Children of syphilitic parents

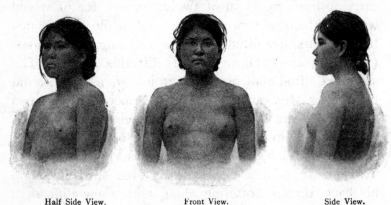

Half Side View.　　Front View.　　Side View.

Tarahumare Girl. The Hair Worn in Mexican Fashion.

show the symptoms soon after birth. Small-pox, too, plays havoc among the population. I have seen some people suffering with cataract in the eyes, and some foot-runners complained that their sight sometimes became impaired during or after a race. The Tarahumares have not any cases of tape-worm, although their sheep have it; probably the large quantities of tesvino drunk during the winter may have something to do with this.

Medicine takes remarkably strong hold of the Indians. One man suffered for two weeks from fever and ague, lost his appetite, and seemed a general wreck; but after a two-grain quinine pill became at once himself again, and a few days later was able to take a message for me to a place forty miles off and return the same day.

The natives do not bathe except in the wet season. When they go to feasts, they wash their hands and faces, and the women comb their hair. Sometimes they may wash their feet, but more frequently they clean their heads. In fact, the regular way of taking a bath is to wash the head. For this purpose they use an agave called sōké. Occasionally they use a white earth from Cusarare, called *javoncillo ;* it is very soft and it is also used as white colour in decorating pottery. When the men go into deep water to bathe they smear fat all over their bodies to guard against all kinds of bad animals in the water ; women do not usually take this precaution.

A Tarahumare does not commit homicide unless he is drunk. There are only isolated exceptions. A *jefe politico* (prefect) told me that in forty years he had heard of only two murders. In both of these cases a drunken husband had killed his wife at a feast, and knew nothing of the crime after he became sober. I have been told that in some rare instances a Tarahumare woman will sit on her child right after its birth to crush it, in order to save herself the trouble of bringing it up. The Tepehuanes are reputed to do the same thing, and for the same purpose. Still with both tribes crimes of this kind are exceedingly rare.

Suicide is never committed unless a person is drunk and angered by some slight or by jealousy. At one time there was a veritable epidemic of suicides among the Indians near Guachochic, the men hanging themselves with their girdles ; one of them even suspended himself by the feet. But it is doubtful whether a pagan Tarahumare ever killed himself.

As a rule, the Tarahumare is not a thief. Only when he thinks himself entirely unobserved, he may appropriate some trifle that particularly strikes his fancy, but the indications are that he learned the art from the Mexicans. Once on our travels we passed a man who was weeding his field. We tried to induce him to give us some information, but he was too busy to talk, and we went on. Soon he noticed that we had accidentally dropped our large axe, and immediately he interrupted his pressing work and came running after us with it. I wanted to compensate him for the trouble he had put himself to, but he would not accept the money I offered, saying that he had not had to go far, and, anyway, he did not bring the axe to get payment for it.

As long as he is in his native state, a Tarahumare never cheats at bargains. He does not like to sell anything that is in any way defective. He always draws attention to the flaw, and if a jar has any imperfection, it requires much persuasion to make him part with it. He shows honesty also in other ways. Often I trusted Indians with a silver dollar or two for corn to be delivered a few days later, and never was I disappointed by them. On the other hand, they are chary of selling anything to a stranger. When a Mexican wants to buy a sheep, or some corn, or a girdle, the Tarahumare will first deny that he has anything to sell. What little he has he likes to keep for himself, and he considers it a favour to part with any of his belongings for money. A purchase, however, establishes a kind of brotherhood between the two negotiants, who afterward call each other "naragua," and a confidence is established between them almost of the same character as that which exists between compadres among the Mexicans.

From outsiders they accept silver coins, but not paper money, because they have been cheated with wrappers from cigarette boxes, and besides, they have no means of keeping such money safe and sound from mice, moisture, etc. Among themselves a little trading goes on, the highlands obtaining from the barrancas in the west copal, chile, ari, ear ornaments made from shells, and goats, in exchange for corn and beans. The Indians from Nararachic go to Rio Concho for the shells from which they make their ear pendants. The powder produced in working the shells is saved and mixed with salt to be used as a remedy for eye troubles.

The tribe has undeniably a certain gift for mechanics. The people are deft with their fingers and do everything neatly. This shows itself in their ingeniously constructed wooden locks and in the niceness with which they stuff animals. They are also very clever in following tracks, and even recognise the hoof-prints of particular horses among others in the same trail. They will also tell you that a tired deer keeps its toes more closely together than an animal just aroused from its lair. And never do they lose their way in the forest, not even when drunk. They love to sit among their corn plants, and will hide among them when strangers approach.

The Tarahumares are inquisitive, and will stand for a long time looking at you from a distance, if anything unusual attracts their attention. They are very critical and there is much gossip going on among them. They also laugh at the Mexicans, and say that the hair on their faces is like the fur on a bear. Squint-eyes also afford them much amusement. They are smart, attentive and patient. They have no qualms of conscience about telling an untruth, but my experience with them shows appreciation and gratitude for benefits received. An Indian whom I had occasion to treat to a good meal, many months afterward at a feast came up and said to me, "You were good to me when I was very hungry," and he proved his thankfulness by assisting me in various ways in establishing friendly relations with his people, which otherwise would have been very difficult to bring about.

Children are bright, and when sent to school learn Spanish quickly. They also master reading and writing without difficulty. They are diligent, eager to learn, and very religious, docile, and easily converted to Christianity.

There is a story about a padre who asked a Tarahumare boy, "What is God doing in Heaven?" The boy said, "The same as the macaw does in the tree." The padre asked, "What does the macaw do in the tree?" and the boy replied, "He eats the good seeds and lets the bad ones drop." A Mexican asked me if God was going to walk on earth again, and my Tarahumare attendant remarked, "No, he is now afraid to come, because people have too many rifles."

When they learn something their ambition runs high, and the boys always want to become generals and presidents of the republic.

The Tarahumares are careful observers of the celestial bodies, and know the Pleiades, the Belt of Orion, and the Morning and the Evening Star. The Great Dipper is of no special interest to them. Near Guachochic the Tarahumares plant corn in accordance with the positions of the stars with reference to the sun. They say if the sun and the stars are not equal the year will be bad; but when the stars last long the year will be good. In 1891, the sun "travelled slowly," and the stars "travelled quickly," and in June they had already "disappeared." Therefore the Tarahumares predicted that their crops would be below the average, which came true. On June 3d I asked an Indian how much longer the sun would travel on, and he told me that it ought not to be more than fifteen days. The Tarahumares are reputed to be good weather prophets among the

Mexicans, who frequently consult them upon the prospects of rain. The Indians judge from the colour of the sun when he rises as to whether there will be rain that day. If the crescent of the moon is lying horizontally, it is carrying much water; but when it stands up straight, it brings nothing. This belief is shared by the Mexicans. When the moon is full and has "a ring around," she is dancing on her patio. At the period of the dark moon she is dead, but will return after three days. Eclipses are explained as collisions between the sun and the moon on the road, when they fight.

The Tarahumare men make bows and arrows, and in the central part of the country are great hunters and clever at shooting. The fore-shaft of their arrows is made of palo hediondo, a wood used also in the making of needles. But the people living near the pueblo of Panalachic and the Barranca de Cobre are poor shots, and their favourite weapon is the axe. The boys still play with slings, which not so long ago were used for killing squirrels. A club with a stone (Spanish, *macana*) is said to have been formerly in common use. The grandfathers of the present generation of Nararachic had flint-tipped arrows. The Indians also know how to prepare excellent buckskin. They peg the hide on the ground and leave it for three days, and when it is sufficiently dry the hair is scraped off with a knife. It is then smeared over with the brain of the animal and hung up in the sun for four days. The next step is to wash it well in warm water in a wooden trough. Then it is well kneaded, and two people taking hold of it draw it out of the water and stretch it well between them. It is dried again and is then tanned with the crushed bark of the big-leaved oak-tree. A natural cavity in a rock is chosen for a vat, in which the skin is left for two days. After this it is well rinsed and squeezed until no water remains in it. Two persons are required for the operation, which is always performed in a place on which the sun beats strongly, while at the same time it is sheltered from the wind by surrounding rocks.

Deer are caught in snares fastened to a bent tree, so that the animal's foot is held, while the tree when released hoists the quarry up. The Indians also chase deer with dogs toward some narrow passage in the track where they have placed sharp-pointed pine sticks, two feet long, against which the deer runs and hurts itself. Blackbirds are decoyed by kernels of corn threaded on a snare of pita fibre hidden under the ground. The bird swallows the kernel, which becomes entangled in its œsophagus and is caught. Small birds are also shot with bow and arrows, or killed with stones.

The Tarahumare is ingenious in devising many kinds of traps for birds and animals. Into the burrow of the gopher he places a small upright frame cut from a piece of bark. There is a groove inside of the frame, and in this the snare runs; and a string is attached to a bough above ground. Another string, on which some grains of corn are threaded, keeps the snare set and obstructs the gopher's passage through the frame. When trying to get at the kernels the gopher cuts the string, the snare is released, and he is caught in his own burrow.

Squirrels are hunted in the most primitive way—by cutting down the tree on which an animal is discovered. Sometimes it will escape when the tree falls, and then the man has to cut down another tree, and thus he may go on felling as many as ten trees before he can bag his game, not a very substantial reward for a whole day's work.

The women make girdles and blankets on primitive looms, inserting characteristic designs in the weaving.

Weaving a Girdle.

It takes four days of constant work to make a girdle, but no woman weaves more than one blanket in a year,

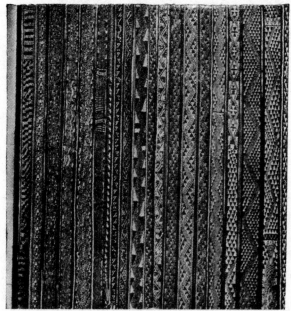

Patterns of Tarahumare Belts.

and it is almost an event when it is finished. The weaving frame consists simply of four sticks—placed on the ground tied together in a rectangle or triangle, and pieces of reed on which the thread is wound, one for each colour, are used as shuttles. Textiles from Pamachic are especially highly valued. The blankets from that locality are sold all over the Tarahumare country and are the finest made by the tribe.

The Tarahumares are not far advanced in the art of making pottery. Their work is crude and not very sub-

Woman Pottery Maker and Some Results of Her Labour.

stantial. The industry is practised only by the women, and the degree of ability varies considerably. The art is often hereditary. The nicest pottery I found in the neighbourhood of Panalachic, where it is decorated with certain designs in red and white. One woman in a western barranca cultivated a specialty of making large jars for holding tesvino. The largest jar shown in the illustration was nearly eight feet in circumference.

Women when making pottery taste a little of the clay before commencing work, ascertaining whether it is the right kind or not. Some of the clay is acid and not good. The clay which is serviceable is a little sweet and of a pale yellow colour. The clay is dried and ground, and then mixed with ground pieces of old pottery instead of sand. To make a piece of pottery, a lump of clay is hollowed out in the shape of a cup, and on this foundation the jar is built up, thin layers of clay being placed on successively, and smoothed carefully over with wet hands, making the walls thinner and thinner. The vessel is built up standing on a bowl filled with ashes and covered with a piece of cotton cloth.

I saw a clever woman make a medium-sized jar in twenty-seven minutes. She was seated in the sun, and finished four vessels in one afternoon. Then, assisted by her husband, she began to even them on the outside with a small, smooth, oblong piece of a gourd. The vessels were then put into the house in order that they might not dry too quickly. After an interval of fifteen minutes, during which she nursed her infant, which had been bothering her all the while, she began work again. First, with the edge of a sharpened stick she removed all irregularities on the outside and on the brim, and then with a stone she polished the vessel. To polish the jars seemed to take the longest time, for each of the workers was engaged on a vessel for over an hour, and even then had not completed the task. They polished outside and a little way inside below the brim. Finally they painted decorations with ochre, and polished again for a long time, but only the outside. Now the jars were again put into the house to dry a little more before the polishing was finished.

To burn the jars, they must first be thoroughly dried, as otherwise the fire would crack them. When the weather is nice the fire may be made outside the

Inside of Bowl. Diameter, 17 ctm.

Height, 13.5 ctm.

Height, 16.5 ctm.

Height, 19 ctm.

Tarahumare Pottery from Panalachic.   Decorations in red ochre and white *javoncillo*.

house ; but usually it is built inside on the ordinary fire-place. Each vessel, one at a time, is turned upside down over charcoal, and pieces of pine bark are built up all around and over it like a square little hut, then ignited. Care is taken that no piece of bark comes so near to the jar as to touch and injure it.   Where bark cannot be readily procured, wood is used.   The heat first turns the clay dark, and afterward a pretty yellow colour.

There is one industry which has a peculiar bearing on the whole life of the Tarahumare, namely, the making of native beer.

Nothing is so close to the heart of the Tarahumare as this liquor, called in Mexican Spanish *tesvino*.   It looks like milky water, and has quite an agreeable taste, reminding one of kumyss.   To make it, the moist corn is allowed to sprout ; then it is boiled and ground, and the seed of a grass resembling wheat is added as a fer-ment. The liquor is poured into large earthen jars made solely for the purpose, and it should now stand for at least twenty-four hours ; but inasmuch as the jars are only poorly made, they are not able to hold it very long, and the people take this responsibility on themselves.   A row of beer jars turned upside down in front of a house is a characteristic sight in the Tarahumare region.

The tesvino forms an integral part of the Tarahu-mare religion.   It is used at all its celebrations, dances, and ceremonies.   It is given with the mother's milk to the infant to keep it from sickness.   In " curing " the new-born babe the shaman sprinkles some over it to make it strong.   Beer is applied internally and exter-nally as a remedy for all diseases Tarahumare flesh is heir to.   No man could get his field attended to if he did not at first make ready a good supply of tesvino, be-cause beer is the only remuneration his assistants re-ceive.   Drinking tesvino at the feast marks the turning-point in a person's life. A boy begins to drink tesvino because now he feels himself a man ; and when a girl is seen at feasts, it is a sign that she is looking for a husband. No marriage is legitimate without a liberal consumption of tesvino by all parties present at the wedding. Hunting and fishing expeditions are accompanied by beer-drinking to insure luck. No matter how many times the Tarahumare changes his abode in the course of his life, he always makes tesvino when moving into a new house or cave. Even the dead would not get any rest, but come back and harm the survivors, if a quantity of tesvino were not set aside for them. In fact, there is absolutely no act of importance that is not, in one way or another, connected with the drinking of this

Basket for Straining Tesvino. Height, exclusive of handle, 14 ctm.

beer. Never is a jar commenced unless some of the liquor is sacrificed before the cross, for the gods are believed to be as fond of the beer as are mortals. Rain cannot be obtained without tesvino ; tesvino cannot be made without corn ; and corn cannot grow without rain. This, in a nutshell, is the Tarahumare's view of life.

There are many occasions during the year, especially during the winter time, when regular symposiums are held, generally inside of the house ; but the people never drink tesvino unless there is some purpose to be attained, be it luck in some undertaking, or good crops, or the health of the family, or some similar benefit. They may dance yúmari for a little while at any of these functions.

It is the custom to appoint one man to distribute the liquor among the guests. In doing this the host offers to the chosen one three drinking-gourds full of tesvino, which the latter empties, and he enters upon his duty by giving to every man present three gourds in succession and to every woman four. The guests, although from politeness hesitating between each gourdful, are only too delighted to comply with this inviolable rule, which speaks eloquently for their constitutions.

The seat beside the distributer is the most coveted. I, too, was always glad to get it, because it gave me the best chance to observe the behaviour of the Indians at the feasts. The dispenser establishes himself close to the big jar, and being immensely popular with everybody he is never left alone. The geniality of the Tarahumares, their courteousness and politeness toward each other in the beginning of a feast, is, to say the least, equal to that of many a civilised gentleman. When the cup is offered to anyone, he most urgently protests and insists that the distributer shall drink ; often this remonstrance is heeded, but the gourd is never emptied ; something is always left in it, and this the guest has to take, and a second gourdful is immediately held out to him. Though he again refuses, he generally allows himself to be persuaded to drink it, and this mock refusing and urging goes on as long as they have their wits together.

To my knowledge, this beer is not known outside of the Tarahumare tribe and their immediate neighbours, the northern Tepehuanes, the Tubars, and some

Mexicans in Chihuahua who have also adopted it. It must not be confounded with the well-known Mexican drink, pulque, to which it is superior in flavour. It is very nourishing, and the Indians as well as the Mexicans are in the habit of abstaining from food before partaking of the beer, which they assert would otherwise not agree with them. But, food or no food, at all feasts and dances they drink such incredibly large quantities that they are invariably completely overpowered by it, though when taken in moderation tesvino is only mildly stimulating.

Another national beverage, maguey wine, is made from a favourite sweet food of many Indian tribes, which a white man's stomach can hardly digest, namely, the baked stalk of the maguey plant, or that of other agaves. To prepare the liquor, the leaves are cut from the bulb-shaped stalk or heart, which looks like a hard white head of cabbage. These hearts contain a great deal of saccharine matter, and are baked between hot stones in earth mounds, being protected against contact with earth by layers of grass.

When the Tarahumares want to make maguey wine they leave the baked stalks in water in natural hollows or pockets in rocks, without any covering. The root of a certain plant called frijolillo is added as a ferment, and after two days the juice is wrung out with a blanket.

An intoxicating drink is also made from another agave, called tshāwí, which, though common on the higher slopes of the barrancas, has only recently become known to science. According to tradition it is the first plant God created, and the liquor made from it is considered by the pagan Tarahumares as indispensable to certain ceremonies. The Tepehuanes, too, put much importance on this brew, and say that the plant is so sensitive that if one passes a jar in which it is being boiled the liquid will not ferment.

Finally it should be mentioned that an intoxicating, though extremely distasteful drink is made from the stalk of the maize plant (*caña*), by pounding this material into a pulp, then allowing it to soak in water for three days, when it is fermented, whereupon the liquor is prepared in the same way as the maguey wine.

CHAPTER XIV

POLITENESS, AND THE DEMANDS OF ETIQUETTE—THE DAILY LIFE
OF THE TARAHUMARE—THE WOMAN'S POSITION IS HIGH—
STANDARD OF BEAUTY—WOMEN DO THE COURTING—LOVE'S
YOUNG DREAM—MARRIAGE CEREMONIES, PRIMITIVE AND CIV-
ILISED—CHILDBIRTH—CHILDHOOD.

FOR a barbarian, the Tarahumare is a very polite personage. In his language he even has a word "rēkó" which is the equivalent of the English "please," and which he uses constantly. When passing a stranger, or leaving a person, he draws attention to his action by saying, "I am going." As he grows civilised, however, he loses his good manners.

In spite of this he is not hospitable; the guest gets food, but there is no room for him in the house of a Tarahumare. A visitor never thinks of entering a house without first giving the family ample time to get ready to receive him. When he approaches a friend's home, good manners require him to stop sometimes as far as twenty or thirty yards off. If he is on more intimate terms with the family, he may come nearer, and make his presence known by coughing; then he sits down, selecting generally some little knoll from which he can be readily seen. In order not to embarrass his friends he does not even look at the house, but remains sitting there gazing into vacancy, his back or side turned toward the homestead. Should the host be absent the visitor may thus sit for a couple of hours; then he will rise and go slowly away again. But under no circumstances will he enter the home, unless formally invited, " because," he says, " only the dogs enter houses uninvited." Never will the lady of the house commit such a gross breach of etiquette as to go out and inform him of her husband's absence, to save the caller the trouble of waiting, nor will she if alone at home, make any statements as to t h a t gentleman's whereabouts.

The Tarahumare never does anything without due deliberation ; therefore he may, for a quarter of an hour, discuss with his wife the possible purport of the visit, before he goes out to see the man. They peep through the cracks in the wall at him, and if they happen to be eating or doing anything, they may

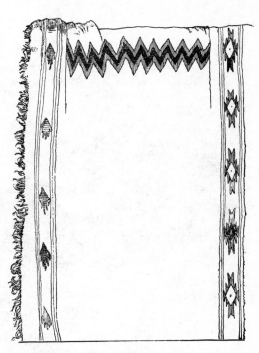

Tarahumare Blanket.

keep the visitor waiting for half an hour. Finally the host shakes out the blanket on which he has been sitting, throws it around himself, and, casting a rapid glance to the right and left as he passes through the door, goes to take a seat a few yards distant from the caller. After some meditation on either side, the conversation, as in more civilised society, opens with remarks about the weather and the prospects for rain. When this subject is exhausted, and the host's curiosity as to where the

man came from, what he is doing, and where he is going
to, is satisfied, the former may go back to the house and
fetch some pinole and meat for the traveller. The object
of the visit not infrequently is an invitation to take part

A Tarahumare Call.

in some game or foot-race ; and as the men are sure to remain undisturbed, they generally reach some understanding.   A friend of the family is, of course, finally invited to enter the house, and the customary salutation is " Assagá ! " (" Sit down ! ")   In this connection it may be noted that the Tarahumares in conversation look sidewise, or even turn their backs toward the person they speak to.

After having eaten, the guest will carefully return every vessel in which food was given to him, and when he rises he hands back the skin on which he was seated. Should occasion require, the host will say : " It is getting late, and you cannot return to your home to-night. Where are you going to sleep ?   There is a good cave over yonder."   With this he may indicate where the visitor may remain over night.   He will also tell him where he may find wood for the fire, and he will bring him food ; but not unless the weather is very tempestuous will he invite an outsider to sleep in the house.

When at home the Tarahumare keeps regular hours, rising and retiring with the sun.   Having slept on a skin on the floor, rolled up in his blanket, without anything for a pillow except perhaps a stone or a chunk of wood, he sits for a while near the fire, which is kept up most of the year at night in the house or cave.   His wife brings him his breakfast of pinole.   While combing out his long black hair with a pine cone, he may ask the boys and girls whether they have attended to the traps he told them to set on the night before.   They run out and soon they come in with some mice. " Here they are," they say, " but they are very poor ! " The father, however, may consider them fat and nice, and the mother affably adds : " Of course, they are fat, since they have eaten so much corn."   They go about to roast them, while the husband looks on.   Generally the Tarahumares have a number of traps set to catch mice. They are so fond of this "game" that, when civilised, they have been known to ask permission from Mexican acquaintances to go through their houses to

Tarahumare Arrow Release.

hunt for them. The mice are skinned and threaded on a thin stick, which is stuck through their necks and serves as a spit.

Having enjoyed the dainty morsel thus set before him, the husband now tells his wife what he is going to do to-day. He will run deer or hunt squirrels, and accordingly takes his bow and arrows or his axe with him. In spring-time he may go to the field. The wife also tells of her plans for the day. The work that engages most of the time of the housewives in Mexico is

the grinding of the corn, on the metate, for corn-cakes ;
and if she has any time to spare she boils beans, looks
for herbs, or works on her weaving-frame ; but she never
sits about idle. She looks as conscientiously after her
duties as any white woman ; she has always something
to do, and many things to take care of in her small way.

About sunset the husband returns, bringing a squirrel or rabbit, which he carries concealed in his blanket,
that no neighbour may see it and expect an invitation to
help to eat it. As he goes and comes he never salutes
his wife or children. He enters in silence and takes his
seat near the fire. The animal he caught he throws
toward her where she is kneeling before the metate, so
that it falls on her skirt. She ejaculates " Sssssssssss !"
in approval and admiration, and, picking it up, praises
its good points extravagantly : "What a big mouth !
What large claws !" etc. He tells her how hard he
worked to get that squirrel, how it had run up the tree,
and he had to cut down that tree, till finally the dog

Height, 16 ctm.   Height, 18.5 ctm.

Tarahumare Baskets.

caught it. " The dog is beginning to be very good at
hunting," he says. " And now I am very tired." She
spreads before him a generous supper of beans, herbs,
and maize porridge, which she has ready for him. And
while he eats she goes industriously to work removing
the fur from the game, but leaving on the skin, not only

because it keeps the meat together while it is boiling, but mainly because she thinks there is a good deal of nourishment in it, which it would be a shame to waste.

When the man is at home, and neither sleeping nor eating, he may sit down and make a bow or some arrows; or, stretched out on his back, he may resort to his favourite amusement, playing his home-made violin. Like all Indians of Mexico, the Tarahumares are fond of music and have a good ear for it. When the Spaniards first came, they found no musical instruments among the Tarahumares except the short reed flute, so common to many Mexican tribes, the shaman's rattle, and the rasping stick. But they soon introduced the violin and even the guitar, and throughout Mexico the Indians now make these instruments themselves, using pine wood and other indigenous material in their construction, sometimes with remarkable skill and ingenuity, and for glue the juice of a certain lily root. Having no idea of the value of money, they frequently sell a tolerably good instrument for fifty or even twenty-five cents.

Toward evening the Tarahumare father of a family gets more talkative and chats with his wife, and then

> " The day is done, and the darkness
> Drops from the wings of night
> As a feather is wafted downward
> From an eagle in his flight."

And as the shadows deepen, he wraps himself closer in his blanket, and before he knows it childlike slumber enfolds him. Frequently he grows hungry in the middle of the night, and reaches out for food, as well as for his violin, devoting himself to music for half an hour, before he drops off to sleep again.

There are more women in the tribe than men, and they are looked upon as of less importance. There is a saying among the people that one man is as good as five women. Her prayers are not of as much value as his, because she prays only to the moon, and her deity is not as big as his, the sun. For this reason her place is behind the man in all dances. Yet she occupies a comparatively high position in the family, and no bargain is ever concluded until the husband has consulted his wife in the matter. I am bound to say, however, that on such occasions every member of the household, even the youngest and smallest child, is asked to give an opinion, and, if one of the little tots objects, the sale will not be closed. In such cases there is nothing for the customer to do but to try to influence the young business man who raised the objection, not directly, but through his parents. This accounts for a good deal of the frightful loss of time incurred in dealing with these Indians. The purchase of a sheep may require

Tarahumare Girl
Carrying Water.

two days, and the negotiations concerning an ox may extend over an entire week.

That a woman of intelligence and character is appreciated even among barbarians is proven by the fact that once a woman was made gobernador, or chief, because " she knew more than men." She did not assume the title, but she is said to have ruled with more wisdom and justice than many of her predecessors and successors.

Husband and wife never show their affection in public except when drunk. Parents kiss their little ones on the mouth and on the stomach, and the youngsters express their love for each other in the same way. On

some occasions I have seen lovers sitting closely together, she holding on to his forefinger. The women
are of a jealous disposition.

The Tarahumare standard of beauty is not in accordance with the classic ideal as we perceive it, nor
is it altogether in conformity with modern views on the
subject. Large, fat thighs are the first requisite, and
a good-looking person is called "a beautiful thigh."
Erect carriage is another essential to beauty. In the
face, the eyes attract more notice than any other feature,
and the most admired ones are "the eyes like those of
a mouse." This is the highest praise that can be bestowed upon anyone's personal appearance. They all
like straight hair, and consider hair very ugly when it
has a curl at the end. I once asked a bright young
Tarahumare how the man must look who is most admired by women, whether his mouth and nose should be
large or small, etc., and he replied, "They must be
similar to mine!" Aside from good looks, the women
like best men who work well, just as in civilised countries a woman may look out for a good *parti*.

But wealth does not make the possessor more attractive to the girls. In Nararachic was an elderly man
who owned forty head of cattle and eighteen horses.
When he became a widower, he had to live with an
elderly woman of bad reputation, as he could not get
another woman to marry him.

The young women enjoy absolute liberty, except
as regards Mexicans, against whom they are always
warned. They are told that they become sick from
contact with such men. Never are they forced to con-
tract what would turn out to be a loveless marriage. A
beautiful Indian girl was much sought for by a Mexican.
He spoke the Tarahumare language very well, and
offered to give her a good house and fine clothes and a

PLATE VI.

Sidney Starr.

whole handful of silver dollars. Her brother, who was
half civilised, and therefore more corrupt than the ordinary Indian, also tried to persuade her to accept the
rich suitor. But she tossed up her head and exclaimed,
" Tshíne awláma gátsha negālé " which, freely trans-
lated, means: " I do not like that fellow; love goes where
it chooses."

The custom of the country requires the girl to do all
the courting. She is just as bashful as the young swain
whom she wishes to fascinate, but she has to take the
initiative in love affairs. The young people meet only
at the feasts, and after she has gotten mildly under the
influence of the native beer that is liberally consumed
by all, she tries to attract his attention by dancing
before him in a clumsy way up and down on the same
spot. But so bashful is she that she persistently keeps
her back turned toward him. She may also sit down
near him and pull his blanket and sing to him in a
gentle low voice a simple love-song :

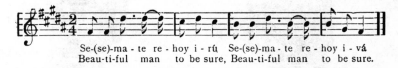

Se-(se)-ma - te re - hoy i - rú   Se-(se)-ma - te   re - hoy i - vá
Beau-ti-ful man   to be sure, Beau-ti-ful man   to be sure.

If occasion requires, the parents of the girl may say
to the parents of the boy, "Our daughter wants to
marry your son." Then they send the girl to the boy's
home, that the young people may become acquainted.
For two or three days, perhaps, they do not speak to
each other, but finally she playfully begins to throw
pebbles at him. If he does not return them, she understands that he does not care for her. If he throws them
back at her, she knows that she has won him. She lets
her blanket drop and runs off into the woods, and he is
not long in following her.

Sometimes the boy, when he likes a girl very much, may make the first advances, but even then he has to wait until she throws the first pebbles and drops the blanket, for, among the Indians, it is the woman who seeks the man, and the fair who deserve the brave.

Front View.   Side View.

Tarahumare, Showing Mode of Wearing Blanket.

Next day they come home together, and after this they do not hide themselves any more. The parents of the girl are advised to make tesvino, as the young couple should not be separated any more, and word is sent out to a few friends and relatives to come to the wedding.

The guests arrive in the afternoon and most of the people remain outside of the house during the ceremony, but the bridegroom and his parents go inside, where they seat themselves on skins spread out on the floor. The mother of the girl has placed a large skin next to a big jar of tesvino, and on this the father of the boy sits down. As soon as he has taken his place, the host offers him three gourds full of the drink and requests him to accept the office of honour, the distribution of tesvino to all present, and he immediately enters upon his duties. He first gives four gourds full to the mother of the bride, as the mistress of the tesvino, and three gourds full to the host, the master ; then four gourds full to his own wife. The bridal couple have been called in and told to sit down side by side, and all the rest of the people come in and stand around the pair. There is no special place assigned to anyone ; but the father of the boy stands up and his mother sits down, while the girl's father sits down and her mother stands up. The boy's father now makes a speech, telling the bridal couple that they must remain together, and never separate nor fight. He specially tells the young man that he has to kill deer and take care always to bring some animal home to his wife, even if it be only a chipmunk or a mouse. He also has to plough and to sow corn and to raise crops, that he and she may always have enough to eat and not go hungry.

The father of the girl next takes the word, addressing himself mostly to the bride. Now that she is united to the man of her choice, she should always comply with her wifely duties. She must make blankets for her husband, and be industrious, make tesvino and iskiate, pinole, tortillas, gather herbs, etc., that her husband may always have something to eat and not go hungry. He names all the herbs singly. She must also help him, in her way, with the ploughing and sowing, so that he may raise plenty of corn to make tesvino that others may help him. She never must be lazy.

The father of the girl now gives tesvino to his future son-in-law, whose father in turn gives some to the bride. The bridal couple are covered with blankets, and in some cases his and her right hands are tied together. There is no other marriage ceremony. But all the guests partake of the liberally flowing bowl, and the festivities end in general and complete intoxication.

About two weeks later, the parents of the bridegroom make a feast exactly the same in character, but now the father of the girl occupies the seat of honour next to the big tesvino jar and acts as distributer. He also makes the first speech. The bridegroom gives to his brother-in-law a flint for striking fire, and six arrows. No matter how many brothers the bride has, they all get this present. It is considered an exchange for the girl. The shamans avail themselves of *jus primæ noctis.*

After the marriage the bridal couple separate, each staying in the old home for several weeks, after which the young man comes to live with his father-in-law for half a year or a year, until he has had time to make a house for himself. In the meantime the young couple are fed, but they receive nothing else. The young man has his own animals, which he got when he was small, and now his father gives him a piece of land.

Among the Christian Tarahumares the fiscal is advised of any contemplated marriage. This functionary has charge of the church edifice and the teaching of the children. It is his duty to take the young couples to the padre to be married. But the padre is far away and comes around only once a year, and sometimes even less frequently, and then the fiscal, so to say, rounds up all the matrimonially inclined. On account of their innate ardour to comply with all religious requirements the Tarahumares are willing to go through the ceremony, though to them it has no significance beyond the payment of one dollar. On this account they do not mind waiting for the padre's blessing for a couple of years, until they get ready to part with the dollar, thereby generally saving an extra trip for baptising.

As the padre's visits are so few and far between, the fiscal even considers it incumbent upon himself to make up matches on his own account, telling the people that when the padre comes they should be ready to get married. But so independent are the Tarahumare girls that it has happened that when the padre asks the portentous question, they cry, " Kæke, kæke " (" No, no "), and run away.

In my time there was a padre (now removed) who emulated the example of the shamans and was frequently in his cups. On one occasion he was unable to perform the marriage ceremonies, and the sacristan accompanying him had to take his place. All this man knew about the rite was to ask the man and the woman whether they would have each other. On hearing their " Yes " he would say, " Where is the dollar ? " and pocketing it send the couple off with, " Now you are all right."

When an addition is expected in the family the chief preparation of the woman is to get ready a quantity of beer, calling on her friends to help her, while the husband goes to look for the shaman. When she feels her time is approaching, she retires to some lonely spot, as she is too bashful to bear her child while others are about. She tightens her girdle around her waist, and bears her child sitting up, holding on to something above her, like the branch of a tree. After the little

stranger has arrived the husband may bring her a jar with
warm water from which she occasionally drinks.   He also
digs a hole, in which, after he has gone, she buries the pla-
centa, placing stones on top of the place on account of the
dogs.   The umbilical cord is cut with a sharp reed or a
sharp-edged piece of obsidian, but never with a knife, for
in that case the child would become a murderer and could
never be a shaman.   I once asked a Tarahumare where
he was born, expecting him to give me the name of
some ranch ; I was rather amused when he pointed to a
big stone a little farther on along the slope.   That was
his birthplace.

The mother may lie down for that day, but the following morning she works as usual, as if nothing had
been the matter with her.   The husband does not work
for three days, because he thinks his axe would break,
or the horns of his ox would fall off, or he would break
a leg.   The third day he takes a bath.

When the baby is three days old the shaman comes
to cure it.   A big fire is made of corn-cobs, the little
one is placed on a blanket, and with the father's assistance the shaman carries it, if it is a boy, three times
through the smoke to the four cardinal points, making
the ceremonial circuit and finally raising it upward.
This is done that the child may grow well and be successful in life, that is, in raising corn.   Then the shaman takes a burning corn-cob from the fire and with
the charred end makes three parallel lines lengthwise
over the child's head and three across them.   He also
sprinkles tesvino on the head and other vital parts of
the body to make them strong, and cures the umbilical cord.   He may, too, anoint the child with the fat
of the rattlesnake mixed with herbs, and leave it in the
sun, that the light may enter its heart.   For his services
the shaman gets a little maize, beans, salt, etc.

On the fourth day the mother goes down to the river to bathe, and while bathing leaves the little one naked, exposed to the sun for at least an hour, in spite of all its wailings, that Father Sun may see and know his new child. The baby is not washed until it is a year old. Then it is cured again, by the shaman, who on various occasions throughout its life repeats his curing, that the child may grow well and that no sickness or bad accidents may befall it. To protect it still further, pieces of palo hediondo or the chuchupate root, the strong smell of which is supposed to avail against disease, are wrapped in a piece of cloth and tied around the child's neck.

The mother nurses the child until it is three years old. In some instances she begins to give it once in a while a little pinole when it is only six months old. When two years of age a child begins to walk and to talk. Sometimes when the mother is busy, for instance at the metate, and will not stop to nurse him, the little rascal may take a stick and in his way try to beat her.

The Tarahumare woman is a faithful mother, and takes good care of her children. She generally has from six to eight, often more. While small the children play with primitive dolls. They dress up corn-cobs with scraps of textiles and put them upright in the sand, saying that they are matachines and drunken women. They also play, like other children, with beans and acorns, or with young chickens with their legs tied together. Of course the youngsters maltreat these. Sometimes they play, too, with stuffed squirrels, but there are no special children's games. The father makes bows and arrows for the boys, and instructs them in hunting and agricultural work. As the girls grow up, the mother teaches them how to spin yarn and weave blankets, "for," she tells them, "otherwise they will become men." She also warns them not to have children too rapidly in succession, for there is no one to carry them for her. Women cannot eat the tenderloin until they are very old, because if they did they could have no children. For the same reason they must not eat the pancreas. The women

Tarahumare Blankets.

who fear lest they may have difficulty in giving birth to a child make soup of an opossum and eat it. Girls must not touch deer antlers, or their breasts would fall off.

A characteristic custom is that the children, no matter how old they get, and even after they are married and have families of their own, never help themselves to anything in the parents' house. The mother has to give all the food, etc., and she gives as long as she has anything.

Parents never inflict corporal punishment upon the young people. If a boy does not behave himself, he gets scolded, and his father's friends may also remonstrate with him at a feast. Otherwise, the children grow up entirely independent, and if angry a boy may even strike his father. A girl will never go so far, but when scolded will pout and weep and complain that she is unjustly treated. How different is this from the way in which, for instance, Chinese children treat their parents! It does not favour much the theory that the American Indians originally came from Asia.

CHAPTER XV

MANY KINDS OF GAMES AMONG THE TARAHUMARES — BETTING AND GAMBLING — FOOT-RACES THE NATIONAL SPORT — THE TARAHUMARES ARE THE GREATEST RUNNERS IN THE WORLD — DIVINATIONS FOR THE RACE—MOUNTAINS OF BETTING STAKES—WOMEN'S RACES.

TO my knowledge there is no tribe so fond of games as the Tarahumares. There are few days in the year when a man has not a game of some kind to play. Even when they become civilised and demoralised, in spite of their depression and poverty this passion of theirs still clings to them. While it is true that there is always something of value, however insignificant, put at stake, their gambling spirit is not vicious. They have some curious practices in their play : when going to run a race, or when intending to play *cuatro* or *quinze*, they do not eat chile. Where holes in the ground are required for a game, as in cuatro and quinze, they are generally made in the level space on a rock.

Very common is it to see two young men amusing themselves with shooting-matches, shooting arrows at an arrow which has been shot out into the ground some fifty yards off as a mark. This arrow, as well as the game itself, is called in Mexican Spanish *lechuguilla*. In Tarahumare the game is called chogírali, and the target-arrow chogira. The arrow coming nearest the chogira counts one point; and if it comes within four fingers' width of the aim, it counts four. The game is for twelve points. The distance is not measured from the points of the arrows, but from the winged parts, one man measuring for all. If a shot arrow strikes so as to form a cross with the chogira, it counts four. If it only touches the point of the latter in the ground it counts two. If two arrows happen to form crosses, neither counts.

Instead of arrows, three sticks may be employed. One is thrown out at a distance and is the chogira, and the other two sticks are thrown toward it, and count in a similar way as the arrows. Often while travelling, the Tarahumares play this game, in either form, as they go along the road, perhaps for the entire distance. Two and three pairs may play together.

There is also a game very similar to quoits, played with stone disks, flat on one side and convex on the other. It is called rixiwátali (rixíwala=disk), and two and two play against each other. First one stone is moistened with spittle on one side to make it "heads or tails" and tossed up. The player who wins the toss plays first. Each has three stones, which are

Stone Disk for Playing. Diameter, 9.5 ctm.

thrown toward a hole in the ground, perhaps twenty yards off. One of each party throws first, then goes to the hole and looks at it, while the other players make their throws. The stone falling nearest to the hole counts one point; if it falls into the hole, it counts four; if the stone of the second player falls on top of the first stone in the hole, it "kills" the first stone. The game is out at twelve. To measure distances, they break off small sticks. Lookers-on may stand around and bet which of the players will win.

Another game is called tákwari, "to beat the ball"; in Spanish, *palillo*. It is played only by women. Two play at a time. One knocks a small wooden ball toward one goal, while her opponent tries to get it to another. This game is also played by the northern Tepehuane women, who sometimes use two short sticks tied together in the middle, instead of the ball. The sticks are thrown ahead from their places on the ground with a kind of

Sticks Used by Tepehuanes for Playing. Length of Sticks about 6 ctm.

quick, prying movement, with the aid of a longer stick.

Civilised Tarahumares, as well as the Mexicans, play with knuckle-bones as dice. The game is called *la taba*,

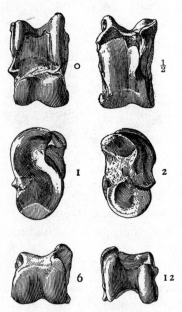

Value of the Different Sides of a Knuckle-bone.

and the bones are taken from either the deer, the sheep, or the goat. Only one bone is used by the two players. Twelve points make a game, and each player has twelve grains of corn with which he keeps count. He makes two rings in the sand, and puts his twelve grains in one ring, and as the game progresses he transfers them into the second ring until the game is out.

Their greatest gambling game, at which they may play even when tipsy, is quinze; in Tarahumare, romavóa. It is played with four sticks of equal length, called romálaka and inscribed with certain marks to indicate their value. Practically

Tarahumares Playing Quinze.

they serve the same purpose as dice, but they are thrown in a different way. The player grasps them in his left hand, levels their ends carefully, lifts his bundle, and strikes the ends against a flat or square little stone in front of him, from which they rebound toward his opponent. The sticks count in accordance with the way they fall. The point of the game is to pass through a figure outlined by small holes in the ground between the two players. The movements, of course, depend upon the points gained in throwing the sticks, and the count is kept by means of a little stone, which is placed in the respective hole after each throw. Many accidents may impede its progress; for instance, it may happen to be in the hole into which the adversary comes from the opposite direction. In this case he is "killed," and he has to begin again from the starting-point. The advance is regulated by a number of ingenious by-laws, which make the game highly intellectual and entertaining. If he has the wherewithal to pay his losses, a Tarahumare may go on playing for a fortnight or a month, until he has lost everything he has in this world, except his wife and children; he draws the line at that. He scrupulously pays all his gambling debts.

The northern Tepehuanes also know this game, and play with sticks eighteen to twenty inches long. As these larger sticks fly quite a distance off when rebounding, the players sit rather far apart.

Wrestling also may be observed, but what may be termed the national sport, of which the Tarahumares are inordinately fond, is foot-racing, which goes on all the year round, even when the people are weakened from scarcity of food. The interest centres almost entirely in the betting that goes with it; in fact, it is only another way of gambling. It is called rālá hípa ("with the foot throw"), the word alluding to a ball used at the race.

No doubt the Tarahumares are the greatest runners in the world, not in regard to speed, but endurance. A Tarahumare will easily run 170 miles without stopping. When an Indian is sent out as a messenger, he goes along at a slow trot, running steadily and constantly. A man has been known to carry a letter in five days from Guazapares to Chihuahua and back, a distance of nearly 600 miles by the road. Even considering short-cuts, which he, no doubt, knew, it was quite a feat of endurance ; for he must have lived, as the Indians always do while travelling, on pinole and water only.

Where the Indians serve the Mexicans they are often employed to run wild horses into the corral. It may take them two or three days, but they will bring them in, the horses thoroughly exhausted, while the men, who, of course, economise their strength, and sleep, and eat pinole, are comparatively fresh. In the same way they will run down a deer, following it for days through snow and rain, until the animal is cornered and easily shot with arrows, or until it is overtaken utterly jaded and its hoofs dropping off.

This propensity for running is so great that the name of the tribe alludes to it. Tarahumare is a Spanish corruption of ralámari, the meaning of which, though somewhat obscure, may doubtless best be given as "foot-runners," because rālá certainly means "foot."

The race is always between two localities, each side being represented by from four to twenty runners. The two parties show in their apparel some distinctive mark; for instance, all of one troop have red head-bands, while the others may wear white ones.

A peculiar feature is that the men toss along a small ball as they run, each party having one of their own. These balls are about two and a half inches in diameter and carved from the root of the oak. The foremost runner kicks it with the toes of his right foot, so as to make it bound along as far as 100 yards, and he and all the men behind him follow in the same trot as before. The first man reaching it again kicks it onward. It must never be touched by the hand, unless it happens to fall in some awkward place, as between stones or in a water-pool, when it is picked up and kicked on.

There is never any laid-out track, but the circuit is determined in a general way by crosses cut in trees. There are certain favourite places always used as race-courses. The runners seem to have a preference for the level tops of low ridges lying in a circle, wherever this is possible. If this is not feasible, they may run forward and back on a ridge, starting always near the middle, from some little plane or other convenient place, where the people gather for the occasion.

Cross Marking the Track of
the Foot-runners.

There is a manager for each party, and the two arrange the time and place for the race to be held, also the number and length of the circuits to be made. A circuit may measure from three to twelve miles in extent, and when the circuits are short as many as twenty may be agreed upon. At one race-course near Carichic, the circuit is about fourteen miles long, and twelve circuits may be run here without stopping. Runners of equal ability are matched against each other, each side being, of course, anxious to secure the best. The managers take care of their men until the race comes off. The training consists mainly in abstinence from tesvino for two or five days before the event. When preparing for a big race the runners may practise; not that they

need training in running, for that comes to them as naturally as swimming to the duck ; but only that they
practise kicking the ball and try the ground.

Much more important are the magical devices by
means of which they endeavour to secure their own success and to defeat their opponents. A daring manager
may go to a burial cave, taking two balls with him. He
digs out a bone, preferably the tibia from the right leg,
and sets it on the floor of the cave in which it has been
found. In front of it he places a jar with tesvino and
some vessels containing food. On either side of these
he lays one of his balls, and in front of all he plants the
cross. The food and the beer are the payment to the
dead that he may help to win the race by weakening
the adversaries.

As human bones are supposed to induce fatigue, some
may be brought to the race-track and secreted there in
such a way that the competing runners have to pass
over the spot, while the manager's own crew are advised
of the danger, to avoid it. The man uses the utmost
care not to touch the bones with his fingers, lest he
should dry up ; instead, he uses sticks in handling and
carrying them.

Scores of remedies are brought to the scene, either
to strengthen friends or to weaken opponents. Certain herbs are thrown into the air or shaken before
the runners to enervate them. Some enterprising
Mexican may bring a white powder or similar substance, declaring that it is very efficacious, and get a
Tarahumare to pay a high price for it. But whatever
means are employed, one way or the other, there is always a counter-remedy to offset its effect. Specially
potent is the blood of the turtle and the bat, stirred together, dried, and mixed with a little tobacco, which is
then rolled into a cigar and smoked. Hikuli and the

Tarahumares Racing by Torch-light.

dried head of an eagle or a crow may be worn under the girdle as a protection.

The services of the shaman are indispensable for the foot-runners. He helps the manager, himself often a shaman, to rub the men with herbs and smooth stones to make them strong. He also makes passes over them to guard them against sorcery. On the day before the races he "cures" them. Food and remedies are placed on a blanket beneath the cross, together with many magical things. The herbs are very powerful and have to be tied up in bags of buckskin or cotton cloth, as otherwise they might break away. The water for the runners to drink is also placed underneath the cross, and candles are set on either side of the pile. The runners bring their balls and stand in a row around the cross. Then the shaman, taking his position in front of the latter, smokes incense of copal over them, and sings of the tail of the grey fox, and other songs. He also makes a speech, warning them not to accept pinole or water in other people's houses. All their food and drink must come from their relatives as a guard against witchcraft and illness. The runners drink three times from the water and the strengthening remedies; then the principal runner leads the others in a ceremonial circuit around the cross, walking as many times around it as there are circuits to be run in the race. The men sleep near the cross, to watch the remedies on the blanket. With them they have some old man, for old men see even when they sleep, and watch against sorcery.

After the ceremony the shaman takes each runner aside and subjects him to a rigid examination in regard to his recent food and his relations with women. Fat, potatoes, eggs, and anything sweet are prohibited, because all these things make the men heavy; but rabbits, deer, rats, turkeys, and chaparral-cocks are wholesome, and such nourishment enables them to win.

An augury as to which side will win is also taken. Water is poured into a large wooden tray, and the two balls are started simultaneously and rolled through the water over the tray. The party whose ball first reaches

Making Wagers at a Foot-race.

the other end will surely win. This test is gone through as many times as there are to be circuits in the race.

A race is never won by natural means. The losers always say that they have been bewitched by the others. Once I was taking the temperature of some foot-runners before they started, and their opponents, seeing this, lost heart, thinking that I had made their contestants strong

to win the race. Often one of the principal runners becomes disheartened, and may simulate illness and declare
that their rivals have bewitched him. Then the whole
affair may come to nothing and the race be declared off.
There are stories about injurious herbs that have been
given in pinole or water, and actually made some racers
sick. It may even happen that some dishonest fellow
will pay to the best runner of one party a cow if he lets
the other party win. But, as a rule, everything goes on
straightforwardly. No one will, however, wonder that
there are six watchmen appointed by each side to guard
the runners from any possible peradventure, and to see
that everything goes on in a proper, formal way. Tipsy
persons are not admitted, and women in a delicate condition are carefully kept away, as the runners become
heavy even by touching such a woman's blanket.

On the day of the race the forenoon is spent in making bets, the managers acting as stakeholders. These
people, poor as they are, wager their bows and arrows,
girdles, head-bands, clothes, blankets, beads, ari, balls of
yarn, corn, and even sheep, goats, and cattle. The stakes
of whatever nature are tied together—a blanket against
so many balls of yarn, a stick of ari against so many arrows, etc. At big races the wagers may amount to considerable heaps of such articles, and the position of
manager requires a man of decision and memory, for he
has to carry all the bets in his head and makes no written record of them. The total value of the wagers may
reach a thousand dollars, and what to the Indians are fort-
unes may change hands in accordance with the result of
the race. One man on one occasion had $50 worth of
property at stake.

The scene is one of great animation. As many
as two hundred people may assemble, among them
women and children. At the gathering-point, which is

called in Tarahumare "the betting-place," all the bets are made, and here the race is started and concluded. Here the managers also place a row of stones, one stone for each circuit to be run, and whenever a circuit is completed one stone is taken away. In this way the count is kept. The runners walk about wrapped in their blankets like the rest of the people. They have had nothing to eat all day but pinole and tepid water, and their legs have been rubbed with warm water in the morning by the managers.

When finally all the people have arranged their stakes the gobernador steps forward and makes a speech, in which he specially exhorts the runners not to throw the ball with their hands; if they do, they certainly will go to hell! He also warns them against cheating of any kind.

At a given signal, quick as lightning, the runners throw off their blankets, and one man in each party, previously selected, throws his ball as far as he can, and all the runners start after it. A second ball is always kept in reserve, in case the first should be lost.

The racers wear rattles of deer-hoofs and bits of reeds tied together on a strip of leather, which they stick in the backs of

Part of Tarahumare Rattling Belt.

their girdle or hang over their backs. The magic rattling keeps them from falling asleep while running, so they say; besides, the deer-hoofs lend them the swiftness of the stag. Some runners adorn themselves with feathers from various birds, preferably the macaw and the peacock, tying them to short sticks. The few Tarahumares who have ever seen a peacock think a good deal of this bird, because it is considered light-

Tarahumare Foot-runners, Photographed After the Race.

footed and mystic, being foreign to their country. Some runners may be seen who paint their faces and legs with white chalk, near Batopilas, for instance.

They do not run at an extraordinary speed, but very steadily, hour after hour, mile after mile. Good runners make forty miles in six or eight hours. At one race, when they covered according to calculation twenty-one miles in two hours, I timed the leading runner and found that he made 290 feet in nineteen seconds on the first circuit, and on the next in twenty-four seconds. At a race rehearsal I saw them cover four miles in half an hour.

The public follows the race with great enthusiasm from beginning to end, the interest growing with each circuit. Many begin to follow the runners, shouting to them and urging them on. They also help them by pointing out the ball so that they can kick it without stopping to look for it. The wives of the contestants heat water and prepare pinole, which they hold out in drinking-gourds to the men as they pass. The latter stop for a few seconds to partake of this their favourite dish; and if this cannot be done, the tepid water is thrown over the shoulders of the runners, by way of refreshing them. As darkness comes on, torches of resinous pine wood are lighted and carried along to illuminate the path for the runners, that they may not stumble, making the scene one of extreme picturesqueness, as these torch-bearers, demon-like, hurry through the forest.

One contestant after another drops out. The excitement becomes wilder; more and more people join in accompanying the few runners left, their principal motive being to shout encouraging words to the runners and urge them to exert themselves to the utmost. And at last the best man comes in, generally alone, the others having either given up the contest or being far behind.

The race usually commences at midday; but often the bets are not finished until late in the afternoon. It may last four hours and even longer. A famous runner, now dead, could run from mid-day until sunrise. There is no prize for the winner himself, except the

golden opinions he earns among the women ; and his
father may accept presents from lucky bettors.   A man
who wins a cow is expected to give two pesos to the

Tarahumare Women Crossing a Stream in Their Race.

victorious runner; in case he wins a goat he gives half
a real.

The race over, the wagers are immediately paid and
the Indians quickly disperse, soon to arrange for another contest.

Sometimes there is an old man's race preceding that
of the young men, the latter being always the principal
event of the day.   Races are also run by women, and

the betting and excitement that prevail on these occasions run as high as at the men's races,
though on a smaller scale.
Instead of tossing the ball
with their toes, they use a
large wooden fork, with two
or three prongs, to pitch it
forward. Sometimes they
have a ring of twisted strips
of yucca leaves instead of
the ball, but more often two
interlocked rings which they
throw ahead with a stick
curved at the end. This
game, which is called rowé-
mala (rōwé signifies a ring),
must be very ancient, for
rings of this kind have sometimes been found in ancient
cliff-dwellings. It is certainly a strange sight to see these
sturdy amazons race heavily

Fork and Wood-
en Ball Used in
Women's Game.
Length of Fork,
69 ctm.; diameter
of Ball, 6.5 ctm.

Stick and
Ring Used
in Women's
Game. Length
of Stick, 85
ctm.; diameter
of Ring, 11
ctm.

along with astonishing perseverance, when
creeks and water-holes come in their way,
simply lifting their skirts *à la Diane* and making short
work of the crossing.

CHAPTER XVI

RELIGION—MOTHER MOON BECOMES THE VIRGIN MARY—MYTHS—
THE CREATION—THE DELUGE—FOLK-LORE—THE CROW'S STORY
TO THE PARROT—BROTHER COYOTE—BELIEFS ABOUT ANIMALS.

THE pagans or *gentiles* in the barrancas say that
they have two gods, but no devil. These gods
are Father Sun (Nonorúgami) and Mother Moon
(Yerúgami). The Sun guards the men in the daytime ; therefore the Tarahumares do not transact business after sunset. He also makes the animals sleep.
The Moon watches at night, and is the special deity of
the women. In her nightly vigils she is assisted by her
son, the Morning Star, who commands all the other
stars, because they are his sons and they are Tarahumares. The Stars advise their brothers on earth when
thieves are entering their houses. When the Tarahumares affirm anything solemnly, they say, " By those
above ! " meaning the Sun, Moon, and the Stars.

But the greater part of the Tarahumares are nominally Christians, though all that they know of Christianity are the words *Señor San José* and *Maria Santis-
sima.* Moreover, they have adopted the words *Tata*
(Father) *Dios* (God) for their Father Sun ; and the
Virgin Mary becomes with them a substitute for
Mother Moon, and in natural sequence the wife of
Tata Dios. They celebrate in their own peculiar way
all the Christian feasts they know, with as much pleasure and as elaborately as their own native ceremonies.

Next in importance is the Devil, whom they fear even more than their own sorcerers.   He is always represented with a big beard, such as the Mexicans wear. He is old and has only one eye, and the shamans have seen him often.   He plays the guitar, but never the violin, because the bow and the strings form a cross. He would like very much to go to heaven, and the shamans have to work hard to keep him from doing so. There is also a female devil, his wife, who bears many children, always twins, who are the original Mexicans.

Their paradise. consists in big ranches, where they will get all the animals which in this life they sacrificed to Tata Dios.   The occupation of Tata Dios in heaven is to run foot-races with the angels, while the Devil vies with the sorcerers in making the lives of the Tarahumares uncomfortable, he being the chief sorcerer of all.

The Tarahumares are the sons of God, and the Mexicans the sons of the Devil.   For this reason the Tarahumares say that it is no crime to eat the cows of the Mexicans; they think the cows do not really belong to the Shabotshi anyway.   Neither do they tell when a Tarahumare steals anything from a Mexican, while they are very quick to find out if one Tarahumare steals from another.

I give here some of the myths and traditions of the tribe.   Those which Christian ideas have entered into will easily be recognised, and it is not necessary to draw special attention to them.

CREATION MYTHS

In the beginning there were many worlds before this, but one after the other came to an end.   Just before the world was destroyed for the last time, all the rivers flowed toward the place where the sun rises.   But now the waters also flow toward the other side, where the sun sets.*

The bears put the world into shape. Before their time it was nothing but a waste of sand.

In ancient times there were plenty of lagoons around Guachochic; but the land was put in order, when the people came and began to dance yūmarí.

The rocks were at first soft and small; but they grew until they became large and hard. They have life inside.

The people grew up from the soil, while the earth was as level as a field ready for sowing. But in those days they lived to be only one year old, and then they died like the flowers.

According to another tradition they descended from heaven with corn and potatoes in their ears, and were led by Tata Dios into these mountains, the middle of the world, having originally come from the north-east or east.

THE SUN AND THE MOON IN THE BEGINNING OF THE WORLD

In the beginning the Sun and the Moon were alone, and they were children. They wore dresses made of palm-leaves, and they lived in a house thatched with palm-leaves. They had neither cattle nor sheep. Both the Sun and the Moon were dark, and the Morning Star was the only one that shed any light on the earth. The Moon was eating lice from the hair of the Sun, and the Morning Star was watching at night. There were 600 Tarahumares at that time, and they were much hampered by the darkness. They could not do their work, and they had to hold each other's hands, and they were

---

* The Rio Fuerte, the only large water-course in the Tarahumare country, empties into the Pacific Ocean.

stumbling all the time. Then they cured the Sun and the Moon by dipping small crosses into tesvino, and touching the Sun and the Moon on the chest, on the head, and on the back. Then the Sun and the Moon began to shine and to shed light.

STAR LEGEND

A man lived with three women. He was making arrows while they went to look for squirrels and wood-chucks, and when they could find none they killed their father. Then they said: " It is of no use to stop here any longer. Let us go away." When the man saw them running away he shot arrows after them. The women were ascending to heaven, holding each other's hands, and he transfixed them to the sky, where they can still be seen just as they rose, as three bright stars in the belt of Orion. The three women remained in heaven, but the man remained in the world and was changed into a coyote.

DELUGE LEGENDS

When the world became full of water, a little girl and a little boy climbed up on a mountain, called La-váchi (gourd), which is south of Panalachic, and when the waters subsided they came down again. They brought three grains of corn and three beans with them. The rocks were soft after the flood, and the footprints of the little boy and the little girl may still be seen. They planted the corn and went to sleep and had a dream that night; then they harvested, and all the Tarahuma-res are descended from them.

The Tarahumares were fighting among themselves, and Tata Dios sent much rain, and all the people per-ished. After the flood he sent three men and three women to people the earth. They planted corn at once,

bringing three kinds, the same varieties still found here
—soft corn, hard corn, and yellow corn.

GIANTS

On the heights once lived giants.   They were as big
as pine-trees and had heads as big as bowlders.   They
taught the Tarahumares how to plant corn, by cutting
down trees and burning them, but they ate children.

A woman bore a giant in a cave, which was situated
very high up on the side of a valley.   She died, because the child was so large, and he was taken care
of by his grandmother.   Once when she was asleep, she
turned over and crushed him.

From Wasivori (near Cusarare) came giants to Nararachic to ask alms.   Tesvino they liked very much.
They worked very fast, and the Tarahumares put them
to hoe and weed the corn, and gave them food and
tesvino.   But the giants were fierce, and ravished the
women while the latter were under the influence of the
Moon ; therefore the Tarahumares got very angry and
they mixed a decoction made from the chilicote-tree
with the corn that they gave the giants to eat, and the
giants died.

TATA DIOS AND THE DEVIL—THE SHEEP AND THE DEER—WHY THE COCKS CROW IN THE MORNING *

Tata Dios came down into the world, and he had in
his house many large jars filled with strong tesvino.   On
the other side of the river Huerachic, in the big arroyos,
lived the Devil.   He was very poor, and he had only
one small jar with tesvino, and that was bad.   The Devil
and his brother invited Tata Dios to come and drink
tesvino with them.   Tata Dios went to the Devil's house,

---

* As related by an old "Christian" Tarahumare woman in Huerachic, on the
upper Rio Fuerte.

and they gave him the jar and the drinking-gourd, and
he sat down to drink ; but he did not get intoxicated
because there was not enough tesvino.   When he had
emptied the jar, Tata Dios said : " Now we will go to
my house and drink tesvino ; I have some, too."   They
accepted the invitation, and all went away together,
and Tata Dios gave them a large jar full of tesvino and
the drinking-gourd.   They drank much, and the Devil
and his brother sang like the Mexicans, until they lay
down on the ground completely overcome.   Later in
the night the Devil rose, and he went to the wife of Tata
Dios.   And when she awoke, she was very angry, and
roused her husband, and he fought with the Devil, until
Tata Dios got killed.   But after a while he rose and
said to the Devil, " Now go away, go below."   " I am
going home to get my weapons," said the Devil.   But
first he went into the house of Tata Dios and robbed
him of his money, and [noticing the reporter's book]
of his books and everything.   He hid all the things in
his house and Tata Dios came to look for them.   Tata
Dios again was very angry, and they fought until he
was killed.   But this time, too, he rose and said to the
Devil, "Go below," and the Devil went below and remained there, and Tata Dios went home.

One day at dawn the people saw the lands full with
sheep everywhere.   On a flat stone Tata Dios drew
figures like the tracks of the deer, and from them all the
deer originated.

When Tata Dios returned to heaven, he carried in
his right hand a rooster, which he placed on top of a
palm-tree.   The cock crowed three times while Tata
Dios ascended to heaven.   After this, whenever the
sun rises in the morning, the cocks on earth respond
when they hear the cocks in heaven crow.

After Tata Dios had gone to heaven he never came back. He is angry with the Tarahumares, and he wants to destroy the world, but the Virgin says: "Let the people alone; I pity the family we left behind." This is the reason why the world stands.

When Tata Dios went away, he said, "I will leave two crosses here." He then put up a cross where the sun sets at the end of the world, and another where the sun rises. The cross in the east he uses when he rises to heaven and when he comes to visit the Tara-humares, and the cross in the west is for the Tarahu-mares when they die and go to heaven. Between these two crosses the Tarahumares live. They would like to go to the crosses and worship before them, but they are prevented from doing so by large bodies of water. They therefore set up small crosses in front of their houses, and before them they hold their dances, and God comes to eat near these crosses. He only eats the soul or substance of the food, and leaves the rest for the people.

THE GIANTS, THE CROW, AND THE BLACKBIRD

The Crow, who is very knowing, told the following story to the Parrot, who told it to the pagans:

The Blackbird and the Crow, long, long ago, saw a contest between two giants, who made a bet as to which of them could throw a stone farthest. The stakes were four deer. One giant, called Gōlí, carried a bird in his hand and threw it instead of the stone; so he won; then he returned to where the Blackbird and the Crow were standing. The Blackbird said to the Crow, "They will not do us any harm until they stoop to pick up a stone." But the Crow replied, "Maybe they bring the stone in their hands." So they flew away, and while they were flying the Crow said, "I am going to the mountain to look for my wife and my son. They went away and have been lost for six days."

THE DEER, THE TOAD, AND THE CROW

The Crow set out for the mountain, where the Deer and the Toad were making a bet. "Let us try," they said, "who can see the sun first in the morning." The stakes were twenty-five Gadflies, and they asked the Crow to be a witness to the contest. In the morning they were ready to watch for the sun. The Toad was looking westward from the highest mountain, but the Deer looked to the east. The Toad said, "Look here, Brother Crow, I have already seen the sun starting," and the Crow said to the Deer: "Brother Deer, you have lost. Give him the twenty-five Gadflies." The Deer asked one day's time to catch the Gadflies, but the Toad thought he was not going to pay him, and said to the Deer, "Let us have a race, that you may settle your bet." The Deer readily consented to this, and a stone was put up as the goal. The Toad went away to call many other toads, and placed them at intervals toward the goal, and when the Deer arrived at the stone the Toad was already sitting on it, and said, "Brother Deer, you have lost." And the Deer went away.

Then the Toad said to the Gadflies: "Go and sting the Deer much, that he may have to run quickly. If you will sting him much, I will never eat you." The Gadflies were vexed with the Deer, because he had put them up on a bet, therefore they were very willing to sting the Deer, and they have been stinging him ever since.

STORY OF THE COYOTE

The Coyote asked permission from Tata Dios to come into the world, and Tata Dios asked him what he would do there. The Coyote replied that he would steal the animals and the corn from the Tarahumares. Then

The Coyote, *Canis latrans.*

Tata Dios gave him permission to go and make a living in this way, because the Coyote did not know how to work.

THE MOUNTAIN LION, THE COYOTE, AND THE GREY FOX

The Coyote challenged the Mountain Lion to a contest, that they might see which of them had the better eyesight and was the smarter. The Lion said, " Let us see who can first shoot an animal." Then he proposed that they should go to a water-hole, and to this the Coyote agreed; so they started out on the hunt. The Lion climbed up on a tree, but the Coyote remained below on the ground, and paid no attention to what the Lion was doing. A deer came, and the Lion struck it dead. The Coyote saw this from where he was hunting, and by and by he found a dead mare. When they met again the Lion said to the Coyote, "Well, how did you get on?" The Coyote replied: "Very well; I killed a mare." But the mare had been dead so long that she was smelling. Therefore the Lion said to the Coyote, "Don't be a liar," and he chased him off, and the Coyote was ashamed of himself.

The Coyote next met the Grey Fox, and told him to go and challenge the Lion. The Grey Fox went to the Lion and said: "How do you do, Brother Lion? I hear you got the best of Brother Coyote." The Lion replied: "No, Brother Grey Fox; the Coyote made a fool of himself." Then the Grey Fox said: "Let us see whether you can get the best of me, and which of us can catch a rabbit first." So they went to the mountain to look for rabbits. At sunrise the Lion took a position facing the north, and the Grey Fox faced south, and both of them watched for rabbits. After spying for a while, the Lion saw one, but by that time the Grey Fox was asleep alongside of him. So the Lion said to the rabbit: "Pass right between us, and then go to the hole in the oak-tree on the rock, and act as if you wanted to go into the hole, but go away to one side." Then the Lion woke up the Grey Fox and said: "Over there is a rabbit. He went into a small hole into which I cannot follow him; but you are small, and you can catch him." The Grey Fox just saw the rabbit's tail disappearing behind the rock, but the rabbit hid himself, and did not enter the hole, as the Lion had told him. "All right," said the Grey Fox, "I will go; but, as you saw the rabbit first, you have won the bet." But the Lion said: "No; you go into the hole, and fetch the rabbit out and eat him." Then the Grey Fox entered the hole, and the Lion made a fire in front of it, and when the Grey Fox came out again he was burned, and his feet were sore from the fire. That is why the Grey Fox always walks so lightly.

And he reproached the Lion, saying that he was very bad, and begged him to let him go and not to kill him. He cried and went to hide himself in a cave, because he was afraid of the Lion. Then the Humming-bird who lived in the cave stung him in the face with his bill and in the eyes, and he went away and never came back again.

THE HENS, THE GREY FOX, AND THE COYOTE

The Woodpecker made a guitar and gave it to the Butterfly to play on, and the Cock danced a pascual, and the Cricket danced with the Locust, and the Hen was singing. While the dance was going on, the Coyote came to see what he could get from the feast, and the Grey Fox also came, and he brought some tunas (fruit of the nopal cactus). They were very nice and sweet, and he gave one to the Coyote and said, "Here, Brother Coyote, take this nice mouthful." He had well rubbed off the spines, and the fruit tasted well to the Coyote. It made his heart glad, and he wanted more. The Grey Fox said to the Coyote, "I will give you more tunas, but you must eat them with your eyes shut." He gave him some tunas from which he had not cleaned off the spines, and as the spines hurt the Coyote he became very angry and wanted to eat the Grey Fox. But the Fox said to him: "Don't be angry, Brother Coyote: I will give you a drink; and don't howl, because there are dogs around." He went to the Cock and to the Hen, and asked them for tesvino, and he brought it to the Coyote and said, "Here, Brother Coyote, drink this." The Coyote drank two gourdsful, and then a third one, and when he had finished this he began to howl, because he was very drunk, and he asked the Grey Fox, "Why are they all dancing?" The Grey Fox replied: "They dance, because Miss

Cricket married Mister Locust; therefore the Butterfly is playing on the guitar, and the Cock dances with delight, and the Hen is singing." But the Coyote said: "I don't want the Hen to sing; I want to eat her." Then the Grey Fox took the Coyote into the arroyo and told him to remain there, while he went to fetch the Hen. But instead of the Hen he got two very fierce dogs and put them in a bag, and carried them into the arroyo, where the Coyote was waiting. He was very drunk and very angry, and he said to the Grey Fox, "Why did you keep me waiting so long, you cursed old Grey Fox!" The Grey Fox replied: "Don't be angry, Brother Coyote; here I bring you some very nice Hens. I was looking for many of them, that is why I remained away so long. Now, shall I let them out one by one, or do you want them all at once?" The Coyote replied, "Let them out all at once, that I may have a good old time with them." Then the Grey Fox opened the bag, and out came the two fierce dogs; and they caught the Coyote and bit him and tore him to pieces. The Grey Fox ran away and hid himself, but afterward he came and got the paws of the Coyote and threw them into a water-pool.

THE MOUNTAIN LION AND THE BEAR

The Mountain Lion killed a deer, and the Bear wanted to take it away from him. They fought, and the Lion won, and the Bear asked his pardon, because the Lion is more powerful than the Bear.

THE FROG AND THE COYOTE

The Frog and the Coyote made a wager as to which of them would gain in a foot-race. They were to run along a ridge, and return to a point close by the starting-point. The Coyote lost, because the Frog jumped directly over to the finishing-point. This happened twice, and the Coyote wanted to kill the Frog, but the Frog dived into a water-hole, where the Coyote could not catch him.

The Bears, whose skin is of the same color as the Tarahumares, are called "grandfathers," ūmúli, and are so to speak their forebears. In ancient times they danced on top of the mountains, where they have roads yet.

Often the bears are sorcerers, who, after death, assumed the shape of these animals. In fact, there are two kinds of bears, one that is real, and another one that is a dead Tarahumare. The people do not know which is which. Only the shamans can make the distinction, and it is useless to try and kill the man-bear, because he has a very hard skin, and arrows cannot pierce it. He is the very devil.

The following curious incident happened near Nararachic a few years ago : A bear had done much damage to a Tarahumare's corn-field. Some forty Indians with over fifty dogs gathered together to kill the bear. In order to make the dogs ferocious, the Indians set them to fight among each other, by way of preparing them for the hunt. The Indians now divided themselves into several parties, and presently one lot encountered the bear. They asked the shaman who was with them whether the creature was a bear or something else, and he replied, "Let the dogs on and see." As the dogs had never seen a bear, they were timid, and did not bark or attack the beast ; therefore the shaman said : "This is not a bear. All is lost. The dogs do not know him, and the bear does not see the dogs with his eyes. He is from hell, and he is a devil, who came here in the shape of a bear, because he wants to eat us.

Let him alone and let us all go away." And they all
retreated.

The mountain lion is a good animal and watches
over the people. When he sees an animal such as the
bear or the coyote approach a man, he roars to warn
the man ; and if the man pays no attention, the lion
attacks the animal to save the man ; therefore strips of
his skin are worn around the ankles and the neck as a
protection.

The grey fox is considered an astute animal and is
feared. If he passes by a house in which there is a sick
person, and calls three times, the patient will die. One
of my Indian men related the following story : One
night he and another man were sleeping in a house
when he heard the grey fox whistle. At first he did
not know what it was, and he said to his companion,
" Listen, what is that ?" The other one said, " This
is a very bad thing, very ugly." He was a man who
knew something, and he said, " If this grey fox returns
for two nights more and whistles outside of the house
of our sick neighbour, that man will die." My informant did not believe this at the time ; but the next night
the grey fox returned and whistled very uncannily, and
on the third night he did it again. And on the following morning a man came and asked the Indian to help
him to bury the neighbour who had died during the
night. They went to the house of the dead man, and
"then," the narrator concluded, " I knew that the grey
fox had said the truth, for the grey fox never tells a
lie."

The grey fox and the rabbit in ancient times danced
rutubúri.

The horned toad holds the world. It says : " Don't
tread on me ! I am the colour of the earth and I hold

the world; therefore walk carefully, that you do not tread on me."

The master of the deer lives inside of the mountains, in the earth; therefore the Tarahumares place small quantities of corn and beans, or three arrows in a jar, on top of the highest mountain to buy the deer from the one below.

The brown ground squirrel (chipawíki), which lives among rocks and seldom ascends trees, is thought to become a serpent. This belief is also current among certain classes of Mexicans. A Mexican told me that a man once smashed the head of a chipawíki in the hollow of a tree, and when he wanted to take his game out, he found that the rest of the animal had the body of a serpent. It cannot be used for sacrifices.

Rats become bats.

The owl is very bad. Whenever it comes to a house and screeches, somebody falls ill. If it calls three times, in three consecutive nights, the sick person will die. The owl is also very smart. It knows when the Tarahumare's blanket (in which he is wrapped when sleeping along the fire) is going to be burned. When the owl hoots near a home it says, "Chu-i, chu-i, chu-i,"— "dead, dead, dead." Owls are killed but not eaten.

The goat sucker makes darts through the air and calls down rain. It has two nice fat young, which the Tarahumares consider a great delicacy.

The crow is much in disfavour because it eats the corn. Only the young crows are eaten.

The large swifts (olamáka) are thought to be witches, who pierce the souls of people and eat them. They are used by the sorcerers, whom they obey like dogs. Once a woman was sitting in a corn-field watching it by the side of a fire, and making yarn, when a swift settled on her skirt. She told a girl to bring a large basket, with which she covered the bird up, caught it and had it for many years. Every night the bird flew away, and then returned in the morning. Once, when the woman was absent at a tesvino feast, the girl killed the bird and roasted it. She could not eat it, however, because it had such a bad smell, and the woman found it on her return in the basket, dead and roasted. The girl ran away and the raccoons ate the corn the woman was watching.

The giant woodpecker during the wet season rises high up toward the sun; that is why he gets his tail burned.

When the Tarahumares handle any kind of fish they take care not to touch their hair, for fear that it may turn grey and they become old.

The rattlesnakes are the companions of the sorcerers and watch to meet them and then talk with them. A Mexican once killed a rattlesnake, and the Indian grew very angry and said that the snake had protected his house; now he had no one to guard it.

Large serpents, which only the shamans can see, are thought to live in the rivers. They have horns and very big eyes.

The dragon-fly has no song; it flies about without making a noise.

Tata Dios put sheep into the world; they are good animals because they give wool from which people can weave blankets, and their meat is good, and they do not weep when they are killed. But goats were put into the world by the Devil; their hair is of no use, their meat is bad, and they howl much when they are killed.

CHAPTER XVII

THE SHAMANS OR WISE MEN OF THE TRIBE—HEALERS AND PRIESTS IN ONE—DISEASE CAUSED BY LOOKS AND THOUGHTS —EVERYBODY AND EVERYTHING HAS TO BE CURED—NOBODY FEELS WELL WITHOUT HIS "DOCTOR"—SORCERY—THE POWERS OF EVIL ARE AS GREAT AS THOSE OF GOOD—REMARKABLE CURE FOR SNAKE BITE—TREPANNING AMONG THE ANCIENT TARAHUMARES.

WITHOUT his shaman the Tarahumare would feel lost, both in this life and after death. The shaman is his priest and physician. He performs all the ceremonies and conducts all the dances and feasts by which the gods are propitiated and evil is averted, doing all the singing, praying, and sacrificing. By this means, and by instructing the people what to do to make it rain and secure other benefits, he maintains good terms for them with their deities, who are jealous of man and bear him ill-will. He is also on the alert to keep those under his care from sorcery, illness, and other evil that may befall them. Even when asleep he watches and works just as if his body were awake. Though real illness is the exception with him, the Tarahumare believes that an ounce of prevention is better than a pound of cure, and for this reason he keeps his doctor busy curing him, not only to make his body strong to resist illness, but chiefly to ward off sorcery, the main source of trouble in the Indian's life. The demand for shamans is therefore great, but the supply is quite equal to it. For instance, in the little village of Nararachic and the neighbouring ranches, where there are about 180 households, twenty-five shamans are living, each of whom takes care of about twenty souls, though only about ten of them enjoy great reputation in the community.

Before a man is allowed to consider himself a shaman, he is examined by a "board" of recognised members of the profession, who pass upon his fitness to enter their ranks.

These priest-doctors have their specialties. Some sing only at rutuburi or yumari dances, others only at hikuli-feasts. A few of them do not sing at all, but are merely healers, although far the greater number also sing at the feasts. Those who make a specialty of the hikuli cult are considered the greatest healers. They all conscientiously fast and pray, complying with the demands of the gods, which impose restrictions and abstinence, and they are therefore called "righteous men" (owirúami). They are the wise men of the tribe ; and as rainmakers, healers, and keepers of the heritage of tribal wisdom and traditions, their influence is powerful.

Their services are never rendered gratuitously ; in fact, what with the payments they receive from singing at feasts and curing the sick, they generally manage to live better than the rest of the people. Whenever a shaman is hungry, he goes to the house of some of his well-to-do clients and cures the family, receiving all the food he wants in payment for his efforts, for what would become of the people if the shaman should die ? The Devil would surely take them away at once. Therefore the best parts of the meat from the animal killed for the feast is given to the shamans, and they generally get all the tesvino they can hold. In winter time, when numerous feasts are being held, the shamans are nearly all the time under the influence of their native stimulants. Yet this does not seem to harm them, nor does it in the estimation of the people detract from the efficacy of their singing ; the curing is no less potent, even though the doctor can hardly keep from falling all over his patient. It is always incumbent on the shamans to be peaceful, and they never fight at the feasts.

The singing shamans invariably have a primitive musical instrument, the rattle, with which they beat time to their singing and dancing.   Ordinarily it is made

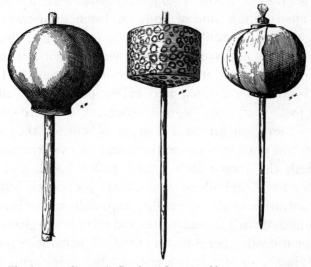

Tarahumare Shaman's Rattles.   Length of longest, 31.5 ctm.

from a gourd filled with pebbles and mounted on a short stick which serves as a handle. Another kind is made from coarse shavings glued together. The latter variety is not infrequently decorated with daubs of red or some similar painting. Sometimes at the feast the shaman, even nowadays, may be seen wearing a head-dress made of the plumes of birds. Through the plumes the birds are thought to impart all that they know. Besides, the plumes are supposed to keep the wind from entering the shaman's body, and thus prevent him from falling ill.

When curing, the shamans may sometimes use rational means. There is in existence around Norogachic for instance, a kind of sweating-bath, made by placing in a hole in the ground, just large enough for a man to sit in, several hot stones, pouring water on them, and covering them up with branches of the fragrant mountain cedar. The steam passing through the latter is credited with curative power.

The Indians know several excellent medicinal herbs. Palo amarillo is a kind of household remedy used extensively in every family. There are many other highly valued herbs and trees, some of which have a wonderfully refreshing and invigorating aromatic scent. Headache is cured by a green herb called pachoco, of which they smell until they begin to sneeze. To cure constipation they boil ari with a grain of salt, or they heat stones and pour water over them and sit over the steam.

Both the sacred little cactus called híkuli and the maguey have undoubtedly medicinal properties, but the administration of these remedies, especially of the former, is connected with so many rites and ceremonies that their therapeutic value becomes obscured. The curative power of tesvino is absolutely magical, and this is the remedy to which recourse is most commonly had. In administering it the shaman makes his customary passes, and exhales over the patient to blow away the disease. He also dips a small cross into the liquor, and with the wetted end taps the sick man on the head, neck, shoulders, and back, and draws crosses over his arms. Finally the patient is given three spoonfuls of the liquor, while all the members of the family stand around and murmur approvingly, " Thank you, thank you." Occasionally tesvino is exclusively used for curing, with the aid of two small crosses, one of red Brazil wood, the other of white pine. If he chooses, a shaman may provoke illness as well as cure it, but he cannot cure the person he made ill.

When a shaman is asked to cure a person of any complaint, real or imaginary, his first move is to find the cause of the trouble. According to his opinion illness is brought on either by the wind or by sorcery. From the former kind of disease nobody dies, although the heart, the liver, or the head may be attacked; but the other kind is serious. Sorcerers may put snakes into the legs, and such animals as centipedes, toads, larvæ, scorpions, or even small bears into the body of some unfortunate person, and these disturbers have to be drawn out at once or else they will eat the sick man's heart. The shaman therefore first feels the patient all over, to find if something—in other words, the disease-bringing animal—is moving underneath the skin. Illness may also result from small stones, or the spine of the nopal placed in the body by the same agency.

A person suspected of having been bewitched is told to hold his mouth open to the sun, that the shaman may see whether the evil entered the body through this aperture. People become bewitched at night through the openings of the body, and the shaman also examines the nostrils, ears, etc. It is also the shaman's business to find out who caused the trouble, and since he can see more than ordinary people he is able to track the offender.

Some people by their mere looks or thoughts are liable to make a person ill. Such illness may be brought on in retaliation for some slight or offence, and may even result in death. The first thoughts of a person falling ill are: Whom have I offended? What have I taken that I should have left alone, and what have I kept that I should have given? Then the shaman may tell him to find the person to whom he had refused to

give food, and the sick one and his wife go from house
to house asking the people: "Was it you whom I refused food? Someone has made me ill, and I want him
to make me well again." If he can find the person

Rubio, the Shaman.

whom he had offended, and arrange matters with him, he
will recover.

The doctor may find that the person's heart is on
the wrong side, and prescribe a liberal allowance of
tesvino to get it back to its proper place. But generally the skill of the shaman is taxed more severely
and he resorts to the more direct and powerful methods of magic. A common occurrence is that of illness

caused by maggots, which the shaman has to extract
from the patient by means of a sucking-tube, a short
piece of reed about three inches long, cut from a kind
of reed different from that of the arrow-shaft. He
places it on the afflicted spot, and after sucking vigorously for a minute or so empties from his mouth into
his hand or into a corn-leaf, what purports to be the
maggots. I never had an opportunity of examining
closely the small white bits of something or other that
he spit out, but they seemed to me to be tiny pieces of
buckskin which the man had secreted in his mouth and
which swelled up when saturated with saliva. To the
shaman they represent maggots ; that is, the embodiment of the disease, and all the people firmly believe
that they are maggots. The corn-leaf and its contents
are buried; a cross is made on the ground over the spot
and a ceremonial circuit run around it. When resting
between operations, the shaman places his sucking-tube
into a bowl of water in which some herbs are soaking.

The mode of curing, however, varies. A common
way in use near Guachochic is to make the patient
stand on all fours and bathe him well with water; then
to place him on a blanket and carry him over a fire toward the cross and the four corners of the world. When
put down on the ground again he lies or kneels on the
blanket, and the shaman places his tube against the
afflicted part and begins to suck forcibly, while the rest
of the people stand around with sticks, ready to kill the
disease so as to prevent it from returning and doing
harm to others. Presently the shaman produces from
his mouth a small stone, which he asserts was the cause
of the disease. While the people are furiously beating
the air, he proceeds at once to bury it in the earth, or in
the bottom of the river, into which he dives. He may
suck out as many as eight stones, but generally contents

himself with four ; and for treating a man in this way
he receives four almuds of maize.

On one occasion, when I had taken a little cold, I
asked a shaman friend whether he could cure me.
"Certainly I can," was the confident reply. He took
from a little basket, in which he kept his hikuli or
sacred cacti and probably similar valuables, three black
stones and said that he would sell one of these to me ;
if I put it into warm water it would cure me. This was
not quite to my liking, as I wanted him to perform the
magical feat of sucking maggots out of the skin. He
complied with my request, and told me to go ahead to
my camp, whither he would follow me soon. On his
arrival I offered him some food, as my case was not
urgent, but he declined, and proceeded to cure me. A
saddle blanket was spread out for me to kneel on, and
my Mexican and Indian attendants were told to retire,
while he made his examination. Having ascertained
that I had a headache, he took my head between his
dirty hands, pressed it, applied his lips to my right ear,
and commenced to suck very energetically. This was
rather trying to my nerves, though not unendurably so.
Presently he let go his hold, and spit out quite a lot of
blood into a cup an Indian boy was holding out to him.
He repeated the operation on my left ear with the same
result. "More pain ?" he asked. "Yes," I said, "in
my right hand." He immediately grabbed that member
in his mouth, biting almost through the skin over the
pulse, and after having sucked for a little while, deposited contents, of a similar nature, into the cup from
his mouth. It was afterward found that the blood was
mixed with a considerable number of grass seeds, which
had been the cause of my illness. I had not known that
I was so "seedy."

The curing is often performed at dances, during the

night, as the family who give the feast expect to receive, in return for all their trouble and expense, the benefit of the shaman's magic powers, whether any of them are ill or not.   Once a man, his wife, and his child had been cured with tesvino, but nevertheless they still anxiously looked to the shaman for more treatment, apparently feeling that they needed more strength against coming

Rubio, the Shaman, and his Wife at Home in their Cave.

evil.   The woman said : " Yesterday I fell into the water and got wet and felt ill, and in the night I dreamed that I was dead and that you cured me." To this the doctor replied, " Yes, that is why I came to cure you." Then, yielding to their beseeching glances, he daubed them again, this time holding their hands and with a little cross in his left hand.   Then he said : " Now you need not be afraid ; I have cured you well.   Do not walk

Shaman Rubio's Cave, Seen from the Outside.

about any more like fools and do not get wet again." And they were content.

There is a shaman near Baqueachic (bāká = bamboo reed) who has a great reputation for curing cattle, or rather for keeping them in health. Every year he makes a tour of the different ranches, and the Indians bring their animals to him to be treated. A large hole is dug in the ground and a fire kindled in it. Then some green branches of the mountain cedar and some copal are thrown in and burned, and the animals driven one by one through the smoke. Since the veterinary gets one animal for each ceremony, he becomes quite rich.

The shamans also undertake to cure the sun and the moon, because these, too, are often ill and have to be righted. Not a feast is held in which some spoonfuls from the jars containing the remedies are not thrown up for the benefit of the sun and the moon. Occasionally, however, special ceremonies have to be performed to cure the celestial bodies, particularly the moon, because from her all the stars receive their light. At the period of the dark moon she is considered to be sick and tied up by the Devil, and the world is sad. Then the shamans assemble to consult about her ailment and the means of curing her. An ox may be killed and tesvino made. In killing the animal, care is taken not to injure the heart, which is treated with great ceremony. The people always avoid touching it, and at sacrifices they hang it with the lungs to a stick raised near the cross. The shamans stand near, with small earthenware dishes containing copal incense ; while the oldest cuts with his knife four crosses on four diametrically opposite points of the heart, and from the upper part all but slices off a piece, which is left hanging down beside the main part. All the blood the heart contained is sacrificed to the four cardinal points with much singing. Then the shaman asks for an earthen bowl which has never been used before, and in this he places the heart and burns it without adding fat or anything else. The ashes he rubs between his fingers until reduced to a fine dust, which he mixes with water and some medicinal herbs. The shamans stand in the middle, and the people around them, and all are unanimous in their prayer that they may see the moon. Each shaman takes three spoonfuls of medicine, the rest of which is thrown on the cross, and the shamans watch all night.

The Christian Tarahumares even feel called upon to cure the church when those buried in and around it have been noisily dancing and damaging the building to make the people give them tesvino. The principal shaman heads the procession, carrying a jar of the liquor. His assistant holds in one hand a bowl containing water mixed with the crushed leaves of the maguey, and in the other some fresh maguey leaves.   The tesvino, as well as the green water, is liberally thrown upon the walls and the floor of the church to lay the perturbed spirits.

How to cure smallpox is beyond the ken of the shamans, but they try to keep off the dread enemy by making fences of thorny branches of different trees across the paths leading to the houses; and snake-skins, the tail of the grey fox, and other powerful protectors or charms, are hung around the doors of their dwellings to frighten the disease away.   The same purpose is accomplished through the pungent smell produced by burning in the house the horns of cows, sheep, and goats.

The shamans also profess to produce springs by sowing water.   They make a hole one yard deep in the rocky ground.   Water is brought in a gourd and poured into it, together with half an almud of salt.   The hole is then covered up with earth, and after three years a spring forms.

High as the shamans stand in the estimation of the people, they are by no means exempt from the instability of mundane conditions, and the higher a man rises the less secure is his position.   The power to see everything, to guard against evil, and to cure illness issues from the light of his heart, which was given him by Tata Dios.   It enables him to see Tata Dios himself, to talk to him, to travel through space at will, for the shamans are as bright as the sun.   But all this supposed great power to do good may at any moment be turned to evil purposes.   There are indeed some shamans whose kindly, sweet-tempered manners and gentle ways enable them to retain their good reputation to the end ; but few go through life who can keep themselves always above suspicion, especially when they grow older; and innocent persons have on this account been cruelly persecuted.   Such a fate is all the more liable to befall them on account of the recognised ability of a shaman to both cure and produce disease.

No doubt the great quantity of stimulants taken by shamans in the course of their career causes them to go periodically through a state of excitement, which, combined with the enthusiasm which they work themselves up to, gradually gives to these men, who frequently are richly endowed with animal magnetism, a supernatural appearance. Advancing years have their share in making such a man look odd and uncanny, not only on account of his grey hair, wrinkled face, and shaggy eyebrows, but still more by his reserved bearing and distinctive personality. Women shamans, too, may turn bad and become witches.

Much as in cases of heresy among Christian ministers, the other shamans hold a consultation regarding a suspected colleague, and may decide that the light of his heart has failed him and that he is no longer one of them. From that time on, good people avoid him ; they no longer give him food, and do not tolerate him about their homes ; they are afraid of him ; and the better a shaman he was before, the more terrible a sorcerer he is now supposed to have become. Soon every accident that happens in the locality is laid at the accused man's door.

There are, on the other hand, many evil-minded persons who pretend to possess supernatural powers to do harm, and accept payment for services of that kind ; in short, who make it a business to be sorcerers. The power of the sorcerer to do evil is as great as the ability of the good shaman to cure it. The sorcerer may rasp on his notched stick, and sing death and destruction to a person   or to attain his ends he may use hikuli, smooth stones, the corpse or the foreleg of some highly venerated animal and powerful rainmaker, as the toad, which is never killed except by bad persons. A terrible thing in the hands of a sorcerer is a humming-bird stripped of its feathers, dried, and wrapped in pochote wool. To the Tarahumares the brilliant little bird, often mentioned in their songs, is a good and mighty hero-god, but the

Rubio, the Shaman, Examining a man accused of Sorcery.

sorcerer perverts his great power to his own evil purposes. The sorcerer is feared by all ; pregnant women, especially, go out of his way, as he may hinder them from giving birth to their children. When Tarahumares see a shooting star they think it is a dead sorcerer coming to kill a man who did him harm in life, and they huddle together and scream with terror. When the star has passed, they know that somewhere a man has been killed, and that now the sorcerer is taking out his heart.

If a man does any harm to a powerful sorcerer, the latter, after death, enters into a mountain lion or jaguar or bear, and watches by the wayside until the offender comes, when he kills him.

Sorcerers are also believed to prevent rain from falling, and therefore the people were once much pleased when they saw me photographing a sorcerer. The camera was considered a powerful rain-maker, and was thought to make the bad man clean. The people may chastise a man suspected of sorcery, to frighten him from doing further mischief. A sick person also is supposed to improve when the sorcerer who made him ill is punished; but if accidents and misfortune continue to happen, the accused man may be killed. Such extreme measures have been resorted to even in recent years, though rarely.

The magical powers of a sorcerer are appalling. When a Tarahumare walks with a sorcerer in the forest and they meet a bear, the sorcerer may say: " Don't kill him; it is I; don't do him any harm!" or if an owl screeches at night, the sorcerer may say: " Don't you hear me? It is I who am calling."

The sorcerer dies a terrible death. Many dogs bark and run away and come back; they look like fire, but they are not; they are the evil thoughts of the sorcerer. The river, too, makes a greater noise as it flows, as if somebody were dipping up water and pouring it out again. Uncanny, weird noises come from every part of the house, and all the people in it are much frightened. Hardly anyone goes to talk to the dying man, and no one bids him good-bye. The Christian Tarahumares do not bury him in the churchyard with other people, but alone in a remote cave, and they bury all his things with him—his machete his axe, and heavy things that other people never take along, but which the sorcerer, because he is very powerful, can carry with him when he goes to heaven.

As we have seen, the medical education of the sha-mans is extremely limited. Their rational *materia medica* is confined to the hikuli cactus and a few roots and plants. Aside from this they have a cure for snake-bites which is really remarkable. The injured man kills the reptile, cuts out its liver and gall, and smears the lat-ter over the wound ; he may also eat a piece of the liver, but it must be taken from the animal that inflicted the injury ; then he will be well again in three days. If people die of snake-bites, it is because the reptile es-caped. The gall of a rattlesnake has a sickening smell ; even my dogs were repulsed by it when I once killed a four-foot rattler. The method may be considered as in accord with the modern theory that the bile of many animals contains strong antitoxins.

However, there is nothing new under the sun. In the Talmud we find recommended as a cure for hydro-phobia to eat the liver of the dog that bites one ; and in the Apocrypha we read that Tobias was cured of blind-ness by the gall of a fish.

Most surprising of all is the fact that this tribe, which to-day shows but very slight knowledge of surgery, should in former times have practised trepanning. That the Tarahumares understood this art is evident from two skulls which I brought back from their country. The skulls were found under the following circumstances :

In 1894 I stayed for a fortnight in a remote part of the Sierra Madre, called Pino Gordo on account of its magnificent pine-trees. The district is separated on the north from the central part of the Tarahumare country by the deep Barranca de San Carlos, and there are no Mexicans living within its confines. The place in which I found one of the skulls is twenty miles north of the mining town of Guadalupe y Calvo. A lonely trail leads through it on which, only occasionally, perhaps once in the course of a month, a Mexican from the ranches at Guachochic may journey to Guadalupe y Calvo.

One day the principal man of the locality, who had been very friendly to me, showed me a burial-cave. I had persuaded him that it was better for me to take away the bones contained in it, in order to keep them in a good house, than to let them remain where they were, "killing sheep and making people sick." "But why do you want them?" he asked. Having been satisfied on this point, he one day led the way to a wild, steep arroyo, pointed at its head, and having thus indicated where the cave was, at once left me. I made my way as best I could up the steep little gorge, accompanied by one of my men. On arriving at the top I found the entrance to the cave completely covered with stones plastered together with mud. A heap of stones was also piled outside against the wall.

The cave I found very small, and, contrary to the exaggerated reports of the Indians, it contained only three skeletons. According to the custom prevailing throughout part of the country of the Tarahumares, these remains had not been buried. The skeletons were simply lying on their backs, from east to west, as if looking toward the setting sun. A few crudely made clay vessels of the ordinary Tarahumare type were found alongside of them. On gathering the three skulls I was at once struck by a circular hole in the right parietal bone of one of them. As they undoubtedly belonged to the Tarahumares, the question at once occurred to me:

Can it be possible that this barbaric tribe, not particularly advanced in the arts, was capable of trepanning? The remoteness of the place entirely negatives the suggestion that a civilised surgeon could have had anything to do with it.

The skull, the lower jaw of which is missing, is that of a Tarahumare woman over fifty years of age. The age of the specimen itself is impossible to arrive at, on account of the peculiar circumstances in which it was preserved. However, the cranial walls still contained some animal matter, were still somewhat fatty to the touch, and retained some odour. A spindle provided with a whorl made from a piece of pine-bark, which was lying

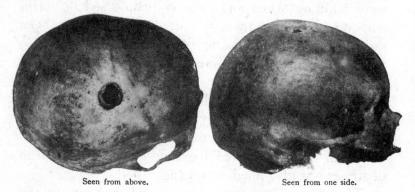

Seen from above.   Seen from one side.

Trepanned Tarahumare Skull, Female.

among the bones in the cave, indicates that the body of this female had not been put there in recent times. This variety of whorl, so far as I can ascertain, has not been observed among the Tarahumares of the present day. It is, indeed, possible that the skeleton may be pre-Columbian.

The skull does not present any deformities or fractures, and the singular aperture is almost exactly round, measuring two centimetres in diameter. A careful examination shows that the cut was made a long time, several years in fact, before death. The regularity of the hole indicates beyond doubt that it is artificial.

Another skull taken from a burial-cave near Nararachic is also that of a female, and the opening here, too, is in the parietal bone, and in almost the same place as the opening in the first skull described. In this second specimen the cavity is almost filled in with new bone, and as in this instance the edges are very regular and uniform, and distinctly beveled, they show that the operation was performed by scraping. This cannot be said of the first specimen found; the almost circular form of the opening, and its perpendicular walls, prove conclusively that in this instance the surgeon did not employ the simple method of scraping the bone. I have never found among the Tarahumares any implement with which such an operation could have been performed. Possibly it was done with a kind of flint wimble with three teeth, much like the instrument used to-day in trepanning by the Berbers in L'Aurés, who cure even headaches by this method. It is, of course, impossible to say now whether the ancients performed the operation simply to relieve the patient of bone splinters, pus, blood, etc., pressing on the brain, or whether it was done to let out an evil spirit. It is the first time that cases of trepanning have been found in Mexico.

CHAPTER XVIII

RELATION OF MAN TO NATURE — DANCING AS A FORM OF WOR-
SHIP LEARNED FROM THE ANIMALS—TARAHUMARE SACRI-
FICES—THE RUTUBURI DANCE TAUGHT BY THE TURKEY—
THE YUMARI LEARNED FROM THE DEER—TARAHUMARE RAIN
SONGS—GREETING THE SUN—TARAHUMARE ORATORY—THE
FLOWING BOWL—THE NATIONAL IMPORTANCE OF TESVINO—
HOMEWARD BOUND.

SINCE the people obtain their subsistence from the products of the soil, they naturally are deeply con-cerned in the weather upon which their crops depend. Rain, therefore, is the focal point from which all their thoughts radiate. Even the plough is dipped into water before it is put to use, in order that it may draw rain. The people may try to force the moon and the sun to give them rain. In times of drought they reproach es-pecially the moon for making the people live on the leaves of the ash-tree and what other poor stuff they can find; on her account they are getting so thin that they can no longer recognise themselves. They scold her, and threaten to denounce her to the sun. The sun himself may be rebuked for lack of rain. At other times they may throw up water to heaven with many ceremonies, that Tata Dios may replenish his supply. Generally, however, their relations with the gods, as with men, are based on the business principle of give and take.

Sacrifices of food, the meat of domestic animals or of game, and of tesvino, are needed to induce Father Sun and Mother Moon to let it rain. The favour of the gods may be won by what for want of a better term may be called dancing, but what in reality is a series of monotonous movements, a kind of rhythmical exercise, kept up sometimes for two nights. By dint of such hard work they think to prevail upon the gods to grant their prayers. The dancing is accompanied by the song of the shaman, in which he communicates his wishes to the unseen world, describing the beautiful effect of the rain, the fog, and the mist on the vegetable world. He invokes the aid of all the animals, mentioning each by name and also calls on them, especially the deer and the rabbit, to multiply that the people may have plenty to eat.

As a matter of fact, the Tarahumares assert that the dances have been taught them by the animals. Like all primitive people, they are close observers of nature. To them the animals are by no means inferior creatures; they understand magic and are possessed of much knowledge, and may assist the Tarahumares in making rain. In spring, the singing of the birds, the cooing of the dove, the croaking of the frog, the chirping of the cricket, all the sounds uttered by the denizens of the greensward, are to the Indian appeals to the deities for rain. For what other reason should they sing or call? For the strange behaviour of many animals in the early spring the Tarahumares can find no other explanation but that these creatures, too, are interested in rain. And as the gods grant the prayers of the deer expressed in its antics and dances, and of the turkey in its curious playing, by sending the rain, they easily infer that to please the gods they, too, must dance as the deer and play as the turkey.

From this it will be understood that dance with these people is a very serious and ceremonious matter, a kind of worship and incantation rather than amusement. Never do man and woman dance together, as in the waltz and polka of civilised people. The very word for dancing, "nolávoa," means literally "to work." The wise old man may reproach laggard, inexperienced younger ones, saying, "Why do you not go to work?" meaning that they should go to the dance and not stand idly about while the feast is going on. If the Tara-humares did not comply with the commands of Father Sun and dance, the latter would come down and burn up the whole world.

The Indian never asks his god to forgive whatever sin he may have committed; all he asks for is rain, which to him means something to eat, and to be free of evil. The only wrong toward the gods of which he may consider himself guilty is that he does not dance enough. For this offence he asks pardon. Whatever bad thoughts or actions toward man he may have on his conscience are settled between himself and the person offended. I once asked a prominent heathen shaman why the people were not baptised, and he said: "Because Tata Dios made us as we are. We have always been as you see us. People do not need to be baptised, because there is no devil here. Tata Dios is not angry with us; why should he be? Only when people do bad things does he get angry. We make much beer and dance much, in order that he may remain content; but when people talk much, and go around fighting, then he gets angry and does not give us rain."

Dancing not only expresses prayers for rain and life, but also petitions the gods to ward off evil in any shape, as diseases of man, beast, or crops. The people may dance also in case too much rain is falling, or for luck in field work, hunting, despatching the dead, etc.; and in this way they also give thanks for the harvest. By dancing and with tesvino they express all their wants to the gods, or, as a Tarahumare told me, "We pray by dancing and the gourd."

With the dances is always connected the sacrifice of an animal; the greater portion of the meat is eaten by the people themselves, who, beside, bring forth all kinds of nice food, the best they have. Such dancing festivals, as a matter of course, are given either by individuals or by the community. It is thought that Tata Dios himself comes down each time to make his demands on the Tarahumares for dancing and sacrificing. He communicates his wishes in a dream to someone, not necessarily a shaman; and in the dry season, when the Indians begin to prepare their fields, most of these notices come and are generally made known to all at a race, where many people always come together. During all these months hardly a day passes without a messenger being sent out from some place in the country to advise one or the other of the principal shamans that God has come down and demanded a feast. Sometimes Tata Dios asks for an ox to be killed; at other times he wants only a sheep. Frequently he indicates that the animal must be white; on other occasions he is not particular about the colour. The threat is added that if the sacrifice is not forthcoming, and the people do not dance soon, all the corn will be burned up, and they will have to die of hunger. Or, if there has been too much rain, the notice may say that, unless they sacrifice and dance at once, all will be drowned, because it is going to rain tremendously. Occasionally it is directed that they dance only a little while, then rest, then dance again; or else they have to keep on dancing for a night and a day, or two nights in succession. When a great many sacrifices have been made and animals begin to be scarce, Tata Dios may have to content himself with iskiate and tortillas. The people may continue to make feasts and to dance, and yet get no other results but fresh messages, ordering still more sacrifices. Then the Indians begin to argue with Tata Dios that he must not be so greedy; he has filled himself up with oxen and sheep and tesvino, and they cannot give him any more. When such revolt seems imminent the shaman may throw out an ominous hint that the sacrifices have to be made; for what would the Tarahumares say if Tata Dios wanted one of them to be killed?

Among the reasons given by the Christian Tarahumares for continued dry weather are the following: The Devil has made Tata Dios sick and has tied him up; or the Moon (Virgin Mary) is sick; or the people have not given Tata Dios enough food and he is very hungry; or the railroad engines of the Americans are making so much smoke that Tata Dios is angry; or, finally, someone at a feast has infringed upon the law of decorum, and thereby annulled its value.

At present domestic animals are considered more valuable at sacrifices than the beasts of the field and the forest; yet squirrels (chipawiki), turkeys, deer, rabbits, and fish are still used to some extent, especially by those who do not possess domestic animals. Twenty men may go out to hunt a deer, or from six to ten men try to bring in four or five squirrels for a communal feast, to which all contribute the corn necessary for the tesvino, say, half an almud, more or less, according to the means of each householder. Never does any one man give all the corn required for a tribal feast, though he may donate all the meat, in the shape of an ox, a cow, or a sheep. Goats are sacrificed only at burial functions. If the people do not give the best they have for the sacrifice, they will obtain only poor results.

The dances are always held in the open air, that Father Sun and Mother Moon may look upon the efforts of their children to please them. They dance on the level space in front of the dwelling, preferably each danced on its own patio. Some people have as many as three such dancing-places, but most of them have to content themselves with one. If a Tarahumare could afford it, he would have ten patios to accommodate more people and dances near his house.

To my knowledge there are six different dances, but of these I will describe only two, the rutuburi and the

The Beginning of the Rutuburi and the Yumari Dance.

yumari, as these are the most important and the two almost exclusively used in the central part of the country. The other four I saw only among the southern Tarahumares.

The rutuburi was taught to the people by the turkey. Generally three crosses are put up, and there are three shamans, the principal one being in the middle; his assistants need not be shamans, but the master of the

house and his son, or some trusted friend, may officiate.
When the dancing is about to begin, these men take a
position in a line before the crosses, facing east, and
shake their rattles continuously for two or three minutes
from side to side, holding the instruments high up in the
air, as the rattling is meant to attract the attention of the
gods. Then, with the singing and shaking of the rattles—now down and up—they move forward in a manner similar to that of a schoolgirl skipping over a rope,
passing the crosses to a point as far east as the starting-
point was to the west, altogether about eighteen yards.
They then turn around and move back to the starting-
point. In this way they keep on dancing forward and
back three times, always in an easterly and westerly direction, swinging their rattles down and up, while passing
from one point to the other, and from side to side whenever they reach it. The down-and-up movement of the
rattle is not a simple down and up, but the down stroke
is always followed by a short after-clap before the arm
rises for the new swing, producing thus a three-part
rhythm. They sing the following stanza, repeating it
over and over again:

INTRODUCTION TO RUTUBURI

Ru - tu - bú - ri væ - ye - na   Ru - tu- bú - ri væ - ye - na
Rutuburi, from one side to the other moving! Rutuburi, from one side to, etc.

Ó - ma wǽ - ka xá - ru - si.   Ó - ma wǽ - ka xá - ru - si.
All!   many!   Arms crossed!   All!   many!   Arms crossed!

This is the introduction and prelude to the whole
dance. After this formal opening the men take their
places in line to the right of the shamans, and the
women to the left. They stand for a few minutes while
the shamans sing and swing their rattles, the men
silently holding their arms folded over their breasts, as

described in the song. This crossing of the arms I take to mean a salutation to the gods. While the Tarahumares of to-day never salute each other by shaking hands, neither is there any trace at present of their ever having saluted each other by crossing arms over the breast, which form was probably never used except with the gods, at ceremonies.

All the people are closely wrapped in their blankets, which they wear throughout the dance. In its general traits, the dance is performed in the same way as the opening ceremony. The shamans, or sometimes only the leader, jumps along as described, but the men just walk to and fro, and have to take long steps in order to keep abreast with the leaders. The women follow the men after the latter have gone several yards ahead, skipping in the same way as the shamans, though less pronounced. They stamp the hard ground with the right foot and run without regard to time, so that the pattering of their naked feet reminds one of a drove of mules stampeding. They overtake the men, so as to turn around simultaneously with them and wait again for a few seconds for the men to get ahead of them. Thus the dance is continued without interruption for hours and hours. This may sound as if the spectacle was monotonous; but such is not the case. On the contrary, there is a certain fascination in the regular, rhythmical movement from side to side—like the double pendulum of some gigantic, unseen clock. The shaman specially captivates the attention of the observer, being the very incarnation of enthusiasm. He swings his rattle with energy and conviction, as if bent on rousing the gods out of their indifference, while he stamps his right foot on the ground to add weight to the words, which he pours forth in a loud, resonant voice from his wide-open mouth. Although the Tarahuhumare, as a rule, has a harsh and not very powerful singing voice, still there are some noteworthy exceptions, and the airs of the rutuburi songs are quite pleasing to the ear. These, as all their dancing-songs, are of great antiquity and strangely enchanting.

RUTUBURI DANCE

Vá - sa - ma du - lú(- hu - ru) - si   Sæ - va-gá wi - lí
In   flowers (is)   jaltomate,*   in flow-ers stands up,

Sæ - va - gá   wi - lí   wú - ka   wú - ka.
In flowers   stands up   getting ripe, getting ripe.

RUTUBURI DANCE

Rā - ya - bó va - mí va - mí - (ru)   rā - ya - bó
(On the) ridge yon - der, yon - der   (On the) ridge

be - mó - ko   rā - ya - bó   be - mó - ko.
fog   (on   the) ridge   fog.

The water is near ;
Fog is resting on the mountain and on the mesa.
The Bluebird sings and whirs in the trees, and
The Male Woodpecker is calling on the llano,
Where the fog is rising.
The large Swift is making his dashes through the evening air ;
The rains are close at hand.
When the Swift is darting through the air he makes his whizzing,
     humming noise.
The Blue Squirrel ascends the tree and whistles,
The plants will be growing and the fruit will be ripening,
And when it is ripe it falls to the ground.
It falls because it is so ripe.

* A kind of tomato.

The flowers are standing up, waving in the wind.
The Turkey is playing, and the Eagle is calling;
Therefore, the time of rains will soon set in.

In the wet season, when the rabbits are about, the shamans sing of the rabbit. In winter time they sing of the giant woodpecker, and in harvest time, when the people begin to make merry, they sing of the blackbird.

The yumari was learned from the deer. According to tradition it is the oldest dance. At the hour appointed, the shaman, facing the cross and the east, here, too, opens the proceedings by shaking his rattle to both sides to notify the gods. Then he begins to walk around the cross, humming a song and marching in time to the rattle, which he now swings down and up. He makes the ceremonial circuit, stopping at each cardinal point for a few seconds. After this he begins his dance, and the rest of the assemblage gradually join in. The dance consists in short walks, forward and backward, with lock-step, the men being arrayed in line on both sides of the shaman, their eyes fixed on the ground, their elbows touching. In this way they swing to and fro, generally describing a curve around the cross, or, sometimes, forming a circle against the apparent movement of the sun. The women dance in a similar way, in a course of their own behind the men; but they frequently break ranks, jumping forward and backward with movements wholly devoid of grace. When the dance goes in a circle, the women move with the sun.

The tones marked with the accent > in each of the following yumari songs are grunts.

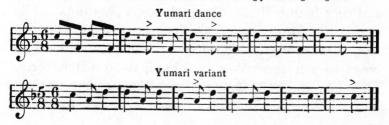

Yumari dance

Yumari variant

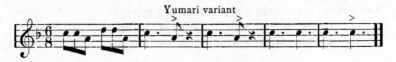

Yumari variant

The yumari songs tell that the Cricket wants to dance; the Frog wants to dance and jump; and the Blue Heron wants to fish; the Goatsucker is dancing, so is the Turtle, and the Grey Fox is whistling. But it is characteristic of the yumari songs that they generally consist only of an unintelligible jargon, or, rather, of a mere succession of vocables, which the dancers murmur.

Unlike the rutuburi, the yumari soon becomes tiresome, in spite of its greater animation. Yet the spectacle has something weird in it, especially when seen by the fitful flicker of the fire, which throws a fantastic light upon the grotesque figures, like goblins moving about on the same space. Many mothers carry their sleeping infants on their backs. Sometimes, the blanket which supports the baby loosens, and the little thing hangs half out of it, following every movement of the parent.

At most feasts both these dances are performed, and the Indians themselves consider them to have the same general purpose. It is, therefore, not easy to see the relation of the two dances to each other. Rutuburi is the more serious dance, and is more efficacious than yumari, though the latter, of course, has its own special value; for instance, it expresses a prayer that the shaman may have strength to cure. In yumari, all sing and dance, and very frequently all the performers are drunk, while during the former dance absolute decorum is observed. Both dances are for the sun and the moon—rutuburi, in order to call them down; yumari, to despatch them. Therefore, the usual dancing-feasts commence with rutuburi. When the function is about to be concluded, an

Dancing Yumari.

hour or two before sunrise, yumari is commenced, and leads over to the second part of the festival, the eating and drinking. After this, yumari may be continued throughout the day, while the Indians get drunk. Rutuburi is also danced at thanksgiving for the harvest, while on such occasions yumari asks for a good year to come. Then, again, rutuburi may be danced throughout the day, and yumari at night; but generally the former dance commences soon after sunset. On one occasion, while I was waiting for the performance to begin, the son of the house, in answer to my query, pointed to the sky, and told me that the dance would not commence until the Pleiades reached a certain spot in the heavens, which I calculated to mean about eleven o'clock. This indicated that the stars have some connection with the dancing.

At the break of dawn busy hands begin to get everything ready for the great ceremony of the sacrifice. For several days the women of the household and their friends have been making tortillas and boiling beans and *tamales* (small quantities of unsalted ground corn, wrapped and boiled in corn-husks). An animal was killed on the preceding day, and the meat has been boiling (without salt) in large jars all day and all night. Tata Dios does not like bones, therefore no bones are cooked with this meat. Several of the women have been dividing their time between dancing and watching the food-supply, to guard it against mishap from any source. A blanket is spread underneath, just to the west of the cross, or the three crosses, as the case may be, and on it in a line they place the jars of tesvino; behind these are set three small earthenware bowls filled with the stringy mass of the meat; then come three baskets of tortillas; and finally three little jars with wooden spoons in each are brought on and

put in their proper places, behind the rest of the food.
The latter vessels contain medicines to be taken, for the
welfare of the people is looked after from every point
of view.

In the meantime the dancing goes on with undimin-
ished force. Nearly every night during the dry season,
for nobody knows how many centuries, the Morning
Star has been looking down upon his sons, the Tarahumares, as they dance in the heart of the sierra, casting
his last rays upon the weird scene around their dying
fires before he flees from the approaching keeper of the
day. Just before the first beam of the rosy light an-
nounces the coming of Father Sun, the dancing ceases,
and the rattles are added to the sacrificial offerings on
the blanket. Everybody now is ready to do homage to
the deity about to appear above the horizon. The shaman greets him with the words, " Behold, Nonorugami is coming ! " and then solemnly proceeds toward
the cross, while the people form a line behind him and
preserve a respectful silence throughout the ensuing
ceremony. He fills a large drinking-gourd with tesvino, and, holding it in his left hand, throws a small dip-
perful of the liquor with his right hand into the air,
three times to each cardinal point, making the ceremonial circuit. Then the meat and the tortillas are sacrificed in the following way : The shaman takes up
from the ground the vessel in front of him, and lifts it
three times toward heaven. Then with his fingers he
takes up a little meat, offers it to the cross with the
word " Koá ! " (Eat), and throws it up into the air.
Next he breaks off a small piece of tortilla, and repeats
the same ceremony. Thus he sacrifices to all the cardinal points. The two assistants of the shaman follow
their principal in every act he performs.

The solemnity of the scene is by no means impaired

Sacrificing Tesvino after a Yumari Dance.   The Cross was, on this occasion, covered
with a Coloured Handkerchief.

by the numerous dogs, which are gathering to see what they can snatch up. Of course, the people drive them away, but in the end they always get Nonorugami's share of the food, while the god is supposed to eat only the nourishing substance.

What is left in the jars or bowls after the sacrifice is placed back on the blanket under the cross. The broth of the meat, too, is sacrificed, and so is the blood of the animal that has been killed for the feast.

Whenever the shaman returns to the people after performing the sacrifice, he says, "This was done on behalf of Nonorugami," and all the people respond: "Matetravá! Matetravá! Kalahúpo!" (Thank you! Thank you! It is all right!)

When the gods have had their share of the tesvino and the food, the curing begins. The medicines are cold infusions of different medicinal plants. The shaman standing directly in front of the middle cross, takes up the jar containing the chief medicine, palo hediondo ; his assistant to the north takes up the bowl containing a root called ohnoa ; and the one on the south maguey water. After having duly sacrificed to the gods, the great shaman himself takes three spoonfuls of the medicine, and gives the same quantity to his assistant to the north, who in turn first takes his remedy and then gives some to the shaman. In the same way the latter exchanges with his assistant to the south, and then the two assistants exchange remedies. The bowls are then handed by the shaman to the owner of the house, who in turn passes them on to the first man in the row, and from him they go from hand to hand to the last man in the line, each man taking three spoonfuls out of each bowl, while each of the women gets four. The man who drinks last gives the bowls back to the owner of the house, who in turn hands them to the shaman, who puts them back on the blanket underneath the cross. Meanwhile the incense-burners have been filled with hot coals, on which the shaman now throws some copal, the smoke of which he waves over all the people. He, as well as the other men, open their blankets a little to get the smoke on their bodies. This finishes the curing act, and now a speech is made. At private festivals the shaman is the orator of the occasion, but at communal or tribal festivals the gobernador is expected to, and generally does, perform this part of the proceedings. Rhetoric is one of the accomplishments of the Tarahumares, though it is not to be judged in accordance with the white man's standard. Here is a speech made by the gobernador at the end of one of the feasts I witnessed :

Listen to me! Stand up in a row and listen to what I have to tell you. All of you stand up in line, men, women, and children, because I am going to give you my words, to present to you the words which the One Above bids me to tell you. Now all is over! We have done something good to Tata Dios, and he has given you life to dance ; and now he is giving you life for another year. All of you will have to make feasts like this. You have no experience ; therefore listen to me and hear what I have to tell you. If you do not believe what I am telling you, the Devil will carry you off. You all are inexperienced, all of you who are standing here in a row around. Be quiet, and do all your business quietly. Drink quietly, talk quietly, sing quietly. And do not fight, because if in the fight you kill somebody, what will you have afterward? Nothing but sorrow and sadness! The One who is above us bids me to tell you, to say to all of you, men, women, and children, that this water, this tesvino that we are drinking is what makes us lose our heads. You know it all, and the One Above knows that this is the truth that I am telling you. Don't fight, don't pull

each other's hair, don't beat anyone in the face until he
bleeds.   For the blood and the hair belong to Tata
Dios, and you pull his hair and shed his blood.   Drink
tesvino to your hearts' content, get much drunk, but
then lie down and sleep, and in the morning you return
to your homes without coming to blows with anyone.

All the time the speech is punctuated with expres-
sions of approval, and at the end they all say : " Mate-

Ready to Begin Eating and Drinking after a Night's Dancing of Rutuburi.

trava ! Matetrava ! Kalahupo !"   (Thank you ! Thank
you !   It is all right !)

A speech is also often made in the beginning of the
feast, when much the same sentiments are expressed.
The orator tells the people to follow the good example
of the host, that sacrificing and dancing may go on
here, there, and everywhere, so that the gods will get
plenty to eat and grant the prayers of the Tarahumares.

He strongly admonishes them to keep away from women, as otherwise the value of the feast would be lost.   This day belongs to Tata Dios, and nothing else is to be thought of.   If anyone transgresses this command, he will have to give an ox or a sheep and tesvino, to make the feast all over again.

While the dancing and singing, sacrificing and speechmaking, are going on, the people behave with decorous solemnity and formality.   The ceremonies are never interrupted by unseemly conduct; everybody deports himself with grave sobriety, and refrains from loud talking and laughing and from making any disrespectful noise.   But after the gods have been given their share, the people go in, no less energetically, for enjoying themselves.

Food and tesvino are never distributed by the same man, nor are men and women waited on by the same functionary;   in other words, one man is appointed for each sex, to dispense the tesvino, and two others to serve the food.

They eat but little of the solids, as it is customary for the guests to take home their portions, the women bringing jars and baskets along for the purpose.   Little or nothing of the tesvino is spared, and it is the avowed intention and aim of everybody to get "a beautiful intoxication."   They all like to get drunk.   An India 1 explained to me that the drunken people weep with delight, because they are so perfectly happy.   Every Tarahumare has in his heart a cross which Tata Dios placed there long, long ago, and this cross they respect. When drunk they remember Tata Dios better.   At their feasts they sit alongside of him and drink with him. The women sit alongside of the Moon and remember ancient times.

But unfortunately this blissful stage of their intoxication does not last long, and then the animal nature in them manifests itself. Under the influence of the liquor, men and women rapidly lose that bashfulness and modesty which in ordinary life are such characteristic traits of their deportment. Furthermore, whatever grudge one man may have against another now crops out, and very likely a fight will ensue, in which the two opponents recklessly pull each other's hair and punch each other's faces. Sometimes in such an outbreak of unreasoning animalism one of the combatants will seize a stone and batter the other one's head to crush it. Afterward, when sober again, the murderer may deeply deplore his deed—if he remembers it at all.

Mothers, when overcome by the spirit of the feast, may unawares allow their babies to fall out of the blankets and into the fire. Children may frequently be seen with bruises and scars which they carry as mementoes of some tesvino feast. I know one man who had no hair on one side of his head, having when a child been a victim of such an accident. But seldom, if ever, is a child allowed to become fatally injured.

Taking it all in all, it is a good-natured, jolly, silly crowd, out for a good time and enjoying themselves. All are good friends, and familiarity becomes unlimited. Late in the afternoon those still able to walk start on their way home. Rarely, however, can they reach their domiciles, if these are any distance off, before nature enforces her rights; and the track is strewn with men and women, who, overcome with the effects of their spree, have lain down wherever they happened to be, to sleep themselves sober. Tarahumare society has not yet advanced far enough to see anything disgraceful in debauches of this kind, which, if viewed from their standpoint, are *pro bono publico;* and we ourselves need go back only to our grandfathers' and great-grandfathers' time to find that inebriety was not at all inconsistent with good morals and high standing. Moreover, no matter how often the Tarahumares indulge in such saturnalia, as soon as they recover their senses they are as decorous and solemn as ever. Their native stimulant does not seem to affect either their physical or their mental faculties, and, all scientific theories to the contrary, their children are strong, healthy, and bright.

Aside from social and religious considerations, the drinking of tesvino is a vital factor in the national life of the tribe. Incredible as it may sound, yet, after prolonged and careful research into this interesting psychological problem, I do not hesitate to state that in the ordinary course of his existence the uncivilised Tarahumare is too bashful and modest to enforce his matrimonial rights and privileges; and that by means of tesvino chiefly the race is kept alive and increasing. It is especially at the feasts connected with the agricultural work that sexual promiscuity takes place.

A large gathering is not necessary in order to pray to the gods by dancing. Sometimes the family dances alone, the father teaching the boys. While doing agricultural work, the Indians often depute one man to dance yumari near the house, while the others attend to the work in the fields. It is a curious sight to see a lone man taking his devotional exercise to the tune of his rattle in front of an apparently deserted dwelling. The lonely worshipper is doing his share of the general work by bringing down the fructifying rain and by warding off disaster, while the rest of the family and their friends plant, hoe, weed, or harvest. In the evening, when they return from the field, they may join him for a little while; but often he goes on alone, dancing all night, and singing himself hoarse, and the Indians told me that this is the very hardest kind of work, and exhausting even to them.

Solitary worship is also observed by men who go
out hunting deer or squirrels for a communal feast.
Every one of them dances yumari alone in front of his
house for two hours to insure success on the hunt; and
when putting corn to sprout for the making of tesvino
the owner of the house dances for a while, that the
corn may sprout well.

In certain parts of the country, near Aboreachic, for
instance, a dance called valixíwami is in vogue. Here
the line of the women faces that of the men, and the two
rows dance backward and forward, following each other
all the time.

In a dance called cuváli, which is found still further
south, the movements are the same as in the dance just
mentioned, but the steps are different. It is danced for
the same reason as rutuburi is, and it makes the grass
and the fungi grow and the deer and the rabbits multiply. This is the only dance known to the Tepehuanes.

In the winter they dance for snow, a dance called
yohé; and finally there is a dance called ayéna, which
calls the clouds from the north and south that they
may clash and produce rain.

I was present at feasts in which four of these dances
were performed, and the order in which they followed
each other was: Rutuburi, yumari, valixiwami, cuvali.

According to one version of the tradition, both
yumari and rutuburi were once men who taught the
Tarahumares to dance and sing. They live with Father
Sun. Valixiwami and cuvali were also men and companions of the former, but much younger.

At certain feasts for the benefit of the moon, three
cigarettes are offered under the cross. The shaman
takes one of them, gives a puff, raising the cigarette at
the same time upward toward the moon and saying:
" Suá" (rise) " vamí" (yonder) " repá" (upward). This

is repeated three times. The master of the house and his wife do the same. The ceremony is performed in order to help the moon to make clouds. Now all present may smoke. The Tarahumare never smokes in the middle of the day ; he would offend the sun by so doing. He indulges in the " weed" mostly at feasts when drunk. When an Indian offers another man to-bacco and a dry corn-leaf to roll his cigarette it is a sign that everything is well between them.

Every year between March and May a large perform-ance takes place on a special patio in the woods. Its purpose is to cure or prevent disease, and much tesvino is consumed. A straw-man, about two feet high, dressed in cotton drawers, and with a handkerchief tied around its head is set up next to the cross. It represents Fa-ther Sun, and the cross is his wife, the Moon. Some-times a stuffed recamúchi (cacomistle, *bassariscus*) is used either in the place of a straw-man or in addition to it. After the feast is over, the manikin is taken to the place from which the straw was obtained, in order to make the grass grow. The Christian Tarahumares keep it in the sacristy of their church.

The latter also celebrate Christmas, and on this oc-casion some of them, the so-called *matachines*, paint their faces and carry on their backs stuffed animals, such as the grey fox, squirrel, or opossum, while dancing to the music of the violin. They jokingly call the skins their *muchachitos*, and hold them as women carry their babies. At present the only object is to make the be-holder laugh ; but of course the play is a remnant of some ancient custom, the meaning of which is now for-gotten through the new associations with which the mis-sionaries of old imbued the ceremonies and rites found among the pagans.

A similar suggestion of antiquity is unmistakably

embodied in the deer masks, as well as in the heads with
antlers attached, which the same men also may wear.

During Easter week live rattlesnakes are carried
about, but the heads of the reptiles are tied together so
that they can do no harm. One man may have as
many as four serpents with him.

CHAPTER XIX

PLANT-WORSHIP—HIKULI—INTERNAL AND EXTERNAL EFFECTS—
HIKULI BOTH MAN AND GOD—HOW THE TARAHUMARES OB-
TAIN THE PLANT, AND WHERE THEY KEEP IT—THE TARAHU-
MARE HIKULI FEAST—MUSICAL INSTRUMENTS—HIKULI LIKES
NOISE—THE DANCE—HIKULI'S DEPARTURE IN THE MORNING
—OTHER KINDS OF CACTI WORSHIPPED—"DOCTOR" RUBIO,
THE GREAT HIKULI EXPERT—THE AGE OF HIKULI WORSHIP.

TO the Indian, everything in nature is alive. Plants,
like human beings, have souls, otherwise they could
not live and grow. Many are supposed to talk and sing
and to feel joy and pain. For instance, when in winter
the pine-trees are stiff with cold, they weep and pray to
the sun to shine and make them warm. When angered
or insulted, the plants take their revenge. Those that
are supposed to possess curative powers are venerated.
This fact, however, does not save them from being cut
into pieces and steeped in water, which the people afterward drink or use in washing themselves. The mere
fragrance of the lily is supposed to cure sickness and to
drive off sorcery. In invoking the lily's help the shaman utters a prayer like this :

" Sūmatí	okiliveá	sævá	rākó	cheeneserová
" Beautiful	this morning	in bloom	lily	thou guard me !

waminámela	ke usugitúami	cheeotshéloaya
drive them away	(those who) make sorcery !	thou make me grow old !

cheelivéva	tesola	chapimélava	otshéloa
thou give me	walking-stick	(to) take up	(in) old age

rimivélava	Matetravá	Sevaxóa
(that I may) find !	thanks	exhale fragrance

wiliróva ! "
standing ! "

("Beautiful lily, in bloom this morning, guard me! Drive away sorcery! Make me grow old! Let me reach the age at which I have to take up a walking-stick! I thank thee for exhaling thy fragrance there, where thou art standing!")

High mental qualities are ascribed especially to all species of *Mammilaria* and *Echinocactus*, small cacti, for which a regular cult is instituted. The Tarahumares designate several varieties as hikuli, though the name belongs properly only to the kind most commonly used by them. These plants live for months after they have been rooted up, and the eating of them causes a state of ecstasy. They are therefore considered demi-gods, who have to be treated with great reverence, and to whom sacrifices have to be offered.

Echinocactus.

The principal kinds thus distinguished are known to science as *Lophophora Williamsii* and *Lophophora Williamsii*, var. *Lewinii*. In the United States they are called mescal buttons, and in Mexico *peyote*. The Tarahumares speak of them as the superior hikuli (hikuli wanamé), or simply hikuli, they being the hikuli *par excellence*.

The Huichol Indians, who live many hundred miles south of the Tarahumares, also have a hikuli cult, and it is a curious and interesting fact that with them the plant has even the same name, although the two tribes are neither related to nor connected with each other. The cults, too, show many points of resemblance, though with the southern tribe the plant plays a far more important part in the tribal life, and its worship is much more elaborate. On the other hand, the Huichols use only the species and variety shown

in the illustration, while the Tarahumares have several.
Major J. B. Pond, of New York, informs me that
in Texas, during the Civil War, the so-called Texas
Rangers, when taken prisoners and deprived of all other

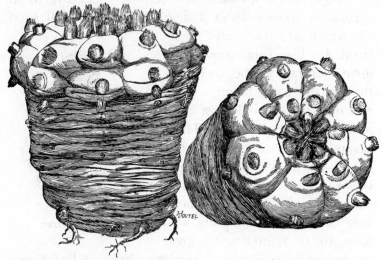

Lophophora Williamsii, var. *Lewinii*.   *Lophophora Williamsii*.
Hikuli or Peyote, the principal sacred cacti.   Nearly natural size.

stimulating drinks, used mescal buttons, or "white
mule," as they called them.   They soaked the plants in
water and became intoxicated with the liquid.

The plant, when taken, exhilarates the human system, and allays all feeling of hunger and thirst.   It also
produces colour-visions.   When fresh, it has a nauseating,
slightly sour taste, but it is wonderfully refreshing when
one has been exposed to great fatigue.   Not only does
it do away with all exhaustion, but one feels actually
pushed on, as I can testify from personal experience.
In this respect it resembles the Peruvian coca; but unlike the latter, it leaves a certain depression, as well as a
headache.   Although an Indian feels as if drunk after
eating a quantity of hikuli, and the trees dance before

his eyes, he maintains the balance of his body even better than under normal conditions, and he will walk
along the edge of precipices without becoming dizzy.
At their nocturnal feasts, when drinking heavily of both
tesvino and hikuli, many persons may be seen to weep
and laugh alternately. Another marked effect of the
plant is to take away temporarily all sexual desire.
This fact, no doubt, is the reason why the Indians, by a
curious aboriginal mode of reasoning, impose abstinence
from sexual intercourse as a necessary part of the hikuli
cult.

The effect of the plant is so much enjoyed by the
Tarahumares that they attribute to it power to give

Dry Hikuli.

health and long life and to purify body and soul. The
little cacti, either fresh or dried, are ground on the metate, while being mixed with water ; and this liquor is the
usual form in which hikuli is consumed.

Hikuli is also applied externally for snake-bites,
burns, wounds, and rheumatism ; for these purposes it is
chewed, or merely moistened in the mouth, and applied
to the afflicted part. Not only does it cure disease,
causing it to run off, but it also so strengthens the body

that it can resist illness, and is therefore much used in warding off sickness. Though not given to the dead, since the dead are no longer in need of remedies, hikuli is always partaken of at the feasts of the dead.

Moreover, hikuli is a powerful protector of its people under all circumstances, and it gives luck. If a man carries some hikuli in his belt, the bear cannot bite him and the deer cannot run away, but become quite tame and can easily be killed. Should he meet Apaches, hikuli would prevent them from firing off their guns at him. It gives luck in foot-races and all kinds of games, in climbing trees, etc. Hikuli is the great safeguard against witchcraft. It sees even better than the shamans, and it watches that nothing bad is put into the food. The Christian Tarahumares, when they partake of hikuli, think that the devil runs out of their stomachs. Hikuli purifies any man who is willing to sacrifice a sheep and to make native beer. There is, however, no remedy for a murderer ; not even hikuli can cure him.

The Christian Tarahumares make the sign of the cross when coming into the presence of the plant, and I was told to lift my hat to it. It is always saluted in the same way as a man, and is supposed to make the customary responses to the salutations. Hikuli is not as great as Father Sun, but sits next to him. It is the brother of Tata Dios; and the greatest hikuli is his twin brother, and is therefore called uncle.

Sometimes these plants are dressed up in pieces of blankets, and cigarettes are placed before them. Boys must not touch hikuli, and women only when they act as the shaman's assistants and have to grind it. As a matter of fact, only shamans can handle it properly, and even they wash their hands carefully, and sometimes elect not to touch it at all, making use of little sticks instead of their fingers. Certain shamans washed their hands and rinsed their mouths immediately after eating from my vessels, because hikuli would be angry with them for eating strange food cooked by strange people.

Hikuli is not kept in the house, because it is extremely virtuous, and might become offended at the sight of anything immodest. It is placed in a special jar or basket, in a separate store-house, and is never taken out until tesvino and meat have been offered to it. If this were neglected, it would eat the Indian's soul. If anything happens to hikuli—for instance, if irreverent mice eat it—the owner fears that he may be made crazy as a punishment for his failure to guard it. If anyone should steal hikuli, he would be sure to go crazy, unless he returned the plant to its original owner. He must also kill an ox and make a big feast, in order to set himself right again with the mighty god and with the people.

After four years, hikuli grows old and mouldy, and loses its virtues. It is then buried in a corner of the cave or the house, or taken to the place where it came from, and fresh plants are obtained instead. According to tradition, when Tata Dios went to heaven in the beginning of the world, he left hikuli behind as the great remedy of the people. Hikuli has four faces and sees everything. Its power is well shown in the following myth :

The Bear in a cave said to Hikuli, " Let us fight and let us first smoke over there." They smoked and they fought, and Hikuli was stronger than the Bear. When Hikuli threw the Bear down, all the wind went out of the Bear ; but the Bear said again, " Let us smoke and let us fight a few times more." And they did so, and Hikuli again threw down the Bear, and the Bear seated himself on a stone and wept, and went away, and never returned.

Hikuli is not indigenous to the Tarahumare country

of to-day. To obtain it long and until recently perilous
journeys have to be undertaken every year to the plateaus
of eastern Chihuahua, in the Sierra del Almoloy, near the
railroad station of Ximenez, and to the Sierra de Margoso,
beyond Santa Rosalia de Camarga, crossing the tracks
of the Mexican Central Railroad. From two or three
to a dozen men start out to get the plants, first purify-
ing themselves with copal incense. It takes a week
or ten days to get to the Sierra de Margoso, where the
plants are chiefly found, and about a month is consumed on the entire journey. Until they reach the
hikuli country, the Tarahumares may eat anything;
but once there, they must abstain from everything except pinole. Upon arriving at the spot, the pilgrims
erect a cross, and near it they place the first plants
taken up, that these may tell where others may be
found in plenty. The second batch of plants gathered
is eaten raw, and makes the men drunk. As speech is
forbidden, they lie down in silence and sleep. The following day, when perfectly sober again, they begin early
in the morning to collect the plants, taking them up with
the utmost care, by means of sticks, so as not to touch or
injure them, because hikuli would get angry and punish
the offender. Two days are spent in gathering the plants,
each kind being placed in a separate bag, because, if they
were mixed together, they would fight. The bags are
carefully carried on the backs of the men, as the Tarahumares generally have no horses.

In the field in which it grows, it sings beautifully,
that the Tarahumare may find it. It says, "I want to
go to your country, that you may sing your songs to
me." It also sings in the bag while it is being carried
home. One man, who wanted to use his bag as a pillow, could not sleep, he said, because the plants made
so much noise.

When the hikuli-seekers arrive at their homes, the people turn out to welcome the plants with music, and a festival at which a sheep or a goat is sacrificed is held in their honour. On this occasion the shaman wears necklaces made of the seeds of *Coix Lachryma-Jobi*. In due time he takes them off, and places them in a bowl containing water in which the heart of the maguey has been soaked, and after a while everyone present gets a spoonful of this water. The shaman, too, takes some, and afterward wears the necklaces again. Both plants, the *Coix Lachryma-Jobi* as well as the maguey, are highly esteemed for their curative properties; and in his songs the shaman describes hikuli as standing on top of a gigantic seed of the *Coix Lachryma-Jobi*, as big as a mountain.

The night is passed in dancing hikuli and yumari. The pile of fresh plants, perhaps two bushels or more, is placed under the cross, and sprinkled with tesvino, for hikuli wants to drink beer, and if the people should not give it, it would go back to its own country. Food is also offered to the plants, and even money is placed before them, perhaps three silver dollars, which the owner, after the feast, takes back again.

During the year, feasts may be held especially in honour of hikuli, but generally the hikuli dance is performed simultaneously with, though apart from, the rutuburi or other dances. On such occasions some shamans devote themselves exclusively to the hikuli cult, in order that the health of the dancers may be preserved, and that they may have vigour for their work.

The hikuli feast consists mainly in dancing, which, of course, is followed by eating and drinking, after the customary offerings of food and tesvino have been made to the gods. It is not held on the general dancing-place, in front of the Tarahumare dwelling, but on a special patio. For the occasion a level piece of ground may be cleared of all stones and rubbish, and carefully swept with the Indian broom, which is made of a sheaf of straw tied in the middle.

Meanwhile some people go into the woods to gather fuel for the large fire which will be needed. The fire is an important feature of the hikuli-feast, a fact indicated by the name, which is napítshi nawlíruga, literally, "moving (*i.e.* dancing) around (nawlíruga) the fire (napítshi)." There seems to be a preference for fallen trees, pines or oaks, but this may be because they are found in plenty everywhere, are drier and burn better, and finally save the men the labour and time of cutting them down. Quite a number of such trunks are brought together, and placed parallel to each other in an easterly and westerly direction; but not until after sunset is the fire lighted.

The master of the house in which the feast is to be held gives some plants to two or three women appointed to the office of shaman's assistants. At an ordinary gathering, a dozen or two of the plants suffice. The women are called rokoró, which means the stamen of the flower, while the shaman is the pistil. The women grind the plants with water on the metate, and then take part in the dance. They must wash their hands most carefully before touching them; and while they are grinding a man stands by with a gourd, to catch any stray drop of liquor that may drip from the metate, and to watch that nothing of the precious fluid is lost. Not one drop must be spilled, and even the water with which the metate is afterward washed, is added to the liquid. The drink thus produced is slightly thick and of a dirty brown colour.

The shaman (sometimes there are two) takes his seat on the ground to the west of the fire, about two yards off. On the opposite side of the dancing-place, toward the east, the cross is placed. The shaman's male assistants, at least two in number, seat themselves on either side of their principal, while the women helpers take a position to the north of the fire. On one occasion I observed that the men grouped themselves on one side of the shaman, the women on the other. Close by the shaman's seat a hole is dug, into which he or his assistants may spit, after having drunk or eaten hikuli, so that nothing may be lost. After this improvised cuspidor has been used, it is always carefully covered with a leaf.

As soon as the shaman has seated himself, he takes a round drinking-gourd, and by pressing its rim firmly into the soil and turning the vessel round, makes a circular mark. Lifting up the bowl again, he draws two diametrical lines at right angles in the circle, and thus produces a symbol of the world.

In the centre he puts a hikuli, right side up; or he may dig a hole in the centre, to the depth of five or six inches, and place the hikuli in this. He then covers it up with the gourd, bottom up, so that the plant stands within a hollow sphere. The gourd may be replaced by a wooden vessel of similar shape; but in any case it is firmly planted in the ground to serve as a resonator for the musical instrument,—the notched stick, which the shaman leans against the vessel, and on which with another stick he rasps an accompaniment to his songs. If he does not plant the gourd carefully in the ground, it will·make a discordant sound, which will vex the demi-god, and he will cause someone in the house to die. The noise produced by the rasping is enjoyed by Hikuli; that is why he is placed beneath the bowl. He is powerful, and manifests his strength by the noise produced.

The notched stick, as well as the rasping-stick, is made from the heavy, hard Brazil-wood, brought from the vicinity of San Ignacio, the hikuli country. The shaman holds the notched stick in his left hand, a little away from himself, so that it touches the vessel at a point below the middle of its length, the part between the shaman's hand and the point of contact being a little longer than the portion from that point to the end of the stick.

The notched sticks which are shown in the illustration, from a Tarahumare burial-cave, are apparently of considerable age. The Indians to whom I showed them did not know them, but they all affirmed that they were rasping-sticks. On two sides of one of them are slanting lines, which symbolize the road of Tata Dios ; on the intervening sides are transverse lines which represent falling rain. As the implements were found near Baborigame, they may possibly have belonged to the Tepehuanes, the northern members of whom also have the hikuli cult.

When the shaman begins to rasp, he starts from the farther end of the notched stick, though not quite at the point, and runs his rasping-stick quickly and evenly, about twenty-six times, toward himself, and away again ; then he makes three long strokes down and outward, each time throwing out his arm at full length, and holding the stick for a second high up toward the east. This is repeated three times,

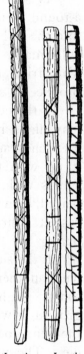

Shaman's
Notched
Stick.
Length,
75 ctm.

Length,
46 ctm.

Length,
40 ctm.

Ancient
Notched
Sticks.

and is the prelude to the ceremony. Now he begins to sing, accompanying himself with even strokes on the notched stick, playing regularly, one stroke as long and as fast as the other, always first toward himself, then down again. His songs are short, lasting only about five minutes.

Presently the shaman's assistants, men and women, rise. They carry censers filled with burning charcoals and copal, and emitting a heavy smoke, and proceed toward the cross, to which they offer the smoking incense, kneeling down, facing east, and crossing themselves. This feature, if not wholly due to Catholic influence, is at least strongly affected by it.

Having offered incense to the cross, they return to the shaman. The women now sit down again in their previous places. The men receive from the shaman rattles (*sonajas*) consisting of deer-hoofs tied with bits of reed to a strap of leather. They are either held in the right hand or slung over the shoulder. When there are not enough rattles for all assistants, a bell may be substituted.

Finally everything is ready for the dance to commence. The men wear white blankets, in which they keep themselves wrapped up to the chin throughout the night; but they have no sandals. The dance is performed by the shaman's assistants, and consists of a peculiar, quick, jumping march, with short steps, the dancers moving forward one after another, on their toes, and making sharp, jerky movements, without, however, turning around. They dance in the space between the fire and the cross, and move in a direction opposite to the sun's apparent movement. Nobody present is allowed to walk in contra-direction to the dancers. After six or eight rounds, they enlarge the circuit so as to include the fire; and whenever a dancer finds himself just between the shaman and the fire, he quickly turns around once, then, dancing as before, moves on to the dancing-place proper. Now and then the dancers give vent to what is supposed to be an imitation of the hikuli's talk, which reminded me of the crowing of a cock. Beating their mouths quickly three times with the hollow of their hands, they shout in a shrill, falsetto voice, " Hikuli vava ! " which means, " Hikuli over yonder ! "

The women take their turns separate from the men, though sometimes they dance simultaneously with them. They move around in silence, and their dance is slightly different from that of the other sex. Sometimes two and two may be seen dancing toward each other. They all wear freshly washed, clean white skirts and tunics, and the entire scene around the big fire is marvellously picturesque.

The dancing may sometimes lag, but the singing and the rhythmical rasping of the shaman are kept up through the night, interrupted only once or twice, when he sees fit. He politely excuses himself to Hikuli, and formal salutations are exchanged with the plant under the bowl both when he goes and when he returns. On such occasions he stops his singing and rasping, and notifies Hikuli by striking the notched stick several times quickly with the rasping-stick, and finishing off with three slow beats.

His songs describe how Hikuli walks with his rattles and with his staff of authority; he comes to cure and to guard the people and to grant a " beautiful " intoxication. To bring about the latter result, the brownish liquor is dispensed from a jar standing under the cross. A man serves it in small quantities from a gourd, which he first carries around the fire on a rapid run, making three circuits for the shaman, and one for the rest of the assemblage. The spirits of the feasters rise

Tarahumare Women Dancing Hikuli at Guajochic Station.

in proportion to their potations. Sometimes only the shaman and his assistants indulge in the drinking ; on other occasions all the people partake of the liquor.

SONG TO THE HIKULI

Allegro.

Hí - ku - li   o - ku - lí - va - va   Ta - mi - sǽ - li - va   re - gá
Hikuli,   uncle!   Our authority   thus!

A - go - ná wi - lí si - nǽ   Na - na - já re - gá we - lá
Yonder standing upright, see!   The ancients thus placed him.

The secondary effect of the plant, depression and drowsiness, shows itself more plainly on the company when they sit down between the dancing, than on the well-trained shaman, who, besides, is kept awake by his occupation. As one or the other of his assistants succumbs to sleepiness, he has to ask permission of Hikuli, through the shaman, to go off and rest for a while, and must properly notify Hikuli of his leaving and returning to duty. Toward morning all the assistants are struggling hard to overcome somnolence, while the shaman sings and rasps as conscientiously and enthusiastically as ever.

But all rouse themselves for the important acts of curing the people by rasping and of despatching Hikuli. Just at daybreak, as the fire is dying out, the shaman gives the welcome signal that the dance is over, by the three final raps on his notched stick. Then the people gather at the eastern end of the dancing-place, near the cross. The shaman rises from his seat, carrying in his hands his rasping implements, and, followed by a boy who carries a gourd with water, he proceeds to confer upon everybody present the benediction. Stopping in

front of each one, he solemnly dips the point of the
rasping-stick into the water, and after touching the
notched stick lightly with the wetted end, first in the
middle, then on the lower end, and finally on the top,
he daubs the head of the person three times with it.
Then he rests the end of the notched stick against the
man's head and rasps three long strokes from end to
end, throwing out his hand far into the air after each
stroke. The dust produced by the rasping, infinitesi-
mal though it be, is powerful in giving health and life.
Now he turns toward the rising Sun, holding out his implements to him ; and, quickly rubbing up and down a
few times at the lower end of the notched stick, he makes
a long stroke from end to end, passing the hand far out
from the stick toward the Sun. By this act, three times
performed, he waves Hikuli home. In the early morning, Hikuli had come from San Ignacio and from Sata-
polio, riding on beautiful green doves, to feast with the
Tarahumares at the end of the dance, when the people
sacrifice food, and eat and drink. The greatest Hikuli
eats with the shaman, who alone is able to see him and
his companions. If Hikuli should not come to the
feasts, there would always be on the Tarahumares the
breath or stain of sorcery.

Having bestowed his blessings, Hikuli forms himself
into a ball, and flies home to his country, accompanied
by the owl, who also flies to its shelter at that hour.

The dust produced by the rasping of the shaman in
the course of the night is carefully gathered up and
kept in a buckskin bag as a powerful remedy for future
use.

After the feast everybody has to wash his face and
hands, a duty esteemed most important.

Besides hikuli wanamé ordinarily used, the Tarahumares know and worship the following varieties :

1. Mulato (*Mammilaria micromeris*).—This is believed to make the eyes large and clear to see sorcerers, to prolong life and to give speed to the runners.

2. Rosapara.—This is only a more advanced vegetative stage of the preceding species—though it looks quite different, being white and spiny. This, too, must only be touched with very clean hands, in the moral sense, it would seem, as much as in the physical, for only people who are well baptised are allowed to handle it. It is a good Christian and keeps a sharp eye on the people around it; and when it sees anyone doing some wrong, it gets very angry, and either drives the offender mad or throws him down precipices. It is therefore very effective in frightening off bad people, especially robbers and Apaches.

3. Sunami (*Mammilaria fissurata*). — It is rare, but it is believed to be even more powerful than wanamé and is used in the same way as the latter; the drink produced

Mammilaria fissurata.

from it is also strongly intoxicating. Robbers are powerless to steal anything where Sunami calls soldiers to its aid.

4. Hikuli walúla sælíami.—This is the greatest of all, and the name means " hikuli great authority." It is extremely rare among the Tarahumares, and I have not seen any specimen of it, but it was described to me as growing in clusters of from eight to twelve inches in diameter, resembling wanamé with many young ones around it. All the other hikuli are his servants. The

reason why so few of these plants are brought to the Tarahumare country is that he is very greedy, requiring oxen for food, not being satisfied with sheep, goats, or anything else. Therefore but few Tarahumares can afford to entertain him in their country. If an ox is not killed for him, he will eat the Indian. He always holds his head down, because he is listening to all the ceremonies that are being held in the Tarahumare land, and he is alway full of thoughts of how he may cure his sons, the Tarahumares. He never dies. When a person is very ill, and there is no such hikuli in the country, the shaman in his thoughts flies to the hikuli country, where "the great authority" stands looking at his children, the people, and offers him the soul of an ox that has been sacrificed. Hikuli accepts the offering, and sends back his blessings by his servants, who are always well dressed and wear straw hats, "like regular Americans," as my shaman friend Rubio expressed it. Only the shamans, however, can see them come, to cure the hearts of the people and to clean their souls.

All these various species are considered good, as coming from Tata Dios, and well-disposed toward the people. But there are some kinds of hikuli believed to come from the Devil. One of these, with long white spines, is called ocoyome. It is very rarely used, and only for evil purposes. If anyone should happen to touch it with the foot, it would cause the offending leg to break. Once when I pushed one of these globular spiny cacti out of my way with a cane, my Indian attendant immediately warned me, "Leave it alone, or it will make you fall down precipices."

At one of the feasts which I witnessed I wished to taste hikuli, as it was new to me. A lively discussion arose between the shamans, and I was finally told that I might sit with them, as it was known that I had some of the sacred plants in my possession. The condition was made, however, that I should take off my sombrero. It happened to be a cold and windy December night, but I obeyed and put my handkerchief over my head, to which no objection was raised. The man who carried the gourd, first danced in front of the shaman, then around the fire, and finally brought it to me. The liquid tasted somewhat bitter, but not exactly disagreeable; and while I drank, the man looked at me with astonishment, as if he had expected that hikuli would refuse to be taken by me.

I drank only a small cupful, but felt the effect in a few minutes. First it made me wide awake, and acted as an excitant to the nerves, similar to coffee, but much more powerful. This sensation lasted for about ten minutes, when it was followed by a depression and a chill such as I have never experienced before. To get warm I almost threw myself into the fire, but not until morning was the feeling of cold conquered. Some Tarahumares told me that they are similarly affected, and for this reason they do not take it. When I told the shaman about the effect hikuli had on me, he asked whether I had rasped on the notched stick, because, he said, hikuli does not give chills to people who rasp. In other words, according to him, the effect might be warded off by physical exercise.

A shaman who agreed to sell me some hikuli took me with him to his house. Then he walked over to a store-house of pine boards, and with a long stick undid the lock from within, taking off a few boards from the roof to get at it. After some searching, he produced a small closed basket. Holding this in his hand, he rapidly ran around me in one ceremonious circuit, and said in a scarcely audible voice: "Thank you for the

time you have been with me; now go with him; I
will give you food before you go." The smoke of copal
was blown over the plants in the basket, that they might
eat; and I had to smell of the incense, so that hikuli
might find pleasure in being with me. The shaman
then opened the basket and asked me to select what I
wanted. I picked out twelve plants, but, as he asked
$10 for them, I contented myself with three.

On my way back to civilisation, I spent some time
at Guajochic, near which place the great hikuli expert,

Shaman Rubio and His Company at a Hikuli Feast.   Photographed after a
Night's Singing and Dancing.   Rubio is Seen to the Right.

Shaman Rubio, lives. He is a truly pious man, well-
meaning and kind-hearted, living up to his principles,
in which Christianity and Paganism are harmoniously
blended. He is highly esteemed by all his countrymen,
who consider him the greatest hikuli shaman in that
part of the Tarahumare country. His profession brings
him a very comfortable living, as his services are constantly in demand, and are paid for by fine pieces of
the animals sacrificed. For curing the people he even
gets money; and what with praying and singing, drinking tesvino and hikuli, fasting and curing the sick, he
passes his days in the happy conviction that he keeps
the world going. From him I obtained specimens of

the various kinds of cacti which the Tarahumares worship,—a betrayal of the secrets of the tribe, for which
the other shamans punished him by forbidding him
ever to go again on a hikuli journey. Though in the
first year he obeyed the sentence, he did not take it
much to heart, feeling himself far superior to his judges,
who, he knew, could not get along without him, and in
the end would have to come to him ; for he is the most
virtuous of them all, and therefore knows the commands
of Tata Dios better than anyone else.

It is to him that I owe a good deal of what I know
about this plant-worship, as well as several songs used
in the cult. He came often to see me, and one day told
me in confidence that the hikuli in my possession would
have to be fed before they started on their long journey
to the United States ; for it was a long time since they
had had food, and they were getting angry. The next
time he came he brought some copal tied up in a cotton
cloth, and after heating the incense on a piece of crockery he waved the smoke over the plants, which he had
placed in front of him. This, he said, would satisfy
them ; they would now go content with me, and no
harm would come to me from sorcerers, robbers, or
Apaches. This was a comfort, for to reach Chihuahua I had to pass through some disturbed country, and
there were rumours of a revolution.

It seems that at present only the districts around
Nararachic and Baqueachic get hikuli from its native
country, and that all the others procure it from these
two. Until recently the people of Guachochic also went
to fetch plants, and a few may yet undertake the journey. One old man showed me some hikuli which he
had gathered thirty-five years ago. At Nararachic they
use hikuli all the year round, that is, as long as they
have corn, because "hikuli wants tesvino." The people

in the barrancas are too timid to go on the expeditions, and they buy the plants at the price of a sheep apiece. The purchaser holds a feast, not only when he brings the demi-god to his home, but also a year after the event. In the eastern section of the country, and in the foot-hills around Rio Fuerte, hikuli is not used at all. It is very rarely planted by the Tarahumares ; the only in-stance I saw of it was in Tierras Verdes.

A significant light is thrown on the antiquity of the cult, as well as on the age of the tribe itself, by a cer-tain variation in the ceremonial which I observed in the southwestern part of the Tarahumare country. There it is the custom of the shaman to draw underneath his resonator-gourd a mystical human figure in the sand, and to place the hikuli in its centre. Regarding this mystical figure, my lamented friend, Frank Hamilton Cushing, informed me that similar or almost identical drawings are found depicted on the lava rocks of Arizona. In a letter dated October 30, 1893, he said :

The figure you sketch for me is closely allied, for ex-ample, to very ancient ritualistic petrographs in the lava regions of Arizona. You will see this at a glance by the figure of one of those petrographs, which I reproduce in juxtaposition with yours :

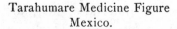

Tarahumare Medicine Figure   Ancient Ritualistic Petrograph,
Mexico.   Arizona.

Others which I have recorded are even more strikingly similar. I have always supposed that these figures were designed for " medicine " ceremonials, but thought of

them rather as pertaining to the medicines of the elements, wind, rain, water, etc., used in connection with
sacrifices (with which ceremonial rites were terminated)
than as connected with actual medicinal ceremonials.
I was led to this belief by finding in connection with
some of them little cup-shaped concavities pecked into
the angles of the figures (as *a, a, a*). You will observe
that a line is drawn from the middle and straight portion of my figure and coiled around the concavity at
the right side, and that the terminations of the upper
cross lines are bifurcated around similar though smaller
concavities. This entire figure represents a water-ani-
mal god, one only of a number of semi-human mystic
monsters. For convenience his heart is drawn out to
one side, and within it is placed the cup of the " chief "
medicine ; while in his left hand is the cup of the
"good" medicine, and in his right hand the cup of
" bad " (*i.e.*, strong) medicine. If in the light of this
you re-examine your figure, you will see with me that it
represents a man-god sitting, his legs doubled under
him and his medicines distributed around and upon him
according to his parts, and in accordance also, probably,
to their importance and the case in hand. He must always have the chief of all medicines placed on his heart,
as the renewer of life. Then, strictly with reference
to the ailment to be treated, and its location in the body
or limbs of the patient (I should say), the other medicines. I throw this out as a suggestion, yet with much
confidence in its at least approximate correctness as indicated by my comparative studies. Probably a consultation of your notes and the remembrance of variations
of the ceremony you have seen, will signify to you
whether I am right or not. Remember that if these
people have this ceremonial in connection with the
treatment of disease, they will also have it in the treatment of the weather, etc., when " diseased," so to say.
You have opened up a new significance of many outlines among the older lava-remains, and if my record of
these in turn has helped to explain your diagram, etc.,
you can judge of my pleasure and appreciation."

CHAPTER XX

THE TARAHUMARE'S FIRM BELIEF IN A FUTURE LIFE—CAUSES OF
DEATH—THE DEAD ARE MISCHIEVOUS AND WANT THEIR FAM-
ILIES TO JOIN THEM—THEREFORE THE DEAD HAVE TO BE
KEPT AWAY BY FAIR MEANS OR FOUL—THREE FEASTS AND A
CHASE—BURIAL CUSTOMS—A FUNERAL SERMON.

THE idea of immortality is so strong with the
Tarahumares that death means to them only a
change of form. They certainly believe in a future life,
but they are afraid of the dead, and think that they

Mourning.

want to harm the survivors. This fear is caused by
the supposition that the dead are lonely, and long for
the company of their relatives. The dead also make
people ill, that they too may die and join the departed.
When a man dies in spite of all efforts of the shamans
to save his life, the people say that those who have gone

before have called him or carried him off. The deceased are also supposed to retain their love for the good things they left behind in this world, and to be trying every way to get at them. So strong is the feeling that the departed still owns whatever property he once possessed, that he is thought to be jealous of his heirs who now enjoy its possession. He may not let them sleep at night, but makes them sit up by the fire and talk. To soothe his discontent, tesvino and all kinds of food are given him, because he needs the same things he needed here. In the course of the year several ceremonies are performed, by which he is actually chased off, and the survivors constantly take precautions against his return to bother them.

Sometimes the dead are sent by sorcerers to harm people and make them ill, but generally they come of their own accord. They enter the house at night and drink the tesvino and eat the food prepared for a feast, and what they cannot eat they spoil. To protect the beer against such mischief the people place bows and arrows next the jars, and cover the vessels with sprigs of the odorous artemisia. The dead will also kill cattle and sheep, and spit and blow in the faces of the people, to make them ill, and possibly cause their death. Sometimes the dead are viewed as spirits, and the shaman sees them flying through the air, like birds. If the spirit of a dead person takes up his abode in a house, the owner of the dwelling will feel a choking sensation, dry up, and die, unless the shaman gives to the dead plenty of tesvino, and drives him away with incantations.

The dead are supposed to be about at night; therefore the Tarahumares do not like to travel after dark, for fear of meeting the dead, who whistle when they pass the living. Only shamans can travel at night, although sometimes even they have to fight with the dead, who come running out of the caves on all fours. In the daytime the Tarahumares are not afraid of the dead, though even then they do not dare to visit burial-places, modern or ancient. I found it difficult to get Indians to carry bones of skeletons excavated from ancient burial-caves, and even the Mexicans would not allow their animals to carry burdens of that kind, for fear that the mules would get tired, that is to say, play out and die.

When a person dies, his eyes are closed, his hands crossed over his breast, and the relatives talk to him one by one, and bid him good-bye. The weeping widow tells her husband that, now that he has gone and does not want to stay with her any longer, he must not come back to frighten her or his sons or daughters or anyone else. She implores him not to carry any of them off, or do any mischief, but to leave them all alone.

A mother says to her dead infant: "Now go away! Don't come back any more, now that you are dead. Don't come at night to nurse at my breast. Go away, and do not come back!" And the father says to the child: "Don't come back to ask me to hold your hand, or to do things for you. I shall not know you any more. Don't come walking around here, but stay away."

The body is wrapped in a blanket almost before it is cold, to be buried later, but food is at once placed around it, and ashes are liberally strewn over and around the corpse, to enable the relatives to discover, by the tracks, into what kind of animal the dead has changed. At night some fox or coyote, polecat or rat, is sure to be attracted by the smell of the food; but the people believe that it was the departed who returned in the form of the animal to get his food. A shaman, without even looking at the tracks, may be able to tell what animal shape the dead assumes.

Within twenty-four hours the corpse is taken away to be buried. It is tied in three or four places to one or two poles and carried by two men. Women never go with them to the funeral. As soon as the undertakers have accomplished their task, they immediately wash their persons well. Upon their return, branches of the mountain cedar are burned inside of the house, to " cure " it.

The body is laid at rest in a shallow grave inside of a cave or just outside of it, with the head to the east and the feet to the west. In some caves, however, this rule is not adhered to, for I found corpses placed in accordance with the formation of the floor of the cave. The body is covered with an inch of earth, then with a row of pine or palm sticks put on lengthwise, and over this a layer of earth is spread five or six inches deep. On top of all, stones are thrown. The bodies of grown persons are stretched out to their full length, but with children the knees are generally drawn up.

This is one way in which the pagan Tarahumares bury their dead. Another mode, equally common, is to place the body lying on its back, on the surface, without any earth to cover it ; in this case the mouth of the cave is walled up with stones, or stones and mud, and several bodies may be found inside.

When exhuming skeletons I have frequently found bits of charcoal, which was explained by the fact that during the first night the mourners keep a fire near the grave, which to-day serves the same purpose as candles. This also accounts for the smokiness of the interior of the burial-caves, even of the ancient ones.

The dead keeps his buckskin pouch and three small gourds with beans. Three ears of corn are placed to the left of his head, as well as a small jar of tesvino. Another small jar of tesvino is placed near his feet, as well as his bow and arrows, the stone with which the arrows are stretched, reeds and sinews, his steel for striking fire, the small stick with which paint is put on the arrows, his sucking-tubes when the deceased has been a shaman, in fact all his light-weight belongings, besides balls of gum from the pine-tree, necklaces of *Coix Lachryma-Jobi*, and a hikuli plant.   Everything heavy, such as his axe, machete, beads, and money, he leaves, as it is thought that the weight would hinder him from rising to heaven.   This is the practical view the Indians have taken since their contact with the whites, as valuables frequently attract marauders.   The dead man's sandals, his violin, and the vessels from which he used to take his food, are kept in a separate place for a year, that is, until after the last function for the dead is over ; then at night the shaman and other men take them away and bury them somewhere, but not with the dead.   The skins on which he died are treated in the same way, and are never used again, lest a very ugly dog might be born of them.   The house is always destroyed, and the metate and many jars and baskets are broken.

On the third day after the death, the relatives begin to prepare the first feast for the dead, which is held within a fortnight.   One or two sheep or goats are killed, and the lungs, the heart, and the windpipe are hung from a stick outside the burial-cave.

As soon as the tesvino is ready the feast comes off, although comparatively little of the liquor is used at this first function.   The relatives, men and women, visit the grave and leave a jar with pinole, a small jar with tesvino, three tortillas, and three cigarettes with the dead, if he was a man ; with a woman, four tortillas, etc., are required.   The size of the tortillas varies with the age of the person.   For adults the ordinary tortilla is used ; to young people over six years old, medium-sized ones are given ; and children get small ones, about an inch and a half in diameter.   I have seen medium-sized ones made into the shape of a cross.

All the mourners talk to the departed, the shaman first.   He tells him that he had better take away everything they have given him, and not come and disturb the people he has left behind.   He should leave them alone, and some day they, too, will have to go where he is.   He should not kill any of the animals belonging to the family, as they have killed a sheep for him and given him the best part, the lungs, that he may eat and be satisfied and not take what now is theirs.

At the first feast I have seen worn in the hair by both men and women a peculiar kind of artificial flower. It is made from a short bit of reed in one end of which four incisions are made, with the parts turned outward to stand out like the corolla of a flower.   It is stuck under the hair-ribbon at one side of the head.   The mourners also make crosses on their foreheads with charcoal.

The second feast is given half a year later, and again animals are killed and a large quantity of tesvino is made.   Three men and three women carry food and tesvino to the grave, the relatives remaining at home. On their return they stop at a distance from the house and throw ashes over each other's heads before entering.

For the third function, which is the largest, an animal is selected from among those last acquired by the deceased, and quantities of food and beer are prepared. This feast is the final effort to despatch the dead.   A large earthen bowl is made especially for the purpose. It is about two feet in diameter and six inches deep.   It is filled with water, and a drinking-gourd placed inside

of it, upside down.   The shaman beats this gourd with
a corn-cob fastened to the end of a little stick.   His assistants help him, one by swinging the rattle, the other
by singing.   After a while the shaman lifts the bowl
up and after carrying it about in three ceremonial
circuits throws it into the air.   It falls to the ground
and breaks into many pieces, and the people dance and
trample on the shreds and on the drinking-gourd.

The young people conclude the function by running
a race of some hundred yards.   The men have their ball,
and as they run they scatter ashes to the four cardinal
points to cover the tracks of the dead.   They return re-
joicing, manifesting their delight by throwing up their
blankets, tunics, and hats, because now the dead is at
last chased off.   If the deceased be a woman, the
women run a race with rings and sticks.

A very elaborate third function, given by a widow,
was described to me as follows : There were five patios.
On one, for the dead, was erected one large cross and
two small ones, and three gourds with tesvino and a
basket with uncooked meat were placed near by.   A
fire was lighted, and one man had to watch here.   On
another patio one cross was raised, and a branch from a
pine-tree placed next to it.   Here, too, a jar with tesvino and a basket with uncooked meat were deposited,
and one man and two women kept watch, but no ceremonies were performed.   A third patio was for the hikuli cult, where the shaman rasped and sang.   On the
fourth patio, yumari was danced, and one large cross
and two smaller ones had been erected.   Finally, on the
fifth patio four torches of resinous pinewood, each a yard
high, were placed at the four cardinal points.   A peculiar
feature was that one man alone danced here between
these four torches, cutting with his knife three times
through each flame as he danced. This he did in reprises.

According to the names which the Tarahumares apply to the three functions for the dead, the main idea of the first is to give food ; of the second, to replenish the first supply ; and of the third to give drink. The three feasts are on an increasing scale of elaborateness, the first being comparatively insignificant. Each generally lasts one day and one night, and begins at the hour at which the dead breathed his last. There is always a special patio prepared for the dead, and another one for the hikuli cult, besides the ordinary dancing-place, and much howling and singing goes on, especially at the last.

At the feasts, the shaman steeps herbs in water and sprinkles this medicine over the people. Hikuli dancing and singing always play a prominent part at all the festivities, for the plant is thought to be very powerful in running off the dead, chasing them to the end of the world, where they join the other dead. Yumari is danced at intervals and much tesvino is used, and at all feasts the survivors drink with the dead.

There are three feasts for a man, and four for a woman. She cannot run so fast, and it is therefore harder to chase her off. Not until the last function has been made will a widower or a widow marry again, being more afraid of the dead than are other relatives.

After the death of a person, anyone who rendered him any service, as, for instance, watching his cattle for a week, claims something of what the dead left. He is satisfied, however, with a girdle or the like.

Once I was present at the burial-feast for a man who had hanged himself a fortnight before, while under the influence of liquor and angry over some property out of which he considered himself cheated. He had changed into a lion. Two men and two women carried food and tesvino ; the wife did not go with them, as the deceased had died alone, and she was afraid of being carried off by him. His father-in-law led the procession, carrying a goat-skin with its four feet remaining. The animal had belonged to the deceased and had been sacrificed for him, and the skin was to be given to him that in his new life he might rest on it. The suicide had been buried in a little cave with his feet toward the entrance. Having deposited the food near the dead man's head, the women sat down on a stone inside, while the men stood up near the mouth of the cave, all faces turned toward the grave. The father-in-law seated himself on a stone near the feet of the dead. It was a dreary winter evening in the Sierra and the scene was singularly impressive. The old man was a strong personality, powerfully built, and a shaman of great reputation, who in his entire bearing showed his determination to keep the dead at bay. He seemed to exercise a reassuring influence over the whole assembly.

I shall not easily forget the solemn and convincing way in which he upbraided the dead for his rash act. Taking the reed flower from his hair and holding it in his right hand, he waved it down and up, as if swayed by the force of his own thoughts, in accentuating his points, and he talked and argued with the dead for a quarter of an hour. The man was a great orator, and spoke so earnestly that my interpreter Nabor was affected almost to tears. The speech was a kind of dialogue with the dead, the speaker supplying the responses himself, and this is the gist of it :

Why are you there?—Because I am dead.—Why are you dead?—Because I died.—Why did you die?— Because I chose to.—That is not right. You have no shame. Did your mother, who gave you birth, tell you to do this? You are bad. Tell me, why did you kill yourself?—Because I chose to do it.—Now what did you get for it, lying there, as you are, with stones on top of you ? Were you not just playing the violin in the house with us ? Why did you hang yourself in the tree ?

Here I leave this tesvino and food for you, the meat and tortillas, that you may eat and not come back. We do not want you any more. You are a fool. Now I am going to leave you here. You are not going to drink tesvino in the house with us any more. Remain here ! Do not come to the house, for it would do you no good ; we would burn you. Good-bye, go now ; we do not want you any more !

All present then said good-bye to him, and all the women added, " Fool!" and then they all ran quickly into a deep water-hole, splashing into it clothes and all, that nothing from the dead might attach itself to them. They changed their wet attire after their arrival at the house. Later in the evening a magnificent hikuli feast was held. The Indians sat around the big fire, which cast a magical light over the tall old pine-trees around the patio, while the dancers moved about in their fantastic way through the red glow. Such a scene makes a deeper impression than any that could be produced on the stage.

The Christian Tarahumares believe that the shaman has to watch the dead throughout the year, or the deceased would be carried away by the Devil. If the feasts were not given, the departed would continue to wander about in animal shape. This is the direful fate meted out to people who are too poor to pay the shaman. Sometimes, if the dead person has not complied in life with the customary requirements in regard to feasts and sacrifices, the shamans have a hard time in lifting him to heaven. It may take hours of incantations and much tesvino to get his head up, and as much more to redeem his body. Sometimes the head falls back, and the shamans have to call for more tesvino to gain strength to lift him up again.

The Tarahumares had no great scruples about my removing the bodies of their dead, if the latter had died some years before and were supposed to have been properly despatched from this world. Where a body had been buried, the bones that were not taken away had to be covered up again. One Tarahumare sold me the skeleton of his mother-in-law for one dollar.

CHAPTER XXI

THREE WEEKS ON FOOT THROUGH THE BARRANCA—RIO FUERTE
—I GET MY CAMERA WET—ANCIENT CAVE-DWELLINGS AS-
CRIBED TO THE TUBAR INDIANS—THE EFFECT OF A COMPLI-
MENT—VARIOUS DEVICES FOR CATCHING FISH—POISONING THE
WATER—A BLANKET SEINE.

ON a cold day in the end of October I started from
Guachochic bound for the upper part of the great
Barranca de San Carlos and the country southward as
far as there were Tarahumares. Everything seemed
bleak and dreary. The corn was harvested, the grass
looked grey, and there was a wintry feeling in the air.
The sere and withered leaves rustled like paper, and as I
made camp near an Indian ranch I saw loose stubble
and dead leaves carried up in a whirlwind, two or three
hundred feet up toward a sky as grey and sober as that
of northern latitudes at that time of the year. We
travelled to the southeast from Guachochic over pine-
clad hills, coming now and then to a lonely ranch.

About seven miles before reaching the barranca I
arrived at a point 8,600 feet high, from which I could
look over this vast expanse of woodland, extending all
the way up to the deep gorge and diminishing in breadth
toward the northwest. At San Carlos, a ranch but recently established in this wilderness, I left my animals,
and immediately prepared for an extended excursion on
foot into the barranca and its neighbourhood.

Nearly the whole country of the Tarahumares is
drained by the river Fuerte, which, with its many tributaries, waters as many barrancas. The main one,

namely Barranca de San Carlos, is from 4,000 to 4,500 feet deep, and sinuous in its course. If there were a passable road along its bottom, the distance from the source of the river to a point a little below the village

View from the North across Barranca de San Carlos, near Guachochic.

of Santa Ana, where Rio Fuerte emerges from the Sierra, could be easily covered in two days; but as it is, a man requires at least a week to travel this distance, so much is he impeded by the roughness of the country.

Having descended into the barranca, which now felt almost uncomfortably warm, after the piercing winds of the highlands, I first visited the plateaus on the southern side, where the Indians have still kept themselves tolerably free from the white man's evil influence and are very jealous of their land. One night, while camping in a deep arroyo with very steep sides frowning down on us, one of the Indian carriers woke us with the startling news : "Get up! A stone is falling and will strike us!" I heard a noise, and instantly a stone, half the size of a child's head, hit the informant himself, as he sleepily rose. He lost his breath, but soon recovered, and no further damage was done.

I secured the necessary carriers and went down again to the river, which I now followed westward from Nogal for about twenty-five miles. The elevation at Nogal is 4,450 feet, about 800 feet higher than the place at which we left the river again. At the outset we came upon two very hot springs, the water of which had a yellow sediment. The gorge was narrow throughout. Sometimes its two sides rise almost perpendicularly, leaving but a narrow passage for the river. We then had either to wade in the water or to ascend some thousand feet, in order to continue our way. But generally there was a bank on one side or the other, and now and then the valley widened, yielding sufficient space for some bushes, or even a tree to grow, though it soon narrowed again. In some such spots we found a shrub called baynoro, with long, flexible branches and light-green leaves. Its small, yellow berries were as sweet as honey, but they did not agree with the Mexicans, who had stomach-aches and lost their appetites after eating them. The Indians made the same complaints, but I felt no ill effects from them.

Along the river we saw the tracks of many raccoons and otters, and there were also ducks and blue herons.

The colour of the water in the deep places was greyish green, and as the river rises in the high sierra, it felt icy cold to wade through. One day we had to cross it eight times. On one such occasion, while wading waist-deep, the Indian who carried the photographic outfit in a bag on his back, forgot for a moment, on account of the stinging cold, how far his burden hung down, and

let it dip into the water. The prospect of being prevented, perhaps for a long time to come, from photographing, was very annoying. Six plate-holders were
so wet that I could not even draw the shutters out, but
luckily I had more elsewhere.

We came upon several ancient cave-dwellings, all of
which were rather small, and attributed by the Tarahumares to the Tubar Indians. One of them was situated about 250 feet above the bottom of the barranca.
A two-storied, rather irregularly shaped building occupied
the entire width of the cave, without reaching to the
roof. The floor of the house was scarcely two yards
broad, but the building widened out very much, following the shape of the cave. The materials used in the
construction were stone and mud or, rather, reddish
grit; and smaller stones had been put between larger
ones in an irregular way. The walls were only five or
six inches thick and were plastered with mud. An
upright pole supported the ceiling, which was rather
pretty, consisting of reeds resting on the rafters, and
covered on top with mud. The ceiling of the second
story had been made in the same way, but had fallen
in. A piece of thick board half covered the entrance.
In the first story I found an additional chamber, and in
it a skeleton, of which I secured the skull and some
typical bones.

Not far from this, and situated in very rough country, was another cave, that contained ten one-storied
chambers of the same material and construction. The
cave was fifty feet long and at the mouth seven feet
high. The apertures of the chambers were fairly
squared, and not of the shape of the conventional ear
of corn. One door was a foot and a half broad, and
two feet and a half high. I crawled through the chambers, which were miserably small. The floor was plas-

Barranca de San Carlos, in its Upper Part.

tered, and in some rooms I noticed circular holes sunk into the ground in the way that I had already observed in Zapuri. There were also small square holes, the sides being six inches long in the front wall.

Twenty miles from here, and just north of the pueblo of Cavorachic, was a third cave which contained thirteen houses in ruins. The material here, too, was the same as before, but the houses were built to the roof of the cave, and were rounded at the corners. Peculiar round loop-holes were seen here, too. Eight of them formed a horizontal line, and one extra hole was a little higher up.

A track could be made out at certain places along the river, but the country was very lonely. In the course of several days only six Indian fami-

One of my Companions in Barranca de San Carlos.

lies were encountered, and two of those lived here only temporarily. We also met five stray Indians that had come down from the highlands to fetch bamboo reeds for arrows, etc. It was quite pleasant to meet somebody now and then, although, unfortunately, no one had anything to sell, except a few small fish, the people being themselves as hard up for food as we were. We carried our little metate on which we ground corn for our meals, but we found it very difficult on this trip of four weeks' duration to secure from day to day corn enough to satisfy our wants. One item in our menu, new to me, but common throughout northern Mexico, was really excellent when we could procure the very simple material from which it was made, namely squash-seeds. These were ground very fine and boiled in a saucepan. This dish, which is of Tarahumare origin, is called pipian, and looks like curds. Mixed with a little chile it is very palatable, and in this period of considerable privation it was the only food I really enjoyed.

But such luxuries were not served every day. Far from it. For several days in succession we had nothing but corncakes and water. Therefore our joy was great when at last we one day espied some sheep on the other side of the river. They belonged to a woman who watched them herself, while wintering among the rocks with her herd of about a dozen sheep and goats. I sent my interpreter over to make a bargain for one of the animals, and as he did not return after a reasonable lapse of time, and as we were all hungry, I went across the river myself to see the dashing widow. I found my man still bargaining, lying on the ground stretched out on his stomach and resting his head on his hands. She was grinding corn on the metate and seemed to pay little attention to either of us, but her personal attractiveness at once impressed me. She was still in her best

years and had fine bright eyes. A ribbon dyed with
the native yellow dye from lichens ran through the
braids of her hair, and was marvellously becoming to
her almost olive complexion.   I could not help saying,
" How pretty she is ! " to which the interpreter, in a
dejected mood, replied : " Yes, but she will not sell
anything, and I have been struggling hard." " Of course,
she will sell," said I, " handsome as she is ! " at which

The Widow Grinding Corn in her Camp.

remark of mine I noticed she smiled.   Though I judged
from the way in which she wore her hair, in two braids,
hanging in a loop in the neck, that she had been in
association with the Mexicans, I did not expect that
she could understand Spanish so well.   I immediately
returned to my camp to fetch some beads and a red
handkerchief to make an impression on my obdurate
belle.   But on my way back to her I met my interpreter, who brought the glad tidings that she had made
up her mind to sell, and that I might send for the animal whenever I wanted it.   The price was one Mexican silver dollar.   So I sent my " extras " along with
the money, and in return received a fine sheep with
long white wool, when all we had hoped for was only a
goat.   There is not the slightest doubt in my mind

that my felicitous compliment brought about this happy
result.

During our travels along the river, every day we
came upon traps for catching fish. The Tarahumares
have various modes of fishing. Sometimes they manage to catch fish with their hands in crevices between
stones, even diving for them. In the shallow parts of
the rivers and in the brooks, following the course of the
stream, two stone walls a foot or two high are built.
These walls converge at the lower end and form a
channel, in which is placed horizontally a mat of stalks
of the eagle fern (*Pteris aquilina*). When the fish attempt to cross this mat, through which the water passes
freely, they are intercepted. Often the fish caught in
this way are only an inch long, but none is too small
for a Tarahumare to reject.

Other similar walls form square or oblong corrals,
where the fish can easily enter, but not so readily find
a way out. After dark the owners come with lighted
torches and carefully examine the corrals, turning up
every stone. The fish are blinded by the glare of the
light and can be caught and thrown into baskets.
Frogs, tadpoles, larvæ, and water-beetles are also welcome.

In the central part of the country they use a spear
made of a thin reed and tipped with thorns of the nopal. Sometimes it is shot from a diminutive bow, like
an arrow. But a more interesting way is to hurl it by
means of a primitive throwing-stick, which is nothing
but a freshly cut twig from a willow (*jaria*) about
six inches long, left in its natural state except for the
flattening of one end on one side. The spear is held
in the left hand, the stick in the right. The flat part
of the latter is placed against the end of the spear,
which is slightly flattened on two sides, while the end

is squarely cut off. By pressing one against the other, the throwing-stick is bent, and sufficient force is produced by its rebound to make the spear pierce small fish. Many a Tarahumare may be seen standing immovable on the bank of a streamlet, waiting patiently for a fish to come, and as soon as he has hit it throwing himself into the water to grab it.

But a more profitable way of catching fish is by poisoning the water. In the highlands a kind of polygonum is used for this purpose. It is pounded with stones and thrown into the small corrals. When the fishing is to be done on a somewhat extensive scale, two species of agave—the amole (the soap-plant) and the soke—are used, and many households join in the sport. First of all maguey plants have to be collected, and wine made, as this is indispensable to the success of the undertaking. At the place selected for the fishing the people assemble, and two managers are appointed, one for each side of the river. It is their duty to see that everything is done in the right and proper way and all the requisite ceremonies are observed.

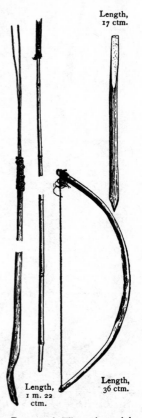

Length, 17 ctm.

Length, 1 m. 22 ctm.

Length, 36 ctm.

Bow and Throwing-stick for the Fish-spear. A modern Fish-spear with iron points, and thrown by hand is seen to the left.

The women are a couple of hundred yards back cooking herbs and making pinole for the men to eat. No pregnant women are allowed to be present, as then the fish would not die.

Half-circular corrals of stone are built to intercept

the fish that drift along, irrespective of any private traps that may be found on the place. Fish caught in the latter belong to those who put up the traps. While constructing these corrals, the men catch a few fish with their hands, between the rocks, open them in the back and give them to the women to broil. When they are done, the men pound the fish to a pulp, mix it with pinole, and roll the mass into a ball two or three inches in diameter. One of the managers then goes down stream, below the corrals, and places the ball in a water pool. It is a sacrifice to the master of the river, a large serpent (Walúla), which makes an ugly noise. Every river, water-hole, and spring has its serpent that causes the water to come up out of the earth. They are all easily offended; and therefore the Tarahumares place their houses some little distance from the water, and when they travel avoid sleeping near it.

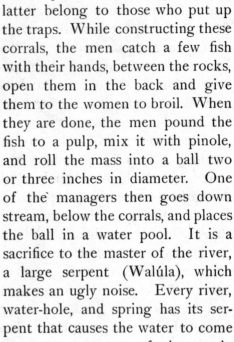

The Amole, a Species of Agave.

Whenever the Tarahumares make pinole while away from home, they sacrifice the first part to the water-serpents, dropping it with the little stick with which the pinole is stirred. They sprinkle it first forward, then to the left, then to the right, and then upward, three times in each direction. If they did not do this, the water-serpents would try to catch them and chase them back to their own land. Besides the sacrifice of the fish ball, they offer axes, hats, blankets, girdles, pouches, etc., and especially knives and strings of beads, to the master of the fish, who is considered to be the oldest fish. This is in payment for what they are going to catch, and the donations are either hung to a cross or a horizontal bar specially erected in the middle of the river, and remain hanging there until daybreak, when their respective owners take them back.

In the meantime eight or ten men have gathered the amole and soke. They wrap the plants in their blankets and bring them direct to the river, where they are to be used. The leaves are pounded with stones and spread out for a while before sunset. As soon as it is dark the men throw them into the water, and trample on them to make the juice come out. Three or four men take turns, standing waist-deep in the water, treading with all their might and howling. The effect of the poison in the course of the night is said to reach down some 300 yards. It stupefies the fish, and although many of them revive, a few are killed and may be eaten, as the poison does not affect the meat.

The managers see to it that everybody does his duty and that no one falls asleep during the night, while the women help by watching the mats, that the otters may not eat the fish caught in them.

A curious detail is that one man on each side of the river is deputed to heat stones and throw them into the river three or four at a time, every half-hour, possibly to frighten off the serpent. During the night not one fish is taken up, but at daybreak the managers go down the river to investigate the effect of the poison, and upon their return the fish are gathered in, the men often diving into deep water for them. The work is done with great earnestness and almost in silence, the women helping the men in catching the fish. While the fishing is going on they do not eat any of the fish, for fear of not getting more, but during the day quantities are broiled and eaten, without salt or chile, however, and the bones are invariably thrown into the fire. Most of the fish are cut open in the back and placed on rocks or on trees to dry for future use. Such fishing may last for two days and nights, and is finished by dancing yumari and drinking maguey wine. On one occasion as much was caught as ten men could carry. Expeditions of this kind may be repeated two or three times a year; but when food is plentiful a whole year may pass without one being undertaken.

Palo de la flecha, too, is used as poisoning material, and seems to be even more powerful than the two plants mentioned. There is a milky juice under the bark of this tree which, when it comes in contact with the human skin, makes it smart like a burn. The water is poisoned by cutting the bark from the trunk and boughs directly into the water, the people taking care to stand to the windward. One man who neglected this precaution got some juice in his eyes and was blinded for three days, though an application of salt water finally cured him.

Although a single man may poison fish in a small way even in winter, he is hardly likely to do so except in summer-time, when provisions are low. The Indians dislike going into cold water; besides, they say that the cold impairs the effect of the poison.

In summer-time the Indians may also improvise a net with the help of their blankets, and drag the river at suitable places. Farther down on the Rio Fuerte, I once saw them make a large and serviceable net by fastening sixteen blankets together lengthwise with a double row of wooden pins. Along the upper edge of this

Tarahumares on the Rio Fuerte Fishing with their Blankets.

net they made a hem three inches deep, and through this they passed vines securely joined together by means of the fibres of the maguey to do duty as ropes. The opposite edge of the net had a hem four inches deep and this was filled with sand to sink it as it was dragged in. The boys and girls were told to go ahead and splash all they could in the water to prevent the fish in the net from swimming out, and it was funny to see them dive heels over head into the water over and over like porpoises, the girls as well as the boys, with their skirts on. The fishermen advanced slowly, as the net was heavy. When it was brought in toward the shore, the women, even those with babies on their backs, helped to drag it. As the two ends of the net reached the bank, the big fish were picked out and thrown landward, while the remainder were brought up with a dip-net made of three blankets. Eighty good-sized suckers were secured, besides a large quantity of "small-fry."

CHAPTER XXII

RESUMPTION OF THE JOURNEY SOUTHWARD—PINUS LUMHOLTZII—
COOKING WITH SNOW—TERROR-STRICKEN INDIANS—A GEN-
TLEMANLY HIGHWAYMAN AND HIS "SHOOTING–BOX"—THE
PERNICIOUS EFFECT OF CIVILISATION UPON THE TARAHU-
MARES—A FINE SPECIMEN OF THE TRIBE—THE LAST OF THE
TARAHUMARES.

FROM this trip I returned to San Carlos, mainly
over the highlands south of the barranca, and
shortly afterward was able to continue my journey
toward the southwest. The cordons here, generally
speaking, have a southerly direction, running parallel to
each other.

Reaching at one place an elevation of 8,800 feet, I
had a fine view of the entire central part of the Tarahumare country, seeing as far as Cerro Grande, at the
northern end of the llano of Guachochic, in which direction the country, as a matter of course, looked quite flat.
Nearest to us were wild-looking arroyos and cordons,
covered in the lower portions with oak-trees, and higher
up with pines. We were in the midst of vast pine forests, and even the country north of us looked like one
uninterrupted forest of pines.

The Tarahumares have names for six kinds of pines.
One species, first met with near Tutuhuaca, was new to
science. Though not a large tree, it is very ornate, owing to its slender, whip-like branches, and its hanging
needles, from eight to ten inches long. It grows here
and there in groups at high altitudes, on decomposed

volcanic tuff. The needles are boiled by the Indians and the Mexicans, and the decoction used as a remedy for stomach troubles. It is not disagreeable to take, the

Pinus Lumholtzii.

taste resembling that of anise-seed. The Tarahumares prefer the wood of this variety of pines for the making of their violins. I found this species as far south as the sierra above Pueblo Nuevo, in the State of Durango.

The vegetation of the Sierra Madre is incomparably stronger and more luxurious than that of the cold North. The pine-trees in higher altitudes, for instance in Norway, appear miserably puny and almost stunted when compared with the giants of the South. Trees of 100 to 150 feet high and 10 to 15 feet in girth are frequent. We noticed some species of pines the needles of which were over a foot long.

The region through which we were passing seemed uninhabited, and there were really but few Indians living here. The cordon nearest to the one on which we were standing was covered with snow, and we climbed without difficulty to a point 9,300 feet high. There was no water, but snow three inches deep in some places, yielding all the water we required, though it had a slight flavour of the pines. The Mexicans did not like it, and said they would not eat food cooked with snow; but after I had shown them that the water obtained in this way was very good, they also took to it.

On our arrival at some Indian ranches, the people screamed with terror, ran away and hid themselves. There was something so unusual about their fright, that the interpreter and I went out of our way to investigate the matter. I saw two children making their escape among the bushes as best they could, a boy leading a three-year-old girl all the time, never deserting her. We found the children and a young woman on top of a rock. After we had succeeded in allaying their fears, they answered our questions readily. It appeared that two men from this place had recently been hanged by some people from Cienega Prieta, the ranch for which we were making. One of the victims had been revived, but the other had died. My Indian boy Patricio knew about the outrage, too.

I had at the outset been warned against robbers

south of Guachochic, and advised never to sleep in houses—a thing I rarely did, anyway, for other reasons. One man especially, Teodoro Palma, had an unsavoury reputation as a "gentlemanly highwayman." In the desolate region where his residence lies, his father had maintained a band of valiant men, who made regular plundering expeditions, driving cattle away, etc. It was a common tale that travellers who had to pass his place were invited to come in, but never came out again. The bodies of the victims, it was said, were buried at night in the cemetery of the Indian village of Chinatu, a few miles distant. Times had changed since then, and the son was more guarded in his operations, but still sufficiently active.

In order to avoid a long detour to the east, I had chosen to follow the track which passes this place, though travellers generally give it a wide berth ; besides, I thought best to take the bull by the horns. When I reached the robber's stronghold, I did not find Don Teodoro at home, though he was expected to return the next day. In the mean time the superintendent showed me around the house and sold me some necessary provisions.

The house looked forbidding enough. A wall of adobe, eighteen feet high, ran all around the establishment, shutting it in securely. It was provided with two small towers, which had loop-holes for rifles.

In the house was a small chapel, in which Don Teodoro and his father before him had frequently knelt to pray. The altar was decorated with the pictures of many saints, and in the centre was a painting of the Christ-child, a crucifix, and an artificial apple.

When the lord of the manor arrived the following day, I immediately went to see him. As I passed through the enclosure he was scolding the superintendent, but on perceiving me he stepped forward to receive me. This modern Fra Diavolo was about thirty years old, rather short of stature, but unusually well built. He wore an embroidered brown jacket and a blue waist-coat, and around his neck was thrown a many-coloured scarf. On one side of his sombrero was a scarlet rosette. Under it gleamed brown, piercing eyes. His hair was cut short. Altogether he was quite good-looking, ex-cept for a cruel, sensual expression of the features. His entire manner, erect carriage, and quick, decisive move-ments told me he was a man of violent temper and extreme determination.

He led the way into a room, and I handed him my letter of recommendation from the Mexican Govern-ment, and explained what I was doing in the sierra. Af-ter he had read the letter, he said that he was my friend. I told him that I had heard there were robbers in the vicinity, and in case I was molested I should apply to him for assistance, since he was a very influential man. Of course I knew as long as he did not rob us we were quite safe. I then photographed him and his house, and he evidently felt quite flattered. He accompanied me for a mile down the road, and then, taking me aside, handed me back the paltry sum I had paid for the pro-visions, saying he did not accept payment from his guests. This was rather embarrassing, but there was no way out of it, and I had to accept it. I afterward sent him a copy of his photograph to even up matters.

The guide with whom Don Teodoro had provided me pointed out to us a place where his master last year killed and robbed a man. "He is a poor shot," he added, "except at close range, and he generally travels at night." In 1895 Don Teodoro Palma himself was killed by the Indians. If half the rumours about him are true, he certainly deserved his fate. He never dared to go down to the lowlands, because " he owed so many dead," as the saying goes.   A few years before my visit, an American had been killed and robbed in the vicinity, and his countrymen in Chihuahua offered a re- ward for the apprehension of the murderer, dead or alive.   Don Teodoro knew that a certain friend of his had perpetrated the crime, and in order to secure the re- ward he invited him to his house and shot him down in cold blood.

I arrived safely in Guadalupe y Calvo, a once flour- ishing place, but now quite dead, since the mines have ceased to be worked.   There are large Mexican ranches southeast of the town, and whatever Tarahumares live hereabout are servants of the Mexicans and frequently intermarry with the Tepehuanes.

I thus traversed from north to south the country over which the Tarahumares once held sway.   To-day we find this tribe, approximately, between Guadalupe y Calvo and Temosachic ; roughly speaking, between the twenty-sixth and twenty-ninth degrees northern latitude.

Civilisation, as brought to the Tarahumare, is not fraught with benefits for him.   It rudely shakes the col- umns of the temple of his religion.   The Mexican Cen- tral Railroad crushes his sacred plants without thought of its anger, which is vented on the poor Tarahumare by sending him bad years and ill-luck.   While the Ind- ians deny themselves the pleasure of smoking tobacco in the daytime for fear of offending the sun with the smoke, the white men's furnaces and engines belch forth black clouds of smoke day after day, keeping the people out of the sight of Tata Dios, and thus preventing him from guarding them.   In the engine itself they see the Devil with a long tongue and a big beard.

Worse than that, the foot of civilisation destroys his home; for the whites draw the boundary line of his country closer and closer. The better class of Mexicans keep to themselves, and seldom, if ever, bother about the Indians at their doors, whose mode of living and way of thinking are so different from their own. The class of whites on the borderland of such civilisation as the Tarahumare comes in contact with is not the kind that will or can improve him, being ignorant and unscrupulous. The Indian civilised by them is a very unpleasant person to deal with. He has learned to cheat and to steal, and he no longer carries out his contracts and agreements. Having learned the value of money, his greed is awakened, and he begins to look out only for his own profit.

The first white men with whom the Indian gets acquainted are the traders who speak his language, and whose sole aim is to enrich themselves at his expense and compel him to deal with them. If the Indian does not want to sell, the lenguaraz loses his patience, throws a few dollars toward him, takes the ox, and goes off. Many will go still further. They force the native to borrow from them, whether he wants the money, the cloth, the mescal, or the use of the horse, or not. Many Indians would refuse mescal, satisfied with their native stimulants, but see no other way of getting rid of the unwelcome and obtrusive white than by yielding to his demand. The agreement is made that he must return the so-called loan on a certain date, two or three months hence; the Indian, of course, having no almanac, easily makes a mistake in his calculation, and the date passes. The dealer has gained his point. He saddles his horse, looks up the Indian, and makes a great to-do about all the trouble he is put to in collecting the debt, charging not only enormous interest for overtime, but adding exorbitant travelling expenses and fees. He succeeds by threats and intimidation in getting his damages adjusted in such a way that, in return for the paltry sum he lent the Indian, he now drives off two or three oxen.

The Indians, being honourable in their dealings, do not at first contact with the whites suspect rascality, and many stories are told illustrating the ease with which they have been cheated.

Once a Mexican bought a sheep from a native on credit, and, after killing it, paid for it with the head, the skin, and the entrails. Another man did still better. He paid for his sheep with the same valuables, and "spoke so well" that the Indian was content to remain in his debt as the final result of the transaction. On another occasion a native was induced to sell eleven oxen, almost his entire stock, to a Mexican. It was agreed that the latter should pay two cows for each ox, but not having any cows with him he left his horse and saddle as security. The Indian is still waiting for the cows. When I expressed my surprise at the ease with which he allowed himself to be swindled, he replied that the Mexican "spoke so well." They are so delighted at hearing their language spoken by a white man, that they lose all precaution and are completely at the mercy of the wily whites, who profit by their weakness.

Some tough lenguaraz is not ashamed to cheat at games until the Indian has lost everything he has. One poor wretch lost several oxen in one game of quinze. Other sharpers borrow money from the natives and never pay back the loan, or else impose fines on the Indians under the pretext of being authorities. Some foist themselves upon the Tarahumares at their feasts, which they disturb by getting drunk and violating women. Where the Indians are still masters of the situation they catch such an offender and take him before the Mexican

authorities, insisting upon his paying for all the requirements for another feast, as he has spoiled the value of
the one on which he intruded. In the central part of
the country, near Norogachic, they may even kill such a
transgressor.

It is generally through mescal that the Indians become peons. When the Indian has once developed a
taste for mescal, he will pay anything to get it, first his
animals, then his land. When he has nothing more to
sell, the whites still give him this brandy and make him
work. And there he is. To work himself free is next
to impossible, because his wages are not paid in money,
but in provisions, which barely suffice to keep him and
his family alive. Indians are sometimes locked up over
night to force them to work.

The children of such parents grow up as peons of
the Mexicans, who deal out miserable wages to the
descendants of the owners of the land on which the
usurpers grow rich. Before the occupancy of the country by the new masters, the Tarahumares never knew
what poverty was. No wonder that the Christian
Tarahumares believe that hell is peopled so thickly with
Mexicans that there is not room for all. Some
have been crowded out, and have come to the Tarahumares to trouble them. The Indians in some districts have been cheated so much that they no longer
believe anything the white men tell them, and they do
not offer food any more to a white stranger if he is
what they call "deaf," in other words, unable to speak
and understand their language and explain what he is
about.

They make very good servants when treated right,
although they often want a change; but they will return
to a good master. I once had a Tarahumare woman in
my employ as cook. She was very industrious and in

every way superior to any Mexican servant I ever had. When not busy with her kitchen work, she was mending her own or her two children's clothes. While very distrustful, she was good-tempered and honourable, and spoke Spanish fairly well, and her eyes indicated unusual intelligence. A white man had deserted her to marry a Mexican woman, and she grieved much, but in time she became reconciled to her fate, though she declared she would never marry again, as all men were bad.

Civilised Tarahumare Boy.

The Tarahumares have made excellent soldiers in fighting for the Government. In one of the civil wars, their leader, Jesus Larrea, from Nonoava, a pure-bred Tarahumare, distinguished himself, not only by bravery and determination, but also as a commander. In private life he was civil and popular.

The majority speak their own language, and in the central and most mountainous part, the heart of the Tarahumare country, they are of pure breed. Here the women object to unions with outsiders, and until very recently light-coloured children were not liked. Mothers may even yet anoint their little ones and leave them in the sun, that they may get dark. The consensus of opinion among the tribe is that half-castes turn out to be bad people and "some day will be fighting at the drinking-feasts." A few instances are known in which women have left their half-caste babies in the woods to perish, and such children are often given away to be adopted by the Mexicans. In the border districts, however, the Indians have become much Mexicanised and intermarry freely with the whites.

Be it said to the credit of those high in authority in Mexico, they do all in their power to protect the Indians. But the Government is practically powerless to control the scattered population in the remote districts. Besides, the Indians most preyed upon by the sharpers cannot make themselves understood in the official language, and therefore consider it hopeless to approach the authorities. In accordance with the liberal constitution of Mexico, all natives are citizens, but the Indians do not know how to take advantage of their rights, although sometimes large bodies have banded together and travelled down to Chihuahua to make their complaints, and have always been helped out—for the time being. The efforts of the Government to enlighten the Indians by establishing schools are baffled by the difficulty in finding honest and intelligent teachers with a knowledge of the Indian language.

Where the Indians have had little or nothing to do with the whites, they are obliging, law-abiding, and trustworthy. Profit is no inducement to them, as they believe that their gods would be angry with them for charging an undue price. As a matter of fact, they sell corn all the year round, whether it be scarce or plentiful, at the same price, though the Mexicans charge them very different prices. The almighty dollar has no devotees among these Indians. They have no need of aught that money can buy, and are swayed by persuasion and kind and just treatment more than by gold. If they have a few coins, they place them in a jar and bury them in some remote cave, taking from the horde only a little when they have to buy some necessity of life.

Among the pagans in Pino Gordo I met the finest specimen of the Tarahumare tribe, a shaman, called Juan Ignacio. Although he had never been as far as Guadalupe y Calvo, and only twice in his life to Babori-

Juan Ignacio and his Son, Pagan Tarahumares.

game, and had thus spent all his life in the mountains among his own people, he showed a courtesy and tact that would have graced a gentleman. He took splendid care, not only of myself, but of my men and animals as well, giving us plenty to eat, sending his man to chop wood for us, etc. He was possessed of the nicest temper, and was truthful, a rare quality among Tarahumares, as well as square in his dealings. His uprightness and urbanity commanded respect even from the lenguarazes, and they did not rob him as much as the other Indians of the district ; consequently he was quite well-to-do.

While living among the heathen, of whom there are yet some three thousand left, I had no fear of being robbed of any part of my outfit. The Indians themselves would not touch anything, and there were no strange Mexicans about. If they had come, the Tarahumares would have immediately warned me. Everything was perfectly safe as long as I had an honest interpreter. The Tarahumare in his native condition is many times better off, morally, mentally, and economically, than his civilised brother ; but the white man will not let him alone as long as he has anything worth taking away. Only those who by dear experience have learned to be cautious are able to maintain themselves independently ; but such cases are becoming more and more rare.

It is the same old story over again, in America, as in Africa, and Asia, and everywhere. The simple-minded native is made the victim of the progressive white, who, by fair means or foul, deprives him of his country. Luckily, withal, the Tarahumare has not yet been wiped out of existence. His blood is fused into the working classes of Mexico, and he grows a Mexican. But it may take a century yet before they will all be made the servants of the whites and disappear like the Opatas. Their assimilation may benefit Mexico, but one may well ask : Is it just ? Must the weaker always be first crushed, before he can be assimilated by the new condition of things?

Future generations will not find any other record of the Tarahumares than what scientists of the present age can elicit from the lips of the people and from the study of their implements and customs. They stand out to-day as an interesting relic of a time long gone by ; as a representative of one of the most important stages in the development of the human race ; as one of those wonderful primitive tribes that were the founders and makers of the history of mankind.

CHAPTER XXIII

CERRO DE MUINORA, THE HIGHEST MOUNTAIN IN CHIHUAHUA—
THE NORTHERN TEPEHUANES—TROUBLES CROPPING OUT OF
THE CAMERA—SINISTER DESIGNS ON MEXICO ATTRIBUTED TO
THE AUTHOR—MAIZILLO—FOOT-RACES AMONG THE TEPE-
HUANES — INFLUENCE OF THE MEXICANS UPON THE TEPE-
HUANES, AND VICE VERSA—PROFITABLE LIQUOR TRAFFIC—
MEDICINE LODGES—CUCUDURI, THE MASTER OF THE WOODS
—MYTH OF THE PLEIADES.

ON my return from an excursion southward from
Guadalupe y Calvo as far as Mesa de San Rafael,
I ascended on January 12, 1895, Cerro de Muinora,
probably the highest elevation in northern Mexico.
I say probably, because I had no opportunity of measuring Cerro de Candelaria. Approached from the north
it looked like a long-stretched mountain, covered with
pines, and falling off abruptly toward the west. It is
conspicuous in the songs and beliefs of the Tepehuane
Indians.

We made a camp about 1,000 feet below the top,
among the pines, with snow lying all around us, and in
the night a flock of parrots flew screeching past the
tents. I was surprised to find the temperature so mild;
there was no ice on the water, not even at night.
The aneroid showed the height of the top to be 10,266
feet (20.60 in. at a temperature of 40° F., at 5.15 P.M.).
I noticed more birds between our camping-place and
the top than I had ever seen before in pine forests.
Blackbirds, the brown creepers (*certhia*), and red cross-
bills were seen on the very top.

From Guadalupe y Calvo I continued my journey to the northwest in order to visit the Tepehuanes, about fifteen hundred of whom still exist here in the northern-most outpost of the tribe's former domain. Only seven-

A Tepehuane Family.

teen miles north of Guadalupe y Calvo is the Tepe-huane village Nabogame (in Tepehuane, Navógeri, "where nopals [nāvó] grow ").

The Tepehuane region includes some fine agricultural land. There are fields there which have been planted for forty and fifty years in succession, as for instance in Mesa de Milpillas ; but here, too, the whites have ap-propriated a considerable portion of the country, though the Tepehuanes are largely in possession of their land, because they are more valiant than the Tarahumares, and can only be deprived of their property through the agency of mescal, for which they have an unfortunate weakness.

The Tepehuanes are less phlegmatic and more impressionable and impulsive than the Tarahumares. One woman laughed so much that she could not be photo-

Old Log-Houses near Nabogame.

graphed. They are noisy and active, and in the fields they work merrily, chatting and laughing. Even when peons of the Mexicans they are not so abject-looking as the Tarahumares, but retain their proud and independent manners. They behave almost like men of the world in comparison with the unsophisticated Tarahumares. In the eyes of some of the Tepehuane women I noticed a fire as bright as in those of Italians.

These Indians live in commodious log-cabins, with interlocked corners. The roofs are gabled and often supported by piles of wood. They are covered with shingles, over which are placed rows of stones to keep them in place. The doors are furnished with jambs.

The Tepehuanes call themselves Ódami, the meaning of which I could not find out. By the Tarahumares they are called Sæló ("walking-stick" insects (*phasmidæ*), in Mexican-Spanish *campamoche*). The Tepehuane language is not melodious, being full of consonants, and hard like the people themselves. They still speak it among themselves, though there are but few who do not understand Spanish. The Mexicans frequently enter into marriage with them.

SONGS OF THE TEPEHUANE TRIBE

LAST SONG SUNG AT THE FEAST WHEN THE MORNING STAR
APPEARS

So - (só-) da - gi   u - ki - (jí-) ru   tu - vá - ni - mi.
(There is) water (*i.e.*, tesvino) in the house ; He is coming down (to us).

As to their religion they are far more reticent than the Tarahumares, and it is difficult to get information on this subject. One reason for this is that they are afraid of being laughed at by the Mexicans. They still keep up their dances and secret rites and their ceremonies, customs, and beliefs. Although in many points they resemble the Tarahumares, in others fundamental differences exist, such as the complex observances of rules in regard to puberty, none of which have been found among the Tarahumares.

Ignorant Mexicans, who have but a faint idea as to who is president of their country, more than once have attributed land-grabbing intentions to my expedition. With my three or four Mexicans and Indians and a dozen pack mules, I have been credited with designs of conquering Mexico for the Americans. Even here in Nabogame a Mexican settler felt uneasy about his holdings and stirred the Indians up, saying that if they allowed "that man to photograph them, the Devil would carry off all of them, and it would be better to kill him." I was to meet the people on a Sunday, and in the morning I received this discouraging letter written by a Mexican for the Indian gobernador or "general," who, to affirm or authenticate the letter, had put a cross, as his mark or signature, underneath his name :

PUEBLO DE NABOGAME, January 29, 1893.
DEAR MR. PICTUREMAKER :

Do me the favour not to come to the pueblo to photograph, which I know is your intention. I believe the best for you to do is to go first to Baborigame, because, as far as this pueblo is concerned, I do not give permission. Therefore, you will please decide not to pass this day in this pueblo photographing.

Your obedient servant,
JOSÉ H. ARROYOS,
General.

TO MR. PICTUREMAKER.

Taking my Mexican attendant with me, I walked over to the place where some twenty Indians and several Mexicans had assembled. The scheming instigator of the trouble had brought his rifle with him, to give weight to his words ; but the Mexican judge was on my side, and after he had read my letters from the Government, he made a speech in which he convinced the people that they must obey the authorities. The Tepehuanes soon saw the force of his argument, and the defeated agitator slunk away. The outcome of the dis-

Tepehuanes from Nabogame.

pute was that the Indians expressed their regret that there were not more of them present for me to photograph ; if I desired, they would send for more of their tribe to come and pose before the camera.

Around Nabogame grows a plant called *maizillo,* or *maizmillo.* It is more slender than the ordinary corn-plant and the ears are very small. It grows among the corn and has to be weeded out, as it injures the good plants. However, several Mexicans assured me that, when cultivated, the ears develop. After three years they grow considerably larger and may be used as food. A man in Cerro Prieto raises this kind only ; others mix it with the ordinary corn. I was told that people from the Hot Country come to gather it, each taking away about one almud to mix with their seed corn. The combination is said to give splendid results in fertile soil.

Can this possibly be the original wild plant from which the ordinary Indian corn has been cultivated ? If the information I received about it in Mexquitic, State of Jalisco, is correct, then this question must be answered negatively, because my informant there stated that the plant is triennial. In that locality it is called *maiz de pajaro,* and it is cultivated as a substitute for the ordinary corn, or for use in making atole. The Huichol Indians also know it and raise it ; they call it tāts.

For about a month I stopped at Mesa de Milpillas, which is a fertile high plateau. The country is now almost open, yet magnificent pines still remain, and Cerro de Muinora stands guard to the south. This is the stronghold of the northern Tepehuanes.

I then descended toward the west to the village of Cinco Llagas, and found the Tepehuanes there pure-bred, although speaking Spanish. Ascending again to the sierra over the mining camp of San José, I arrived in Baborigame (Tepehuane, Vāwúlile = "where there is a large fig-tree"). The pueblo is finely situated on a llano one mile and a half in diameter, and surrounded by pretty hills. I took up my abode in a Tepehuane shanty in the neighbourhood of the village. The owner asked for the rent in advance, and for the amount of fifty centavos Mr. Hartman and I secured the right of occupancy, without time limit. I stayed there from March 31st to April 30th. There are a couple of Mexican stores at Baborigame, and the village is more Mexican than Indian. The Tepehuanes live on their ranches, and come in only on festive occasions, to mingle with their "neighbours," as the Mexicans are designated by the Indians in all parts of Mexico.

I was told that native travelling merchants from southern Mexico, called Aztecs and Otomies, pass through Baborigame every five years, to sell their goods. They bring articles of silk and wool, wooden spoons, needles and thread, and do nice embroidery work, and make or mend garments.

The Tepehuanes of the north have much the same games and sports as the Tepehuanes, and at Easter-time, foot-races *à la* Tarahumare were arranged as part of the general festivities of the season. Two hundred and ninety people assembled, among them a few Tarahumares. There were several races, the runners being divided into different groups, men and women (married and unmarried), and children. As among the Tarahumares, two parties opposed each other in each race, and the men ran with balls, the women with rings. The married women, although fat and heavy, made better time than the young girls.

The runners who distinguished themselves most were the married men, ranging in age from eighteen to thirty years, the best of whom made thirteen circuits in three hours and one minute and a half. I measured the circuit, and found it to be 9,223 feet long; therefore the total distance run was nearly twenty-three miles. The two men who came in first, one a Tepehuane, the other a Tarahumare, showed no signs of fatigue. By way of comparison, I will add that the best one among some young Mexicans, who raced at the same time, took twelve minutes for the circuit, and all arrived breathless, and would apparently not have been able to continue much longer. I was credibly informed that eight years ago a man who had died but a short time before could make twenty-seven circuits, or more than forty-seven miles, on this race-course. This runner was well known in that part of the sierra. His antagonist made twenty-six circuits, then fell down exhausted, while the victor indulged in a prolonged dance the next day. The race lasted from noon until eight o'clock in the evening.

Some of the Tepehuane customs have been adopted by the Mexicans. For instance, after the harvesting is over, the owner or his son is tied on to a horse, and has to carry a cross made from three ears of corn. The horse is led to the house, and is received with rifle shots; and the men tell the women in the house that the man on the horse has stolen the corn, and they will not let him go unless they are given tesvino and a ball. The demand, of course, is acceded to, and drum and violin furnish the music for the dance.

The Tepehuanes around Baborigame now frequently rent their lands to the Mexicans for a term of years, but rarely get it back, for the "neighhours" have a powerful agent in mescal. The enormous profit accruing from trading in this brandy with the natives may be judged from the fact that a demijohn of the liquid costing $5 contains 24 bottles, for each of which the trader gets from the Indians one sack of corn, worth $1. On this quantity he realises elsewhere at least $5. In other words, on an outlay of, say, $50, he earns a gross $1,200; deducting expenses for transportation of the corn, etc., leaves still a net profit of at least $1,100.

The Tepehuanes have medicine lodges in remote places, where they secretly gather once a month, or

Tepehuane Medicine Lodge near Mesa de Milpillas.

every other month. The name of the lodge is Vākir Nuídadu (vākir = the inside of the house; nuídadu = where there is singing; *i.e.*, "the house where there is singing inside"). Here they sing to call down their god Túni, whom they also call their brother-in-law (Gunósi). He instructs the shaman how to proceed to get rain, and to avert evil, by making tesvino and by dancing.

The gathering at the medicine lodge begins at dusk, three shamans being present. A cross is raised and many kinds of flowers from the barrancas are attached to it. Eagle feathers, too, are hung to it, as well as strings of beads. From each arm of the cross is suspended an "eye of the god" (Vol. II, Chap. XI), called in Tepehuane, yágete. There are three jars with tesvino, and three bowls with meat are placed before the cross.

The fire is put out, and the shamans begin to sing different songs with different melodies, continuing until nearly midnight, when a noise is heard on the roof, as if somebody were walking there. The Indians sing on, and the walking on the roof is heard three times. At last the roof opens, and behold somebody jumps on the floor three times. The singing stops, and Tuni (Tata Dios) is among the people. He looks like a Tepehuane, with a breech-cloth and tunic, but without blanket, and with a bandana around his head. The borders of the breech-cloth and of the tunic are of gold, and so are the ends of his hair. Only the shamans see him. He greets them with the usual salutation, "Váigase!" and the assemblage responds in the same way. He plays with the Indians, and calls them his brothers-in-law. Three cigarettes are made and placed near the tesvino. "Smoke, brother-in-law!" they say, and all laugh and make merry with Tuni. He then makes a speech, telling them to make plenty of tesvino in their houses, in order that the world may not come to an end. He is invited to drink, and to sing three different songs, in which all the men join. He then drinks tesvino, with such a gurgle that all can hear it. "How strong it is," he says; "I may not even be able to get home!" He also sprinkles tesvino over them. Anyone who wants to drink simply stretches out his arm, saying nothing, and a full drinking-gourd is placed in his hand. When

empty, the gourd vanishes.   Such a person will remain
drunk until morning, for Tuni's hand is strong.

He remains for about half an hour, and when he
leaves he says that he will come back if the people
make tesvino for
him.   He vanishes
like a breath, noise-
lessly.

Immediately after
he has gone, a fe-
male deity comes,
whom they call San-
ta Maria Djáda
(mother; that is, the
moon).   The same
salutations are ex-
changed, and the
women ask her to
sing.   She, too, re-

A Well-known Tepehuane Shaman.

ceives tesvino, and makes a speech, the trend of which
is that they must go on making the liquor through the
year, lest their father should get angry and the world
come to an end.   Afterward the Snow and the Cold also
come to play with the people in a similar way.

Cúcuduri is the name of the master of the deer and
the fish.   He also makes rain and he is heard in the
thunder.   He is a small but thick-set man, and in foggy
weather he rides on a deer over the mountain-tops.
When there is much fog and rain, a Tepehuane may
go to a wrestling-contest with Cucuduri in the forest.
He throws an arrow on the ground, and the little man
appears and agrees to put up a deer against the arrow.
They wrestle, and often Cucuduri is thrown, although he
is strong.   Then the man will find a deer close by, and
shoot it.

The fisherman hears in the ripple of the flowing water the weeping of Cucuduri, and throws three small fish to him. If he should not do this, he would catch nothing. Cucuduri would throw stones into the water and drive the fish off, or he would even throw stones at the man himself.

The Tepehuanes never drink direct from a brook, but scoop up the water with their hands, else in the night the master of the spring might carry them inside of the mountain.

They never cut their finger and toe nails, for fear of getting blind.

They say that the seat of the soul is between the stomach and the chest, and they never wake up a man who is asleep, as his soul may be wandering about. Sometimes a man is ill because his soul is away. The doctors may be unable to make it come back, and still the man lives. Soul is breath; and when a man dies, his soul passes through the fontanels of the head, or through the eyes or the nostrils or the mouth.

If anyone steps over a man, the latter will not be able to kill another deer in his life. A woman can be passed in this way without such danger.

When the wind blows hard, it is because a woman delayed curing herself.

The reason the Tepehuanes make four feasts to despatch a dead woman from this world, and only three for a man, is their belief that a woman has more ribs than a man.

Unmarried women are not allowed to eat meat from the spinal column of the deer, as those bones look like arrows. If they ate this meat, their backs would grow curved and they would have back-aches.

The Tepehuanes do not eat pinole with meat, because their teeth would fall out. After eating pinole they rinse their mouths.

One kind of squirrel is thought to change into a bat, another into a parrot. The ground-squirrel changes into a serpent. Catfish become otters, and larvæ on the madroña-tree are transformed into doves.

When a hen crows, an accident is going to happen, unless the hen is immediately killed.

The moon sometimes has to fight with the sun. If weather depended only on the moon, it would rain always, for the benefit of the Tepehuanes.

The Pleiades are women, and the women of this world are their sisters. They were living with a man who used to bring them their food. One day he could not find anything, and drew blood from the calf of his leg, and brought it in a leaf from the big-leaved oak-tree. He told the women it was deer-blood, and thus he sustained them. On discovering that it was his blood, they became very angry and ascended to heaven, where they are yet to be seen.

When he came home in the afternoon he missed them, and followed their tracks, but could not find them. He slept alone, and in the night he said to the mice, which he took for the women, "Come, come to boil the deer-blood!" He continued his search until he reached the place where they had disappeared. The women, seeing from above how he went around looking for them, laughed, and he caught sight of them and called out, "Tie your girdles together that I may get up also." He climbed up; but when he had almost reached them, the oldest of the women told the others to let him drop, because he had deceived them. He became a coyote and has remained in that shape ever since. If he had succeeded in getting up, he would have become a star, the same as the women.

The three stars in the Belt of Orion are deer.

CHAPTER XXIV

ON TO MORELOS—WILD AND BROKEN COUNTRY—THE ENORMOUS FLOWER-SPIKE OF THE AMOLE—SUBTROPICAL VEGETATION OF NORTHWESTERN MEXICO—DESTRUCTIVE ANTS—THE LAST OF THE TUBARS—A SPECTRAL RIDE—BACK TO THE UNITED STATES — AN AWFUL THUNDER-STORM — CLOSE QUARTERS — ZAPE — ANTIQUITIES — WHEN AN "ANGEL" DIES — MEMENTOS OF A REIGN OF TERROR—THE GREAT TEPEHUANE REVOLUTION OF 1616—THE FERTILE PLAINS OF DURANGO.

AFTER having at last succeeded in getting men, I continued my journey to the northwest, over the very broken country toward the town of Morelos, inhabited almost entirely by pagan Tarahumares. There were, of course, no roads, only Indian trails, and these in many places were dangerous to travel with beasts of burden. The barrancas during the month of May are all but intolerably hot, and it was a relief to get up now and then on the strips of highland that intersperse the country and look as fine as parks. At the higher altitudes I noticed a great number of eagle ferns, and the Indians here plant corn in the small patches between the ferns, merely putting the grains into the gravelly red ground without tilling the soil at all.

Lower down were groves of big-leaved oak-trees. Their leaves are sometimes over ten inches long and of nearly the same breadth, and are frequently utilised by the Indians as improvised drinking-vessels.

On the summits of the barrancas, and on the slopes over which we descended into the valleys, an astonishing number of parasites and epiphytes was observed, especially on the pines and oaks. The round yellow clusters growing on the branches of the oaks sometimes give the entire forest a yellow hue. In the foot-hills I saw a kind of parasite, whose straight, limber branches of a fresh, dark green colour hang down in bunches over twenty feet in length. Some epiphytes, which most of the year look to the casual observer like so many tufts of hay on the branches, produce at certain seasons extremely pretty flowers.

Salvia elegans, var.
sonorensis.

In the valleys of the western inclines of the sierra there is nothing suggestive of tropical luxuriance or romance in the landscape, which impresses one chiefly with its towering mountains and vast slopes. Grass is plentiful enough among the stones and rocks, and groups of fresh green trees indicate where ground is moist and water to be found. The country is dry, and from January to June there is no rain. Yet an aloe, which smells like ham, is so full of juice that it drips when a leaf is broken. This, too, is the home of the agaves, or century-plants, and I know of nothing so astonishing as the gigantic flower-spike that shoots upward from the comparatively small plant called amole. One fine day in May I came upon one, which I measured. It was by no means the largest one to be found, but the spike itself, without the stalk, was 15 feet 8 inches in height, and 31 inches in circumference at its thickest part. It seemed a pity to cut down such a magnificent specimen, but, as I wanted to count the flowers, I had one of my men fell it with a couple of blows of an axe. After counting the flowers on one section, I estimated that the entire spike bore at least 20,000 beautiful yellow blossoms, each as large as a tulip. It required two men to carry the spike, and as they walked they were followed by a multitude of humming-birds, which remained fear-

The Flower-Spike of the Amole.

lessly at work among the flowers of what they evidently considered their own private garden. They might have to fly miles before finding another like this. The flower-stalk of the maguey is eaten before it flowers. It looks like a big bamboo stick, and when roasted in the hot ashes is very palatable, sweet, and tender.

Below the Indian village of Coloradas stands an isolated peak 400 to 500 feet high, in regard to which the Tarahumares have the following legend: A Tepehuane once cut bamboo reeds and tobacco, down on the river, and being followed up by the Tubars changed himself into this stone. The man's girdle can still be made out.

At the village my interpreter asked me for the cover of a copy of London *Truth*, and for the wrapper on my photographic films, that with these pictures he might adorn the altar of the old adobe church.

The country is but thinly populated east and north of Morelos, and the steepness of the valleys through which the Indians are scattered, makes it difficult to reach them. At the time of my visit these Indians had absolutely nothing to sell us but the sweet mescal stalks. In the end of May I reached Morelos, an old mining place, about 1,800 feet above sea-level.

Cereus cæspitosus.

The surrounding hills and mountains were covered with the typical Mexican vegetation of the warm regions. The many odd-shaped cacti form a strong contrast to the light and pinnate leaves of the numerous leguminous shrubs, acacia, sophronia, etc. The chilicote, or coral-tree (*erythræa*), with scarlet flowers, is seen everywhere; also palo blanco, with a white stem, looking like an apple-tree. The year 1893 was an exceedingly dry one throughout northern Mexico. My mules, obliged to travel under a scorching sun, sometimes had to be without water for twenty-four hours. Still, in those hot barrancas, I saw no difference in the vegetation. The trees and plants did not seem affected by rain or no rain. The only exception I noticed was that the flat, leaf-like joints of the nopal cactus shrivelled up a little on the surface, but the fleshy inside seemed as juicy as ever. Even during the dryest season the trees and shrubs here blossom and bear fruit, and mornings and evenings the air is filled with the perfume of acaciæ, cacti, and other plants. One is at a loss to understand how the cattle can subsist on these shrubs, but they have adapted themselves to circumstances, and are able to chew up the thick stems of the cacti, in fact the whole plant, with the result, however, that their stomachs are so filled with spines that the Mexicans cannot utilise the tripe. The frugal Indian is the only one who does not reject it, but manages to burn off the biggest spikes while toasting the tripe on cinders.

Near Morelos are ancient house ruins, some round and some square, and also traces of circular fortifications built of loose stones. Several of the latter were from sixteen to twenty yards in diameter and located on the top of mountain ridges. The remains are attributed to the Cocoyomes.

The commonly accepted idea that in southern latitudes anything may be easily cultivated is often proved by actual observation to be fallacious. Sometimes there may be too much rain, sometimes not enough. The worst enemies of plant-life in the warm countries are the many pests. One evening my host, Don Manuel Perez, showed me some of the foes he had to combat in order to maintain his garden. Certain kinds of ants bite off the flowers and leaves and carry away the pieces. The insects come out at night and may strip a tree of its leaves and fruits before morning. It was an astonishing sight to see the dark stem of an elder looking as if it were green, on account of the multitude of ants, each of which carried a bit of green leaf half an inch long. Every evening a man went around to burn them off with a torch of resinous pine-wood.

Some Tubar Indians were induced to come to Morelos to be measured and photographed. The few representatives of the tribe I saw had good figures and small

hands and feet. They seemed to be shy, but rather
kind-hearted, jolly people, resembling the Tarahumares
in appearance. They are found from the village of San
Andres, three miles from Morelos, as far as the village of

Front View.   Side View.
Tubar Man.

Tubares. According to tradition their domain extended
in former times much higher up on both sides of the river,
to where Baborigame is now. But they were gradually
restricted to the locality on which the remnant of the
tribe at present resides. They are said to have been
fierce and constantly fighting the Tarahumares. There

are now not more than a couple of dozen pure-bred Tubars left, and only five or six of these know their own language, which is related to the Nahuatl. The name of the tribe as pronounced by themselves is Tuvalím.

Tubar Women.

Most of the Tubars are found in the pueblo of San Miguel, seventeen miles from Morelos, down the river. An old woman told me that she did not know what the Tubars had done that they were disappearing from the world. The few remaining members of the tribe were related to one another, and the young people had to marry Mexicans. The customs of the Tubars evidently resembled much those of their neighbours, the Tarahumares, who until recent years invited them to their dances. The Tubars danced yohe, and the dancers accompanied their singing by beating two flat sticks, like two machetes. They did not use hikuli. In the sacristy of the church in the old Tubar village of San Andres, I found a complete tesvino outfit, jars, spoons, etc., the vessels turned bottom up, ready for use. The saints, too, must have tesvino, because they are greedy and exacting, and have to be propitiated. The Tubars are said to have worn white girdles.

Mr. Hartman, whom I left in San Miguel to conclude some investigations, returned a few weeks later to the United States. On the small plateaus near San Miguel, two hundred feet or more above the river, he found interesting old tombs, which were well known to the inhabitants under the name of *bovedas*. The presence of a tomb was indicated on the surface by a circuit of stones from three to five feet in diameter set in the ground. There were groups of ten or twelve circuits, and the tombs underneath were found at a depth of five or six feet. They consisted of small chambers excavated in the clayey soil, and were well preserved, though they contained no masonry work; still at one place a yoke of oxen while dragging the plough had sunk down into the subterranean cavity. The entrance to such a tomb is from one side, where a large slab, placed in a slanting position, protects the inside. Nothing was discovered in the four tombs that were opened but some curious slate-coloured beads of burnt clay. People of the district reported, however, that small jars of earthenware had been found in the *bovedas*. No doubt the absence of skeletons was due solely to the length

Beads of Burnt Clay, from Tubar Tombs. Natural Size.

of time that had elapsed, for even in the cemetery of the church Mr. Hartman found similar tombs that contained several skeletons. These tombs were indicated by the same kind of stone circuits as the rest, but were only about three feet down in the hard clay, and had no slabs in front of the entrance. In one of them Mr. Hartman found six corpses more or less decomposed, the sepulchre having evidently been used for a long time. In the same cemetery the Mexicans buried their dead.

I continued my journey down the river through the country once inhabited by the Tubars. As the heat was intense, I availed myself of the light of the full moon and travelled at night. Now and then the road touched the big river where the croaking of the frogs was intensely doleful and monotonous, but withal so loud that on a quiet night like this they could easily be heard two miles off.

Warm winds fanned me to sleep, and only when my mule ran me against some spiny branch, did I wake to find myself in a fantastic forest of leafless, towering cacti, that stood motionless, black, and silent in the moonlight, like spectres with numberless arms uplifted. The overwhelming noise of the frogs seemed to voice their thoughts and forbid me to advance farther. But the mule accelerated its pace, the shadows glided quicker and quicker, up and down the stony, slippery path that wound its way through this ghostly forest.

In the daytime there was a disagreeably strong, warm wind blowing, making it difficult even to get the saddles on our mules, but the nights were calm. At the pueblo of San Ignacio nobody speaks the Tubar tongue. Blue herons have a permanent breeding-place here on an almost perpendicular rock, four to six hundred feet high, where I counted twenty nests.

In travelling down to Tierra Caliente there is one

place at which one must leave the river and ascend to the pine region. This is below the village of Tubares. The river narrows here and forms rapids, and it has been calculated that the water in flood-time rises sixty-five feet. Alligators do not go above these rapids. In two days' journey from Morelos one may reach the undulating country of Sinaloa, *la costa*, which is warmer even than the barrancas.

At San Ignacio I left the river, and turned in a northeasterly direction to Batopilas. After five days' pleasant sojourn at Mr. Shepherd's hospitable home there, I again ascended the sierra, and, after visiting the Indians of Santa Ana and its neighbourhood, arrived at Guachochic. Leaving my mules here in charge of my friend Don Carlos Garcia, I soon started again toward the northeast on my way back to the United States, passing through tne Indian ranches, and finally arriving at Carichic (in Tarahumare Garichi, "where there are houses," probably ancient) on July 31st. At less than an hour's distance from the place I was over-taken by a thunder-storm, the heaviest my Mexicans or I had ever experienced. In a few minutes the almost level fields were flooded as far as the eye could see, and the road we followed began to run with brown water. As we advanced through the mud, the small arroyos were rapidly filling. The rain did not abate, and the force of the currents steadily increased. When only three hundred yards from the town we found ourselves at the edge of a muddy stream, running so rapidly that it tore pieces from the bank, and carried small pines and branches of trees with it. As it was impossible to cross it, we had to wait, however impatiently, for the rain to subside sufficiently to allow us to wade through the water. And all the next day was spent in drying my things.

One year later I was again in Carichic, and from there I made my way to Guachochic. One night I had to spend in the house of a civilised Indian, as it rained too heavily for us to remain outdoors. The house was made of stone and mud, without windows, and the door had to be closed on account of the dogs. There was no way for air to get in except through the chimney, over the fireplace. There were nine people and one baby in the small room. Strange to say, I slept well.

My mules and outfit had been well taken care of at Guachochic, and I now arranged with Don Carlos Garcia to take most of my belongings to Guanazevi, a mining town in the neighbouring State of Durango, while with a few of the best mules I crossed Barranca de San Carlos near Guachochic, and pursued my way through regions inhabited by Tarahumares and Tepehuanes. A stammering Tarahumare was observed, the only Indian with this defect that has come to my notice.

The road I followed to Guanazevi from Guadalupe y Calvo leads through a part of the Sierra Madre which is from nine to ten thousand feet high and uninhabited, and for two days we met nobody. In winter the region is dreaded on account of the heavy snowfalls that are liable to occur here. Several people are said to have perished, and one freighter on one occasion lost twenty-seven mules. In the wet season bears are numerous, and, according to trustworthy information, have attacked and eaten several Tarahumares.

We camped one night at a place where a man had been killed by robbers some time before, and one of the Mexicans shudderingly expressed his fear that we should probably hear the dead man cry at night. This led to a discussion among the men as to whether the dead could cry or not. The consensus of opinion was that the dead could cry, but they could not appear. This, by the way,

is the common Indian belief.   My Tepehuane servant
took an intense interest in the arguments.   His face became suddenly animated with fear, and the thought of
the dead changed him from an indolent fellow into a
valuable aid to my chief packer in watching the animals
at night.   His senses became so keen as to be quite reassuring in regard to robbers at night, and from that
time on he was really a valuable man, active and alert.

There is a small colony of Tarahumares living a few
miles north of Guanazevi, near San Pedro.   Here I excavated some corpses that had been buried several years
before on a little plain.   The graves were about four feet
deep.   In Guanazevi a silver "bonanza" was in full
blast and much activity prevailed.

We were now outside of the sierra proper; but on
the route south, which I followed for several days, I
was never farther away from the mountain range than
thirty miles.   At Zape, about twenty miles to the south,
there are some ancient remains.   As the principal ones
have been described by E. Guillemin Tarayre, who explored Mexico under Maximilian, it is not necessary for
me to dwell on the subject.   Suffice it to say that walls
constructed of loose stones are commonly seen on the
crests of the low hills and are attributed to the Cocoyomes.   Circles and squares made of stones set upright
in the ground may also be seen, and nicely polished
stone implements are frequently to be found near by.

Outside of Zape are a number of ancient burial-caves,
which have been disturbed by treasure-seekers.   As a
curiosity, I may mention that a Mexican once brought
to light a big lump of salt that had been buried there.
It was given to the cattle.

One afternoon a gay little procession of men and
women passed my camp, some on horseback, others
walking.   One of the riders played the violin, another

one beat a drum. An old woman who just then stepped up to sell something explained to me that " an angel " was being buried. This is the designation applied to small children in Mexico, and I could see an elaborate white bundle on a board carried aloft by a woman. My informant told me that when a child dies the parents always give it joyfully to heaven, set off fireworks and dance and are jolly. They do not weep when an infant dies, as the little one would not enter Paradise, but would have to come back and gather all the tears.

The way southward led through undulating country devoid of interest. To judge from the clusters of ranches, so numerous as to form villages, the land must be fertile. There were no more Indians to be seen, only Mexicans. All along the road we observed crosses erected, where people had been killed by robbers, or where the robbers themselves had been shot. A man's body is generally taken to the cemetery for burial, whether he was killed or executed, but a cross is raised on the spot where he fell. The crosses are thus mementos of the reign of terror that prevailed in Mexico not long ago. Most of the victims were so-called Arabs, or travelling peddlers, sometimes Syrians or Italians, but generally Mexicans.

The most important place I passed was the town of Santiago de Papasquiaro, which is of some size, and situated in a rich agricultural country. The name of the place means possibly "*paz quiero*" ("I want peace"), alluding to the terrible defeat of the Indians by the Spaniards in the seventeenth century. There is reason to believe that before 1593 this central and western part of Durango had been traversed and peopled by whites, and that many Spaniards had established haciendas in various parts of the valley. They held their own successfully against the Tepehuanes until 1616, when these, together with the Tarahumares and other tribes, rebelled against them. All the natives rose simultaneously, killed the missionaries, burned the churches, and drove the Spaniards away. A force of Indians estimated at 25,000 marched against the city of Durango, carrying fear everywhere, and threatening to exterminate the Spanish ; but the governor of the province gathered together the whites to the number of 600, "determined to maintain in peace the province which his Catholic Majesty had placed under his guardianship." He routed the enemy, leaving on the field more than 15,000 dead insurgents, without great loss to his own troops. The Indians then sued for peace, and after their leaders had been duly punished, they were dispersed to form pueblos. The insurrection lasted over a year, and many bloody encounters between the natives and their new masters occurred in the course of the following centuries, the result being that the Indians in the State of Durango have not been able to maintain themselves, except in the extreme northern and southern sections.

There was an epidemic of typhoid fever in some of these ranch-villages, and in one place I saw two dogs hung up in a tree near the road, having been killed on account of hydrophobia. A strong wind was blowing day and night on the llanos along the river-course, which annoyed us not a little. It was a real relief to get up again on the sierra, about fourteen miles south of Papasquiaro, and find ourselves once more among the quiet pines and madroñas.

CHAPTER XXV

WINTER IN THE HIGH SIERRA—MINES—PUEBLO NUEVO AND ITS
AMIABLE PADRE—A BALL IN MY HONOUR—SANCTA SIMPLI-
CITAS—A FATIGUING JOURNEY TO THE PUEBLO OF LAJAS
AND THE SOUTHERN TEPEHUANES — DON'T TRAVEL AFTER
NIGHTFALL! — FIVE DAYS SPENT IN PERSUADING PEOPLE TO
POSE BEFORE THE CAMERA — THE REGIME OF OLD MIS-
SIONARY TIMES—STRANGERS CAREFULLY EXCLUDED — EVERY-
BODY CONTEMPLATING MARRIAGE IS ARRESTED — SHOCKING
PUNISHMENTS FOR MAKING LOVE — BAD EFFECTS OF THE
SEVERITY OF THE LAWS.

THE sierra for several days' journey southward is about 9,000 feet high, and is not inhabited, except in certain seasons by people who bring their cattle here to graze. I doubt whether anyone ever lived here permanently. The now extinct tribes, to whose territory this region belonged, dwelt, no doubt, in the valleys below. The high plateau consists of small hills, and travelling at first is easy, but it becomes more and more rough as one approaches the big, broad Barranca de Ventanas.

Having passed for several days through lonely, cold, and silent woods, now and then interspersed with a slumbering snow-field, it was a real pleasure to come suddenly, though only in the beginning of February, upon plants in full bloom on the high crest that faced the undulating lowlands of Sinaloa, which spread themselves out below, veiled in mist. The warm air wafted up from the Hot Country brings about this remarkable change in the flora of the precipitous inclines toward the west.

451

The air was filled with perfume, and it was lovely to be on these high, sunny tops. Foliage trees, especially alders, began to appear among the pines, basking in the dazzling sunshine. I also noticed some fine ferns spreading out their graceful fronds.

A few miles farther and much lower I made camp above the Indian pueblo of San Pedro, as far as I could make out the most eastern extension of the northern Aztecs (Mexicanos or Mexicaneros, as they are called here). From here southward I found them in many of the warm valleys of the Sierra intermingled with Tepehuanes and Coras.

There is an excellent road zigzagging down to the mining place of Ventanas ("Windows," from the formation of a rock) for the greater part of the distance ; but at the outset the way, at two places, is so narrow that parties coming from opposite directions could neither pass nor turn back, which is not pleasant with a yawning chasm of a couple of thousand feet so close at hand.

I was anxious to secure men to go up again into the sierra and farther south ; but the people were afraid of the cold, and nobody seemed to know anything about the country except the postmaster, and he only in a vague way. Mazatlan is not much more than 100 miles off and Durango 125 miles. There are here a great many dykes of porphyry of different ages, but neither slate nor granite in the immediate vicinity, though there is some granite farther up the river.

Among the mine-owners who lived in Ventanas I was surprised to find a Swedish gentleman. They all received me hospitably, providing me also with two men, whom I badly needed. We had to ascend on the other side of the barranca as high as we had been north of this place, and for a day we travelled through snow and rain. Corn does not grow here. From one point the

Pacific Ocean can be seen. We then descended again a couple of thousand feet to the village of Chavaria, which is the only Mexican village I have seen where the houses had gable roofs covered with shingles. The walls of the houses were adobe, but I was told that the earth at this place is not suitable for making the usual flat roofs.

While camping here I saw, on the 15th of February, a flock of six giant woodpeckers pass by in the morning. Except in the pairing season these birds are not seen in such numbers. The journey over a high part of the Sierra Madre to the Mexican village of Pueblo Nuevo requires two days. On the second day I obtained a magnificent view toward the east and southeast. The high peak towering in the distance is Cerro Gordo, very broad at the base and conical in shape. Patches of snow were visible on it, and snow lay in the crevices wherever we travelled.

I descended through magnificent groves of cedar-trees to Pueblo Nuevo, making my camp on top of a hill, from which I overlooked the little settlement and the valley in which it nestles. As every house is surrounded by its little garden of orange-trees, aguacates, and guayabas, the landscape presented a mass of verdure of different shades, the ugly, often dilapidated houses being almost lost in the green. Lemons grow wild, and therefore there is no sale for them. Lemon juice mixed with milk is in many parts of Mexico considered a remedy for dysentery.

A young priest, who exercised a supreme but judicious authority in this secluded spot, treated me with much consideration. He took an honest pride in the development of his little village, and showed me its sights, first the church, which he was embellishing in many ways, and then the spring which supplied the place with water, and where the women gathered to wash their clothes and gossip.   We met many graceful figures carrying jars on their shoulders, as in ancient times.

In order to give me an opportunity to see the people, el Señor Cura allowed them to come and dance on his veranda.   His organist was a musical genius, and a composer of no mean ability, and on the cabinet organ the priest had brought from Durango on muleback he played not only hymns, but also excellent dance music.

The climate here was delightful, the valley fragrant with the perfume of oranges, and one felt reluctant to leave this restful camp.   But I was soon reminded that nothing in this world is perfect, as one night a storm lifted my tent up and carried it several yards off, leaving me to sleep as best I could till morning.   The wind was so powerful as to fell trees.

The Pueblo Nuevo was once inhabited by Aztecs. The present inhabitants, though amiable, are indolent and lazy, and there is a saying that in Durango not even the donkeys work.   I therefore had considerable trouble in finding a guide, the difficulty being aggravated by the fact that nobody seemed to know anything about the country toward Lajas, the Tepehuane village I was making for.

The sierra to the south where the Tepehuanes live is not frequented by the people here, who maintain communication only toward the east, principally with the city of Durango, where they market their garden crops of chile and tomatoes.   Nevertheless, some of the Tepehuane pueblos belong to the Cura's parish, and he seemed to be the only one who could give definite information about the country southward.

The track leading down to the San Diego River runs through an idyllic valley where picturesque brooks trickle down the slopes between groves of semi-tropical vegetation. In one of the limpid streams a couple of pretty girls were bathing and washing their clothes, as is the custom among the poorer classes of Mexico, who rarely possess more than the clothing they wear. As we appeared on the scene, they gracefully slipped into a deep pool, leaving nothing but their pretty faces, like water-lilies, floating above the crystal-clear water, and thus nodded a friendly greeting toward us.

Not more than ten miles' travel brought us to the San Diego River. Its source is said to be in the sierra, apparently toward the north, and it flows in a southerly direction. It was not very difficult to cross, but in flood-time it must be large. Its elevation at this point was about 3,300 feet.

Here began the ascent into the sierra again. Although the road on the first day was very good, it required rather hard climbing to get to the top. I was anxious to reach my destination that day, which was Saturday, in order to be in time for the gathering of the Indians in the pueblo on Sunday. I therefore travelled on after nightfall, though the road was much longer than I expected, leading through extensive pine forests, the monotony of which was interrupted only once by the appearance of a couple of beautiful macaos.

Just as the moon rose, we entered on the "spine of the coyote," as the Tepehuanes call a narrow ridge, six to eight yards broad, with yawning abysses on both sides. Then we came on grassy slopes covered with trees. What a magnificent view there must be here, by daylight, of this wild country! To the southeast could clearly be seen a sloping table-land among hills; I even could distinguish some small houses on it. That was Lajas. It appeared to be but a league off, but in reality it was still three times as far away.

We descended among oak-trees, when suddenly the track ran down a precipitous volcanic rock, utterly impracticable for the mules to follow. Evidently we had strayed on a side trail; and while we guarded the mules, a man was sent back to look for the main track, which luckily was found after a short time. The worst of it was that the animals had to be led back one by one, along the side of a dangerous precipice, and it was a wonder that none of them rolled down the steep sides. I was glad when we could safely proceed on our way.

It is disagreeable to travel with a pack-train after nightfall, even on a moonlight night like this, but particularly when without a guide and on an unfamiliar track. The journey seems interminable. The fear of losing one's road, or having something happen to the animals, or dropping some part of the pack; the uncertainty regarding what camping-place one may find; and the anxiety lest the backs of the animals may become sore, while the men are getting hungry and in as bad a temper as one's self,—all tend to demonstrate the advisability of going into camp when the sun is still well above the horizon.

Another harassing consideration, which, however, does not apply to this part of the country, is the possibility of arousing a suspicion that pack-trains which travel at night carry treasures.

After a continuous journey of ten hours and a half we arrived without further mishaps at Lajas at 9.30 P.M., the middle of the night in that part of the world. One of my men, who had a habit of singing whenever we entered a village, had been ordered to keep silent, that the people in this lonely place, susceptible as they are, might not become alarmed at the sudden arrival of such a party.

A few houses lay scattered about in the dim moonlight, and I with my chief man rode ahead. " Ave Maria ! " called out Catalino, knocking at the door of a hut. " God give you a good night," he continued, but there was no response. After having in this way tried several huts, we at last succeeded in getting an answer, and learned where Crescencio Ruiz lived, to whom the priest in Pueblo Nuevo had given me a letter of introduction, and who was a kind of secretary to the Indians. We now directed our steps toward his house, aroused him from his slumbers, and after some parleying brought him to the door. He was a small-statured, kindly-looking man, a half-caste, who displayed a friendly manner and showed me where I could camp near his house. As he was very talkative, it was late in the night before I could retire.

The name of the village is San Francisco de Lajas, the word *laja* (flat stone) referring to stones which abound in the neighbourhood. The Indian name, "Eityam," has the same meaning. The next day many Indians came fearlessly and curiously up to see me. They wore the ordinary dress of the working-class of Mexico, except that their flat straw hats were trimmed with black and red woollen ribbons and some flowers. The women had flowers and leaves in their hair, which they wore in Mexican fashion, in two braids. Some of the men had their hair put up in one braid and fastened at the end with a narrow hair-ribbon, but most of them had it cut short. I was surprised to see many bald-headed men, some not over thirty years old. Surely it must be more healthy for the hair to be worn long.

Fortunately for me the Indians had just come into the pueblo for a week to repair the old adobe church, in which work Don Crescencio greatly assisted them. This man, nine years ago, was sent to the place as a

teacher by the Mexican authorities in Durango. On his arrival he was met at the old curato by 140 children, none of whom had ever seen a Mexican before, and, of course, they did not understand a word of Spanish. They soon went back to their homes, and five days afterward the preceptor was left without a pupil. He induced the parents to make the children return, and 48 came back. Out of these, five remained with him for six months. At the close of that period they were able to read and to write their names. Of late years, however, teaching has been given up altogether. The fact is that the Indians do not want schools, "because," as an intelligent Huichol afterward told me, "our sons lose their native tongue and their ancient beliefs. When they go to school, they do not want to worship the Sun and the Water any more." The white teacher's aim should be to incite the desire for instruction rather than to force his pupils to listen to his teachings; not to destroy the Indian's mental world, but to clear it and raise it into the sphere of civilisation.

Tepehuane Sling made from Maguey Fibre. Width, 10 ctm.

But Don Crescencio remained with the Indians as their "secretary" (escribano), attending to whatever correspondence they had with the authorities, and gradually becoming their factotum and adviser. As he was an honourable and straightforward man, his influence was all for their good. To swell his meagre income, he carries on a small trade, going twice a year to Durango to replenish his stores; and so invaluable has he become to the Indians that they send some men along with him to watch that he does not remain with the "neighbours." He has learned the language tolerably

well, and has risen to such importance that the gobernador, as I saw myself, visited him every morning, asking his advice in every movement.

These Indians visited me all day long, accompanied
by their wives and children, undauntedly seating themselves in front or out-
side of my tent. In re-
sponse to my expressed
desire to see and buy
articles made by them,
they brought me, during
my short stay here, gir-
dles and ribbons of wool
or cotton, as well as a
great variety of bags of
all sizes, knotted from
twine of maguey fibre.

The people here do
business on a basis en-
tirely different from that
of the " neighbours,"
inasmuch as they have
a fixed price for every-
thing. There is no
bargaining with them ;
when they have once
told the price of a thing
(and it is always a high
one), they adhere to it

Tepehuane Pouch made from Maguey
Fibre.   Width about 16 ctm.

firmly, and as money is
no object to them, they make trading rather difficult.
On my tours among the people, I found them hospitable.
They always asked me to come in and sit down, and they
have good manners.

The one thing they strenuously objected to, and

which they were deadly afraid of, was the camera, and it took Don Crescencio's and my own combined efforts for five days to induce them to pose. When at length they consented, they looked like criminals about to be executed. They believed that by photographing a person I should be enabled to carry his soul off to eat it later, at my ease, if I chose. They would die as soon as their pictures arrived in my country, or some other evil would result, anyhow. The women disappeared like frightened quails, when I was about to perform the dreadful operation on the men. However, most of them returned to see how their spouses stood the painful ordeal. When I then asked for some women to pose, they ran away, in spite of the demonstrations of the men ; only three sturdy ones with "great souls" remained and were "taken" after having been duly "shaken" with fears.

The Tepehuanes feel at home only in their ranches. They clear land in the numerous little valleys of which their rugged country consists, and plant corn in places where no plough could ever be used.

They always have sufficient corn for their wants. Their store-houses are square upright cribs of bamboo sticks held in place with withes on a framework of pine poles. Sometimes they stand at considerable distances from the dwellings. The floor is raised about a foot above the ground, and the entrance is made from the top. The ears of corn can plainly be seen behind the bamboo sticks. In March they are taken out and shelled, and the corn is put in home-made sacks and replaced in the store-houses.

The Tepehuanes make pulque, but not tesvino, and cotton is cultivated on a very small scale. They gather the fibre of the maguey and other plants, and make sacks and ropes of excellent quality, for their own use as well as for sale in Durango, to which market they also take any fruit not required for home consumption.

Their only amusement is to drink mescal and pulque. No games are in use, and to stake money or valuables in any of the " neighbours' " games is forbidden.

The commonest disease here, strange to say, is malaria, which sometimes proves fatal. The first thing a

Tepehuane Store-house, near Lajas.

Tepehuane does in the morning is to wash his head, face, and hands with cold water, letting it dry without wiping it off. He starts to do his work with the water dripping from him.

The Southern Tepehuanes perform a religious dance called by the Mexicans *mitote;* it is also found among the Aztecs, the Coras, and the Huichols. In the vicinity of Lajas is a circular plain set pleasantly among the oak-trees. This is the dancing-place. At its eastern side is a jacal, a gable-shaped straw-roof resting on

four poles, the narrow sides standing east and west. Inside of it is found an altar, consisting simply of a matting of large, split bamboo sticks (*tapexte*) resting on a
framework of four horizontal poles, which in turn are
supported by two pairs of upright forked sticks. On this
altar the people put the food used at the dances, and
many ceremonial objects are placed here or hung under
the roof of the jacal.

In regard to their native religion, they are as reticent
as their northern brethren, if not more so. " I would
rather be hanged than tell anything," said one shaman
to me. Still, all things come to him who waits. This
very man, who was so tragic, became my friend, and
when we parted he asked me to write my name on a
piece of paper, that he might salute me every morning.
A name is a sacred thing, and they never tell their real
native names.

Nowhere else in Mexico have the institutions
founded by the missionaries of early times remained intact as in Lajas. Not only so, but the regulations are
carried even further than was originally intended, and
this in spite of the fact that the Indians have not given
up their own ancient religion. No priest is now living
among them ; and only at rare intervals does the Cura
come from Pueblo Nuevo to baptise and marry.

The native chosen civil authorities are composed
of fourteen, the ecclesiastical of seven members. The
gobernador has supreme authority with both bodies, and
when important matters are at issue the people are
brought together and consulted. The decisions or orders
are given to the so-called captain, who sees that they are
carried into effect. The officers are elected every year,
and meet in sessions almost every day, to settle the
affairs of the people, and to inflict punishment even on
the shamans when necessary. They have recently reno-

vated the prison, and put in a new set of stocks; and the whipping-post is still in constant use, to supplement the laws of the Mexican Government, which are considered altogether too mild.

The punishments which these people inflict are severe and barbarous. I have heard that Mexican criminals, who have been caught and punished by them, on complaining of their harsh treatment to the government authorities, did not receive any sympathy, the latter no doubt considering it meritorious rather than otherwise, on the part of the Indians, to maintain order so effectually without the aid of soldiers. The captain in Lajas is on duty day and night, watching that nothing untoward may happen to man, beast, or property. But few strangers come to this remote pueblo, and no one can pass it unnoticed. The only trail that runs through the place is swept every afternoon with branches of trees, and the next morning it is examined by the captain to ascertain if anyone has gone by. White men are wisely prohibited from settling here ; and when a " neighbour " comes, his business is at once inquired into, and sufficient time, perhaps a night and a day, is given him to attend to it, after which he is escorted out of the village.

Safety to life and property is thus insured among these Indians. " I guarantee you that none of your animals will be stolen here," Crescencio said to me the first night, and a very short experience convinced me that he was right. Theft is practically unknown here, unless some "neighbour" tempts an Indian with a promise of a part of the booty.

Murder is committed only by intoxicated individuals, and then the culprit is chained in the stocks for three or four weeks, and gets a whipping at regular intervals. Afterward he is sent to the Mexican authorities in the city of Durango to be dealt with according to the law.

There is no capital punishment for murder in Mexico, and when criminals have served their terms and return to their native village the Indians may even send them back to Durango, saying that they are better off without them.   Suicide is unknown.   When murder or theft has been perpetrated, they do not at once try to apprehend the suspected person, but first call the shaman to ascertain by divination who the culprit may be, by placing ceremonial arrows, smoking tobacco, and waving plumes.

I was told that three years ago two travelling Mexican peddlers arrived here, and after having done a little trading went away without informing the authorities of their departure.   This aroused the suspicion of the Indians, who began to look around to see what was missing.   Two cows, it seemed, had disappeared, and in two days the peddlers were overtaken, brought back, put in the stocks, and held in prison for eight days, and three times a day they received a thrashing.   They had very little food.   They were finally taken to Durango.

Once two cows and an ox were stolen from Crescencio, and the Indians followed the tracks of the thieves, their leader frequently touching the earth with his hands to assure himself by the smell that they were going in the right direction.   After a while two Tepehuanes and their accomplice, the " neighbour " who had put them up to the crime, were caught.   The "neighbour," as soon as he arrived in the village, was given twenty-five lashes, and for two hours was subjected to the agonizing torture of having his head and his feet in the stocks at the same time.   Next day he was given ten lashes, and the following day five, and eight days later they took him to Durango.   His two Indian associates, father and son, were also put in the stocks, and for two weeks each of them got daily four lashes and very little food; besides which their blankets were taken away from them.

Although the Tepehuanes keep up their ancient rites and beliefs along with the new religion, they strictly comply with the external form of Christianity, paying due attention to all the Christian feasts and observances. Every day the bells of the old church are rung, and the saints " are put to bed," as the Indians express it. When Crescencio first came here he found the people on Sundays in the church, the men sitting on benches and the women on the floor. They had gathered there from habit, though nobody knew how to pray, and they sat around talking and laughing all the time. It was their Christian worship. Crescencio has now taught them to say prayers.

The teachings of Christianity, however, are for the most part forgotten. No trace of the religion of charity remains among them, but the severity of the early missionaries survives, and their mediæval system of punishment. Evidently the tribe always entertained extreme views regarding the relation of the two sexes toward each other, or else the spirit of the new law would never have been imbibed so eagerly. " The slightest want of modesty or exhibition of frivolity is sufficient reason for a husband to leave his wife, and for young women never to marry," says Padre Juan Fonte, of the Tepehuane Indians. There is no sign of relaxation in their strictness, or of any inclination to adopt more modern views on marital misdemeanour.

In the greater number of cases husband and wife live happily together " till death doth them part." If either should prove unfaithful, they immediately separate, the wife leaving the children with the husband and going to her parents. Then the guilty one and the co-respondent are punished by being put in the stocks and given a public whipping daily for one or two weeks. Neither of the parties thus separated is permitted to marry again.

If a girl or widow has loved "not wisely, but too well," she is not interfered with until her child is born. A day or two after that she and the baby are put into prison for eight or ten days, and she is compelled to divulge the name of her partner. The man is then arrested and not only put into prison, but in the stocks besides. There are no stocks for women, only two horizontal bars to which their hands are tied, if they refuse to betray their lovers. The two culprits are kept separate, and their families bring them food. Twice a day messengers are sent through the village to announce that the punishment is about to be executed, and many people come to witness it. The judges and the parents of the delinquents reprimand the unfortunate couple, then from two to four lashes are on each occasion inflicted, first upon the man and then upon the woman. These are applied to an unmentionable part of the back, which is bared, the poor wretches standing with their hands tied to the pole. The executioner is given mescal that he may be in proper spirit to strike hard. The woman has to look on while the man is being punished, just as he afterward has to witness his sweetheart's chastisement. She opens her eyes "like a cow," as my informant expressed it, while the man generally looks down.

Many times the judges are ashamed to go through this performance, the character of which is below the standard of propriety of most primitive tribes ; but, strange to say, the parents themselves compel them to let the law have its course. Afterward the girl is handed over to her lover in order that they may become officially married by the Church the next time the priest arrives. This may not happen for two or three years, but the two are meanwhile allowed to live together, the girl going to her lover's home. To avert all the misery in store for her, an unfortunate woman may try to doctor herself by secretly taking a decoction of the leaves of the chalate, a kind of fig-tree.

Sometimes punishment is dealt out to young people for being found talking together. Outside of her home a woman is absolutely forbidden to speak to any man who does not belong to her own immediate family. When fetching water, or out on any other errand, she must under no circumstances dally for a chat with a "gentleman friend." Even at the dancing-place it is against the law for her to step aside to exchange a few words with any young man. If discovered in such a compromising position, both offenders are immediately arrested, and their least punishment is two days' imprisonment. If their examination by the judges proves that their conversation was on the forbidden topic of love, they get a whipping and may be compelled to marry.

Some of the boys and girls who have been punished for talking together in this manner, are so frightened that they never want to marry in Lajas, but the more defiant ones deliberately allow themselves to be caught, in order to hasten their union and steal a march on their parents. For these Indians are by no means beyond the darts of Cupid, and both men and women are known to have arranged with a shaman to influence the objects of their tender thoughts, and have paid him for such service. A woman may give a shaman a wad of cotton, which he manages to put into the hand of the young man for whom it is intended. Afterward the shaman keeps the cotton in his house, the affection having been transmitted by it.

On the other hand, men and women, to subdue their natural instincts, go into the fields and grasp the branches of certain sensitive plants. As the plant closes its leaves, the girls pray that they may be able to shut themselves up in themselves. There are two kinds of sensitive plants growing in the neighbourhood of Lajas (*Mimosa floribunda*, var. *albida*, and *Mimosa invisa*), and recourse may be had to either of them. Many men emigrate to other pueblos, though they may in time return. Others remain bachelors all their lives, and the judges in vain offer them wives. "Why should we take them?" they say. "You have thrashed us once, and it is not possible to endure it again." The legitimate way of contracting marriage is to let the parents make the match. When the old folks have settled the matter between themselves, they ask the judges to arrest the boy and girl in question, whereupon the young people are put into prison for three days. The final arrangements are made before the authorities, and then the girl goes to the home of the boy to await the arrival of the priest.

When the Señor Cura is expected in Lajas, all the couples thus united, as well as all persons suspected of harbouring unsafe tendencies, are arrested. On the priest's arrival, he finds most of the young people of the place in prison, waiting for him to marry them. For each ceremony the Indians have to pay $5, and from now on every married couple has to pay $1.50 per year as subsidy for the priest. No marriage in Lajas is contracted outside of the prison. Crescencio himself, when about to marry a Tepehuane woman, barely escaped arrest. Only by threatening to leave them did he avoid punishment; but his bride had to submit to the custom of her tribe.

Contrary to what one might expect, unhappy unions

are rare. Probably the young people are glad to rest in the safe harbour of matrimony, after experiencing how much the way in and out of it is beset with indignities and leads through the prison gates. However, imprisonment for love-making does not appear so absurd to the aboriginal mind as it does to us, and the tribe has accommodated itself to it. I learned that some of the boys and girls after a whipping go to their homes laughing.

The obligation to denounce young people whom one has found talking together, under penalty of being punished one's self for the omission, does not create the animosity that might be expected. Besides, the law on this point is none too strictly obeyed or enforced.

According to Crescencio, the census taken in 1894 enumerated 900 souls belonging to Lajas, and there may probably be altogether 3,000 Tepehuanes here in the South. As far as I was able to ascertain, the following Tepehuane pueblos are still in existence:

1. San Francisco de Lajas.
2. Tasquaringa, about fifteen leagues from the city of Durango. The people here are little affected by civilisation, though a few Mexicans live among them.
3. Santiago Teneraca, situated in a deep gorge. The inhabitants are as non-communicative as at Lajas, and no Mexicans are allowed to settle within their precinct. This, as well as the preceding village, belongs to Mezquital, and the padre from there visits them.
4. Milpillas Chico, where the Indians are much mixed with Mexicans.
5. Milpillas Grande. Here the population is composed of Tepehuanes, Aztecs, and Mexicans.
6. Santa Maria Ocotan, and
7. San Francisco, both little affected by civilisation.

8. Quiviquinta, about fifteen leagues southwest of Lajas.
    The latter three villages belong to the State of
    Jalisco.

   On the road from Durango to Mazatlan, passing
Ventanas, there are no Tepehuane pueblos.

CHAPTER XXVI

PUEBLO VIEJO—THREE LANGUAGES SPOKEN HERE—THE AZTECS—
THE MUSICAL BOW—THEORIES OF ITS ORIGIN—DANCING MI-
TOTE—FASTING AND ABSTINENCE—HELPING PRESIDENT DIAZ
—THE IMPORTANCE OF TRIBAL RESTRICTIONS—PRINCIPLES OF
MONOGAMY—DISPOSITION OF THE DEAD.

THERE are two days journey over rough country
to Pueblo Viejo, my next objective point.   Again
I had great difficulty in finding a guide, as the two villages were at loggerheads about some lands.   The guide
furnished me by the authorities hid himself when we were
about to start.   All the other Indians had gone back
to their ranches, except one, whom I finally persuaded
to show me the way at least as far as the ranch of the
shaman with whom I had made friends, where I hoped
that through him I might get another guide.   On our
way, we passed Los Retablos ("Pictures drawn on a
Board"), the rather fantastic name of a magnificent
declivity of reddish rock, across which the track led.
At this place, tradition says, the Tepehuanes of Lajas,
in the war of independence, vanquished 300 Spanish
soldiers, who were trying to reach the city of Durango
from Acaponeta.   The Indians had hidden themselves
all around and above the steep slope, and from their
ambuscades rolled stones down on the Spaniards, every
one of whom was killed.

Having gotten my mules safely over this dangerous
track, where they could never have been rescued if they
had lost their footing, I arrived after a while at the

home of the shaman, near which I camped.   When I
went up to the house, I found it empty, and was
barely in time to see a woman making her escape with a
child as best she could.   I realised that if the shaman
did not return that evening or early next day, I should
have to return to Lajas.   The plaintive trumpet sound
of a giant woodpecker about sunset—as far as we could
make out, the only living being in the vicinity—did
not detract from the gloominess of the prospect.

Luckily, however, my shaman friend came to my
tent at daybreak next morning, and thus relieved my
anxiety.   Though exceedingly busy cutting down trees
and shrubs to clear his field, he spared one of his helpers
to show me the way to Hormigas (ants), charging only
three reales for the accommodation, and one real extra
(twelve cents in Mexican money) to be paid to the man
in case I should want him to go farther and show me
the way to Aguacates.   I also improved the opportunity
to get from him some ethnological information and a
short Tepehuane vocabulary.

Thus with lightened heart I started off through a
country that, while it did not present any remarkably
steep ascents and descents, was very rough and hard to
travel.   The main sierra is here very narrow, and the
large mountainous mass broken up into irregular ridges
and steep valleys.   The next day, much of the time
we followed a high, rocky ridge, the highest point of
which is called Mojoneras.   Here, ten miles north
of Pueblo Viejo, the boundary line of the territory of
Tepic is said to run.   For several miles on the road,
and particularly from the last-mentioned ridge, magnificent views of the wild country northward present themselves, over the steep descent into the cañons and gorges
of the western part of the Sierra Madre.   Only three
Tepehuane ranches were observed.

I arrived without any mishap at Pueblo Viejo, which is inhabited mainly by Aztecs. Of late years they have become much mixed with the Tepehuanes, who have here taken refuge from drought and the advancing "neighbours." Indian settlers who thus come from other pueblos are called poblanos. They receive land from the community in return for the services they render, and the two tribes freely intermarry, although "neighbours" are never allowed to settle within the confines of the village. Still the people, who have considerable intercourse with Acaponeta, and who also go some distance to work in the mines of Sinaloa, speak Spanish quite well. Indeed, of the three languages spoken here, Spanish is the one most generally heard. Several Nahuatlan words have been forgotten, and in making out my list of collections I had great difficulty in getting designations for some of the objects, for instance the word for "quiver," and for the curious rattling anklets used by dancers. Only elderly people speak Nahuatl correctly, and the Tepehuane influence is strong here, even in the ancient religion of the people. It was curious to note that many people here, as in Lajas, eat neither hens nor sheep, while they freely partake of beef.

People here are more intelligent and much less reticent than in Lajas. Women when addressed will answer you, while in Lajas the inhabitants are guarded, and suspicious even of other Indians, not to speak of "neighbours." Another difference is that very few drink mescal.

At a meeting I had with the Indians, I remarked, in my desire to please them, that the Mexican Government was interested to know whether they were getting on well or whether they were coming to an end. To this the principal speaker at once laughingly rejoined: "Of course, they want to know how soon they can 'finish' us!"

The Indians here have the usual trouble from "neighbours" trying to encroach upon their territory. Once a delegation from this and the neighbouring pueblos undertook a journey to the City of Mexico in order to settle the troubles about their land. They stopped eleven days in the capital and were well received by the Ministerio del Fomento; but their money gave out before they finished their business, and they had to walk all the way back without having accomplished anything.

I found these Indians law-abiding and obliging, and I had no great difficulty in securing permission to be present at a mitote, which was to be given at a ranch in the neighbourhood. On March 24th, a little before sunset, we started out on a ride of an hour and a half, ascending some 3,000 feet on a winding Indian trail up to a high mesa. It was a starlit, beautiful night, but the magnificent view which this mesa commanded could only be surmised. There are a few ranches here owned by people from the pueblo below, a man sometimes living in his ranch here during the wet season, while for the remainder of the year he occupies one in the pueblo. As we entered on the plain we could distinctly hear the beating of the tāwitól, the musical instrument of the Tepehuanes. At this distance it sounded like a big drum.

We passed the ranch which was giving the mitote, and a hundred yards farther on we came upon a picturesque scene. Here on a meadow the Indians were grouped around the many fires whose lights flickered among the trees. There was just a pause in the dancing, which had begun soon after sunset. I could at once discern a little plain set apart for the dancing.

On its eastern side was an altar of the usual description, fenced on two sides with felled trees, on which were hung the paraphernalia of the dancers, their bows, quivers, etc. In the centre of the dancing-place was a large fire, and to the west of it the shaman was seated on a stool. Behind him, similar though smaller stools were set for the owner of the ranch and the principal men.

Strange to say, the shaman was a Tepehuane. I learned later that the Aztecs consider the shamans of that tribe better than their own. In front of the shaman was the musical instrument on which he had been

The Musical Bow of the Tepehuanes of the South, and of the Aztecs.
Length of Bow, 1 m. 36.5 ctm.

playing. This was a large, round gourd, on top of which a bow of unusual size was placed with its back down. The shaman's right foot rested on a board which holds the bow in place on the gourd. The bow being made taut, the shaman beats the string with two sticks, in a short, rhythmical measure of one long and two short beats. When heard near by, the sonorousness of the sound reminds one of the 'cello.

This is the musical bow of America, which is here met with for the first time. It is intimately connected with the religious rites of this tribe, as well as with those of the Coras and the Huichols, the latter playing it with two arrows. The assertion has been made that the musical bow is not indigenous to the Western Hemisphere, but was introduced by African slaves. Without placing undue importance on the fact that negroes are very rarely, if at all, found in the northwestern part of Mexico, it seems entirely beyond the range of possibility that a foreign implement could have become of such paramount importance in the religious system of several tribes. Moreover, this opinion is confirmed by Mr. R. B. Dixon's discovery, in 1900, of a musical bow among the Maidu Indians on the western slope of the Sierra Nevada, northeast of San Francisco, California. In the religion of that tribe also this bow plays an important part, and much secrecy is connected with it.

The shaman's song sounded very different from the songs I had heard among the Tarahumares. As his seat was high, he had to maintain a stooping position all the time he played.

The dancers, men and women, made much noise by stamping their flat soles vigorously on the ground, as they moved in double column around the fire and the shaman, in a kind of two-step-walk forward. They danced in a direction against the apparent movement of the sun, the men leading, the women following. I noticed that the step of the women was slightly different from that of the men, inasmuch as they lifted themselves on their toes at each step. At times the columns would suddenly stop and make the same kind of movements backward for a little while, with the same small jumps or skips as when walking forward. After a few seconds they would again go forward. These movements are directed by the leader, the man who dances first.

Both men and women wore flowers, the former fastening them to their straw hats, the latter in their hair with the stem behind the ear. The flowers were apparently selected according to individual taste, but the kind I saw most frequently was a white blossom called *corpus*, the delicious fragrance of which I noticed every time the women danced by. Two boys had a peculiar kind of white flower fastened with a handkerchief tied around their heads. It is called *clavillinos*, and looks like thick, white hair. The shaman wore a narrow hair-ribbon, but no flower. Around their ankles the men had wound strings of dried empty pods of a certain palm, which made a rattling noise during the dancing. Five times during the night, ears of corn and plumes were brought from the altar, and then the men always removed their hats. The women wore veils (*rebosos*), but it is considered improper for them to use sandals on such occasions; these are worn only by the men.

There were five pauses made in the course of the night, and, to prepare the people for them, the shaman each time began to strike more slowly. The dancers continued until they arrived in front of the altar, where they commenced to jump up and

Rattle for Ankle, made from Empty Pods of a Palm.

down on the same spot, but with increasing rapidity, until the music stopped, when they separated and lay down.

Those who did not take any part in the dancing were lying around the various fires, the number of the dancers changing with the different songs, according to the degree of enthusiasm among the people. Many went to sleep for a while, but this is not deemed very polite to the owner of the ranch, as the effect of the dancing is much greater upon the gods when everybody takes part. I was told that to keep the people awake a man sometimes goes around spurting cold water over the drowsy and nodding heads.

The function had been opened by the owner of the ranch making alone five circuits around the fire, carrying the musical instrument and the two playing-sticks and doing reverence to the sun every time he passed the altar. Just before sunrise the mitote concluded with the dramatisation of the killing of the deer. Deer-skins were brought from the bower of the altar, and the men put on their bows and quivers, each of which contained twenty-five arrows and had two slings attached to it. The men held the deer-skins in their hands and danced five circuits. Two light-footed boys next appeared on the scene to play the part of the deer. They had deer-skins on their backs, and in their hands held deer-heads with antlers. These they showed five times, alternately to the shaman who furnished the music, and to the altar. Then they began to run, followed by the dancers, who shouted and shot arrows, also trying to catch the deer by throwing lassos that had been kept in the bower. Often they had to flee from the deer, who chased them off the dancing-place. But they returned, and at sunrise the deer were captured on a matting spread before the altar, where the dancers now took positions. Starting from here they next made five circuits around the dancing-place in the direction of the apparent move- ment of the sun, then five circuits in the opposite way. The shaman's beating slowed down, once more all the dancers jumped up quickly, the music stopped, and the dancing was finished.

Now the feasting began. The food, that had been placed on the altar, pinole and toasted corn, was brought forward, and the host and his wife ate first. After they had thus broken fast, all sat down, and to each one the following dishes were served on little earthenware platters or bowls : A small slice of deer-meat that had been cooked between hot stones in an earth mound, and a handful of toasted corn ; a ball made of pinole mixed with unbroken beans; four tamales, and one ball of deer-meat and ground corn boiled together. The last-named course is simply called chueena (deer). The boys who served it had on their backs three bundles, each containing three tamales, which the boys afterward ate.

The host always asks his guests to submit for four days longer to the restrictions that are necessary to insure the efficiency of the dancing. These refer mainly to abstinence from mescal and women, and are conscientiously observed for five days before and five days after the occasion, by the family who arranges the dance. The shaman, on whom the obligation to observe these formalities is greater than on anyone else, may have to officiate at another mitote before the time limit for the first has expired, therefore much of his time is spent in privations.

After the feast, the tapexte, that is to say, the matting, which constituted the top of the altar, is hung up in a tree to be used again the next year. The trees that have formed the bower near the altar are left undisturbed. The ceremonial objects are placed in the trees for four or five days, and then put into a basket which is hung in some cave. At Pueblo Viejo no more tribal mitotes are given, and it seems that no family anywhere makes more than one a year.

When a newly married couple wish to give their

first mitote, they go away from the house for a month. Both of them bathe and wash their clothes, and impose restrictions upon themselves, sleeping most of the time. When awake they talk little to each other, and think constantly of the gods.   Only the most necessary work is done ; he brings wood and she prepares the food, consisting of tortillas, which must not be toasted so long that they lose their white colour.   A thin white gruel, called atole, made from ground corn, is also eaten, but no deer-meat, nor fish with the exception of a small kind called mítshe.   Neither salt nor beans are allowed. The blankets they wear must also be white.   During all this time they must not cut flowers or bathe or smoke ; they must not get angry at each other, and at night they must sleep on different sides of the fire.

Fasting and abstinence form an integral part of the religion of these people.   A man who desires to become a shaman must keep strictly to a diet of white tortillas and atole for five years.   His drink is water, and that only once a day, in the afternoon.   The people here once fasted for two months, in order to aid General Porfirio Diaz to become President of Mexico ; and they told me that they were soon going to subject themselves to similar privations in order to help another official whom they wanted to remain in his position.

Fasting also plays an important part in the curing of diseases.   The patient, with his doctor, may go out and live in the woods and fast for many days, the shaman smoking tobacco all the time.   An omen as to whether the patient will live or die is taken from the colour of the tobacco smoke.   If it is yellow the omen is bad.   Or if the smoke remains dense the patient will live ; but if it disperses he will die.

A very interesting ceremony is performed over a child when it is one year old.   The parents go with the shaman into the field and fast for five days before the anniversary and for five days afterward.   An hour or two after sunset a big fire is made and four arrows and the ceremonial object called god's eye are placed east of it.   The parents and those present look east all the time. The shaman first makes four ceremonial circuits, then puffs tobacco-smoke on the god's eye and on the child. He sings incantations and again makes four ceremonial circuits, and smokes as before.   Next he places his mouth to the child's forehead, and draws out something that is called the cochiste, the sleep or dreams, spitting it out in his hand.   He makes a motion with his plumes as if he lifted something up with them from his hand, and holds the plumes over the god's eye for a while. The people now see that two small, white balls are attached to the plumes, and he shows them to all present, to prove that he does not deceive them.   Then he crushes the balls in his left hand with a sound as if an egg was cracked, and throws them away.   In the morning salt is offered to the fasters.

The cochiste is taken away from boys twice and four times from girls.   A boy cannot get married until the cochiste is taken away.   A girl at the age of puberty is pledged to a year of chastity, and the same ceremony is performed on her as in babyhood, to be repeated in the following year.   Should she transgress during that time the belief is that she or her parents or her lover will die.   The principle of monogamy is strictly enforced, and if a woman deviates from it she has to be cured by the shaman, or an accident will befall her—a jaguar or a snake will bite her, or lightning strike her, or a scorpion sting her, etc.

She gives the shaman a wad of white cotton, which he places on the god's eye.   When he smokes tobacco and talks to the god's eye, information is given to him through the cotton, which reveals to him whether she has more than one husband, and even the name of the unlawful one. He admonishes her to confess, explaining to her how much better the result will be, as he then can cure her with much greater strength. Even if she confesses, she is only half through with her trouble, because the shaman exacts heavy payment for the cure, from $10 to $20. If she cannot pay now, she has to come back in a month, and continue coming until she can settle her account. By rights, the man should pay for her, but often he runs away and leaves her in the lurch. Since the Indians have come in contact with the Mexicans this happens quite often. When at length the money is paid and she has confessed everything, there is nothing more for the shaman to do but to give an account of it to the god's eye, and she goes to her home absolved. One year afterward she has to come back and report, and, should she in the meantime have made another slip, she has to pay more. From all the cotton wads the shaman gets he may have girdles and hair-ribbons made, which he eventually sells.

The custom related above is of interest as showing the forces employed by ancient society to maintain the family intact. Fear of accidents, illness or death, more even than the fine or anything else, keeps the people from yielding too freely to the impulses of their senses.

The treatment accorded to the dead by these people, and their notions regarding them, are, in the main, the same as those obtaining with the tribes which I visited before them, but there are some new features that are of interest. Here, for instance, near the head of the dead, who lies stretched out on the ground in the house, the shaman places a god's eye and three arrows; and at his feet another arrow. He sings an incantation and smokes tobacco, though not on the dead, while the widow makes yarn from some cotton, which she has first handed to the shaman. When she has finished the yarn, she gives it to the shaman, who tears it into two pieces of equal length, which he ties to the arrow standing at the right-hand side of the man. One piece he rubs over with charcoal; this is for the dead, and is tied lower down on the arrow. He winds it in a ball, except the length which reaches from the arrow to the middle of the body, where the ball is placed under the dead man's clothes. The other thread the shaman holds in his left hand, together with his pipe and plumes. After due incantations he divides the white thread into pieces of equal length, as many as there are members of the family, and gives one piece to each. They tie them around their necks and wear them for one year. Afterward they are mixed with some other material and from them a ribbon or girdle is made.

On the fifth day the dead is despatched from this world. In the small hours of the morning the shaman, with his plumes and pipe, and a jar of water into which some medicinal herbs have been thrown, leads the procession toward the west, while the people, including women and children, carry branches of the zapote-tree. They stop, while it is still dark, and the shaman steps forward and despatches the deceased. He returns very soon, and sprinkles water on the people and toward the west, where the dead has gone.

CHAPTER XXVII

INEXPERIENCED HELP—HOW TO ACQUIRE RICHES FROM THE MOUN-
TAINS—SIERRA DEL NAYARIT—THE CORAS—THEIR AVERSION
TO "PAPERS" — THEIR PART IN MEXICAN POLITICS — A
DÉJEUNER À LA FOURCHETTE—LA DANZA.

IT is practically impossible to travel from tribe to
tribe in Mexico without changing muleteers, not
only because the men generally object to going so far
from their homes, but also because it is not advan-
tageous to employ men who do not know the country
through which they are passing. Whenever the Indians
understood something about packing mules, I preferred
them to the Mexicans, because I could learn much from
them on the way. The latter part of my travels I
employed none but Indians.

The unwillingness of desirable men to leave their
homes makes a frequent change very embarrassing. My
next destination from Pueblo Viejo was Santa Teresa,
the most northern of the Cora pueblos, and everybody
thought it was too far away. I had finally to take
whatever I could get in the way of carriers. For
instance, I had only one man on whom I could depend, a civilised Tepehuane, who was bright and knew
his business well, but he was hampered by an injured arm. Then I obtained another man, somewhat
elderly. He, too, became suddenly aware that his right
arm was crooked and not strong enough to lift heavy
burdens, while the two remaining carriers had never
loaded a mule in their lives. The first two directed

the other pair how to proceed, and thus I was treated to the ludicrous spectacle of four men engaged in packing one mule. Naturally it took all day to load my ten animals, and when this was accomplished, it was too late to start, so that the day's work turned out to be nothing but a dress-rehearsal in the noble art of packing mules. The result was that I had to take a hand myself in putting the aparejos on the animals, shoeing them and curing the sore backs, which, as a matter of course, developed from the inexperience of some of the men.

On the second day, by a stupendous effort, we started, but could go only eight miles to a beautiful llano surrounded by oaks and pines. A few ranches are all that remains of the village that once existed here. On one of them lived a rich Cora who had married a Tepehuane woman. All Coras get rich, the Indians here assert, because they know better how to appease the gods. They submit to fasting and restrictions for a month, or even a year, and then go "to the richest mountain the ancient people knew." The master of the mountain comes out and the two make a bargain, the Cora agreeing to pay for the cattle, deer, corn, and other possessions, with men that he kills. The belief that the mountains are the masters of all riches—of money, cattle, mules, sheep, and shepherds—is common among the tribes of the Sierra Madre.

When it devolves upon a Cora to make good his agreement and kill a man, he makes from burnt clay, strips of cloth, etc., a small figure of the victim and then with incantations puts thorns through the head or stomach, to make the original suffer. He may even represent the victim on horseback, and place the figure upside down to give him pain. Sometimes a Cora makes a figure of the animal he wants, forming it of wax or burned clay, or carving it from tuff, and deposits it in a cave in the mountain. For every cow, deer, dog, or hen wanted, he has to sacrifice a corresponding figure.

The next day we followed for some time the camino real, which leads from Acaponeta to the towns of Mezquital and Durango. We then descended without difficulty some 3,000 feet into the cañon of Civacora, through which flows a river of the same name, said to originate in the State of Zacatecas. It passes near the cities of Durango and Sombrerete, this side of Cerro Gordo. In this valley, which runs in a northerly and southerly direction, we found some Tepehuanes from the pueblo of San Francisco.

The Indians here were defiant and disagreeable, and would not even give us any information about the track we were to follow. They had the reputation of stealing mules and killing travellers for the sake of the corn the latter are likely to carry. I therefore put two men on guard and allowed them to fire off a rifle shot as a warning, something they always like to do. The sound reverberated through the still night with enough force to frighten a whole army of robbers. The next morning I sent for the most important Tepehuane, told him the object of my visit, and asked him about the track. He gave me what information he could, but he was unable to procure a guide for a longer time than that day. We were then left to ourselves, with the odds against us. Twice we lost our way, the first time passing a mitote dancing-place, and coming to a halt before a steep mountain wall, passable only for agile Indians. The second time we landed at the edge of a deep barranca, and there was nothing to do but to turn back to a ranch we had passed some time before. Luckily we met there a Tepehuane and his wife, who assured us that we were at last on the right track. However, we did not advance farther than the confluence of two arroyos, which the man had pointed out to us deep down in the shrubbery. Before leaving us he promised to be at our camp in the morning to show us the road to Las Botijas, a small aggregation of ranches at the summit. In a straight line we had not gone that day more than three miles.

When passing one of our guide's ranches—and he had three within sight—I noticed near the track a small jacal about 100 yards off. The man told me that he was a shaman and that here he kept his musical outfit, ceremonial arrows, etc. ; though he appeared to be an open-hearted young man, I could not induce him to show me this private chapel of his, and we had to go on. He parted from us on the summit, but described the road so well that we encountered no difficulty during the remaining two days of our journey.

I was glad to be once more up on the highlands, the more so that we succeeded in finding there arroyos with water and grass. On reaching the top of the cordon we had been following, we came upon a camino real running between the villages of San Francisco and Santa Teresa, and now we were in the Sierra del Nayarit. I was rather surprised to find another barranca close by, parallel with the one we had just left. As far as I could make out, this new gorge begins near the pueblo of Santa Maria Ocotan, high up in the Sierra ; at least my old Mexican informed me that the river which waters it rises at that place and passes the Cora pueblos of Guasamota and Jesus Maria. We travelled along the western edge of this barranca, within which there are some Aztec, but mainly Cora villages. There is still another barranca to the east of and parallel to this, and in this the Huichols live.

What is called Sierra del Nayarit is in the beginning

a rather level and often narrow cordon, and the track south leads near the edge of the Barranca de Jesus Maria for ten or twelve miles. Along this ridge hardly any other kind of tree is to be seen than *Pinus Lumholtzii.* A variety of pine which resembles this very much, but is much larger, and which I think may also be a new species, was observed after leaving Pueblo Nuevo.

The cordon gradually widens, and open, grass-covered places appear among the pines, which now are of the usual kinds, and throughout the Sierra del Nayarit are high, but never large. A few Coras passed us leading mules loaded with panoche, to be exchanged in Santa Maria Ocotan for mescal.

The most conspicuous things in the Cora's travelling outfit are his rifle and one or two home-made pouches which he slings over his shoulder. There is an air of manliness and independence about these Indians, and this first impression is confirmed by the entire history of the tribe.

We passed a few ranches on the road, and at last reached the little llano on which Santa Teresa is situated. It is always disagreeable to approach a strange Indian pueblo, where you have to make your camp, knowing how little the people like to see you, and here I was among a tribe who had never heard of me, and who looked upon me with much suspicion as I made my entry.

There were many people in town preparing for the Easter festival, practising their parts in certain entertainments in vogue at that season. At last I met a man willing to show me where I could find water. He led me outside of the village to some deep and narrow clefts in the red earth, from which a rivulet was issuing. I selected my camping-place near by, at the foot of some low pine-covered hills, and then returned to the pueblo.

" Amigo ! " shouted a man as he came running toward me from his house. It was the alcalde, a tall, slender Indian with a slight beard and a very sympathetic voice. I told him that we were entirely out of corn, to which he replied that we could not get any in the pueblo, only on the ranches in the neighbourhood. I asked him if he wanted us to die from starvation, and then another

Cora Men and Women from Santa Teresa.

man offered me half a fanega. I inquired of the judge whether he did not want to see my papers. " We do not understand papers," he replied. Still it was agreed that the Indians should meet me next morning, and that my chief man, the Tepehuane, should read my letters from the Government, because the preceptor of the village was away in the city of Tepic, and no one else was able to read.

Santa Teresa is called in Cora Quemalúsi, after the

principal one of the five mythical men who in ancient times lived in the Sierra del Nayarit. Reports say an idol now hidden was once found here. A few miles east of Santa Teresa is a deep volcanic lake, the only remnant of the large flood, the Coras say. It is called " Mother," or " Brother," the last name containing a reference to their great god, the Morning Star, Chulavéte. There are no fish in it, but turtles and ducks. The water is believed to cure the sick and strengthen the well, and there is no ceremony in the Cora religion for which this water is not required. It is not necessary to use it pure ; it is generally mixed with ordinary spring water, and in this way sprinkled over the people with a red orchid, or a deer-tail stretched over a stick.

Early next morning a good-looking young Indian on horseback rode up to the tent to pay me a visit. He spoke Spanish very well. I treated him with consideration and proffered him some biscuits I happened to have. In the course of the conversation he offered to sell me a fowl, if I would send a man to his ranch for it, which of course I was glad to do.

As he was taking leave, I expressed my admiration for the handsome native-made halter on his horse. " Do you like it?" he asked, and he immediately removed it from the horse and presented it to me. I wanted to pay for it, but he said, "We are friends now," and rode off. The fowl he sent was the biggest he had in his yard, an old rooster, very strong and tough. Could there be food less palatable than a lean old rooster of Indian breeding? The broth is worse than that made from a billy-goat.

I went to the meeting, and all listened silently while my letters from the Government were read. Anything coming from Mexico impresses these people deeply.

Yet with the suspicion innate in their nature, the Indians could not hear the documents read over often enough. We had meeting after meeting, as the arrival in the pueblo of every man of any importance was a signal that my papers would have to be read over again.

The alcalde introduced me to the teacher's wife, a Mexican, who apparently took her lot very contentedly among "these people whom no one ever knows," as she expressed it. She liked the climate, and the security of life and property. Her husband had been working here for four years. The children, of course, have first to learn Spanish, and there is no school from June till September. The youngsters seemed bright and well-behaved, but the Coras told me that they had not yet learned to read.

Most of the Cora Indians are slightly bearded, especially on the chin. In this respect, however, there was no uniformity, some being absolutely beardless, while others looked rather Mexican. They all insisted, nevertheless, that there is among them no intermixture with Mexicans, or, for that matter, with the Tepehuanes, and the Cora women have very strong objections to unions with "neighbours." On the other hand, it should be remembered that during the latter half of the last century the tribe was subjected to a great deal of disturbance, incidental to the revolution of Manuel Lozada, a civilised Aztec from the neighbourhood of Tepic, who, about the time of the French intervention, established an independent State comprising the present territory of Tepic and the Cora country. He had great military talent, and it was said that whenever he liked he could gather thousands of soldiers without cost. He was able to maintain his government for a number of years, thanks chiefly to the Coras, who were his principal supporters. At one time they had to leave their country, and to live for five years in an inaccessible part of the Sierra Madre above San Buena.

Among themselves, the Coras use their own language, but all the men and most of the women speak and understand Spanish to some extent. Though the people now dress like the "neighbours," they are still

Cora Pouch, of Unusual Shape, made of Wool. Patterns represent Flying Birds and a row of Deer. Length about 25 ctm.

thoroughly Indian, and proud of it. There are about 2,500 pure-bred among them. They call themselves Nayariti or Nayari, and in speech, religion, and customs they are akin to the Huichol Indians, who, however, do not care very much for their relatives, whom they call Hashi (crocodiles). Yet some intercourse is maintained between the two tribes, the Coras bringing to the Huichols red face-paint, wax, and the tail-feathers of the bluejay, while the services of the Huichol curing shamans are highly appreciated by the Coras. An interesting home industry is the weaving of bags or pouches of cotton and wool, in many beautiful designs.

The Coras are not good runners; they have neither speed nor endurance, and they run heavily. It is astonishing how small the bones of their limbs are, especially among the females, though this, by the way, is the case with all the Indians I have visited. A Cora woman made for me a shirt as an ethnological specimen, which I thought she must have made too small at the wrist-bands, as they measured about 4¾ inches (barely twelve centimetres); but she showed me how well they fitted her. Still they always have well-developed hips and better figures than the Mexican women. The teeth of the Coras are not always perfect; I have seen several individuals whose front teeth were missing.

Strange to say, in spite of the high elevation, there is fever and ague here; the alcalde told me that he had an attack every second day.

As Easter was at hand, there was quite a concourse of people, nearly 300 Indians assembling. Oxen were killed, and general eating and feasting went on. I attended the communal feast, and dishes of food were brought to me. In accordance with the Indian custom not to eat much on the spot, I had my men carry some of the food to the camp, as a welcome addition to our monotonous diet and scanty stores; and we found that, aside from the usual Indian dishes, they comprised bananas, salted fish, honey, and squashes.

The authorities newly elected for the ensuing year gave a similar entertainment to their predecessors in office. At the home of the "Centurion," the principal official of the Easter festival, a rustic table and benches had been erected outside of the house. I was invited to sit down among the men of quality, and it was phenomenal to be present at an Indian banquet served on a table, the only occasion of the kind in my experience. As the table was small, the diners were served in turns, one set after another. Each guest had a man to wait on him, but there was neither table-cloth nor knife, fork nor spoon. It was, if you like, a *déjeuner à la fourchette*, except that you were supposed to handle the solid food with pieces of tortilla, that were broken off, folded over, and used as a fork, or rather, spoon, and were eaten with the meat. After the meat had all been fished out, you drank the soup from your bowl or plate. If you could not manage with the tortilla, you were excused for using your fingers. When a bowl or plate was set before an

Indian guest, the latter took it up and immediately handed it to his wife, standing behind him, who emptied it into the jars she had brought for that purpose. There was meat with its broth ; meat ground on the metate, boiled, and mixed with chile ; and atole to drink with it, all fresh and excellent. As I was hungry, I pitched in, although at first I was the only one who ate, which was rather embarrassing. But by and by the others, too, began to eat, perhaps out of politeness. They were pleased, however, that I enjoyed their food, and I did enjoy it, after the poorly assorted diet we had been obliged to maintain. Although the variety of dishes of primitive man is exceedingly limited, such of them as they have are well prepared. The dinner was the best I ever had among Indians. The party was pleasant and animated, and the banquet-hall extended to the pines and mountains around and the azure sky above.

During the night there was dancing on the tarima, a broad plank resting on stumps. Dancing on the plank is said to be customary throughout the Tierra Caliente of the northwest. One man and one woman dance simultaneously, facing though not touching each other. The dancing consists in a rhythmical jumping up and down on the same spot, and is known to all the so-called Christian Indians wherever the violin is played, although nowhere but among the Coras have I seen it executed on the plank. It is called *la danza*, and is distinct from the aboriginal sacred dances, although it may have been a native dance somewhere in Mexico. *La danza* is merely a ventilation of merriment, indulged in when the Indians are in high spirits after church feasts, and may sometimes be executed even in church.

Gradually the people submitted to being photographed, even the women. One evening when I changed plates under two wagon-covers in an old empty house, a curious crowd gathered outside and knocked at the door, wanting to know what was going on and to see the secret rites I was performing.

After a few days of deliberation the Indians consented to show me their dancing-place, or, as they expressed it, their tūnamóti (the musical bow).

CHAPTER XXVIII

A GLIMPSE OF THE PACIFIC FROM THE HIGH SIERRA—A VISIONARY IDYL—THE CORAS DO NOT KNOW FEAR—AN UN-INDIAN INDIAN —PUEBLO OF JESUS MARIA—A NICE OLD CORA SHAMAN—A PADRE DENOUNCES ME AS A PROTESTANT MISSIONARY—TROUBLE ENSUING FROM HIS MISTAKE—SCORPIONS.

A FTER a fortnight's stay I said good-bye to Santa Teresa. The alcalde, who had become quite friendly, accompanied me over the llano on which his pueblo lies, extending, interspersed with pine forests, for about three miles west. He begged me not to forget the Coras when I came to the Governor of the Territory of Tepic, and to ask the Mexican Government to let them keep their old customs, which he had heard they were going to prohibit. This fear, I think, was unfounded. He also wanted me to use my influence toward preventing the whites from settling in the vicinity, since they were eager to get at the big forests.

I had found a friend in a Cora called Nuberto, a kind-hearted and frank fellow, sixty years old, who became our guide. The trail leads along the western side of the Sierra Madre, sometimes only a few yards from where the mountains suddenly give way to the deep and low-lying valleys and foot-hills. As we approached the end of the day's journey, a perfectly open view presented itself of the Tierra Caliente below, as far as the Pacific Ocean, which by mules is a week's journey distant. The wide expanse before us unfolded a panorama of hills that sank lower and lower toward the west, where the salt lagoons of the coast could be clearly discerned as silver streaks in the reddish-grey mist of the evening. Acaponeta was right in line with the setting sun. Here, 8,000 feet above the level of the sea, everything was calm and mild; not a breath of air was stirring. A *prunus* was in flower, and oak-trees were growing on the brink of the ridge toward the sea. In every other direction were to be seen the immense silent pine forests that shelter the Coras, but no trace of human life. Everything seemed undisturbed, peaceful, quieting, nerve-resting.

Would it not be delightful to settle down here! Life would be so easy! The Indians would help me to make a hut. I would marry one of those beautiful Cora girls, who would be sure to have a cow or two to supply me the civilised drink of milk. None of the strife and turmoil of the outer world could penetrate into my retreat. One day would pass as peacefully as its predecessor; never would she disturb the tranquillity of my life, for she is like the lagoon, without ever a ripple on its surface. Once in a while the spirit of the feasts might inspire her to utter an angry word, but she would not mean much by it, and would soon resume her usual placid rôle, moving along in the even tenor of her daily life. What a splendid chance for studying the people, for knowing them thoroughly, and for familiarising myself with all their ancient beliefs and thoughts! Perhaps I might solve some of the mysteries that shroud the workings of the human mind. But— I should have to buy my fame at the price of living on tortillas and pinole and beans!

> "We may live without poetry, music, and art;
> We may live without conscience and live without heart;
> We may live without friends, we may live without books,
> But civilised man cannot live without cooks."

Concluding that the eminent authority cited was right, I came back to realities and continued my journey.

By and by I arrived at a fertile little slope partly covered with corn stubble. At the farther end of it was a large Cora ranch called La Cienega, and in front of it grew two or three magnificent oak-trees with light-green stems and equally light-coloured leaves. The people here were well disposed and sold me some necessary supplies, so I stopped with them for a day.

While descending to the famous pueblo Mesa del Nayarit, one gets a magnificent view of the high mountains which form the western border of the Huichol country and stretch themselves out on the opposite side of the cañon of Jesus Maria like a towering wall of a hazy blue colour. The pueblo lies on a plain less than a mile in extent in either direction, on the slope of the sierra, with an open view only toward the east. There is an idol of the setting sun standing on the mesa above the village, "looking toward Mexico," as the Indians express it. This mesa is the one called Tonati by the chroniclers, while by the Coras it is called Naya-riti, and the whole sierra derived its name from it. The same name is given to a cave in that locality, where the Coras, as well as the Huichols, deposit ceremonial objects and other offerings. The setting-sun god is worshipped equally by the two tribes. The Indians jealously guard this cave, which is never shown to outsiders. This is practically the terminus of the Sierra del Nayarit. The sierra from now on is lower and gradually falls down to Rio de Alica, or Rio Grande de Santiago, where Sierra Madre del Norte ends.

The people here, though friendly, were less sympathetic and much more reserved than those of Santa Teresa, and I could find no one who would divulge tribal secrets. They had received a message from their sister pueblo telling them they had nothing to fear from me, but the Coras are not easily scared, anyhow. A stranger may enter a house without any further ceremony than the customary salutation, "Āxú!" One day when I approached a dwelling, a nice-looking little girl, scarcely three years of age, came running out with a big knife in her little fist, her mother following after her to catch her. The small children curiously approach you, rather than run away. My two dogs intruded into a house and met in the doorway a little girl, about four years old, who was just coming out. The family dog was inside and began at once to bark at the new-comers, ready to fight, but the little one continued her walk without in the least changing the quiet expression of her face.

Although the Coras here maintain their traditions and customs more completely than in other places, I did not see any of the adults wearing the national dress, buckskin trousers and a very short tunic reaching only below the breast and made of home-woven woollen material dyed with native indigo-blue. Only one of the boys was seen with this costume, and his father was said to have it also. Yet the Coras do not want to be confounded with the "neighbours." When the principal men submitted to be photographed, I wanted a picture to show their physique, and therefore asked them to take off their shirts, which they refused to do. But when I remarked, "You will then look like neighbours," the shirts came off like a flash.

The gobernador here was an original and peculiar character. First he wanted me to camp in La Comunidad, to which I objected ; but he was bent upon having me as closely under his supervision as possible, and I had to agree to establish my camp only half the distance that I had intended from the village. As soon as my tent had been put up, he came, accompanied by one of his friends. He had a passion for talking, which he indulged in for two hours, interrupting himself about every twenty seconds to spit. His companion wrapped himself in his blanket and began to nod, and whenever the gobernador stopped for expectoration, the other one would utter an assenting "hay" ("yes"). The Cora language is guttural, but quite musical, and when I heard it at a distance it reminded me in its cadence of one of the dialects of central Norway. However, the go-bernador's monologue soon became very tiresome, and finally I made my bed and lay down. After a while they retired, but every evening as long as I stayed in the place, his Honour came to bore me with his talk. I generally took him out to my men, who entertained him as long as they were able to keep awake. He wanted to hear about other countries, about the bears we had met, and the great war, because he thought there must always be war somewhere. When everybody was asleep after midnight, he would retire. He was a widower, and he was the most un-Indian Indian I ever met.

About five miles east of Mesa del Nayarit the descent toward the pueblo of Jesus Maria begins. The valley appears broad and hilly, and the vegetation assumes the aspect of the Hot Country. Specially noticeable were the usual thickets of thorny, dry, and scraggy trees, seen even on the edge of the mesa. They are called *guisachi*, and in the vernacular of the common man the word has been utilised to designate a sharper. A man who "hooks on," as, for instance, a tricky lawyer, is called a *guisachero*. It is the counterpart of the "lawyer palm" among the shrubs of tropical Australia.

Jesus Maria looks at a distance quite a town, on a

Cora Indians from Mesa del Nayarit.

little plain above the river-bank. A fine, grand-looking old church, in Moorish style, a large churchyard surrounding it, and the usual big buildings connected with the churches of Spanish times, make an extraordinary impression among the pithaya-covered hills. The rest of the houses look humble enough. I went a little beyond the pueblo to the junction of arroyo Fraile with the river of Jesus Maria. As a violent wind, caused by the cooling off of the hot air of the barranca, blows every afternoon, I did not put up my tent, but had my men build an open shed. The wind lasts until midnight, and the mornings are delightfully calm and cool. The Coras consider this wind beneficial to the growth of the corn, and sacrifice a tamal of ashes, two feet long, to keep it in the valley.

The Cora of the cañon, and probably of the entire Tierra Caliente, is of a milder disposition than his brother of the sierra, but he looks after his own advantage as closely as the rest of them.

The houses of the village are built of stone with thatched roofs, and, having no means of ventilation, become dreadfully overheated. I frequently noticed people lying on the floor in these hovels, suffering from colds. In the summer there is also prevalent in the valley a disease of the eyes which makes them red and swollen. Although the country is malarial, the Indians attain to remarkable longevity, and their women are wonderfully well preserved. All Indian women age very late in life, a trait many of their white sisters might be pardonably envious of.

There are twenty Mexicans living here, counting the children; they are poor, and have no house or lands of their own, but live in the Convento and rent lands from the Indians. The Coras, of course, are all nominally Christians, and the padre from San Juan Peyotan attends to their religious needs.   I was told that as recently as forty years ago they had to be driven to church with scourges.   Some families still put their dead away in caves difficult of access, closing up the entrance, without interring the bodies, and they still dance mitote, although more or less secretly.

The Indians catch crayfish, and other small fish, with a kind of hand-net of cotton thread, which they hold wide open with their elbows while crawling in the water between the stones.   Where the river is deep they will even dive with the net held in this way.

The day after my arrival I was requested to come to La Comunidad, that the people might hear my letters read.   This over, I explained that I wanted them to sell me some corn and beans, a blue tunic of native make, and other objects of interest to me, that I also wanted them to furnish me two reliable men to go to the city of Tepic for mail and money; that I wished to photograph them and to be shown their burial-caves, and to have a real, good old shaman visit me, and some men to interpret.   The messengers were duly appointed, but it took them two days to prepare the tortillas they had to take along as provisions.   My desire to see the burial-caves was looked upon with ill-favour.   The old shaman, however, was promptly sent for.   He soon arrived at the council-house, and without having seen me he told the Indian authorities that "it was all right to tell this man about their ancient beliefs, that the Government might know everything."   When he came to see me he took my hand to kiss, as if I were a padre, and I had a most interesting interview with the truthful, dear old man, who told me much about the Cora myths, traditions, and history.   I gathered from what he said that he could not be far from a hundred years old, and he had not a grey hair in his head.   His faculties were intact, except his hearing, and while I was interviewing him he was making a fish-net.

I had him with me one day and a part of the next, but by that time he was a good deal fatigued mentally, and I had to let him go.

There was an Indian here, Canuto, who could read and write, and, as he took a great interest in church affairs, he acted as a kind of padre. I was told that he ascended the pulpit and delivered sermons in Cora, and that he aspired even to bless water, but this the padre had forbidden him. He was very suspicious and intolerant and quite an ardent Catholic, the first Indian I had met who had entirely relinquished his native belief. He actually did not like mitote dancing, and the other Indians did not take kindly to him. All the time I was here he worked against me, because the priest of San Juan Peyotan, as I learned, had denounced me before the people.

Two traders from that town, who had been visiting Santa Teresa while I was there, had reported to the padre the presence of a mysterious gringo (American), who had a fine outfit of boxes and pack-mules, and who gave the Coras "precious jewellery" to buy their souls, and visited their dances. The padre, without having ever seen me, concluded that I was a travelling Protestant missionary, and one day after mass he warned the people against the bad Protestant who was on his way to corrupt their hearts and to disturb this valley in which there had always been peace. "Do not accept anything from him, not even his money; do not allow him to enter the church, and do not give him anything, not even a glass of water," he said. This padre, so I was told by reliable authority, made the judges at San Juan and at San Lucas punish men and women for offences that did not come under their jurisdiction. The men were put into prison, while the women had fastened to their ankles a heavy round board, which they had to drag wherever they went for a week or two. It caused them great difficulty in walking, and they could not kneel down at the metate with it.

His speeches about me made a deep impression upon the illiterate Mexicans in that remote part of the world, who in consequence of it looked upon me with suspicion and shunned me. Not knowing anything better, they invented all kinds of wild charges against me : I was surveying the lands for Porfirio Diaz, who wanted to sell the Cora country to the Americans ; I appealed only to the Indians because they were more confiding and could be more easily led astray, my alleged aim being to make Freemasons out of them. A Freemason is the one thing of which these people have a superstitious dread and horror. Even my letters of recommendation were doubted and considered spurious. However, one old man, whose wife I had cured, told me that Protestants are also Christians, and in his opinion I was even better than a Protestant. Fortunately, the Indians were less impressionable, and as their brethren in the sierra had not reported to them anything bad about me, they could see no harm in a man who did not cheat anyone and took an interest in their ancient customs and beliefs, while the padres had always made short work of their sacred ceremonial things, breaking and burning them.

When at last my messengers returned, after an absence of twelve days, I was surprised to note that they were accompanied by two gendarmes. The Commandant-General of the Territory of Tepic had not only been kind enough to cash my check for about $200, but had deemed it wise to send me the money under the protection of an escort, a precaution which I duly appreciated.   As the return of the men was the only thing I had been waiting for, I now prepared to move up the river to the near-by pueblo of San Francisco, where the population is freer from Mexican influence.

When my hut was broken up, I found among my effects ten scorpions.   The cañon is noted for its multitude of scorpions, and I was told that a piece of land above San Juan Peyotan had to be abandoned on account of these creatures.   The scorpion's sting is the most common complaint hereabout, and children frequently die from it, though not all kinds of scorpions are dangerous.   The consensus of opinion is that the small whitish-yellow variety is the one most to be dreaded. The Cura of Santa Magdalena, State of Jalisco, assured me that he had known the sting of such scorpions to cause the death of full-grown people within two hours.

The scorpions of Mexico seem to have an unaccountable preference for certain localities, where they may be found in great numbers.   In the city of Durango the hotels advertise, as an attraction, that there are no scorpions in them.   For a number of years, according to the municipal records, something like 60,000 scorpions have been annually killed, the city paying one centavo for each.   Some persons earn a dollar a night by this means.   Yet some forty victims, mostly children, die every year there from scorpion-stings.

The cura quoted above thinks that there is a zone of scorpions extending from the mining-place of Bramador, near Talpa, Territory of Tepic, as far north as the city of Durango, though he could not outline its lateral extent.   At Santa Magdalena the scorpions are not very dangerous.

CHAPTER XXIX

A CORDIAL RECEPTION AT SAN FRANCISCO—MEXICANS IN THE EM-
PLOY OF INDIANS—THE MORNING STAR, THE GREAT GOD OF
THE CORAS—THE BEGINNING OF THE WORLD—HOW THE RAIN-
CLOUDS WERE FIRST SECURED—THE RABBIT AND THE DEER—
APHORISMS OF A CORA SHAMAN—AN EVENTFUL NIGHT—HUNT-
ING FOR SKULLS—MY PROGRESS IMPEDED BY THE PADRE'S BAN
—FINAL START FOR THE HUICHOL COUNTRY—A THREATENED
DESERTION.

AT the pueblo of San Francisco, prettily situated at the bend of a river, I was made very welcome. The Casa Real, another name for the building generally designated as La Comunidad, had been swept and looked clean and cool, and I accepted the invitation to lodge there. It was furnished with the unheard-of luxury of a bedstead, or rather the framework of one, made of a network of strong strips of hide. As the room was dark, I moved this contrivance out on the veranda, where I also stored my baggage, while my aparejos and saddles were put into the prison next door. Two Indians were appointed to sleep near by to guard me. When I objected to this I was informed that two fellows from Jesus Maria had been talking of killing me as the easiest way of carrying out the padre's orders. I felt quite at home among these friendly, well-meaning people, and paid off my men, who returned to their homes. I thought that whenever I decided to start out again, I could get men here to help me to reach the country of the Huichols. A shaman who knew more than all others was deputed to give me the information I wanted about the ancient beliefs and traditions of the Coras.

The people also agreed to let me see their mitote, which at this time of the year is given every Wednesday for five consecutive weeks in order to bring about the rainy season. The fourth of this year's series was to be on May 22d. As to burial-caves, they at first denied that there were any skulls in the neighbourhood, but finally consented to show me some. Later on, however, an important shaman objected to this, strongly advising the people not to do so, because the dead helped to make the rain they were praying for, at least they could be induced not to interfere with the clouds.

A few Coras here were married to " neighbours," and some Cora women had taken " neighbours" for husbands. For the first time, and also the last, in all my travels, I had here the gratification of seeing impecunious Mexicans from other parts of the country at work in the fields for the Coras, who paid them the customary Mexican wages of twenty-five centavos a day. The real owners of the land for once maintained their proper position.

I saw hikuli cultivated near some of the houses in San Francisco. They were in blossom, producing beautiful large, white flowers. The plant is used at the mitotes, but not generally.

On both sides of the steep arroyo near San Francisco were a great number of ancient walls of loose stones, one above the other, a kind of fortification. In other localities, sometimes in places where one would least expect them, I found a number of circular figures formed by upright stones firmly embedded in the ground, in the same way as those described earlier in this narrative.

The pueblo, *mirabile dictu*, had a Huichol teacher, whom the authorities considered, and justly so, to be better than the ordinary Mexican teacher. He was one of nine boys whom the Bishop of Zacatecas, in 1879, while on a missionary tour in the Huichol country, had picked out to educate for the priesthood. After an adventurous career, which drove him out of his own country, he managed now to maintain himself here. Although his word could not be implicitly trusted, he helped me to get on with the Coras, and I am under some obligation to him.

A prominent feature in the elaborate ceremonies of the tribe, connected with the coming of age of boys and girls, is the drinking of home-made mescal. The lifting of the cochiste, as described among the Aztecs, is also practised, at least among the Coras of the sierra, and is always performed at full moon.

The people begin to marry when they are fifteen years old, and they may live to be a hundred. The arrangement of marriages by the parents of the boy without consulting him is a custom still largely followed. On five occasions, every eighth day, they go to ask for the bride they have selected. If she consents to marry the man, then all is right. One man of my acquaintance did not know his " affinity " when his parents informed him that they had a bride for him. Three weeks later they were married, and, as in the fairy-tale, lived happily ever afterward. His parents and grandparents fasted before the wedding. In San Francisco I saw men and women who were married, or engaged to be married, bathing together in the river.

Fasting is also a notable feature in the religion of the Coras, and is considered essential for producing rain and good crops. Abstinence from drinking water for two days during droughts is sometimes observed. The principal men on such occasions may undertake to do the fasting for the rest of the people. They then shut themselves up in La Comunidad, sit down, smoke, and keep their eyes on the ground.

The Coras of the cañon are not always in summer in accord with Father Sun, because he is fierce, producing sickness and killing men and animals. Chulavete, the Morning Star, who is the protecting genius of the Coras, has constantly to watch the Sun lest he should harm the people. In ancient times, when the Sun first appeared, the Morning Star, who is cool and disliked heat, shot him in the middle of the breast, just as he had journeyed nearly half across the sky. The Sun fell down on earth, but an old man brought him to life again, so that he could tramp back and make a fresh start.

The Morning Star is the principal great god of the Coras. In the small hours of the morning they frequently go to some spring and wash themselves by his light. He is their brother, a young Indian with bow and arrow, who intercedes with the other gods to help the people in their troubles. At their dances they first call him to be present, and tell their wants to him, that he may report them to the Sun and the Moon and the rest of the gods.

A pathetic story of the modern adventures of this their great hero-god graphically sets forth the Indian's conception of the condition in which he finds himself after the arrival of the white man. Chulavete was poor, and the rich people did not like him. But afterward they took to him, because they found that he was a nice man, and they asked him to come and eat with them. He went to their houses dressed like the "neighbours." But once when they invited him he came like an Indian boy, almost naked. He stopped outside of the house, and the host came out with a torch of pinewood to see who it was. He did not recognise Chulavete, and called out to him: "Get away, you Indian pig! What are you doing here?" And with his torch he burned stripes down the arms and legs of the shrinking Chulavete. Next day Chulavete received another invitation to eat with the " neighbours." This time he made himself into a big bearded fellow, with the complexion of a man half white, and he put on the clothes in which they knew him. He came on a good horse, had a nice blanket over his shoulder, wore a sombrero and a good sabre. They met him at the door and led him into the house.

" Here I am at your service, to see what I can do for you," he said to them.

" Oh, no !" they said. " We invited you because we like you, not because we want anything of you. Sit down and eat."

He sat down to the table, which was loaded with all the good things rich people eat. He put a roll of bread on his plate, and then began to make stripes with it on his arms and legs.

" Why do you do that ?" they asked him. " We invited you to eat what we eat."

Chulavete replied : " You do not wish that my heart may eat, but my dress. Look here ! Last night it was I who was outside of your door. The man who came to see me burned me with his pine torch, and said to me, ' You Indian pig, what do you want here?' "

" Was that you ?" they asked.

" Yes, gentlemen, it was I who came then. As you did not give me anything yesterday, I see that you do not want to give the food to me, but to my clothes. Therefore, I had better give it to them." He took the chocolate and the coffee and poured it over himself as if it were water, and he broke the bread into pieces and rubbed it all over his dress. The sweetened rice, and boiled hen with rice, sweet atole, minced meat with chile, rice pudding, and beef soup, all this he poured over himself. The rich people were frightened and said that they had not recognised him.

"You burned me yesterday because I was an Indian," he said. "God put me in the world as an Indian. But you do not care for the Indians, because they are naked and ugly." He took the rest of the food, and smeared it over his saddle and his horse, and went away.

The Coras say they originated in the east, and were big people with broad and handsome faces and long hair. They then spoke another language, and there were no "neighbours." According to another tradition, the men came from the east and the women from the west.

In the beginning the earth was flat and full of water, and therefore the corn rotted. The ancient people had to think and work and fast much to get the world in shape. The birds came together to see what they could do to bring about order in the world, so that it would be possible to plant corn. First they asked the red-headed vulture, the principal of all the birds, to set things right, but he said he could not. They sent for all the birds in the world, one after another, to induce them to perform the deed, but none would undertake it. At last came the bat, very old and much wrinkled. His hair and his beard were white with age, and there was plenty of dirt on his face, as he never bathes. He was supporting himself with a stick, because he was so old he could hardly walk. He also said that he was not equal to the task, but at last he agreed to try what he could do. That same night he darted violently through the air, cutting outlets for the waters ; but he made the valleys so deep that it was impossible to walk about, and the principal men reproached him for this. "Then I will put everything back as it was before," he said.

"No, no!" they all said. "What we want is to make

the slopes of a lower incline, and to leave some level land, and do not make all the country mountains."

This the bat did, and the principal men thanked him for it.   Thus the world has remained up to this day.

No rain was falling, and the five principal men despatched the humming-bird to the place in the east where the rain-clouds are living, to ask them to come over here.   The clouds came very fast and killed the humming-bird, and then returned to their home.   After a while the humming-bird came to life, and told the principal men that the clouds had gone back.   The people then sent out the frog with his five sons.   As he proceeded toward the east he left one of his sons on each mountain.   He called the clouds to come, and they followed and overtook him on the road.   But he hid himself under a stone, and they passed over him. Then the fifth son called them on, and when they overtook him he, too, hid himself under a stone.   Then the fourth son called the clouds and hid, then the third son called, and then the second, and finally the first, who had been placed on a mountain from which the sea can be seen to the west of the sierra.   When the storm-clouds went away again, the frogs began to sing merrily, which they do to this day after rain, and they still hide under stones when rain is coming to the Cora country.

The rabbit in olden times had hoofs like the deer, and the deer had claws.   They met on the road and saluted each other as friends.   Said the deer : " Listen, friend, lend me your sandals, to see how they feel.   Only for a moment."   The rabbit, who was afraid the deer would steal them, refused at first, but at last he agreed, and the deer, putting them on, rose and began to dance. "Oh, how beautifully it sounds !" he said.   He danced five circuits, and began to dance mitote and sing.   The rabbit sat looking on, and was in a dejected mood, fearing that the deer might not give him back his sandals. The deer then asked permission to run five big circuits over the mountains. The rabbit said no, but the deer went away, promising to come back directly. He returned four times, but on the fifth round he ran away. The rabbit climbed up on a mountain and saw the deer already far off. He wanted to follow him, but he could not, because his feet were bare. The deer never returned the hoofs to the rabbit, and hoofless the rabbit has remained to this day.

I had many interesting interviews with the old shaman whom the authorities had appointed to serve me. He confided to me that for many years he had faithfully fulfilled his office as the principal singing shaman of the community, but that the people had once suddenly accused him of practising sorcery and wanted to punish him. Being very intelligent and upright, he was of great assistance to me, and the more eager to do all he could for the grudge he bore his compatriots for accusing him of sorcery. No doubt he was glad of my coming, as it gave him a chance to rehabilitate himself, since, for the first time in three years, he had been engaged to sing at the dance. Be this as it may, I obtained much valuable information from him. He could elucidate the trend of Indian thought better than any shaman I had hitherto met, and his talk was full of aphorisms and opinions with reference to Indian views of life.

Referring to the many regulations and observances the Indians have to comply with in order to insure food, health, and life, he said : "A man has to do a good deal to live. Every tortilla we eat is the result of our work. If we do not work, it does not rain." That the "work" consists in fasting, praying, and dancing does not detract from its hardship.

Other sayings I picked up are as follows:

We do not know how many gods there are.

The Moon is man and woman combined ; men see in her a woman, women see a man.

It is better to give a wife to your son before he opens his eyes very much ; if not, he will not know whom he wants.

Illness is like a person ; it hears.

Everything is alive ; there is nothing dead in the world. The people say the dead are dead ; but they are very much alive.

My friend went with me in the afternoon to the place where the mitote was to be given. As the preparations of the principal men consume two days, and I was bent on seeing everything, I went to the place the day before the dance was to come off. It was a few miles away in a remote locality, on top of a hill the upper part of which was composed mainly of huge stones, some of them as regular in shape as if they had been chiselled. Here and there in the few open spaces some shrubbery grew. An opening in the midst of the great mass of stones had been prepared to serve as a dancing-place. The big stones looked dead enough, but to the Indians they are alive. They are what the Coras call Táquats or ancient people. Once upon a time they went to a mitote, just as we were doing now, when the morning star arose before they arrived at their destination, and all were changed into stone, and ever since have appeared like stones. My companion pointed out the various figures of men, women, and children, with their bundles and baskets, girdles, etc., and in the waning light of day it was not difficult to understand how

The Sacred Dancing-Place of the Coras, called Towta, the supposed residence of the great Taquat of the East of the same name. Photographed after the Dancing was over. The Main Altar is on the Right. The Musical Bow has been Removed from its Place in Front of the Bench.

the Indians had come to this conception of the fantastic forms standing all around the place. Even a mountain may be a Taquat, and all the Taquats are gods to whom the Coras pray and sacrifice food ; but it is bad to talk about them.

It had often been a puzzle to me why primitive people should make for themselves stone idols to whom they might sacrifice and pray ; but what is to us a rock or stone may be to the Indian a man or a god of ancient times, now turned into stone. By carving out features, head, body, or limbs, they only bring before their physical eyes what is in their mind's eye. This peculiar kind of pantheism can never be eradicated from the Indian's heart unless he is from infancy estranged from his tribal life.

In the centre of the dancing-place stood a magnificent tree not yet in leaf, called *chócote*, and there was some shrubbery growing about and around the place, which is very old. Only a few yards higher up among the rocks is a similar spot, with traces of still greater antiquity. The Indians had promised me that on this occasion one of their shamans would make a god's eye for me, and I was shown the stone on which he would sit while making it. It was near the tree ; and back of it, arranged in a circle around the fire, were six similar stones, in place of the stools I had seen in Pueblo Viejo. The principal men had swept the place in the morning, and since then had been smoking pipes and talking to the gods.

There were also present a female principal, an old woman, with her little granddaughter who represented the moon. These too, it seemed, had to attend to certain religious duties which they perform for five years, the child beginning at the innocent age of three. During her term she lives with the old woman, whether she

is related to her or not.   The old lady has charge of
the large sacred bowl of the community, an office vested
only in a woman of undoubted chastity.   This bowl is
called " Mother, " and is prayed to.   It consists of half
of a large round gourd, adorned inside and outside with
strings of beads of various colours.   It is filled with
wads of cotton, under which lie carved stone figures of
great antiquity.   None but the chief religious authority
is allowed to lift up the cotton, the symbol of health
and life.   The bowl rests also on cotton wads.   On
festive occasions the woman in charge brings the bowl
to the dancing-place and deposits it at the middle of the
altar.   Parrot feathers are stood up along the inner
edge, and each person as he arrives places a flower on
top of the cotton inside of the bowl.   This vessel is
really the patron saint of the community.   It is like a
mother of the tribe, and understands, so the Indians say,
no language but Cora.   The Christian saints understand
Cora, Spanish, and French ; but the Virgin Mary at
Guadalupe, the native saint of the Mexican Indians,
understands all Indian languages.

Leaving the principales to prepare themselves further
for the dance, my friend and I early next morning went
to see a sacred cave where the Huichols go to worship.
It was situated in the same hill, outside of the country
of that tribe.   There were a great many caves and cavities between the stones over which we made our way,
jumping from one to another.   Near the lower edge of
this accumulation of stones I noticed, down in the dark,
deep recesses, ceremonial arrows which the pious pilgrims from beyond the eastern border of the Cora land
had left.   Soon after passing this point we came to a
cave, the approach of which led downward and was
rather narrow.   With the aid of a pole or a rope it can
easily be entered.   I found myself at one of the ancient

places of worship of the Huichol Indians, the cave of their Goddess of the Western Clouds. It was not large, but the many singular ceremonial objects, of all shapes and colours, accumulated within it, made a strange impression upon me. There were great numbers of ceremonial arrows, many with diminutive deer-snares attached, to pray for luck in hunting; as well as votive bowls, gods' eyes, and many other articles by which prayers are expressed. In one corner was a heap of deer-heads, brought for the same purpose. As my companion entered, a rat disappeared in the twilight of the cave.

I wanted to take some samples of the articles, but he begged me not to do it, as the poor fellows who had sacrificed the things might be cheated out of the benefits they had expected from them. He had, however, no objection to my taking a small rectangular piece of textile fabric, with beautifully colored figures on it. "This is a back shield," he said, "and the Huichols do not do right by those things. They place them in the trails leading out of their country, to prevent the rain from coming to us. Lions and other ferocious animals are often represented on them, and they frighten the rain back."

God's Eye, made by the Cora Tribe as a Prayer for my Health and Life. Length, 80 ctm.

On our return to the dancing-place I found the man who had been deputed to make the god's eye lying in a small cave in quite an exhausted condition, having fasted for many days. The ceremonial object had already been made, under incantations. It was very pretty, white and blue, and had a wad of cotton attached to each corner. Its efficacy was, however, lost as far as I was concerned, as I had not been sitting beside the man while he made it, praying for what I wanted. This is a necessary condition if the Morning Star is to be made to understand clearly what the supplicant needs.

On the altar, beside the sacred bowl of the community, had been placed food and many ceremonial objects, not omitting the five ears of seed-corn to be used in raising the corn required for the feasts. In the ground immediately in front of the altar were four bunches of the beautiful tail-feathers of the bluejay.

Opposite to this, on the west side of the place, was another altar, a smaller one, on which had been put some boiled pinole in potsherds, with tortillas and a basket of cherries. This was for the dead, who if dissatisfied might disturb the feast. Afterward the pinole is thrown on the ground, while the people eat the rest of the food.

The fasting shaman came forth on our arrival and took his position opposite the main altar, talking to the gods for half an hour. The newly made god's eye had been stuck into the ground in front of him. On his left side stood the little girl, and behind her the old woman, her guardian, and a man, who was smoking tobacco. Two young men, one at the right, the other at the left, held in their hands sticks with which they woke up people who fell asleep during the night while the dance was going on.

The shaman prayed to the Morning Star, presented to him the ears of corn that were to be used as seed, and asked him to make them useful for planting. The gods know best how to fructify the grains, since all the corn

belongs to them. "And as for this man," he added,
speaking of me, "you all knew him before he started
from his own country. To us he seems to be good, but
you alone know his heart. You give him the god's eye
he asked for."

A little after dark the singer for the occasion began
to play a prelude on the musical bow, which the Coras
always glue to the gourd, uniting the two parts to form
one instrument. The gourd was placed over a small ex-

CORA MITOTE SONG, FROM SANTA TERESA.

cavation in the ground to increase its resonance. The
singer invoked the Morning Star to come with his
brothers, the other stars, to bring with them their pipes
and plumes, and arrive dancing with the rain-clouds
that emanate from their pipes as they smoke. The
Morning Star was also asked to invite the seven principal Taquats to come with their plumes and pipes.

The Coras dance like the Tepehuanes and the
Aztecs, but with quicker steps, and every time they
pass the altar the dancers turn twice sharply toward it.
At regular intervals the old woman and the little girl
danced, the former smoking a pipe. The little girl
had parrot feathers tied to her forehead and a bunch of
plumes from the bluejay stood up from the back of her

head.   In the middle of the night she danced five circuits, carrying a good-sized drinking-gourd containing
water from a near-by brook, which originates in the
sacred lagoon.

The shaman sang well, but the dancing lacked animation, and but few took part in it.   When the little
girl began to dance with her grandmother, I seated
myself on a small ledge not far from the musician.
Immediately the shaman stopped playing and the dancing ceased.   In an almost harsh voice, and greatly
excited, he called to me, "Come and sit here, sir!"
He was evidently very anxious to get me away from
the ledge, and offered me a much better seat on one of
the stones placed for the principal men.   I had inad-
vertently sat on a Taquat!   This sacred rock of the
dancing-place had a natural hollow, which the Indians
think is his votive bowl, and into which they put
pinole and other food.   "Never," my friend told me
next day, "had anyone sat there before."

Later in the evening, when there was a pause in the
performance, I noticed that all the men, with the singing shaman, gathered in a corner of the dancing-place,
seating themselves on the ground.   They were discuss-
ing what they should do in regard to the skulls I had
asked for.   One of the principal men told them that
a dream last night had advised him not to deny the
"Señor" anything he asked for, as he had to have a
"head" and would not go without one.   "You are
daft, and he comes here knowing a good deal," the
dream had said.

They all became alarmed, especially the man who
had steadily opposed their complying with my request,
and they agreed that it was better to give the white man
what he wanted.   The gobernador even raised the question whether it would not be best to let me have the

skulls early next morning, together with the other things I was to get; or, if not then, at what other time? My shaman friend diplomatically proposed that I should set the time for this.

Next morning I got the god's eye as well as a splendid specimen of a musical bow with the gourd attached, the playing-sticks, etc., all of which were taken out of a cave near the dancing-place. There was another cave near by, into which the principal men are accustomed to go to ask permission from the sun and moon and all the other Taquats to make their feasts.

The morning saw the feast concluded in about the usual way. Tobacco was smoked over the seed-corn on the altar, and sacred water was sprinkled from a red orchid over everything on the altar, including the sacred bowl and the flowers on top of it, as well as over the heads of all the people present, to insure health and luck. This is done on behalf of the Morning Star, because he throws blessed water over the whole earth, and on the corn and the fruit the Coras eat. The flowers are afterward taken home, even by the children, and put in cracks in the house walls, where they remain until removed by the hand of time.

The people of Santa Teresa and San Francisco, at certain rain-making feasts, fashion a large locust (*chicharra*) out of a paste made of ground corn and beans, and place it on the altar. In the morning, after the dancing of the mitote, it is divided among the participants of the feast, each eating his share. This is considered more efficient even than the dancing itself.

It is evident that the religious customs of the cañon of Jesus Maria are on the wane, mainly because the singing shamans are dying out, though curing shamans will remain for centuries yet. As the Indians now have to perform their dances secretly, the growing generation has less inclination and little opportunity to learn them, and the tribe's ritual and comprehensive songs will gradually become lost.

My shaman friend in San Francisco complained to me that the other shamans did not know the words of the songs well enough. Tayop (Father Sun) and the other gods do not understand them, he said, and therefore these shamans cannot accomplish anything with "los señores." It was like sending a badly written letter: "the gentlemen" pass it from one to another, none of them being able to make out its meaning.

In the mean time my efforts to obtain anthropological specimens were more laborious than successful, because it was very difficult to get anyone to show me where they could be found. To make things worse, suddenly another man dreamed that I had enough "heads," and so I was not permitted to search for them any more. But I did not intend to content myself with the few I had secured. I had made arrangements with a Cora some time before to show me some skulls he knew of, and after much procrastination on his part I at last got him to accompany me.

We rode for fifteen miles in the direction of Santa Teresa. The country was rough and but sparsely inhabited. In fact, I passed three deserted ranches, and near one of them I killed a Gila monster that was just making its burrow. There lay an air of antiquity over the whole landscape. About half a league before reaching the caves we sought, I came upon quite an extensive fortification; I also noticed a number of trincheras in one arroyo; and above it on a mesa, running along the edge, we found a wall built of loose stones. The mesa, 300 by 200 feet in extent, was a natural fortress difficult of access, except at one point where a little cordon, like an isthmus, led to it. Here, however, I found no vestige of ancient inhabitants.

There were two shallow caves close to each other in the remote valley into which the guide had led me. In the larger one, which was eight feet deep and twelve feet broad, nine skulls were found. In the other were only a few bones, and I noticed indications of partitions, in the shape of upright stones, between the skeletons. The bodies must have been partly buried, with the heads protruding, in spaces a foot square.

It was nearing dusk and I had to get back to my camp that evening. On the road my mule gave out, and for the last part of the way I had to walk. I refreshed myself with some zapotes, which were just in season. This native fruit of Mexico has the flavour of the pear and the strawberry, and is delicious when picked fresh from the tree; but as soon as it falls to the ground it is infested with insects.

Contrary to expectation, when I was ready to leave the village, I found it exceedingly difficult to get men. As the Coras here do not understand the mule business, I had to resort to the Mexicans in the valley, who, however, acting under instructions from the padre, would have nothing to do with me. They even shunned those who were seen in my company. One man who used to carry on some trading with the Huichols was more daring than the rest. He declared that he would serve the devil himself if he got paid for it, and tried to make up a party for me, but failed. He was ruining his reputation for my sake, he told me; even his compadre (his child's godfather), on account of his association with me, ran away when he saw him coming. The situation finally became so exasperating that I was compelled to write to the Bishop in Tepic, and lay the case before him. I stated that the padre, without having seen me, had placed me in a bad light before the people, and had then left the country, making it impossible for me to convince him of his error of judgment; that if it were not for the strong recommendations I had from the Government and the Commanding General of the Territory, it would be impossible for me to stay here, except at great personal risk.

To await an answer, however, would have involved too great a loss of time. Luckily I found three dare-devil fellows, but recently come into the valley for a living, who were willing to go with me. These, together with the man already mentioned and one Cora Indian, enabled me to make a start. Thus I parted from pretty San Francisco, and the nice Indians there, who had believed in me in spite of the wickedness the Mexicans had attributed to me. The Coras are the only primitive race I have met who seem to have acquired the good qualities of the white man and none of his bad ones.

On an oppressively hot June morning, when I finally got away, the alcalde rode along with me for a couple of miles. We soon began to ascend the slope of the mountains that form the western barrier of the Huichol country, which, among the Mexicans, is reputed to be accessible only at four points. Next morning, while packing the mules, the father of one of my Mexicans ran up to us with a message that seemed quite alarming. Immediately after I left San Francisco yesterday, the Mexican authority at Jesus Maria had come over to tell me that the Huichols were on the warpath and determined not to allow me to enter their pueblos. The messenger impressed upon my men the necessity of turning back and implored them not to run any risk by accompanying me. The chief packer came hastily to me with this news, which I at once declared to be false. But the men, nevertheless, stopped packing, and proposed to go back. They declared that the Huichols were bad, that they were assassins, that there were many of them, and that they would kill us all.

Now, what was I to do? To turn back from the tribe the study of which had been from the outset my principal aim was not to be thought of; even to delay the trip would be impossible, as the wet season was fast approaching, in which one cannot travel for months. I tried to reason with them and to ease their minds by pointing out the great experience I had had with Indians in general. I also appealed to their manly pride and courage. "Have we not five rifles?" I said. "Cannot each one of you fight fifty Indians?" Still they wavered, and it looked as if they were going to desert me, when the cook courageously exclaimed: "*Vámos, vámos!*" ("Let us go on!") They again began to pack, and I managed to keep my troupe together.

The real danger for me lay in the evil rumours the Mexicans had spread, and in the fact that the whites were afraid of me. The Indians do not follow the "neighbours" in their reasoning; they only think that a white man of whom even the Mexicans are afraid must certainly be terrible. The reason why I had chosen this route was that a friend of mine in far-away Guadalajara had given me a letter of recommendation to an acquaintance of his, a half-caste, who acted as escribano (secretary) to the pueblo of San Andres, or, to give its name in full, San Andres Coamiata. I had been told that this man was temporarily absent, in which case I should be at the mercy of the strange Indians.

The immediate prospect looked dark enough to make me consider the advisability of the long detour to the town of Mezquitic, to get assistance from the government authorities there and to enter the Huichol country from the east by way of Santa Catarina. Against this plan, however, my men urged that they could not be back in their country before the wet season set in, to attend to their fields. Finally, I decided to risk going to San Andres. If Don Zeferino was not there, I would come back and then try Mezquitic. Two days later, after a laborious ascent, I sent my chief packer ahead to San Andres, which was still about eight miles off. What a mountainous country all around us! The Jesuit father Ortega was right when he said of the Sierra del Nayarit: "It is so wild and frightful to behold that its ruggedness, even more than the arrows of its warlike inhabitants, took away the courage of the conquerors, because not only did the ridges and valleys appear inaccessible, but the extended range of towering mountain peaks confused even the eye."

My messenger returned after two days, saying that Don Zeferino was at home and would be at my disposal. In the meantime it had begun to rain ; my men were anxious to return home to the valley, and I started for San Andres.

END OF VOL. I.